SOUTHERN PASSAGE

Soundings Overland:
Tijuana to Tierra del Fuego

Also by Sandy McMath

AFRICA ALONE

COLUMBUS AND COMPANY *publishes original personal accounts of discovery, travel, innovation and ordeal by observers whose primary occupations may be other than writing but who, for a variety of reasons, have found themselves involved with the unusual and written about it. Expedition narratives, natural history research papers, Peace Corps journals, war letters, flight and cruising logs, product–invention histories, archeological field notes and survival diaries are examples. Send descriptions only of available manuscripts unless otherwise requested. A finders fee for exceptional material is available, contingent upon publication. Suitable ventures underwritten.*

Cover photo: *Gazer into passageway, San Pedro Village, Lake Atitlán, Guatemala.*

Back photo: *Igarapé Acara Camp, Reserva Florestal Ducke, Brazilian Amazon.*

SOUTHERN PASSAGE

Soundings Overland:
Tijuana to Tierra del Fuego

Sandy McMath

COLUMBUS AND COMPANY
SAN FRANCISCO
Discoverers' Press

Copyright 1993 by Sandy S. McMath
Published 1993 by Columbus and Company
Printed by Pine Hill Press, Freeman, South Dakota
Typeset by Brevard Business News Inc.
West Melbourne, Florida 32904 (407–951–7777)

COLUMBUS AND COMPANY, SAN FRANCISCO
Discoverers' Press, 10 Liberty Ship Way, P. O. Box 1492
Sausalito,California 94966
Orders and enquiries: 501–225–4333

ISBN 0–9622515–2–6

Library of Congress Catalog Card Number 92–72218
        McMath, Sandy
        Southern Passage
        Soundings Overland: Tijuana to Tierra del Fuego

COLUMBUS AND COMPANY, SAN FRANCISCO
Discoverers' Press, 1993

Maps by Evelyn Backman Phillips
Frontispiece by Marc Davey

All Columbus and Company Books are produced on
acid–free paper that exceeds the minimum standards set by
the National Historical Publications and Records Commission.

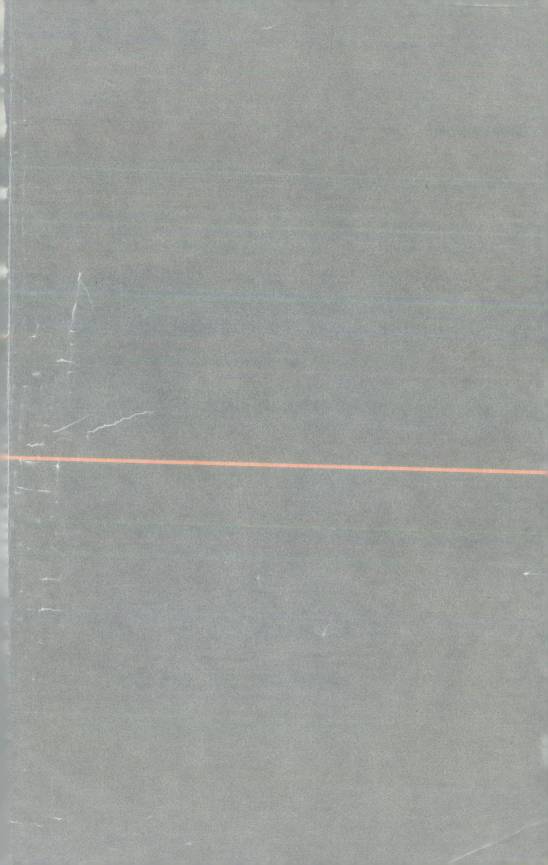

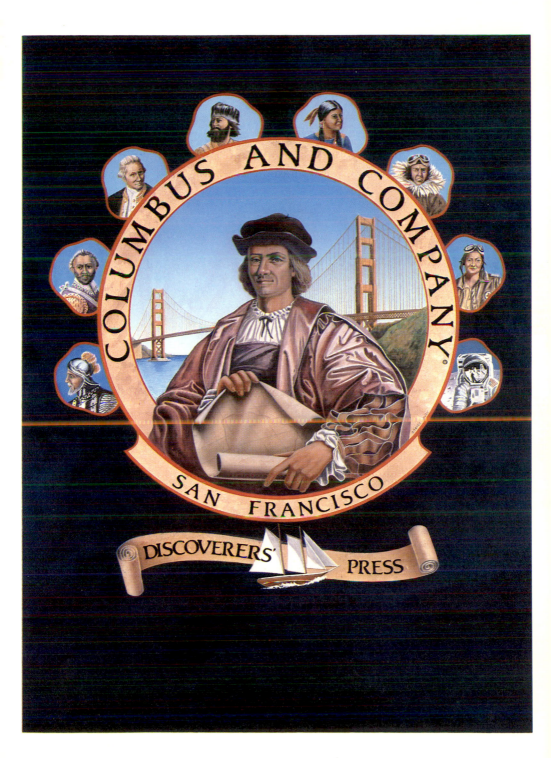

COLUMBUS AND COMPANY

SAN FRANCISCO

DISCOVERERS' PRESS

Advance Praise for
SOUTHERN PASSAGE

Southern Passage is a gigantic accomplishment. It will be the definitive work on Central and South America for the armchair traveler and the scholar.

> — John Monks, Jr.
> *No Man is an Island*

I have read three times the manuscript of *Southern Passage* and find that it is an eminently readable work. It is chock full of insights, very sophisticated ones, on Latin America, its peoples, cultures and geography. The author is well read and this circumstance enhances his observations and gives meaning to the traveler and reader. The book is a veritable guide, a handy *vade mecum* ... squarely in the genre of quality travel literature.

> — Dr. Richard E. Greenleaf,
> Director of the Center
> for Latin American Studies and
> Former Chairman of the
> Department of History,
> Tulane University

Southern Passage is a lively and honest account of just how things are in Latin America these days.

> — Charles Portis
> *True Grit*

SOUTHERN PASSAGE

1	MALARRIMO	31
2	CABO	45
3	ACAPULCO	57
4	CUERNAVACA	63
5	CATEMACO	71
6	CHICHÉN ITZÁ	81
7	NIZUC	99
8	CAY CAULKER	107
9	ATITLÁN	131
10	UTILA	153
11	TEGUCIGALPA	165
12	MANAGUA I	185
13	MANAGUA II	203
14	SAN JOSÉ	227
15	COLÓN	247
16	MIRAFLORES	267
17	LURIGANCHO	281
18	NAZCA	297
19	MACHU PICCHU	317
20	MARAJÓ	339
21	ITAITUBA	361
22	DUCKE	397
23	ORURO	437
24	PERITO MORENO	455
25	USHUAIA	483
	EPILOGUE	497
	Notes	499
	Table of Photographs	525
	Selected Bibliography	533
	About the Author	541

Acknowledgments

The late Professor John Pine transported his students into the history he taught. His field was Latin America. I can still smell the sweat and gunpowder and hear the women, men and horses screaming in that classroom. One of the few honors in a singularly undistinguished undergraduate career was my selection as a research reader for Dr. Pine, who was blind. My first debt is to him.

Carol Holland, Christa Black and Bob Dunn dutifully provided mail—forwarding, film and other logistical backup, often under difficult conditions.

Alan Davis shared his Lima home, affording me a secure base of operations, badly needed rest and storage for the jeep while I was on the Amazon. Hospitality was also extended by a great many others. I am especially indebted to Edith Swift in Rancho Santa Fe, Carlos López in Maxcanú, Emilie Daniel in Balboa, Anthony and Suely Anderson in Belém, and Bill Magnusson and Marc Hero in Manaus.

Special kindnesses were shown by Rosa Elba Balles and Juan Acre and their family on Cedros Island, Katherine "Mom" Lee and Sue Williams in Belize, Barry and Matilda Row and Esteban and Cecilia Koosau in Lima, Maria Reiche in Nazca, Hernán Luza Calvo in Cuzco, Steve Bunker in Belém, Virgilio and Lili Viana in Belterra, Rob Bierregaard and Tom Lovejoy in Manaus, Belém and Robert Torres and Eric and Jeanette Sletten in Buenos Aires, and Bill and Caroline Greenwalt and Francesca Sepe in Trelew.

In Idaho, Steve and Kate Duininck, Bill and Lisa Mirams, Lisa Lesher and Charley Nichols made available their homes at various times and were faithfully supportive throughout my time there.

Forrest and Cheryl Hymas turned over their "Sky Ranch" cabin at Smiley Creek in the Sawtooth Mountains whenever I needed it, once for nine months. Located in the valley of the Salmon, The River of No Return, it is without equal in the Lower Forty—Eight as a place to think and write, especially when embanked in dead—of—winter snows.

The officers and staff of the Community Library, Ketchum, Idaho, were invaluable. I am particularly indebted to Librarian Ollie Cossman and her associates, Ellie Lister and Ann Stone, and to the chairwoman of the Library Committee, Sana Sears. Ellie Lister's ability to locate obscure tomes and arcane data in distant libraries was remarkable.

Grateful acknowledgment is made to the following publishers:

Alfred A. Knopf, Inc., New York, for permission to quote from *The Enigma of Arrival* by V.S. Naipaul, copyright (c) 1987 by Alfred A. Knopf, Inc., and from *Distant Neighbors: A Portrait of the Mexicans* by Alan Riding, copyright (c) 1984 by Alfred A. Knopf, Inc.

Grove Weidenfeld, Inc., New York, for permission to quote from *The Labyrinth of Solitude* by Octavio Paz, copyright (c) 1961 and 1986 by Grove Press, Inc.

The University of California Press, Berkeley, for permission to quote from *Many Mexicos* by Professor Lesley Bird Simpson, 4th Edition, Revised. Copyright (c) 1966 by Lesley Bird Simpson.

The National Geographic Society, Washington, D.C., for permission to quote from "The First Americans: The Dental Evidence," by Professor Christy Turner, III, *National Geographic Research*, Winter 1986, copyright (c) 1986 by *National Geographic Research*.

Interciencia of Caracas, Venezuela, for its generally granted permission to quote from all works published by it. Specific citations occur in the text.

Columbia University Press, New York, for permission to quote from *Human Carrying Capacity of the Brazilian Rainforest* by Philip M. Fearnside, copyright (c) 1986 by Columbia University Press, New York.

Random House, Inc., New York, for permission to quote from *Nicaragua: Revolution in the Family* by Shirley Christian, copyright (c) 1985, 1986 by Shirley Christian.

Robin McKinney Martin, Kaali Frances O'Brien, Martha Morton, and Bill and Adrienne Roth subjected the draft manuscript to severe criticism. "Gentleman Derelle" Smith labored above and beyond the call of friendship, spotlighting gaps, lassoing typos and trimming surplusage. Bill Roth became my editor and skillfully and tenaciously guided the project to completion. I did not always take their advice, though perhaps I should have. Mine alone is the responsibility for the final product.

Steadfast support throughout was shown by my father and mother, Sid and Anne McMath, and by my mother–in–law, Helen Boyer.

Mike Brinkman, Selina Koosau, Penny Mailliard, Pamela and Marc Davey, Jay Freis, Doug Greene, Betsy and John Harris, Henry Morris, Rich Bray, Debbie Spitzer, Cheryl Welch, Tom Wallerich, Charley Cook, Ancil O'Neal, Ethyl Cook, Matt Wells and Ed Walton were most helpful and each is due a special word of thanks.

Finally, to my wife, Allison, without whom the book would never have seen fruition, I am immeasurably grateful.

— SSM

Dr. John Pine

SOUNDINGS

I have a small law practice with my father and brothers and a few old friends. We represent people destroyed by drunk drivers, nursing homes, insurance companies, defective products, pirouetting politicians and other hazards.

The work is rewarding. It is also imprisoning. The law steals nights, pockets weekends, swallows vacations. Many submit to these importunities of the jealous mistress. Others forsake her for short trysts with boat, rod or gun. Those alone cannot renew my spirit.

Early on, I knew that I must seize determinative time to breathe the forest, taste the ocean and look into the eyes of distant wisdom. So every few years I set my affairs in order and hit the road.

Travel restores body and soul if it is done well: leave your self–important baggage behind, live modestly, avoid cities and other crowds where you can, seek people one–on–one, break bread with them, listen, and keep a journal.

My partners tolerate my absences. We work on contingency; I'm not paid while away. I manage to save a little between trips by not collecting houses, furniture, cars, gold watches and other weighty possessions.

Until it burned, my residence was a three–room frame house. One neighbor lived in the home her father built and where she was born; another had been in hers for six decades. Because it lay hidden behind a major thoroughfare, few people knew our neighborhood existed. Now it has been rezoned and the old houses are falling to bulldozers. So are the trees, great rustling elm, oak and sycamore that were saplings in the War of the Rebellion, seedlings at the Louisiana Purchase. The mighty Arkansas River hushes past with Colorado snowmelt and Oklahoma clay, bound for the Mississippi and the Gulf of Mexico. In spring and summer, its banks sing with willow, wildflowers and honeysuckle.

The only vehicle I owned was the one described in these pages. For 17 years, it navigated the thickets of justice and jungle equally well.

A loving wife and a growing son and daughters now require more well–appointed lodgings. And the old jeep has been replaced by a larger, softer wagon. But when the next call comes, we shall set forth together, as before: lighthearted and unburdened. Toward that day, we are building a little ship that will "take us up the shimmering path to the sun." We will seek the brave Ulysses, Amelia and the others. But that is yet to come.

This passage, from Tijuana, Mexico to Tierra del Fuego at the southern extremity of South America, took 397 days. A variety of transport was used, from riverboat to bush plane. The primary

conveyance was a 1974 Toyota Landcruiser, *jeep*, the color of
Mississippi mud, an Indian pot or lightly creamed morning coffee.
Some readers will recognize it as the same machine, repainted and
refitted, that traversed Africa in 1976–77 and Alaska, the Yukon and
Northwest Territories in '81.

The endeavor was mostly single–handed, and there were
immense periods of solitude. Yet I was never, finally, alone. Whatever
the ordeal or sweetness, I was eventually blessed with the Great
Companions: honest, generous men and women — the same spirits
who stirred Walt Whitman, that most robust of takers to the open
road. The poet would surely agree, had he been along, which in a way
he was. Stashed in my kit was a well–worn copy of "Leaves of Grass."
When I thirsted for reasonableness, or when new friends had heard
only our electric mourners and shouters, I summoned a verse from
Whitman, Sandburg or Frost — or one of Jimmy Driftwood's ballads
— and America sang again.

The journey began at Tijuana, and resolved into four broad
episodes:

> 1. Down the length of the Baja
> California peninsula to Cabo San
> Lucas, thence by ferry to Puerto
> Vallarta, along the Pacific to Acapulco,
> then north to Mexico City and Nuevo
> Laredo.
> 2. From Matamoros to Veracruz,
> around the Gulf of Mexico and the
> Caribbean coasts of the Yucatán,
> through Central America to Panama.
> Thence, by sea and air to Guayaquil,
> Ecuador and by land again to Lima,
> Peru.
> 3. The Amazon, from the mouth at
> Marajó Island, Brazil to Iquitos in
> Peru.
> 4. From Lima to Ushuaia on the
> Beagle Channel in the Argentine
> Tierra del Fuego.

Total distance actually covered was just over 25,000 miles and
included a rail stretch in Peru, Arequipa to Machu Picchu via Lake
Titicaca and Cuzco, and legs by air: Guerrero Negro to Cedros Island
off the Baja California coast and back; Panama to Ecuador to meet
the sea–shipped jeep; Lima, Peru to Belém, Brazil to begin the

Amazon ascent; back to Lima from Iquitos; and zigzag hops through Patagonia and the southern Andes.

Because the distance between fuel supplies was not as great as on my African trek, I carried four instead of eight jerry cans. Together they held an extra 20 gallons of gas. With them, and the regular, 15–gallon, and spare, 23–gallon, tanks, I had a range of 750 miles.

A shortwave radio gave access to local chatter and a link to the world via the Voice of America and the BBC. Two stainless steel boxes, placed flush beneath the rear seats, carried tools and spare parts. These were padlocked to hasps welded into the bulkheads and could be removed for storage or to lighten up for short trips.

A top rack carried the jerry cans, a five–gallon water jug, spare firewood and a footlocker with the camping and cooking gear. A North Face mosquito tent was home on the road. A smaller steel box beneath the driver's seat served as a dry "safe." In it I kept an old laminated compass, passport, International Drivers Permit, introductions from an editor and former publisher, car title and currency. Also stowed there was the standard AAA *Carnet de Passage,* issued against a letter of credit for $2,000, the "Blue Book" value of the Landcruiser. The Carnet is a wide booklet of tickets, each perforated into three exact copies. It permits transit without tariff, sometimes double or triple a vehicle's value. One copy is taken when you enter a country and another when you leave.

I began with $1,500 in cash and twice that in traveler's checks. The dollars were an unrenewable resource after Panama, where the greenback is the official currency. Except in Belize, where the exchange rate is rigidly set at 2 to 1, and Panama, all currencies were constantly moving, usually downward, against the dollar. Thus, I rarely changed more than 200 dollars at a time. Traveler's checks were a nuisance to cash for other than official rates, for which you lose from 10 to 50 percent. Yet with persistence it can be done. Dollars are always accepted, sometimes at double or more their pegged value.

Approximately a third of nights were spent camped or hammocked on sooty riverboats, a quarter with friendlies who offered a roof, and the rest in *pensiones* or small hotels. The Grand Hotel de Costa Rica in San José was home for a week, as was the less grand Hotel Lancaster in Buenos Aires. "Cheap" does not always mean uncomfortable in Latin American lodgings. Indeed, a good night's sleep may be inversely proportionate to the price of the room. "First class" hotels are not only harshly expensive, but almost always undergoing noisy repairs. The food is coldly prepared and served, and the "ambiance" feigned or nil.

Local food, especially fish along the Pacific and up the Amazon, was fresh and delicious, although salmonella and amoebae were sometimes a problem. Vegetables prepared personally were boiled, or washed in iodine — five drops per gallon. For the miseries, there was Lomotil and Flagil, prescribed before leaving and difficult to refill, and Pepto Bismol. Bottled mineral water was favored for drinking. When that was not available, I filled the canteens with boiled river water or, a last resort, water sterilized with Halazone or iodine. Two malaria pills were on the menu every Sunday. Otherwise, I had no need of medication.

The so–called Pan American Highway was sometimes followed, but more often not. Contrary to popular belief, it is not a single grand thoroughfare but a frequently unmarked patchwork of local routes. The old Potosí – Río de la Plata colonial silver route was generally followed through Bolivia and Argentina. The ascent of the Amazon was chosen over a float downriver for greater shore visibility and slower traveling. Downriver–bound boats deadhead in midstream.

Travelers, particularly those with a historical eye, are ever forming impressions of the places through which they pass with the larger "world picture" in mind. It is human nature to overemphasize or attach greater significance to conditions and events that one personally witnesses or that occur while one is in a place. I am certainly no exception to this rule. Every effort, therefore, has been made to present as fact only that which was personally observed or which was related by those deemed reliable, or under conditions where misstatement or deception was unlikely. The statements of a great many persons appear, but these are attributed and the circumstances described so that the reader can form his or her own opinion of their accuracy. Pseudonyms are used where names were unavailable and in those situations where revealing identities would result in an invasion of privacy, ridicule or reprisal. This has also been done to protect confidential sources. Descriptions of some such persons have been altered. In certain instances, composites have been created from several individuals. Some events have been edited and compressed for readability and continuity. All, however, are authentic. Published sources are footnoted where appropriate, and a selected bibliography is included.

Most Americans assume that the words "country," "nation" and "government" have the same meanings elsewhere as those to which we are accustomed. To us, they imply a commonwealth of purpose, a regular, if not always efficient, authority and service, a kind of bloodhound reliability, if you will — slow, sometimes bungling, but more or less consistent. Such assumptions, however, are mistakenly applied to the cartographical entities of Latin America and the powers that operate within them. There, with the possible exception of Costa Rica, a citizen's contact with his government, regardless of its ideological bent, is more likely than not to consist of an encounter with a convoy of troops that one day rolls into the barrio or village in search of *contrabandistas,* smugglers, who are often merely a local family who have managed to sock in a few spare sacks of rice or corn without sharing with the local tyrant. Or they may be looking for *revolucionarios* or others operating without pretense as *pistoleros.* Dismounting, the troops will hiss and fondle the young women and enter shops and market stalls, taking whatever suits their fancy, particularly cigarettes, beer and comic books, knowing that the merchants will obsequiously waive payment. Some will deploy about asking for *papeles,* identity papers, and severely question those without them and some of those with them. A neighbor or loved one may be loaded up and driven away. Young men unlucky enough to be in the village when the army arrives will be summarily conscripted. At first there is anguish, but this subsides with the realization that, with its regular pay, commissary and relative prestige, the life of a soldier is not all that bad, even when there is a war. Latin American wars, in spite of what the media have told us, are notable for their paucity of engagement.

The most revealing messages of a place can come through the nose. It is far easier to imagine scenes than odors, but no true "picture" of Latin America can be had without its scents and aromas: A seduction of roses, a lure of gardenias, a melancholy of lilacs, a hospitality of garlic; or its more constant nauseas — of uncovered feces, dysfunctional toilets, dead animals, smoldering garbage, fish meal plants, and open effluent. And then there is noise, noise that transcends mere decibels: bedlams of television, Armageddons of tail pipes, pummelings of rock, even — especially — from "discos" in residential neighborhoods. Complaints are few. Such deafenings are not only tolerated; they seem to be required. I often wondered what it would have been like for a sensitive person, or a traditionalist, to live in such a place, forced nightly to endure the explosion of the village universe by the synthesized whinings and shriekings of an alien, adolescent decadence.

From Guatemala through Panama, and later in Peru, there was rarely a time when the menaces of ambush and abduction did not intrude into my thoughts, at times vaguely, at others with perilous immediacy. Travelers told of being robbed or shot or of others who had been. Each place had its own obscure legend of kidnap, mutilation and lifetaking — often with no word of the victim, though the worst was assumed. "Insurgents," some said of the perpetrators; "bandits," said others. To many, the assailants belonged to cabals of police and guardsmen bent upon plunder and score settling and the eradication of any who opposed them, whether Marxist, libertarian or cutpurse. But no one really knew and that uncertainty was as chilling as the atrocity itself.

In Central America there was forever evidence of the despair, blindness, fear and ennui that has pervaded that contorted isthmus since long before the Powers made of it a proxy field of their Cold War conflict. My unease was exacerbated by the knowledge that I was a citizen of one of these, whose century of extraction, and collusion with the forces of political darkness, belied in the minds of many its present avowal of democratic purpose — an affirmation that, in my own mind, I firmly believed, and still believe.

I had read the history of the place; not just the revisionists, but the master students — Prescott, Stephens, Morley. I climbed the temples of cannibal gods, gazed into *cenotes* where bewildered women were drowned in terror, and touched the stone faces of aboriginal Caesars, to whom were rendered the fruits of human toil and the hearts of those who did the toiling — and both in vain. And I knew that the scales of the Spanish tax collectors and their successors, and their priestly coparceners, gave not good weight. There had been more, far more, at work than Yankee fruiterers and battleships.

More recently, with a population explosion lowering the median age to 15 years and the precipitate advent of popular culture, consumer goods, travel and television, inevitable comparisons with the better life elsewhere began to be made. Dissent spread faster than the ability of *régimes ancianos* to murder and co–opt the dissenters. Yet neither of the resultant Marxist states in Cuba and Nicaragua, nor for that matter the "social democracies" of Peru, Argentina, Brazil, and elsewhere have been able to generate the commerce and commonweal essential to breaking the insidious inertia of poverty and corruption. Indeed, it has become legitimate to ask whether any governance, whatever its faith or form, can do this. Or is the hemisphere south of the Rio Grande doomed to implode ignominiously under its human burden, bypassed by the greater world?

But Europe in the Middle Ages was also hopeless, as was the non–Roman world at the time of Christ. Indeed, history offers so many examples of the rise of the weak and the fall of the powerful, and both with rapacious rapidity, that such judgments are hazardous. Withal they are best left to the reader.

The reader is also left to judge the passage of the great forests through which I wove my journey, and whose abatement by fire, saw, cattle and machine is chronicled herein. Some hear in their spreading silences an economic bustle; others the rattle of planet death. To still others they are but muted chorus toward a time when man will be, if at all, incidental — his own passage shrouded in a newer greenness whose fossils will, in their turn, puzzle the stratigraphy above the shards of Progress.

To my reader, then, I offer one American's window toward the south. Its glass is not rose-colored with marketeering optimism or collectivist convention. Nor is it prinked with literary smartness, smug detachment, contrived suspense, "adventure" or travelogue. For those, you must look elsewhere. I have tried, though, in its telling, to impart the spiritual essence of the journey. Travel, as the true journeyer knows, is more — far more — than passage through space.

To the Jaguar
And for Allison, McKenzie, Savannah and Ian

La Cucaracha! La Cucaracha!
Ya no puede caminar.
Porque le falta
Porque no tiene
Las dos parejas de atrás.

     — Song of the Mexican Revolution,
       ca. 1914

—

Expanding northward 20,000 years ago from a north China Sinodont parent population with a generalized microlithic tool tradition, three branch populations developed in geographic isolation. The most westerly bands moved ... to the Arctic continental shelf of Siberia on which they crossed to Alaska in search of large and small game in the bitterly cold, sparse Arctic steppe habitat ...

Migration southward occurred slightly before 12,000 years ago when Clovis people appeared in the southwestern United States and shortly later when they appeared in South America ... completing the longest overland migration in the history of mankind.

     — Professor Christy G. Turner II, 1986

—

The pyramidal form is one that suggests itself to human intelligence in every country as the simplest and surest mode of erecting a high structure upon a solid foundation. It cannot be regarded as a ground for assigning a common origin to all peoples among whom structures of that character are found ...

[I] have a conclusion far more interesting and wonderful than that of connecting the builders of these cities with the Egyptians or any other people. It is the spectacle of a people skilled in architecture, sculpture, and drawing, and [other] arts not derived from the Old World, but originating and growing up here, without models or masters, having a distinct, separate, independent existence: like the plants and fruits of the soil, indigenous.

     — John P. Stephens, 1840

Human sacrifices have been practiced by many nations ... but never by any on a scale to be compared with [the Aztecs] ... Scarcely any author pretends to estimate the yearly sacrifices throughout the empire at less than twenty thousand, and some carry the number as high as fifty ...

At the dedication of the great temple of Huitzilopochtli in 1487, the prisoners, who for some years had been reserved for the purpose ... were ranged in files, forming a procession nearly two miles long. The ceremony consumed several days, and seventy thousand [were killed].

[The Aztecs] did not feed on human flesh merely to gratify a brutish appetite, but in obedience to their religion. Their repasts were made of the victims whose blood had been poured out on the altar[s] of sacrifice ...

[Victims] were urged along by blows, and compelled to take part in the dances in honor of the Aztec war–god. The unfortunate captives, then stripped of their sad finery, were stretched, one after another, on the great stone of sacrifice. On its convex surface, their breasts heaved up conveniently for the diabolical purpose of the priestly executioner, who cut asunder the ribs by a strong blow with his sharp razor of *itztli,* and, thrusting his hand into the wound, tore away the heart, which, hot and reeking, was deposited on the golden censer before the idol. The body of the slaughtered victim was then hurled down the steep stairs of the pyramid ... and the mutilated remains were gathered up by the savages beneath, who soon prepared with them the cannibal repast which completed the abomination.

— William H. Prescott, 1843

—

How small the caravels were that crossed the Atlantic and intruded into the evenness of the history on the other side; how few the men in those small vessels, how limited their means; how barely noticed. But they went back. They changed the world in that part forever.

— V.S. Naipaul, 1987

[T]he grossest corruption [is] far from uncommon. Nearly every public officer can be bribed. The head man in the post office sold forged [documents]. The governor and prime minister openly combined to plunder the state. Justice, where gold came into play, was hardly expected by any one ... With this entire want of principle in many of the leading men, the people yet hope that a democratic form of government can succeed!

— Charles Darwin, 1839

—

The wealthy and privileged of New Spain were as irresponsible as the Indians they despised, and, when their wealth and privileges were threatened, they acted like spoiled children and threw things around. It was this recklessness and frivolity that made it impossible to set up a working government after Independence ... It was a lawless society [that] had destroyed law. So it fell an easy prey to the first uniformed brigand who had the power to enforce his will.

— Professor Lesley Byrd Simpson, 1941

—

The concept of commonweal barely exists and community approaches to shared problems are rare ...

[C]orruption is essential to the operation and survival of the political system. [It] has in fact never lived without corruption and it would disintegrate ... if it tried to do so.

— Alan Riding, 1984

—

[L]ending to South America has from the beginning been marked by numerous disasters ... Every South American State has been in default at least twice and still it has always been possible for these states to secure funds.

— American Economic Review, May 1935

[T]here is no community of interests or of principles between North and South America.

— John Quincy Adams, 1823

—

I put no trust in the moral sense of my countrymen, and without republican morality there can be no free government ... [Latin] America is ungovernable. He who sows a revolution ploughs the sea.

— Simon Bolivar, 1830

—

The North Americans are credulous and we are believers; they love fairy tales and detective stories and we love myths and legends. The Mexican tells lies because he delights in fantasy, or because he is desperate, or because he wants to rise above the sordid facts of his life; the North American does not tell lies, but he substitutes social truth for real truth, which is always disagreeable. We get drunk in order to confess; they get drunk in order to forget. They are optimists, we are nihilists — except that our nihilism is not intellectual, but instinctive and therefore irrefutable. We are suspicious and they are trusting. We are sorrowful and are sarcastic and they are happy and full of jokes. North Americans want to understand and we want to contemplate. They are activists and we are quietists; we enjoy our wounds and they enjoy their inventions. They believe in hygiene, health, work and contentment, but perhaps they have never experienced true joy, which is an intoxication, a whirlwind. In the hubbub of a fiesta night our voices explode into brilliant lights, and life and death mingle together, while their vitality becomes a fixed smile that denies old age and death but that changes life to motionless stone.

— Octavio Paz, 1961

—

The ability of the most credit–worthy [Latin American] governments to avoid default must necessarily be impaired if [loan money] has not, in fact, been put to the use for which it was intended.

— Royal Institute of International Affairs, 1937

The debt is unrepayable; it can never be repaid.

> — Jesus Silva Herzog,
> Mexican Finance Minister, 1985.

The *caciques* stole the money and took it to the north. Why should the people now have to pay it back to the gringos?

> — Ramon García, ex–seminary student, 1985

—

There is only one solution: SUSPENSION OF PAYMENTS.

> — Mexican Workers Party Poster, 1986

—

"I spent 33 years and 4 months in active military service as a member of our country's most agile military force — the Marine Corps. [D]uring that period I spent most of my time being a high–class muscle man for Big Business, for Wall Street and for the bankers. In short, I was a racketeer, a gangster for capitalism. ... I helped in the raping of half–a–dozen Central American republics for the benefit of Wall Street. I helped purify Nicaragua ...

> — Major General Smedley Butler,
> Former Commandant, US Marine Corps, 1935

—

Marxism–Leninism is the scientific doctrine that guides our Revolution, the instrument of analysis of our Vanguard for understanding its historic role and for carrying out the Revolution; ... Without Sandinismo we cannot be Marxist–Leninists, and Sandinismo without Marxism–Leninism cannot be revolutionary; that is why they are indissolubly linked and that is why our moral force is Sandinismo, our political force is Sandinismo, and our doctrine is Marxism–Leninism.

> — Comandante Humberto Ortega,
> Sandinista Minister of Defense, 1981

The trouble with you Americans is that you no longer *believe* in anything. Not in capitalism, not in democracy; those are just names people give your system. But most Americans don't know or care where it is your country is going or what values it carries.

In history, you know, it is those who *believe* in themselves and who are willing to fight for victory, who survive. But it is unfashionable among your thinkers — your writers, your journalists, your professors — to talk of the victory of democracy. And your politicians, except for a very few, are sheep, slaves to their television images.

— Eden Pastora, "Commander Zero," 1986

—

We camped at a point of land between the two rivers. It was extraordinary to realize that here about the eleventh degree we were on such a big river, utterly unknown to the cartographers and not indicated by even a hint on any map. We spent a day at this spot, determining our exact position by the sun, and afterward by the stars, and sending on two men to explore the rapids in advance. They returned with the news that there were big cataracts in them, and that they would form an obstacle to our progress. They had also caught a huge siluroid fish, which furnished an excellent meal for everybody in camp. This evening at sunset the view across the broad river, from our camp where the rivers joined, was very lovely; and for the first time we had an open space in front of and above us, so that after nightfall the stars, and the great waxing moon, were glorious overhead, and against the rocks in midstream the broken water gleamed like tossing silver.

— Theodore Roosevelt, 1914

Present trends in the use of fossil fuels and the expansion of agriculture into forested lands could lead to sufficient accumulation of carbon dioxide in the atmosphere before the middle of the next century to warm the earth an average of 1.5 to 4.5 degrees Centigrade ...

Carbon dioxide–induced temperature increase from all sources is eventually expected to melt polar ice, beginning with sea ice and the West Antarctic ice sheet, raising mean sea level by five meters.

Such a rise would flood many of the most populous parts of the globe, as well as much of the Amazon region ...

Once critical temperatures [have] been attained ... the long delays for equilibration of oceanic CO_2 would render ineffective any human countermeasures initiated at that late date, such as reduced CO_2 emissions.

— Philip M. Fearnside, 1985

—

Allons! Whoever you are, come travel with me!
Traveling with me you find what never tires.

The earth never tires,
The earth is rude, silent, incomprehensible at first, Nature is rude and incomprehensible at first,

Be not discouraged, keep on, there are divine things well envelop'd,

I swear to you there are divine things more beautiful than words can tell.

— Walt Whitman, 1855

—

¿Quién te quita lo bailado?

— Argentine proverb

1

MALARRIMO

Certain egrets and pelicans seemed, as
they soared and plunged, to conduct
me on my journey.

Five hundred miles south of Los Angeles the harsh desert of
Vizcaíno shoulders out into the Pacific to form the western hump of,
Mexico's Baja California peninsula.

Beyond the parched oasis village of San José de Castro the
extrusion is uninhabited, save for occasional packs of coyotes who
scrounge for a living amongst a dozen species of sparse and forbidding
cactus.

Vizcaíno's northern rim is a pronounced crescent that, like a big
net, catches anything drifting south on the California Current. For
thousands of years before European contact, Indians came to the
beach to collect driftwood for fires and for the carving of their sacred
tablas. Legend says anything lost at sea will eventually wash up here.
Wrecks, from junks to galleons, have made the beach their landfall.
In 1751 the Jesuit explorer Fernando Consag found Chinese porcelain
among ship timbers studded with iron so ancient it crumbled when
touched. Not surprisingly Playa Malarrimo, the cartographical name,
became known by sailors and other hearties as "Scavengers Beach."

At the upper end is the mouth of Scammon's Lagoon, locally
Laguna Ojo de Liebre or Jackrabbit Spring. A bizarre and treacherous
intrusion of the sea, the lagoon is the mating ground of the gray
whale. In its shallows British and Nantucket whalers mutilated and
butchered thousands of these leviathan virtually to extinction before
1900, but not without risk. Scammon's narrow channels could ground
an unwary plunderer in his own bloody pools; savage *huracanes*
lashed and pummeled others. A yacht's nameplank, *Confidence*,
inplied more recent retribution.

This wilderness became an early objective of my southward
journey.

Anne, a friend from San Francisco, had volunteered for the Baja
stage of the trek. She was a shrewd observer, a good photographer,
and had a keen interest in desert geology. We were now three weeks
south of Tijuana, having taken our time meandering between the
Pacific and the Sea of Cortés. Intermittently, we returned to
"Highway 1," a shoulderless strip of asphalt with lanes just wide
enough for two warily passing motorists. Trucks meeting each other,

31

or a car approaching one, must put two wheels in the desert. Completed in 1973, the *carretera* replaced a percarious patchwork of tracks that gave "Baja" an aura of peril commensurate with the Sahara's.

Many of those old trails yet exist, leading one to mission ruins and traces of an even earlier California. Near the isolated hamlet of San Francisquito, for example, are thousand–year–old cave paintings of deer, coyote, big horn sheep, cougar and the men who hunted them.

October was early for the whales that usually do not come until December. Off San Quintín Bay, through whose pinched neck tidal currents surge like cataracts, Anne thought she saw two of the animals rolling. Her unaided eyes were better than mine with the binoculars. Or the whales had dived when I looked. Later, from a precarious camp we installed on the weather edge of a wind–twisted waste of dunes, Anne said she saw them again and they appeared to notice her. But, again, for me they were not.

Near Guerrero Negro, a salt shipping port to the northeast, was a road toward the lagoon now called *Parque Natural de las Ballenas Gris*, whale preserve. At some point a haggard soldier, his face flecked with sand, stepped from a guard box, wrote something on a clip board and waved us on. Choosing haphazardly at successive junctions of polders, forced once to double back, we at last came to Scammon's shore. Stubby reeds and marsh grass sprouted in sulfur–scented mud. Leathery algae made blue–green carpets on sun–cracked tidal beds.

A crude sign indicated a restricted launch site. Private boats, including canoes and kayaks, were forbidden. The official craft, a holed and splintered dory, had clearly seen its last flotation. We crept along the bank, cupping our hands against the sun. Alas, there were no *ballenas*.

Looking about we found a hut dug into a sand hill; its sentinels a trackless bulldozer, three mangled truck chassis and an early Frigidaire. An unfriendly dog slinked behind a wall of old tires. Smoke penciled from a stovepipe. My shouts of *"¡Hola! ¡Buenas tardes!"* went unanswered. The only sound was the dog's, a growl alternating with a whimper.

I'd hoped to find a branch trail or at least navigable open desert skirting the periphery of the lagoon but the road dead–ended. Tidal ooze and an ambiguous shoreline made pioneering unwise. We would have to try reaching the beach by the vague tracks that, according to an old map, led from San José de Castro. A footnote said the tracks followed a steep chasm frequently barricaded by rockslides.

Giant cactus in boulder field north of Guerrero Negro, Baja California Norte.

Backtracking to the asphalt we continued to El Arco, a small irrigation district, and headed west on the corrugated earth road toward Bahía Tortugas, a turtling and fishing station on the desert's southwestern coast. At midnight we camped beneath the Vizcaíno mountains just beyond San José.

Next morning, workers returning from Tortugas — their truck groaned and rumbled for an hour before appearing — led us to tracks northward across a pebbled emptiness. A few scrawny cattle had used the tracks that morning. Skulls of their predecessors implied poor grazing, no water. The gravel continued for 13 miles, halting abruptly at the rim of a dead river's gorge. The Pacific, crisply green, waited in the distance — from the map, another 20 miles.

We each swore we heard the surf long after the odometer said we should have met the ocean, yet bend after bend brought only banks gnarled with scrub and elephant trees. Several of the promised rockslides threatened to topple us as we crept over them. Then, when we had stopped expecting it, the sea was there: at the end of a briny delta that extruded into the surf like a cadaverous tongue.

Thirty miles out, barely visible on the horizon, beckoned the peaks of *Isla Cedros*, Cedar Island, a volcanic anomaly mistakenly named for the stunted junipers that struggle there. Twenty–three miles long and four to eleven wide, the island is a geologist's laboratory with a rich variety of rock forms.

Canyon walls reveal epochal happenings elsewhere obscured such as movements of the planet's tectonic plates. Unlike most of the rest of the continent, Baja is moving westward, led by Cedros. To the east, the movement is opening the Sea of Cortés — less romantically known as the Gulf of California, erstwhile receptacle of the Colorado River before its diversion to Los Angeles. The southern extension of the San Andreas Fault runs down that trough.

The week before we'd left the jeep at the government's Hotel La Pinta in Guerrero Negro and flew out to Cedros. The economy consisted of *Pesquería del Pacífico*, a government fish cannery, and the ocean shipping depot for Guerrero Negro's salt. Tugs pushing barges plodded between Guerrero Negro and the pier: salt piled high like minipyramids, chalky swatches in a grège sea.

We hired a skiff to take us to Punta Norte, the island's northernmost point, where we tented in a cactus forest. Hardscrabble lobster fishermen at a seasonal camp a mile away generously supplemented our cookies and corned beef with fresh *langosta*. The men told of drifting alongside whales in Scammon's Lagoon and of beachcombing at Malarrimo. They were vague about their findings. "Many dead things," said one; "Broken boats," another. Getting there by land was hard but it was worth the effort, they said. They were right.

The riverbank offered a partial shield from the unrelenting west wind. I braced a plastic tarpaulin between two poles seaward of the fire. A rusted refrigerator shelf found with a packing crate made an excellent grill; the crate's pine, quick kindling. After gathering more substantial firewood, I left Anne to her turn at supper.

The surf was docile; 200 feet out you were still only waist deep. The shore ran straight for a way then swung abruptly to the southwest where sheer headlands intruded. You could plainly see the big trap nature had set to clean her ocean of litter. Beyond the end of the cape a barren islet named *Isla Natividad* reached toward Cedros, now vanishing into pink twilight clouds.

Not far away I found an empty trunk and short logs wired together into a raft of sorts and rigged with the imaginings of a mast and shroud. My expectations for the morrow's combings were heightened.

Anne surprised me with her favorite *comida*: shrimp, from the market in Guerrero Negro, delicately fried in garlicky olive oil; mildly hot salsa, made with fresh tomatoes, lime, cilantro and jalapeños; hot canned frijoles, rice, and corn tortillas warmed over from town but still tasty. Iced–down bottles of Dos Equis and Pacífico accompanied.

In what had become a nightly ritual, we sky–watched with the binoculars. Orion, the dippers, the Pleiades — all were vivid. We could distinguish multiple stars where to the naked eye there were only single ones. Jupiter, on its westward journey, was a regular guest. I wondered whether I could see its larger moons or if those pricks of "light" to one side of the disc were illusory. Galileo saw them and his glass wasn't much better than J.C. Penney's.

"Do you think Rosa and her family will always be poor?" Anne asked as a satellite lost itself over Cedros. Our thoughts turned again to the curious island, the high–point of our travels so far.

"Maybe Juanito will find the gold in that old French mine," I replied.

In 1914 the French owners had dynamited the mine, in a mountain near Punta Norte, just ahead of troops dispatched to the island by Pancho Villa. Said to contain one of the richest lodes in Mexico, the government kept it closed against future contingencies, a kind of strategic reserve. It hadn't been worked since the Revolution so nobody knew for sure what was there. In fact, no one we met claimed to know its exact location except Juanito, the 14–year–old son of Juan Arce and Rosa Elba Balles.

Señora Balles, wife of one of the camp's top fishermen and mother of five, was the unofficial mayor of Punta Norte. The first rain in a year began just as we came ashore. She insisted that we wait it out in her shack, one of the camp's dozen scrap–board huts. The only permanent structure was a concrete water tank, the water boated from a spring three miles down. She served us tea, hot tortillas and honey while the camp's 20 children looked on — Juanito, not the oldest, was the most mature among them.

"You made everyone happy by coming to see us," he said. "Not many strangers come and they are always in a hurry."

Except for infrequent yachtsmen and trawler crews, the only foreign visitors to Cedros were "hard rock" geologists and their chisel–dangled graduate students. They swooped in from time to time, pecked through the furnace–hot arroyos, then flew away. Not all were academics. There were rumors of oil. On the dirt airstrip south of town, a PEMEX Cessna was taxiing as our patched–wing DC–3 shuddered in.

Welcoming us was one of Cedros' three taxis: a finned Detroit Chromosaurus rex with colorful objects of religious significance depended from the rearview mirror. With eight people in the vehicle, the fare was 500 pesos, about a dollar–forty. There followed a moonscape with cactuses dusted by the taxis to an earthen hue.

The *dueña* of the only hostelry, the Eagle Guest House, lived above the town's arroyo, which seeped with refuse, producing a saccharine stench. The taxi waited below, enveloped in the cloudlet of its arrival dust. I announced myself through a screen door to an unseen male voice. After intense murmurings a hand delivered a metal plate. Attached was a key to Room Number 9. On the front was a message in English that guaranteed postage. Drop in any mailbox.

Anne rode in front and I in the back with the last local passenger, a burly fellow with few teeth and glazed eyes who smelled of beer. He winked lewdly, tilting his head toward my companion and slapping his palms together.

Everyone in the pueblo worked for the salt pier or cannery or ran one of the little stores under cannery license, except the marines and police. They lived in barracks apart and their only contact with the people was during nightly *papeles,* identity papers, inspections. Young officers strutted about demanding *"sus papeles"* from whomever of the island's inhabitants happened to be in the street at the time. Riflemen, who crowded in close and stared hard into the eyes of the person being asked for *sus papeles,* accompanied the officers.

Juanito and his mother, Rosa Elba Balles,
Punta Norte, Cedros Island, Mexico.

The fishermen considered themselves independent. They kept
their own hours and did not respond to the cannery's mill whistle.
Some lived at one of the island's three remote fish camps: Punta

Norte was the smallest. The only buyer for their catches was the cannery.

The Eagle, 1000 pesos, two days payable in advance, had no pretensions. Its walls retained the 100–degree heat well into the night. Water, gravity piped from a distant spring across arid canyons, gurgled reluctantly — and not at all after noon except to the barracks and the mill bosses' barbwired compound. Sharing the yard outside our window were two starving dogs, a naked child badly in need of a diaper, a teenager with a radio, a wandering pig and a flock of mosquitoes.

A punch of salmonella disabled us for a day. I persuaded Anne to join me for a walk in the cloud–sheltered cool of the second afternoon. She mistakenly followed rather than preceded me in a close passage and young men going in the opposite direction fondled her. My challenge brought snickers and flight. Pursuit into unknown knives was foolhardy.

These indignities — there were others, none life–threatening, but all wickedly petty molestations — both angered and sorrowed Anne. Suggestive whistling and a choppy hissing sound may precede or accompany such assaults. A woman is most vulnerable when alone or momentarily out of sight of a male friend.

Nearby, a sheet splotched with blood flapped on the clothesline of some newlyweds: another gesture of *machismo* or of chastity.

A statue of a large–breasted nude girl holding the pelt of a seal faced the sea from the center of the town's small plaza. To one side was a matronly Victorian bust of the wife of Benito Juárez, Mexico's "Lincoln."

Antonio, self–appointed courier for the fish camps, was our boatman. He spooked deer with a whistle and butted his *lancha* toward rookeries of sea lions. At our request he drew close to La Palmita, a sudden spring feeding a stand of palms.

For two–and–a–half centuries this had been the first stop of the Manila galleons after their four–month journey across the Pacific. The crews — rotting with dysentery, scurvy, sunburn — would anchor off the spring for a week before descending to Acapulco and Lima with cargoes of silk, balm, gems and tales of the East. Commercial trawlers and yachts still take on water there.

At the mouth of Canyon Grande, a nine–mile gash through the island, were a half dozen goats: descendants of those marooned as a source of fresh meat by early whalers.

Six miles up the arroyo was the site of the principal Indian village — called by them "Wamalgua" — when Cedros was discovered by Cortés' pilot Francisco de Ulloa in 1540. The natives were left alone until 1732 when they were "evacuated" by the Jesuits to their

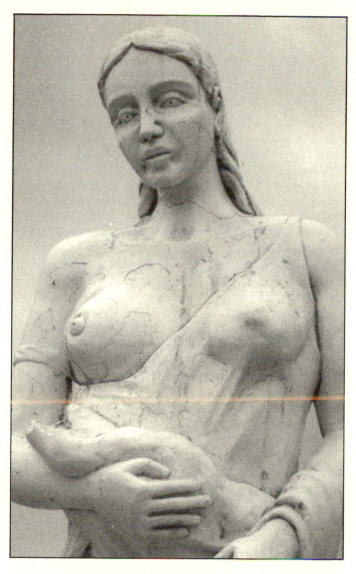

Statue of girl with seal pelt, Cedros Island, Mexico.

mission at San Ignacio on the mainland. Fewer than 100 of 2,000 survived the relocation, most dying of smallpox.

Except for gold prospectors, Cedros remained uninhabited until the fish cannery was established in 1920. I imagined what it was like during the 200–year détente between Spaniard and islander: their only contact the thirsty galleons at La Palmita.

Antonio's arrival at Punta Norte brought virtually everyone to the beach. In addition to two scruffy gringos, he freighted ten cases of Carta Blanca beer and the week's mail, much of it from the United States. Most every one there had a relative working somewhere in "El Norte." Indeed, it was an inquiry from Juanito, "You know where ees Bakersfeel?" that brought him to our attention. Though we'd never been to Bakersfield, much less seen an uncle who lived there, the lad quickly marshaled a portaging of our gear, an antlike procession of tots that, at his mother's gentle admonition, ended at their shanty.

When the rain abated late that afternoon, we moved across a wide arroyo into a cactus forest. At nightfall, a hypnotic six–second beacon commenced its blinkings from an automated lighthouse on the point, a warning to sailors of their approach to Ulloa's last known landfall. Beating north from Cedros, the great pilot had disappeared forever.

For three days we explored the tip of the island. Anne found an empire of seals in sheltered coves just west of camp and spent hours observing them. I climbed the summit of the nearest peak, from which I could see Anne and her shadow groping in tandem through the cactus and along the steep bluffs. Later I hiked up the canyon until it ended in a stairstep of falls. The ground was terribly saline as was most of the freshly captured rainwater, the pools ringed with crystalline froths of drying salt. A few contained sweet water. It was cool and delicious.

Despite two determined attempts I missed the trail that Juanito said led to the mine. In several places there were lengths of old communication or blasting wire. These invariably played out. I disturbed passels of lizards and webs of spiders. A four–point buck whirled, stared at me disdainfully, then bolted.

Such were our wistful musings of Cedros — a place, it must be said, that we were quite ready to leave at the end of a week — that we fell asleep without washing the dishes. Malarrimo's alert coyotes did not let the opportunity pass.

I rustled out at first light and set aboil a strong batch of cowboy coffee, grounds and all. As I lit the fire I noticed an unruly . congregation of paw prints. Feathered scavengers had also been at work. Every pan and foil wrap had been thoroughly licked and pecked. The pint of leftover shrimp and rice I'd figured for lunch was history. So was my Teflon skillet.

The author's camp at Punta Norte, Cedros Island.

I set these impertinences aside as I anticipated my own imminent scavenging. What treasures waited on that eternity of unspoiled beach? Washing down a handful of raisins, I headed out to try my luck. The Manila galleons, the vanished Ulloa, the Chinese porcelain, the mysterious *Confidence* struggling in heavy weather — all sailed through my mind.

The residue of commerce of a different order soon dislodged such thoughts. Malarrimo, I discovered, was not a galleon graveyard but a final display aisle. Flung ashore in high tide arc–sweeps of intertangled kelp were eternal shelf lives of punch–out pill packets; six–pack loops in two of which fish had grown distortedly before dying; Planters' peanut cans, the dapper logo smiling from the label; Clorox jugs; Easy Off oven cleaner jars; pop bottles; a jumbo container of Pine Sol toilet scourge; and hundreds, thousands, of milk cartons bearing the forlorn and faded Polaroid likenesses of children snatched, discarded or escaped from the ethnic smorgasbords of Southern California.

How odd that, had they survived, the Baja aboriginals could have followed from here the history of man — from the age of balsa to the age of silicon. I imagined the alarmed grimace of some pensive primitive as he pondered the origin of this manifestly metaphysical flotsam. Looking forward, I fancied the smile of the geologist from Cygnus 351 whose excavation of quaternary Earth yields a Dagwood stratum of compressed retailing.

I continued for miles, pausing at times to examine particular artifacts. Certain egrets and pelicans seemed, as they soared and plunged, to conduct me on my journey.

Here and there sank surly little canine indentations, perhaps of the thieves of the night before. From their freshness, their authors could not have long preceded me.

Plaza, San Ignacio Oasis, Baja California Sur.

2

CABO

She threw overboard bottles containing notes,
'hundreds of them by now.' On them she wrote the
date, the ship's name and position, and her
address. She asked the finder to reply.

A hundred thousand Indians inhabited the entirety of Baja California when the Spanish arrived in the bay of La Paz in 1533. By 1850 all had disappeared except for a few hundred far to the north in the Colorado River Delta and in the mountains behind Ensenada on the upper Pacific coast. In addition to smallpox, their extinction can be attributed to the loss of dignity and self–reliance attendant upon forced relocation and the displacement of their hunter–gatherer culture.

Mestizaje, the interbreeding that subsumed the Amerindian race throughout most of New Spain, did not occur in Baja since many tribes remained widely dispersed over the inhospitable terrain. The mission settlements were also remote and few Europeans migrated to the peninsula.

The 1533 landing party was composed of mutineers who had murdered their captain. All but a handful were in turn dispatched by the Indians. Cortés, himself, headed a 1535 party which included four hundred Spaniards and three hundred Negro slaves. But this enclave was starved out in less than a year. It was not until 1697, 160 years later, that the first permanent settlement took root in Loreto, an island–shielded harbor 150 miles to the north. The Jesuit missionary Juan María Salvatierra was its founder. Thirty further missions were begun over the ensuing 140 years by the Jesuits and their successors, the Dominicans and Franciscans, who, under Father Junípero Serra, pushed far to the north to found San Diego in 1769 and San Francisco in 1776.

Pearl divers and expeditions seeking a route for the Manila galleons around the "island" of California had intermittent contact with the Indians during this period, mainly along the gulf coast. Aside from the missions there was little activity from Cabo San Lucas up the Pacific until independence from Spain in 1821.

During the US–Mexican war in 1848 the United States Navy occupied San José del Cabo, as well as Loreto and La Paz, and proclaimed Baja California's annexation as an American territory. The peninsula was not retained though in the Treaty of Guadalupe

Hidalgo that ceded half$_1$ of Mexico to the United States for $15 million.

In 1853 the ubiquitous American adventurer–nuisance William Walker proclaimed himself president of "The Republic of Lower California." Evicted, he turned his efforts further south, where in 1855 he took over Nicaragua with a band of mercenaries and was "elected" president. Ousted two years later, he ended his career before a British–inspired Honduran firing squad in 1860.

No other threat to Baja from the north occurred. The land was far too arid and inhospitable for the kind of Anglo migration and settlement which had led Texas to independence and eventual statehood.

Cabo San Lucas is the end of California. When I first visited the place sixteen years before I was put ashore by a small fishing trawler, the *México*, I'd hitched on out of Ensenada. What I found then was a fly–in marlin fishing resort with an old–style hacienda, a run down hotel, a modest pensión and two buses a week to La Paz. Curious children followed my progress from the little bay, up over dunes, to the Pacific. There an avaricious surf grasped into crevices and clutched at red–orange monoliths. The Templar rocks were still there. But my old campsite was now the parking lot of the Hotel Solmar, a split–level accommodation that sprawled across the top of the beach. Under construction next door were "time–share condominiums exclusively offered" by a Los Angeles Realtor.

With perhaps undue optimism the buildings lay not 40 feet from high tide. The hotel encouraged its guests to sit in their little partitions of patio and "watch the ocean come to you." Wearied from two weeks' dusty camping, Anne and I seized the only vacancy. For $9 we bought two wooden recliners from a street peddler in Cabo town. They were made of unseasoned pine and oozed resin in the warm sun. We sat halfway between our patio and the surf; the ocean responded, playfully at first, then petulantly as the tide rose. A *huracán*, I thought, would one day be vengeful. Far down the beach, against the cliffs of land's end, was a well–hidden hotel sign in Spanish that warned of a powerful undertow and admonished that swimming here is *"muy peligroso."*

The town, too, had changed since my previous visit. The principal thoroughfares had been asphalted; the main road to the pier paved. The small harbor had been dredged agape to three times its natural size. The fish cannery at its entrance was closed — the building but a faded shell. Its former workers were now waiters, *taxistas* and guides for the occupants of the white boxes mushrooming on the cape's desert hillsides. In what had been a broad plain, there was an imposing, fenced compound for vehicles awaiting the ferry. An embarcadero and customs house had been built. A billboard with a cloud painted above a tranquil sea welcomed you on behalf of FONATUR, the "National Fund for the Development of Tourism."

A Norwegian cruise ship, that I recognized as the one in a popular television program, rode at anchor. Throngs of elderly American women, brought ashore by the ship's sleek shuttle launch, defiled along souvenir stalls that extended from a concrete pavilion across to the marlin dock. There, superbly equipped motorboats were collecting armamentaria of tackle and beer. The enormous rods and reels invited Lilliputian comparisons.

Soldiers in fatigues and carrying M14 rifles were on patrol. Two of them were ejecting a peddler of miniature wooden fish and other hand–painted toy animals. A T–shirt merchant — "Life's a Beach; Sun your Buns in Cabo"; "Another Day in Paradise" — next door had complained that the peddler was sniping his customers. The man resisted and more soldiers came. His basket of wares fell to the ground and overturned. A crowd of Mexicans gathered and stared at the peddler and at the toys as if they expected them to move. He was led to a police van. When it drove away a soldier returned and gathered the toys into the basket and took them to an army truck. The sergeant in charge was holding hands with a girl in tight shorts who caressed his rifle.

Across the compound, plainclothes officials were inspecting vehicles queued for the ferry to Puerto Vallarta. There were 18 large trucks and some 50 autos, pickups and campers, about evenly split between US citizens and Mexicans. Inspection of the Americans was cursory but that of the Mexicans, relentless. Armloads of items for which there were no purchase or tax receipts satisfactory to the bantamlike *jefe* of the inspectors were being confiscated. Soldiers from the truck were called to help carry television sets and other appliances from the vans of some young Mexicans. The occupants protested, but to no avail.

"¡Ladrones! ¡Ladrones! ¡Chinga tu Madre!" Thieves and worse, shouted one of the drivers. A soldier stepped forward, placing himself at port arms between the young man doing the shouting and the bantam *jefe*. A woman passenger was weeping.

"Es todo que tenemos ... Es todo que tenemos ... ," she was saying. It is all that we have. They had purchased the items in San Diego and were transporting them back to the mainland to sell.

"The Giggling Marlin — You Hook 'Em; We Cook 'Em" was a single large room — a kind of converted meeting hall filled with tables, each covered with plastic red–and–white checkerboard tablecloths. Above, in each corner of the room and midway on either side, were six 31–inch color television sets.

47

On screen an earnest, dimpled hydra was talking sincerely, then stopped and looked down and to the right and another six heads began talking. There were six scenes of a flood and people clinging to the roofs of houses and of a helicopter landing. A policeman in sunglasses was interviewed. The second head stopped talking and the dimpled one said something briefly and the camera backed away showing the first person sitting alone at a desk but with other persons in the background.

Next, two attractive people at a breakfast table were drinking coffee. There was a close—up of the coffee cup steaming; then another close—up of a jar, and the two people smiling at each other intensely; and then another close—up of the jar. The woman was wearing an ambiguous white blouse as if she were ready for either housework or a commute. The man wore a shirt and tie.

Next, a dozen bikini—clad young women cavorted with two bronzed males, one of whom offered the other a cigarette and then several of the young women were smoking as well. Doral. There is no prohibition in Mexico against such commercials. Most tobacco is sold by subsidiaries of American companies or under their franchises.

I recalled Gail and Alfredo, owners of "Alfredo's Sport Fishing" camp up the gulf at Loreto, telling of their daughter. At 18 she'd elected to become a Mexican citizen. Her mother was from Tennessee. The following year she'd become "Miss Mexico" and a runner—up in the Miss Universe contest. The principal sponsors were beer and cigarette companies, and she spent her time now doing promotional tours and television commercials for them. "Linda is on TV so much it's like having her at home," her mother said proudly.

There was a hoist between two steel construction beams at the end of the marlin pier. The tourists who had caught very large fish would stand there with the animal hanging, head down, next to them. Each person being photographed carried a placard on which was chalked his name, hometown, type of fish — today they were all "Blue Marlin," the tackle, the time needed to reel the fish to the boat, the weight of the fish, name of the boat, its captain and the date. The name of the photographer appeared at the bottom of the placard in bright yellow and was the only part of the sign that was permanently painted in. It said simply, "Photo ROGELO."

Unless the person considered his fish a "trophy" — was willing to pay a large sum to have it mounted, with glass eyes and plywood fins attached — it was then turned over to the cleaners who were working frenetically just behind the scales. The meat from only a small marlin is enough for a banquet, so there is an embarrassment of surplusage after the steaks are taken to the hotel chefs for the tourists.

That afternoon two groups, one from Houston and the other from Los Angeles, had just returned. Two in each party had landed fish that might have been considered trophies, though only one was so chosen. The largest was 420 pounds. It belonged to a portly young man from New Braunfels, Texas. I asked him later at the Solmar bar why he did not have his marlin mounted.

"I'd have to sell one hell of a lot of cars to afford that," he replied good-naturedly.

They were a group of automobile salesmen who had a good year and were being treated by their boss to five days in Cabo. It was also a sales meeting, I was carefully told by a colleague. "The IRS can be pretty tricky about these things, you know." This was the fellow with the smallest of the four fish, but the one that would be the "trophy."

While the car dealers were weighing their catches, a crowd of scavengers waiting to grab strips of discarded fish meat and viscera before they fell to the frenzy of pelicans beneath the pier, shoved against the cleaners. A teenage boy briefly tussled with an old woman over a generous portion, then left her to it as he pounced on another. As each fish was hauled by the boat crews over to the cleaning place, other scavengers appeared, staring hungrily at the meat and warily at each other and at the two soldiers detailed to keep order. There was a surge when the great marlin of the New Braunfels car salesman was passed to the butchers. Even the soldiers joined in, the others obsequiously making way for them.

A lone *lancha* approached powered by a venerable Evinrude. The fisherman, a robust fellow in his late 30s, handed up a string of hefty Dorado to a boy on the pier, and tied his *lancha*, the *Mirabelle*, unobtrusively beyond the hubbub. I walked over and called out *"Buenas tardes"* and complimented the catch. The boy, who looked about ten, held up two big ones and asked if I wanted to buy them. But the fisherman, his father, took them, saying they were not for sale.

"For the fiesta," he said, smiling. His name was Roberto.

"Do you guide?" I asked.

"Sí, cómo no," he replied. Ten dollars an hour or 40 for a day, which ran until I wanted to quit. Tomorrow, then, we agreed.

Outside the harbor were anchored a sloop without a name and a ketch, *Shades of Blue*, out of San Francisco and Seattle. They were bound for Costa Rica, with the sloop intending to cross to the Marquesas in February. It was now November and the annual flotilla of American yachts bound to La Paz for the winter was arriving. Cabo was a favorite stopover.

Near a narrow strip of sand just shy of the cape called "Lovers Beach," Roberto plumbed for squid, caught several, baited the hooks and set an easy troll up the Pacific.

"What kind of book you write about Mexico?" he asked, trying a bit of English.

"The countryside; what people are doing, thinking. Politics," I replied.

"People don't like talk about politics things," he said. And then after a pause, "It is worthless talk, and can be very dangerous."

When we reached an old lighthouse, about three miles to the north, he cut the motor and we drifted. He replaced the squid with some small, live mackerel. Before too long we had each hauled in a couple of passable snapper.

"Muy macho, este cabrón;₂ ... ¡machísimo!" he exclaimed, as he netted my best one.

The conversation turned to work, *trabajo*. When the fish cannery closed back in the '70s he had done odd jobs with FONATUR. The employees had been told they would all get better paying jobs there, but it hadn't worked out that way.

"Some of us worked for a little time at the beginning," he said. "But we were not members of the *sindicatos*." Construction unions were expensive to join and even then you had to bribe the union bosses to get a job and keep it, he added.

A marlin smack cruised past on its way up the coast, eight pale passengers attentive on deck. Two of the big lines were already trailing.

"Sacan mucho pescado hoy," he said. They'll catch a lot today. I asked how he knew. *"El Patrón,"* he replied. By *El Patrón,* The Boss, Roberto meant the governor₃ of this Mexican state, Baja California Sur. The sight of the gubernatorial party shook loose an answer to an earlier question that had been ignored with a grunt: "Mexico made more money than even the gringos from the oil. Billions of *dólares*. But, the politicians and the bankers, they steal all of it. And what do they give the people? Inflation, that is what. The peso is not even worth ten percent of what it was just five years ago."

He spoke rapidly, all in Spanish now, becoming more agitated the longer he talked, once conspicuously ignoring a fish on his line.

"You know the politicians are *cabrones* for what they have done to Mexico. I do not believe that this time the people will forgive and forget. I am only a fisherman, but I know that the big changes are coming very soon. *Tenemos que cambiar muchas cosas."* We must change many things.

Politics took us well past four, when the last soda and *cerveza* had long been dispensed from Roberto's polyfoam cooler. On the way in we came alongside the sloop. Its skipper talked of their plans and

50

of "reliable word" passed along that the Sandinistas had been boarding passing yachts on the pretense of searching for contraband, that when "found" resulted in stiff fines. "One boat was hit for five grand." Nicaragua, he said, was to be given wide berth, "At least 150 miles out, and then I wouldn't relax."

The scales at the dock deflated my pride by registering only three pounds for the largest snapper, although a Dorado brought six. I split the catch with Roberto and we cleaned them on the pier, his son Adolfo, who met us wearing a yellow Caterpillar cap, taking the guide's share home. I delivered mine to the *dueño* of the restaurant "Guadalajara" with instructions to cook a batch *a modo de ajo,* in garlic, and ice down the rest. There turned out to be enough for three days for Anne and me, even after the *dueño's* wife, who was the cook, unexpectedly retained a substantial portion for the kitchen.

Anne flew home from Los Cabos airport about 35 miles to the north. Her visa recorded that she had entered by car, and there was a hassle as we went from one official to another, until finally one wrote "accompanied" on hers and "responsible party" on mine. One must leave the same way one arrived. This supposedly keeps gringos from selling cars without paying the import tax.

The ferry was scheduled to leave a half hour after her plane so we said our goodbyes and I hurried back to the embarcadero to find the boat canceled. Not enough passengers. The next one was Sunday so I drove 40 miles up the Pacific to near Todos Santos and camped on the beach.

It was a surfer's beach and some students from Los Angeles and a party of singing Mexicans caravaned out early the following morning. They sat on the sand and drank beer and strummed guitars and waited for the perfect wave. I walked over to visit.

While we were talking, a couple from Phoenix in a rented Volkswagen drove in and took their surfboards off the roof. An older fellow, I supposed about fifty but who was in good training, curled in on a tall wave. He was followed by another with long braided hair. They said there was a strong undertow.

The Mexicans decided to return to town, somehow boarding eleven adults and two tykes into a dauntless '58 Plymouth. The vans full of Americans followed. The older guy, Sid, and I walked over to my camp for tea. The other fellow climbed an outcrop where he sat in apparent meditation.

Sid said he drove the peninsula once a year, usually in the fall. He was partially retired having made his stash in "software."

"I like it down here. 'Fella could live the rest of his life on next to nothing. I know a dozen good folk who've made the move, permanently. Nice houses, too; servants, the lot. One guy even nested

51

down in Tapachula near the Guatemala line. Better in Baja, though, than the mainland. The Mexicans here are a better quality. They have to work and stay out of trouble or they get shipped back. So less thieving and rape and the rest."

"What do you spend a week, more or less?" I asked.

"Oh, a hundred, I guess. Maybe two. But I eat in restaurants and probably spend half my nights in hotels."

There was a lull and I thought I heard a scream.

"Hey, did you hear that?" Sid asked.

"Yeah, I heard it too. Came from over there, I think." I pointed beyond the rocks where the guru had gone to sit.

"Could just be horseplay."

The scream came again, this time rising low in a throat, then hurtling to the top of the horror scale. I ran to the jeep and grabbed an empty five–gallon water jug I kept wrapped with 40 feet of twine, an improvised buoy I had fancied tossing out to Anne — or vice versa.

By the time I got to the water, Sid had plunged out with Olympian strokes. His companion was nowhere to be seen.

Beyond Sid's direction of swim was a yellow form splashing against what was obviously a retrograde current. You could see the rustling water there, undisturbed by the overriding breakers — an ugly riptide. Then I saw two more people even further out, one of them with a bandanna — the guru!

Sid reached the woman just as she went limp in the transparency of a wave. The way I saw her was surreal, the way you see fish sometimes inside waves. I had just the night before seen two — a big one and its prey — knifing through a swell close–in, just before it hit the beach. I'd wondered at the time if dinner had been caught before the deluge.

They were all too far out for the jug, though I noticed that everyone was headed upcoast *with* the current, not fighting it. The experts had won control. In a few minutes they'd worked in behind the jetty and made standing depth. Shortly all were sprawled on the sand, exhausted.

The rescued went to their Volkswagen and stood around, shaking. They waved off an offer of hot tea. The guru resumed his lotus and Sid popped a beer. Soon the Mexicans returned, this time with three clunkers filled with surfers and guitars. The Californians were not far behind.

When I arrived at the embarcadero Sunday to get a ticket I was told there was no record of my reservations. There might be a place for me, but not for the jeep: *"No es posible, Señor."* There was a line of 30 with the same problem. I was not sanguine.

"Don't worry," a tall fellow, about 55, counseled. "Everybody always gets on. They just want you to sweat a little. Maybe get you to contribute to the retirement fund."

"Oh, they said I could get a ticket, but the jeep couldn't make it."

"They always say that. Good for business — if you know what I mean. The name's Bob Elliot; this is my wife, Micaela. You have a Southern accent, don't you?"

He was a "merchant seaman," he said, heading down to a little seaside town named Barra de Navidad where they had built a house. I knew the place, having spent a couple of days there once while hitching down to Manzanillo. Huge, constant swells roll up on the town's beach. And it's perfectly safe to swim, even for children. Off the beaten trail, few tourists know about it. Maybe because of this, a lot of Mexicans go there for holidays with their families.

"How long you been in the Merchant Marine," I inquired.

"Twenty–eight years. Another two, and I'm taking full retirement."

When I asked what his job was he was evasive so I didn't pursue it. But when Micaela replied that she was a ship's librarian, he said they worked on the same vessel.

I told them I'd once turned a hand as a basic seaman/purser's clerk on a ship they had probably heard of, the "President Wilson" of American President Lines out of San Francisco.

They looked at each other and smiled. Then he opened the paperback he was reading. It was rubber stamped, "520392 S.S. *President Wilson*," over a ship's silhouette. He was the captain!

"Of course," he said, "It's not really the same ship, the old two–stacker. It's altogether different, strictly cargo. Well, I shouldn't say that, we do have cabins for 12 passengers, but they ride where the freight goes. We only have 48 crew — a lot fewer than your old passenger liner. More comfortable, too. It's enjoyable being aboard."

"Yes, eet ees so nice. I geet Bob to take me with heem," Micaela said.

"She's a good librarian. Keeps the books catalogued and restocked. She likes to collect a new batch whenever we're in port."

Bob turned out to be correct about getting aboard. It was necessary to "tip" the cargo master — but he was happy with ten dollars. When the second–class lounge where I had planned to throw my sleeping bag proved crowded and noisy, my new friends offered the couch in their cabin.

"We've had more trouble than we had bargained for with the house." Bob grew more talkative later in the main bar. "The Mexican relatives of the seller that we let stay there now seem to think it's theirs." So they spent their vacations with the interlopers, who refused to vacate.

"We've had friends who built a completely new home only to find it occupied when they returned — confiscated by people who said the land belonged to them. The local authorities will do nothing, of course — unless you want to make a contribution. And it's not just one contribution, but many. They never stop once you start. Not a pleasant way to depart with your life's savings."

Micaela, a German–Argentine, and Bob had met on one of his voyages to Buenos Aires in the late '50s. They'd been together 25 years. No children, though Bob had two from an earlier marriage. They were accompanied, however, by a miniature dachshund, sneaked aboard, who had just dumped under the cabin bed. The dog eyed me suspiciously.

"Shees really a goot dog," Micaela managed in defense. "Shee never potties in the bed. Shee jees sleeps under the covers and wakes up with her head on the pillow. I even burp her after her dinner ..." The animal sailed with them on the *Wilson*.

Micaela had developed a peculiar pastime. She threw overboard bottles containing notes, "hundreds of them by now." On them she wrote the date, the ship's name and position, and her address. She asked the finder to reply.

"She must have flipped 15 bottles a day over the side," Bob said. "It got to be we were spending half our time writing these notes in longhand. So I started Xeroxing forms for them."

"She's got letters from India, Thailand. That one was a German on vacation. Even got one from Bangladesh. A Swiss couple sailing a catamaran around the world found one near the Turks and Caicos Islands. And a woman in Aruba who lost her man, she said, because he had to leave the island to find work when the refinery closed."

"And from Sri Lanka, too, and from Taiwan, too, and from Korea," Micaela said proudly.

After a long pause, Bob said — not to me but to her — "The young fellow from Taiwan said that he watched the bottle for over an hour, coming and going in the surf, before he finally decided to pick it up."

Mexican Workers Party, Marxist, poster, La Paz.
"You are drugged up if you think we can pay the foreign debt.
The only solution: suspension of payments!"

3

ACAPULCO

*Puzzled mariachis trumpeted at red–awninged tables of
burritos and Coca–Cola and Dos Equis and to collapsible
stalls of sarapes and wooden donkeys, maracas and
castanets. Elegists and harbingers.*

The ferry *Azteca* docked at Puerto Vallarta early the following
morning after an easy cruise across the mouth of the Sea of Cortés.

Motorists were forbidden to descend to the parking deck for two
hours while ship and customs officials argued. When word came to
proceed we found a chamber of diesel fumes and carbon monoxide.
Even truckers at the very rear of the four queues were revving and
racing their engines.

The implied order of leaving was one vehicle alternately from
each line but the customs men with pistols and riot batons favored
the trucks. Speeding the freight on its way was not the idea. Waybills
and taxes were disputed. There was shouting and horn–blowing from
behind until those in front paid their fines.

I was whistled through as if I had been the cause of everyone's
delay and briskly skipped the town, having visited it once before.
There on the left was Moby Dick's, a cavernous eatery and bar for
American tourists and retirees. Already there was a crowd of
sunburned patrons in khaki shorts and surfer jams.

It is said that Puerto Vallarta is "the city built by a movie." That
is true. The place had been an unhurried fishing settlement when
Richard Burton and Elizabeth Taylor made "Night of the Iguana"
there in 1961. Within months it became a *de rigueur* pilgrimage for
every celluloid noble and lackey. The audience followed in Airstreams
and Winnebagoes, and in ten years the population grew from fewer
than 3,000 to half a million. All begun with a film.

I crept south along the coastal highway. Bob and Micaela passed
in their van. We exchanged waves. I thought of her urgent bottles.
How many of them were still adrift? Doubtless, one would be
shrugged ashore at Malarrimo to be found by the likes of me or by an
idle fisherman. Or perhaps it would merely sink into the breccia —
another artifact awaiting cosmic notice.

There were groves of coconut with high pyramids of the nuts set
smoking to dry. An old woman with a pole and a rope of fish walked
in front of a pregnant young woman who led a small horse. A child
was riding bareback and another tagging along, a little girl trundling
with a bouquet of flowers.

Ahead walked strong, thickly mustached young men with intense brown eyes. Machetes were carried open, no scabbards, but open, with the blade held inboard against the flesh of the arm. Vigilant, unbefuddled, stalwart, ready to be led. Later there were others on horseback and in enormous sombreros, also with machetes, but in scabbards, and with rifles cradled across their saddles. They surprised me at a curve on a hill and did not yield but continued the way that they were going, a cohort of leather and dust.

It is possible to drive long distances in Mexico without seeing another vehicle. This can be discomfiting, raising the severe notion of an unofficial curfew. I learned to detect a village by the appearance of denuded hectares strewn with refuse: tomato paste cans, corn oil jugs, cannibalized refrigerators, accordioned compacts. The autos were compressed at unforgiving speeds, surely among them the perpetrators of those innumerable patches of roadside crosses. Here and there someone would have set a fire which smoldered long after its ignitor had gone — a pungency of grass, offal, plastic, rubber and disposable diapers. Its smoke obscured livestock and pedestrians. *Topes*, speed bumps, seemed insidiously placed not only at community limits and bridges but at no place in particular, possibly at someone's private whim. The bridges narrowed often to a single lane, and their surfaces were buckled and heaved.

Electricity is still a luxury, even in communities with power lines. By night one senses nearness of habitation by the flickering of candles, lanterns and flashlights. Unlit trucks can be stalled or parked dead ahead. Oncoming cars are discerned by their soft yellow parking lights. Suddenly appearing buses with double–bright headlamps force lesser traffic onto speculative shoulders with mangled visions of brown children and vengeful machetes. Broken glass garnishes the roadway as if strewn by some pernicious Appleseed. Girls on porches preen when truckers pass. A *camión* is a suggestion of means.

I was now eight weeks into the trip. Though I'd set no rigid schedule, I knew that I had to keep moving if I was to have the time and energy essential for a thorough look at South America. Baja was the culprit. Its splendid beaches, mountains and deserts had proven irresistible. Plus the fact that it had been the first part of the trek, the freshness and vigor of finally being underway, had let it eat deliciously of the time.

Acapulco was like a neglected widow whose children only came around once in a while. Its crescent bay was ringed with silent steel and concrete clones of Miami siblings, teenage monsters gaping at the ocean's edge with crazed, fixed eyes of windows, vaguely conscious of lesser cousins rooting up the last traces of open beach through vulnerable alleyways and seawall crevices. Puzzled mariachis trumpeted at red–awninged tables of burritos and Coca–Cola and Dos Equis and to collapsible stalls of sarapes and wooden donkeys, maracas and castanets. Elegists and harbingers.

A bargain was the Motel Acapulco at eight dollars a night — and within a block or two of McDonalds and Kentucky Fried Chicken. There was a high wall around the parking lot and a full–time night attendant. Always in such places one is assured, *"No hay problemas; no hay problemas,"* the speaker affecting a bereaved indignation, as if it were rude to inquire about security: There is no problem here with thieves, señor. This is an honest and well–guarded establishment. At the desk were brochures of a harbor excursion firm: See the spectacular sunset, the famous cliff divers, the hidden bays, the hideaway cottages of the Past's Inevitables.

Four boys, none yet 14, swirled like hungry seals in the short lee of the boat. They wore webbed feet and goggles and scanned the passenger rails furtively, waiting for a coin to be thrown into the brown bay, whereupon they kicked at the sky and disappeared for long moments before one of them surfaced with the prize.

The boat was a salvaged ferry crewed by eight young men with biceps, mustaches, tangled hair and sunglasses, who pulled heroically on mooring lines and rushed about the deck attending to departure preliminaries. They then cooked *hamburguesas* and oily fries, tended bar and became a sextet of horns with a xylophone and drum.

There was a festive group of about 40 who danced and drank a great deal. Secondary students clustered in shy patches of blue and gray and maroon. Reserved collegians loitered at the fantail — the boys in white shirts and gray checkered slacks and the girls in yellow and pink and white–laced blouses. Some couples held hands and spoke softly with sudden, exaggerated laughter. There were very old couples who held hands and said nothing.

As we cinder–belched past plunging granitic bluffs, a scratchy recording informed in Spanish, then in malaprop BBC: "Dis house, over there to the right, belong to the late *actur* John Wayne, who has disappeared. And over there, once again to de right, the long red one on the top, many others, North American *acturs*, their mansion, many of them have likewise disappeared, among them Mr. Steve McQueen. …"

There followed the ruins of an actors' guild retreat and the private villas of the more celebrated. Next came the "honeymoon bungalow" of John and Jackie Kennedy. The vessel listed noticeably to starboard as my 243 fellow passengers rushed to distinguish this special shrine.

I watched the disembarkation from the second deck, then went ashore through a queue of wedding revelers, avoiding the streets converging near the *zócalo* discharging rivers of catalytically unconverted engines into the beachfront boulevard. Mufflers were inefficient and impatient. Escaping the traffic I savored odors from a carnival of street kitchens: sizzling beef and goat, tortillas, chickens slowly browning in electric rotisseries and others over driftwood fires — the wood borne in from far up the coast by old women and children in buses and by young men in battered pickups — all basted with sage and greater spices and *huachinango*, caught and marketed that very afternoon. One taco vendor could have dealt four tables of blackjack, so swift was he at carving and chopping the beef, onions, garlic and peppers.

As I paused to order a plate of *chilaquiles* from one of the carts, I noticed a discretely hand–lettered sign in the window of a general merchandise store: *Se venden aparadores baratos. Pida.* Cheap apparatuses sold here. Ask. Cloistered behind bolts of polyester and shelves of school paper and soccer balls, was a glass–enclosed display of condoms in ascending sizes, from about three to eight inches long, and various colors. At the bottom were a number of pale green plastic oak and maple leaves with nylon tails attached and an assortment of small mirrors. In a booklet nearby were instructions from a Dr. Joaquín Marcuse Torres entitled, *"Cómo Evitar El Embarazo,"* How to Keep from Getting Pregnant. Even such hesitant suggestions would have been unthinkable ten years before.[4]

I climbed an hour from the beach. Ancient Bluebird buses exploded past, shuttling workers to a factory somewhere. Also on board were drummers with tubs of fish and tortillas. These plied the lesser markets of the barrios, endless tracts of scrap wood hovels overlooking the city. For a tenth the price of a tourist lunch you could eat your fill in one of these: *tacos, chilaquiles, pollo asado, pozole,* the latter a chunky fish, hominy and vegetable soup sprinkled with diced onions and hot green salsa and served from a crock. At one stall with stools for four and a shelf that opened to the street, a butcher and a fish hawker were slurping bowls of *pozole.* I declined the salsa and took mine plain.

A thin girl, clutched from behind by a tiny brother, came with a deep bowl that the señora filled carefully and covered with cloth. Into a separate cloth she wrapped a stack of hot tortillas. *"Dile a tu madre que espero su mejor salud,"* she told the child, wishing her mother good health. "She cannot walk now for more than a month," she told the butcher when the girl had gone.

A full Bluebird pulled up on the street side. While the passengers watched she served the driver in his own metal pot which he handed back for seconds. Three of the passengers also ate. The

60

drummer hurried out lugging his empty fish bucket. A toothless old woman with an impossible burden of firewood patiently waited for the driver to load her bundle onto the roof. The señora held out a bowl for her, saying *"No te preocupes,"* when the *anciana* said she had no money. The drummer took the wood and passed it up to the driver's assistant. The old woman flashed a gaping smile as she devoured the soup.

The motel desk clerk was an ex—Jesuit seminarian whose English was very good. We sat out back in those resin—seeping lawn chairs I'd bought in Cabo and that continued to serve for such occasions through Argentina. He asked if I'd taken the Pacific highway alone. When I said yes, he smiled and said, "You are very lucky, my friend. There are many people who are robbed and killed by the rebels of Guerrero. The government calls them bandits but they are rebels."₅ I thought of the determined men on horseback.

"I had a friend in seminary whose brothers fought alongside them. He insisted that they were Marxists but no one believed him. Two of his brothers were killed in an army raid. The soldiers also burned his father's house. Shortly after this he left the seminary. I received a letter from him a year later after I too had resigned. He said only that he was back home 'working with the people' — his words. He asked me to come for a visit but I haven't gone. That's not really my thing."

I asked him for the name of a good seafood restaurant. He had heard, he said, that Beto's was not bad but he could not afford such places. I asked if he would care to join me. He politely declined, saying he was obligated to attend a family dinner that evening.

Beto's was a lavish restaurant on the Condesa Beach, the Acapulco main drag. The menu was expensive but I found a supreme *huachinango*, on special, family style. I ordered Corona, for 300 pesos, expecting a quart for such a price; but it was a squatty, midget bottle, less than half the size of the 90—peso regular you got at the *agencia* — a packaging innovation by Corona's secret owners, Anheuser Busch. This one's for you, Buddy. The horsemen of Guerrero would not have been amused.

Beto had, perhaps inevitably, made the discovery that Americans are uncomfortable eating without noise. Lacking MuZak, he had "arranged for your listening pleasure" some melodies machined in Nashville. Two pulsating Sansuis bludgeoned the air: "Sometimes a man's gotta be a man … jis me an' muh pickup truck … you picked a fine time to leave me, Lucille." America does not export the big—hearted songs of her Ozarks, her Mississippi, her Chicago.

61

4

CUERNAVACA

A peasant's liberal allies, unless liquidated, will invariably replace the old regime as his oppressors.

Cuernavaca. One of the oldest and most Castilian of Mexican towns. I am reminded always of Granada here. It is a place to find the past, long and recent. You can *touch* history in Cuernavaca.

Throughout all Mexico one rarely sees a statue, bust, or painting of the country's three most determinative figures: Hernán Cortés, Antonio López de Santa Anna and José de la Cruz Porfirio Díaz. No plaque commemorates them. There is a statue of Cortés here but it is sequestered in the foyer of the Casino de la Selva, a first class tourist hotel. And the conqueror also appears in a painting, a powerful historical mural in what was once his own home, his *palacio*. In it he is portrayed not as a hero but as a monster.

Santa Anna led 11 of the 50 governments Mexico had during its first 30 years of independence. He served more times as *presidente* than anyone, in the process losing half the nation to the United States. One wonders why there is no memorial in Washington to James K. Polk, the president who delivered Texas and California to the Union, fulfilling Manifest Destiny.

Porfirio Díaz was a great builder and developer, the man who brought in foreign capital and marshaled the labor to build railroads and cities and factories and yank Mexico out of the Middle Ages into the 19th century — fiscally, some would say, even into the 20th. In the process, he lined his pockets and those of his retinue literally with gold. But of him also there is not a trace in public memory or praise. It is as if he never existed. Yet a great many are revered who had far less constructive impacts on Mexico. For example, Hidalgo and Iturbide and the Child Heroes, so called, of Chapultepec.

An egomaniacal priest, Hidalgo is credited with instigating the War of Independence from Spain. Yet his vanity and incompetence resulted in the death and mutilation of tens of thousands of peasants and the eventual defeat of his cause. Not for twelve years, and only after the Napoleonic imposition weakened the Spanish monarchy, was independence achieved. And that was wholly illusory for the peasants who had followed Hidalgo in his military comedy of errors.[6] In a final whimper, the prelate recanted the rebellion in an obsequious written confession[7] just before his execution.

63

A more competent revolutionary was also a priest, José María Morelos, after whom the state containing Cuernavaca is named. Instead of stirring up a mob of undisciplined plunderers, he formed small, selective guerrilla units and trained them harshly in the tactics of insurgency. They annoyed the royalists for five years, capturing Oaxaca and Acapulco in the process, before Morelos was himself captured and passed before a firing squad on December 22, 1815 — although not before revealing, under torture, the strengths and deployments of his confederates.

Iturbide, the first *presidente*, when faced with George Washington's choice of monarchy or democracy had no hesitation in proclaiming himself "emperor." He was swiftly deposed and murdered, spinning the nation into thirty years of *santanísmo*, the brigandage of Santa Anna and his cronies. The "Child Heroes" were really cadets who, loyal to Santa Anna, defended their citadel to the last, the survivors reportedly leaping to their deaths, *seppuku*, rather than surrender. They died in vain. The victory went to General Winfield Scott, supported by the United States Marines and two bit–players, Ulysses S. Grant and Robert E. Lee. The year was 1847.

The beginning of the ninth week of the trip found me in Cuernavaca at the Pensión las Canarias, a catacomb of modest but tidy rooms separated from each other by a few feet of space so that they appeared to be cabins. Upon registering, I was required to sign a voucher entitled *Control de Toallas,* Towel Control, and tender the night's lodging of 2,000 pesos, about five dollars, plus a 1,000–peso deposit, whereupon I was handed my key and two towels. The towels had to be returned with the key when checking out. Parked along the sinuous streetlet within were a variety of delivery vans, Chevelles, Mazdas, even a Rolls–Royce, the latter belonging to a friend of the owner and attended by a chauffeur who caressed it with a handkerchief. Two pistol–strapped guards looked on admiringly.

The owner and his friend watched silently as I registered. They were fortyish, thin faced but well–nourished. As I drove the jeep nearer to my assigned room, they emerged from the office, each with a leather purse under his arm, carried snugly like a football. Doors were opened and they were driven away.

On red–tiled patios in overgrown courtyards, some patrons sat reading. One, who could have been an Oxford don from his stacks of scholarly books in English, nodded condescendingly but did not return my ¡Buenas tardes¡ Two women, knitting, sat on mattresses they had pulled outside hoping to catch a breeze. It was not a place one would expect business to be conducted, yet serious men in suits confided in one another, gesturing to papers spread on tables and floors.

Captured in traffic on the way in, I had heard a discordant shriek of brass and glimpsed tubas countermarching. The gear and jeep secured, I walked back down toward the plaza where, I was told at the desk, the principal ceremonies of the morrow, commemorating the 75th anniversary of the revolution, would be held. Cruising clunkers tinning ditties exploded through formerly sedate colonial avenues, now one–way piston chambers. There were barricades near the plaza.

An almost medieval commonalty pervades holidays in Mexico. Everyone is eager to participate in some outward way, as if publicly to reaffirm his or her connection to the nation–spirit. Few citizens approach even strangers without some greeting or recognition, which acknowledges the special occasion being celebrated. Americans do this at Christmas only.

Cuernavaca means "horn of the cow"; it is a Spanish corruption of "Quauhnahuac," Tlahuican for "near the woods." This was their capital. They were a vassal of the Aztecs, furnishing not only tribute in crops and sacrificial victims, but a semitropical spa of repose unequaled in the empire. Although its elevation is 5,050 feet, it is protected from cold winds by the mountains to the north and is totally open to exposure from the southern sun. Perhaps because of this, the Aztec nobility frequented the place and kept a substantial garrison here to ensure its loyalty. Mexican nobility, colonial, gilded and revolutionary, continued the tradition.

When in April 1521 Cortés conquered the city, he is said to have claimed it as his own, his personal spoil, his place of refuge and retirement after the conquest. And for a time it was. During the better part of four years, 1531 to 1535, Cortés lived there as the marquis of the Valley of Oaxaca, the title with which he was conferred by the Spanish Crown in recognition of his martial labors. It was the last act of regal gratitude. Shorn of all gubernatorial power by the royal decree establishing the *Audencia* in Mexico City — he was forbidden for a time even to enter the city and refused to return after 1531 — he set about building up his estate at Cuernavaca. He introduced large herds of cattle and sheep and brought in sugar cane from Cuba and even silkworms, for which he transplanted acres of mulberry trees.

Restless again for adventure he organized the two Gulf of California expeditions of 1533. When they failed, he himself assumed command of the third which established the fateful settlement at La Paz in 1535. That also ended in disaster and two years later he returned to Cuernavaca. Briefly he licked his wounds before sailing to Spain in 1540 to appeal personally to the king about the newly installed viceroy's order excluding him from further California explorations. He was given the runaround[8] for seven years by the vain and supercilious Charles V and died near Seville in 1547 from dysentery while preparing to return to Mexico. Later, his bones were reinterred in the Hospital de Jesús in Mexico City.

His palace still stands off the main plaza and is the seat of the Morelos state legislature. Within, frescoes of the Communist muralist Diego Rivera depict Cortés as an evil–looking hunchbacked plunderer, contrasted with the heroically portrayed Cuauhtémoc, in spite of the latter's superintendence of brutal and grisly sacrifices of not only Spanish prisoners, but thousands of his brother Indians during the last days before the final Aztec capitulation.[9]

Rivera's paintings were executed in the 1930's following the artist's two–year sojourn in the Soviet Union. There he was greatly influenced and enthused by the propaganda poster art of the period, of which his own work then became the best known examples.[10]

Rivera's ultimate hero was the Morelos mule skinner and broncbuster, Emiliano Zapata. In a sense, Rivera made Zapata larger than life, ensconcing him at the pinnacle of the national pantheon. His Marxist canonization would come as a surprise to Zapata, who went to great lengths to reaffirm his Christian faith.[11]

In what might be called Zapata's Twin Laws of Revolution, it could be held that a rebellion that does not extend itself beyond its own province is doomed to failure; and, that a peasant's liberal allies, unless liquidated, will invariably replace the old regime as his oppressors as soon as the fighting is over. Zapata failed. The cause of land reform for which he fought has been resolved into one of history's most cleverly perpetrated frauds. Its myth is maintained, its promise is kept alive, and peasant political tensions are thereby checked. But it is a carrot at the end of a stick that forever remains the same distance away. Mexico's richest and most productive land, even in his native Morelos, remains in the hands of elites. They are either the descendants of the original owners or the heirs of the generals of the revolution, who confiscated the properties not for the people, but for themselves.[12]

I strolled the plaza, listening to a military band and a cluster of folk guitarists, then made my way to the Café Viena a short block away. A section of trumpets followed, stopping briefly to serenade some students who had taken all the sidewalk tables and were well into their *cerveza*.

The waiters wore starched jackets and glided about pompously. The coffee was a substantial espresso or you could have the house blend of rich *Chiapas*. This was a rarity since choice native–grown beans are exported, leaving for the Mexican cup, Nescafe, with its annoying taste of rusty water. When served with powdered milk it is a concoction to be avoided. One learns to ask before sitting down, "*¿Tiene café colado?*" Do you have percolated coffee? Some places will make it if you ask, even from your own beans. In the bush this was no problem, since I always carried reasonably fresh coffee beans which I would grind with the hammer on a rock then filter–drip or boil up cowboy style.

I sat next to an animated couple in their early 20s, the girl tall with close–cropped hair and high, full breasts. Her face was resolute, eyes sensitive yet wild. Her male companion was subdued but purposeful. They appeared to be going over a list of names, checking some and marking out others. Behind them sat an old man, 80 at least, dressed immaculately in a dark pinstripe suit, navy blue tie. A cane leaned against the empty chair across from him.

A waiter hurriedly bussed a long table as the maître d', with unaccustomed servility, ushered in a party of sumptuously attired patrons, among them a stunning woman, thirtyish, in a scarlet evening dress. She had pronounced Indian features and carried herself so that it was unmistakable that she was the arbiter of her coterie as well as of the cafe itself, whose drone of conversation momentarily stalled. Her husband was, I learned, a senior lieutenant to President Miguel de la Madrid Hurtado and was here for the ceremonies. They were accompanied by an entourage of ten, including a portly, gem–laden matron in black and a much smaller, aged, woman companion. The matron was the mother of the lieutenant, who attended upon her with filial deference.

"What a splendid performance," the matron said to their table generally when they were seated. "Never have I heard such excellent music." The others murmured agreement.

They had come from a chamber concert in the home of one of Cuernavaca's magnates, a grand nephew of Calles, who, with Obregón, were the two strong men finally to emerge from the revolution. Between them they ran Mexico for fifteen years, from the murder of Carranza in 1920 until Calles' handpicked successor, Cárdenas, turned on his mentor and packed the meddlesome old fellow off on a plane to exile in Los Angeles in 1935.

The town is the retreat for Mexico's wealthiest, many of whom maintain second residences there. Although Calles and his successors have held power in the name of the revolution, they and their families have enriched themselves beyond the dreams of the *porfiristas* who preceded them. Almost every presidential family has a "summer" mansion in Cuernavaca in which to hold court. The most magnificent are situated along what is locally called, "The Street of the Forty Thieves."

There was a dedicatory speaking the next day, November 20, sponsored by the PRI in a pavilion set up for that purpose. Fifty army officers, half of them colonels and generals, were awarded medals and promotions. The "long history of the great Mexican *fuerzas armadas* in the defense of *La Patria*" was extolled. Party officials lauded the past and each other. The sacred names were spoken: Hidalgo, Morelos, Zapata, Villa, Carranza, Obregón ... de la Madrid. Morelos received by far the greatest applause.

There were two bands, one each from the army and police, and two drill teams from the navy and marines. Each had its accompanying drum and bugle corps. I recognized in uniform several of the "civilian" trumpeters of the night before. The bands played an arrangement of patriotic airs, ending with a bouncy rendition of *"La Cucaracha,"* the popular song of the revolution.

During all this, the presidential lieutenant of the Café Viena consulted with the governor of Morelos, each gesticulating forcefully, and with some MPs and detectives. The latter peeked punctiliously under every tarpaulin.

Plainclothesmen watched the crowd suspiciously.

Later came a parade, the *gran desfile.* Soldiers, musicians and school children strutted between Rotary jalopies, clowns and joyously creped floats with shy, young, brown girls smiling.

5

CATEMACO

*'What choice do the people
have if their own
government is their enemy?'*

"Let me tell you, I am more Mexican now than American ..."

The old Vermonter lived in a decrepit great house on the shores of Lake Catemaco, a volcanic lagoon of the Gulf of Mexico near Veracruz that is a repository of living fossils.

The house had been built in the 1940s by his wife's first father–in–law, the late son of President Carranza. The bearded autocrat succeeded Huerta, murdered Zapata and was himself shot by Obregón in an official "suicide" on the road to Veracruz. From Quetzalcóatl to Cortés, from Santa Anna to Winfield Scott, from Maximilian to Porfirio Díaz and Carranza — most major actors on the stage of Mexico have made their exits and their entrances on the road to Veracruz.

The place bore evidence of military planning: high walls, roof parapet, hidden moorings for speedboat escape.

It had once been an elegant chateau. Now its gardens had fled to seed and the interior smelled of mildew, neglected kitchen remnants and a riotous menagerie of dogs and cats.

The dogs perched on an outcrop of the roof overlooking the entryway. Upon the approach of anyone, even servants such as Manuel, the estate's handyman of 25 years, they galloped down the stairs into the courtyard and lunged at the gate, jaws snapping and drooling. They clearly would have attacked invitee or trespasser without the presence of their owner or upon the slightest suggestion from him of enmity or alarm.

"We have to have them," my host said, sensing my discomfort. "If we didn't, the Mexicans would steal everything we have. No one can be trusted here, not even the ones who work for you.

"You just have to accept that a Mexican will steal. It's ingrained into them. On the whole, they're good people — no worse than most gringos and a lot of them a damned sight better.

"My parents sure loved it here. I brought Mom and Dad down in '81. They died here, and we buried them in the little plot up the way.

"Daddy was completely paralyzed from a stroke. But he could talk with his eyes. He could just look at me and I'd know what he wanted.

"'Rum,' that's what you want, I'd say, and his eyes would get big, and I knew he wanted his preprandial jolt.

"Mother had decided to put him in a nursing home. She even made arrangements to follow him there. But I found out and brought them both down here.

"Nursing Homes! Hah! We don't do that in Mexico. We live and die as a family in Mexico."

Kenneth P. Finnbeck, 64, had been the American consul in Catemaco, but that was long ago.

"They decided it was too expensive to have consuls in out–of–the–way places like this." Catemaco had about 15,000 inhabitants.

"It was light duty. Expired tourist cards, calls home, minor accidents." Then one night a couple in a rented Volkswagen ran into the back of a truck.

"The truck driver said he was moving and had lights, but he lied. They stop, just like that, on the road — or on the side, so they're half on and half off. No flares, no reflectors, nothing. You can't see them until — Bam!

"The woman had been sleeping in the back. She was dead when the police got there. The guy was cut up a bit, but he wasn't badly hurt.

"Do you know what those bastards did? They locked him up, kept him in that dungeon down there for almost three months. That was one of the saddest things I've ever seen. He was heartbroken over his wife. I almost went mad thinking about him.

"They buried her up there in the local graveyard. Wouldn't even let him go to the funeral. Not that they even had one. Just dug a hole and put her in it. Oh, they made her a box. Charged him for it too. Went on his bill. It was a hell of a bill. Relatives up in the States had to raise the money.

"I did my best arguing with the local authorities. They claimed he was speeding, drunk, which I didn't believe. He was a real solid, gentle guy, an engineer as I recall.

"Anyway, I relayed messages back and forth. You should have seen the paperwork. Then they let him go — after he paid the *multa*, of course. Fifteen thousand dollars I think it was. I don't recall exactly.

"That was cruel, but that's how they do things here. You have to be prepared for it. Whenever they see anyone, but particularly a gringo, in a vulnerable situation like that, they'll move in like hyenas, go for everything they can."

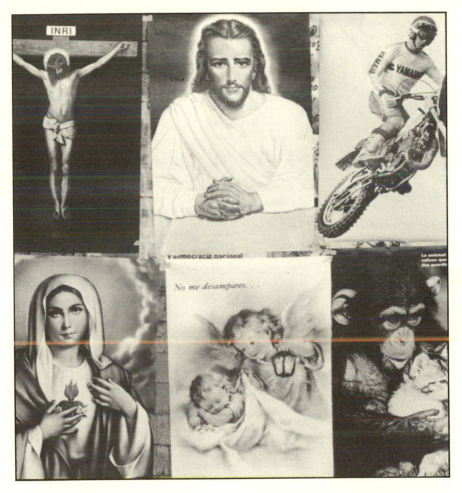

Sidewalk poster display, Veracruz.

Ken's father had been a renowned fishing magazine editor back in the 20s and 30s. He not only wrote, but drew his own illustrations.

"They're all collectors' items now," Ken told me.

He fussed around in a musty book case then tossed a volume on the dining table, startling two scrawny cats.

"Here, take a look at this."

There were water colors of partridges, quail, ducks and other game birds done in old sports–mag deco with almost too much detail, but good for the time.

"Daddy got me an adult card at the Dartmouth library when I was only twelve. I knew right away I wanted to go into ornithology. And I was a whiz at geology. By 1940, I was convinced that Wegener[13] was right. But I was thought of as loco. Now I'm having lots of fun."

He was writing a book, he said, that would "irrevocably substantiate" the theory of continental drift, largely through biological examples drawn from the lagoon and the surrounding area.

"This lake is 1,185 feet above sea level. It's an ancient caldera. It empties out to the sea through a series of rivers that flow west, not east as you'd expect." He drew a napkin map to illustrate.

"The species here represent a Pleistocene boundary — two to two–and–a–half million years old. They're the same as they were then because the westward drift of the plate lifted up the crater and cut it off from the sea. No tidal flow from the gulf gets this far, and the falls at Salto de Eyipantla are steep enough to keep any sea or river life from reaching the lagoon.

"For example, we have the *cichlidae*, what the Mexicans call the *mojarras* or *tilapia*. These are mouth breeders. The female lays her eggs, then scoops them into her mouth where the male fertilizes them. She keeps them there until they hatch. They can breed anywhere, just like salmon. Like salmon, they can last three to four months on their fat reserves.

"If you compare fossils found here from the Jurassic with those from the same period, even later, in Africa and New England and Europe, you'll see they're the same. The only conclusion is that the continents were all together as one, then drifted apart, taking their common gene pool with them."

Ken had attended Dartmouth before World War II, during which he served as an OSS special agent — parachuting repeatedly into Nazi–occupied France.

His last mission, he said, was the day before D Day when he and two other paratroopers dressed as German MPs "directed traffic," tanks and troops, away from the landing zone. They later watched the bombardment from an abandoned farmhouse.

After the war he'd finished his BA at Kansas then completed a Ph.D. there in ornithology. His love of Mexico stemmed from childhood trips with his father into Sonora and Chihuahua. He began living in Mexico in 1947, the year he met Clara. When her husband died a few years later, they were married. They had twin daughters who were now sixteen and rode the bus to the *secundaria* in Catemaco. According to their mother they were excellent students.

The girls spoke little English and had yet to visit the United States, although they planned to become American citizens, one said.

Living with them was a retarded daughter in her 20s from Clara's first marriage. Lolita was rarely addressed and moved about like a shadow. Yet I sensed that her perception belied appearances.

Ken asked me to join him for a cup of coffee in the cafe of the lodge next door where I'd spent the previous night. I listened as he lectured on drift theory and exile living. He supplemented his income, he said, by throw–line fishing in the gulf with a group of local *pescadores* and bird guiding. Because of its many species of birds, the lagoon was a favorite stop of US Audubon Society field trips. As "resident ornithologist," Ken took them to the best sites. "Good fees, good tips," he grinned slyly. Except for regulars the price was always haggled separately with each group, in true Mexican fashion. Just as we ordered a third cup an unexpected charter busload of birders pulled in and Ken sauntered out to ply his trade.

While he was gone, I noticed the old woman with the burn–scarred face who had cooked dinner for me the night before.

I praised her salsa once again. Flattered, she volunteered the recipe: diced fresh jalapeños and sweet green peppers, finely chopped garlic, fresh scallions — all topped with freshly squeezed lime juice added just before serving. All was then souffléed, whipped up with a texture almost like tapioca.

She chuckled as I wrote it down. You should have a little plain vinegar on the side for those who want it, she said, but not mix it in beforehand. And she didn't like cilantro or cucumbers — both considered essential by most chefs.

Ken returned with a fat grin. The tourists would stop over for two days on their return to Veracruz at midweek. We resumed our gabfest during which I told some Arkansas fish tales. At length, he insisted that I go out into the gulf with him and his compadres. I accepted.

We drove on a difficult earth road not shown on the map to the hamlet of Calamaca, about fifteen miles up the coast. Ken led in his pickup and I followed. Along the way he stopped for one of the fishermen, a rotund and amiable fellow introduced as a former fighter mechanic with Mexico's famed Philippines Squadron that distinguished itself in combat against the Japanese in World War II.

The road led through the heart of some of the richest farmland in Veracruz state. Its verdure shouted at you the farther you worked your way over the foothills of the great volcano San Martín, which commands the lagoon to the north. The mountain is the source of the basalt with which the Olmecs sculpted the 18–ton heads at San Lorenzo. To this day, the monoliths remain an enigma to archaeologists. Once, as we approached a ridge, a fog dropped over the emerald meadows, then vanished so quickly the grass might have gulped it.

Beyond Calamaca we came to the high bank of the Laguna de Sontecomapan. Other fishermen had already gathered at a small farm there. Some had ridden horses and mules which were grazing, hobbled. We drank beer and planned the next day's fishing. Later, Ken and I retired to a cabin he leased from the farmer. There were swarms of mosquitoes, so I strung the net.

At dawn we filled a long aluminum boat with ten men, *cerveza* and simple but efficient tackle — three hooks to a line, the hooks medium, catfish–sized ones splayed out from each other, bolerolike.

The gulf pawed and toyed with the boat and the fish responded but in explosive bursts followed by wide parentheses of beery tedium. The snapper here were only a half to a third the size of those in the Pacific. These men had never heard the word *huachinango* used to describe them.

Finnbeck was wholly in his milieu. Physically as fit as a 40–year–old, he could cut bait, tie lines, banter, bluster and haul in fish with the best of them, including several *machos* in their twenties. Even the "captain," the farmer from whose landing we set out and who evidently owned the boat, acted toward Ken with a respect which exceeded deference to a competent senior. His advice was generally followed as to where we should next throw down and his was first refusal on every opening of the cooler. Ken Finnbeck would surely, I felt, have found his way to the Nantucket whaling yards instead of Dartmouth had he lived in the 19th century.

That afternoon we returned to the cabin which was rather a thatched, earth–floored shack. Next door, through a sty of quiet pigs, was a tidy close dominated by a white house. It belonged to Judith López Alvarado, wife, mother of two, master chef, horticulturist, chicken farmer and fighting lawyer.

"… the establishment cliques denied vehemently that continents could move. They said animals just floated across, rafted, from one continent to another."

Ken was lecturing. He hadn't touched his plate which was heaped with succulent spiced chicken and dressing, Mexican country style. He was one of the few people I ever met who would rather talk than eat home cookin' after a hard day.

The vegetables were superb, I told Judith. She grew them all in the family plot out back, she said. Though raised on a farm, she had perfected her green thumb with years of study and seed experimentation. She took special pride in the chickens. Strictly yard–fed. "No chemicals; just bugs and scraps."

Her husband, who looked to be in his mid–30s, and their two children, ages four and eight, listened but kept on eating.

"… Like I was saying … I told them early on that frogs die if they get any salt on them — yet we have frogs everywhere. They surely didn't raft across. And they're too similar everywhere to be the result of parallel evolution.

"The only answer is, then, that the continents drifted apart, taking the same DNA with them as they left.

"Let me give you an even better example, the *galaziad*, the southern hemisphere trout. Almost the exact same fish lives in New Zealand, Tasmania, the tip of South America and South Africa. Although each has differentiated into a well–marked subspecies, they're still the same fish — belong to the *saloniformes*."

Seeing that his food was getting cold, Ken began making up for lost time.

"He's a lawyer, too," he managed to say to the señora, thrusting his fork in my direction.

"Do you represent people or bosses?" She asked.

"People," I replied. "My clients are mostly workers hurt on the job and mistreated by insurance companies."
She warmed to that.

"I help people, too." She got up to make coffee. Her husband went into the front room with the kids.

"Here we have much trouble with the land. The farmers used to own it, but the speculators came from Mexico City, starting, oh, about ten years ago and began buying it up. What they couldn't buy they stole."

She thought the invasion was caused by high prices paid for Mexican beef by US fast food chains and people with new money seeking a haven from inflation. Prices had skyrocketed.

"Some speculators claim they buy from the real owner which is not true but they have a deed signed by someone with the same name who maybe even had lived there and said it was his.

"Sometimes they just build fences around what they want. When the people protest, the police evict them. Many have been evicted from their own very houses in this way."

Poor record keeping and the reluctance of many farmers to register their property increased the opportunity for fraud.

She told of several cases. A few had been successful, but most were left pending for years, lost in a bureaucratic maze of fact–finding and appeals. A few thousand pesos here and there, she said, could buy indefinite delay. For a speculator in possession and running cattle, that was all he needed. One clearly meritorious case had gone on now for 10 years.

Stoically, many of the farmers took jobs working for the interlopers, some on their own land.

One client, a young fellow with five children who lost the family farm, shot his evictors, one a powerful banker, in a bar. He was arrested and held for six months, then escaped.

The police considered Judith a harborer of such fugitives. They would drop in and search the house. "It is mainly for harassment," she said. "But they cannot intimidate me."

In spite of everything, she eschewed violence.

"I always follow the law, even when it is used against us unfairly. Sooner or later the justice of our cause will prevail," she insisted.

In this vein, she counseled against talk of revolution.

"I think it is a waste of time. And it is dangerous. But there is much more of that now than ever before."

Her husband left the table, for a smoke he said. The children followed.

She had tried to get the local PRI leadership to back her up but they were either in the pocket of the speculators or too timid to buck them.

So she joined a rural reform group, the *Movimiento Nacional de los 400 Pueblos.*

At a recent meeting she told them she was tired of no redress for her clients and was thinking of marching the lot, some 2,000 of them, to Mexico City to sit in front of the presidential mansion to demand action. But her colleagues had dissuaded her, at least for the time being.

She used her card as *Agente de Investigaciones Políticas,*[14] political detective, with the national police to investigate complaints and file formal reports of abuses of farmers and their supporters.

"But nothing is ever done. The *caciques* have more friends there than I do."

I asked her who it was that talked about revolution and what they said.

"This is not what I do," she replied sternly. She averted her eyes and asked if we all wanted more coffee, which we did. Her husband came and stood in the doorway. The children could be heard playing quietly behind him.

"You're asking too many questions," Ken admonished. "She does her work like she told you. She doesn't get into politics other than to represent her clients."

"No, Ken, I don't mind telling him what I think." Judith said. "It is just that they already say we are *comunistas*. There are radicals, it is true. Some have decided there is no other way. But not me, not now."

Ken interjected: "You know, these people aren't really 'peasants.' You keep using that word, *campesinos*, but that's not accurate. These farmers are — or were — owners of their own land. Some of them have 50 to a 100 hectares — that's 300 acres. They don't really think of themselves as peasants."

Judith agreed, vigorously.

Ken continued: "Here you don't have a bunch of peons they're stealing from, but fairly well–off, by Mexican standards, anyway, fairly prosperous small farmers.

"They've always treated the Indians and the peasants like dirt when they got in their way. But now it's your landowners who're getting shoved around. And the government either does nothing or sends the cops to help the bad guys. That's not good."

"But it is true! What choice do the people have if their own government is their enemy? What must they do? Tell me!"

The husband had suddenly joined the conversation.

Carnival Clown, Veracruz.

6

CHICHÉN ITZÁ

*All eyes were fixed on the speaker and, thus
emboldened, Carlos proceeded to harangue the
cantina.*

"I will be *El Presidente* of Maxcanú. And if I am a good president
of Maxcanú, then who knows? Maybe one day I will be *El Presidente
de la República.*"

Carlos López was 24, married, the father of two, a skilled
organizer and a clever bureaucrat. He knew how to use the political
system for his *clientes.* They were unusual clients, indeed: 200 Maya
farmers, some of the more than 3 million descendants of the builders
of Chichén Itzá who still inhabit the Yucatán.

In Arkansas or Iowa he would have been a county agent. His job
was teaching those whose ancestors were arguably the most efficient
farmers of antiquity how to farm the modern way. New skills
included irrigation,[15] crop rotation, fertilizer, and, lately, credit and
marketing: how to borrow money, how to use it, and how to get the
best price for sisal, cotton, sugarcane, rice and maize in what was
usually a buyer's market.

I met him on the way to Edzná, a Classic[16] Mayan site.
Suddenly, at a crossroads, there was a hitchhiker — not the usual
white–smocked peasant with a trussed pig at his feet, but a slicker in
a button–down shirt and polyester slacks, toting a briefcase.

"Buenas. ¿Adónde vas?" Where are you headed, I asked.

"Campeche," said a big smile.

"¿Norteamericano?" He asked as he settled in.

"Sí. ¡Gringo vagabundo!"

Now in the 12th week of the trip, I had that morning left the
dusty market junction of Escárcega, a hundred miles to the south,
stopping for a long lunch where the road hit the Gulf of Mexico. There
were enormous conch shells on the beach and I sacked some to ship
home to nieces and nephews.

Edzná was a 45–mile detour suggested by some students at a
carnival fiesta. They looked like victims of a paint store explosion —
faces smudged with red, green, yellow, orange and black. School had
let out early, and they were running madly about, tackling the
unvarnished and smearing them with mud pies of color. They insisted
on photographs. When a teacher asked if I was interested in *ruinas*
they shouted in unison, "Edzná ... Edzná ..."

"They are spectacular," my new rider confirmed. "Would you like for me to show them to you?"

The ruins were just north of the hamlet of Champotón. A pyramid rose above a tight central plaza, with a lesser tower off to the right. In the foreground, at the top of steep, grass–covered steps, were a kind of "bleachers."

Sixty–four steps led from the courtyard to the summit of the pyramid. A narrow platform lipped out from the pinnacle, laced with stone slats, some overlapping to form grill–like openings. From them, an observer, who wished himself to remain unseen, could spy out the goings–on at the ominous "heelstone" below.

Carlos López said that the Mayans of Edzná sometimes sacrificed hundreds if the rains were late but that they had eventually found a more reliable way to conjure water: canals.

Between A.D. 633 and 810, according to deciphered dates on Edzná monuments, its dwellers built an extensive irrigation system for the town and its supporting plots. Traces of these ditches, long since caved in and overgrown, still radiated from the complex.

Edzná prospered in bulk–goods marketing with larger cities in the interior. Cotton, salt and dried fish went inland in exchange for jade, ceramics and tobacco. Militarily, Edzná allied itself with Tikal and Palenque.

It was almost dark when we reached Campeche. *"Barato pero bueno,"* I told Carlos when he asked what kind of lodging I required. Cheap but decent.

He immediately recommended the Castilmar, where, he said, his agency put up visitors from Mexico City. His wife and kids had stayed there once but that was expensive, so he tried to go home at least twice a month. He was hoping for a transfer to Mérida where they had just moved.

"Un cuarto tranquilo," Carlos told the receptionist as she eyed me suspiciously but relented when he said I was his friend.

I parked the jeep in the street next to the door, assured by the bellman it would be safe.

The Castilmar was a weathered Latin establishment of musty rooms. Humid air was churned by overhead fans with two speeds — grating–squeak and propeller–wash. From the balustrade, one looked down into a tiled interior courtyard bounded by baroque arches opening onto a lobby and vaulted passageways to other rooms below. Noises of everyday life echoed upward: a remote hammering, a small child babbling at play, a scolding aunt.

Ruins of 18th Century church, Maxcanú, Yucatán.

In some acoustically auspicious place, a parrot squawked: *"Ya es tarde, ya es tarde... a comer... a comer..."* The child encouraged it. A maid, puzzled but obedient to my request, shrouded its cage, enabling me to fall back half asleep until the aunt rebuked her and unveiled my tormentor to resume its croakings.

Carlos had suggested breakfast at the Restaurante Plaza around the corner on the main drag. He would try to drop over for coffee, though there was an important meeting that morning, a Monday, and it was doubtful. Top of their menu, he said, was *huevos mortulenos*. Never heard of it, so I gave it a try. It was delicious, if bizarre: On a well–done, crispy tortilla was a bed of lettuce, yellow cheese, thick slices of fresh papaya, a very rich goat cheese, ham and fried plantain covered with three *huevos rancheros*, all topped with a tangy lime–based fruit sauce.

A water delivery man came with a great barrel, horse–drawn on a two–wheeled cart. He filled buckets from a tap at the rear and carried them to the kitchen, then drove the contraption to other eateries around the square. *"Agua potable,"* I was told by the waiter. The municipal supply was saline and *sucio*, he said.

The coffee at the Plaza was *colado*, a welcome respite from mornings of Nescafe. After the third cup I left a message for Carlos to meet me at the hotel, then took a walk through the town.

Campeche had retained its colonial ambience. Narrow Mediterranean–style streets were lined with expansive brick and stucco buildings with great slatted shutters that opened onto lazy, wrought iron balconies. Many of the streets were still cobbled passageways. The brick had been fired before Hidalgo, when the leonine pennant of Castile floated invincibly above the *ayuntamiento*.

A quietude, abnormal in Mexico, pervaded the streets. Perhaps this was due to there being little through traffic. But there was also a crusty disdain for hurrying, an amiable lassitude that savored silence.

The only breaches of the softness were Yamahas piloted by young men, young women *atrás*, sidesaddle in spotless dresses, some nonchalantly clutching small implicit bundles of recent motherhood while clinging sensuously to belts buckled with bulls' heads bent from rough silver.

Hidden down an inconspicuous back street was the local museum of history and archeology. Inside I was accosted by what at first I thought was a fellow browser but who proved to be a "retired professor of history." He sought my proper instruction: The brochure I had been handed by the ticket lady, he whispered, was woefully inadequate.

Drinking water delivered to restaurant, Campeche, Yucatán.

Edzná was, of course, featured but there was also a collection of artifacts from the island of Jaina just up the coast. There Mayan nobility buried their dead in the eighth and ninth centuries, the height of the Classic period.

Statuettes from Jaina have an uncannily oriental look about them. Some subjects sit in Buddhalike meditation or grimace under burdens with a realism unusual for Mesoamerican sculpture. Others, though superbly crafted, adhere to more traditional motifs, ignoring the mundane and glorifying the powerful. The "realist" figurines bear a marked resemblance to those of the Moche people of coastal Peru with whom the Maya were contemporaneous. There is no known evidence, though, of contact between the two cultures.

Reverentially displayed in a back room was a sacrificial stone, carved with a dip and hump to ease the victim's restraint by four *chacs*, or acolytes. The priest would then slit open the victim's chest and rip out his heart. My guide's voice trembled, his speech running with excitement, as he demonstrated the rendering and the cannibal banquet that followed. Afterward, he was too exhausted to do more than grunt at the 1,000 pesos I tipped him — or perhaps he felt underpaid.

Carlos was waiting back at the hotel. "Would you come home with me for the weekend? I would like for you to meet my family." Sure, I said. When could we leave? "Tomorrow, Friday. On the way we can see Uxmal. Also, you'll get a chance to meet some of my *clientes*." He had already sent a letter telling his mother to expect him a day early with a surprise guest. I protested that he had gone to a lot of trouble. He would have none of it. *"El gusto es todo el mío,"* he repeated. The honor is all mine.

We spent the better part of the afternoon at Uxmal, one of the three member cities of the so–called "League of Mayapán," once thought to rule the Yucatán between 1000 and 1200. Recent archeology indicates that Uxmal had declined by 1000. One of the city's rulers was a "Lord Chac," who in the 10th century built temples with phallic motifs and a great pyramid, said to be the best surviving examples of the massive Puuc style of architecture — basic, unadorned foundations with elaborate summits.

Maxcanú was a plantation settlement begun on aboriginal foundations but which owed its 20th century life to sisal, the ubiquitous fiber crop of the Yucatán. Markets for it have dried up over the years in the face of competition from synthetic rope substitutes. The plant is nonetheless subsidized by a government fearful of agrarian unrest.

The door of Carlos's house opened onto a secondary dirt street of the town. There were a half dozen well used pickups parked outside.

Word of my coming had spread and a good many neighbors, as well as virtually the entire extended family, had come to see the "gringo loco" who was driving to Argentina alone in a jeep. In the front common room 28 people sat on the floor talking. Some drank soda, none beer.

In the midst of an intensive but friendly interrogation, Carlos pulled me away to meet his father–in–law, a large gentleman who looked every bit like one of those Maya lords in the frescoes. He was polite but perfunctory.

My friend's clients were meeting at a *cantina* in the town. He had instructions for them concerning a loan their cooperative had just been authorized from the *Banco de Crédito Rural,* Banrural. He begged leave from his mother.

The plaza was vibrating with heavy American rock, amplified from a monstrous public address system over the door of a youth center. Gyrating 16–year–olds in brightly colored dresses and in floral shirts and designer jeans raised dust from the street. Shyer peers lolled about self–consciously.

The rock blended with mariachi laments from a *cantina* where the co–op members sat sober and apart from other patrons. One of them motioned us to his table. He was Alfredo Dominguez, a thin, no–nonsense looking gent with aquamarine eyes and a thick mustache. Several others copied his appearance. Blue eyes and Iberian names were not uncommon among the descendants of Hunac Ceel, Jaguar Paw and Curl Snout, although the majority had no European antecedents. Felipe Balam, who could have been a model for one of those powerful rulers, ordered a companion to seize two empty chairs from a nearby table.

I was surprised by the youthfulness, vitality and bearing of these men. None appeared to be much older than thirty and most were clearly in their early to mid–twenties. Carlos, at 24, was their contemporary. Somehow, I had pictured them as haggard, beaten–down peasants, similar to the old hitchhiker with the pig I'd gathered up near Edzná. These fellows were manifestly deliberate and collected in their demeanor, radiating a resolve I had not noticed in other parts. Carlos, though obviously liked and trusted by them, was still an outsider. Their conduct toward me was correct, reserved — friendly but not convivial.

The publican hailed Carlos, waving away a helper so he could take our order.

"*Dos Montejos,*" Carlos said.

When he returned with the beers he asked if Arkansas was close to Texas and was pleased that it was. A brother worked in Marshall.

The farmers resumed their conversation, switching from Mayan to Spanish and back again so that it was hard to follow. They were discussing the loan and how best the money could be used. A fellow named Fausto kept insisting on *"dos tractores nuevos."* Two new tractors. At length they asked how Carlos and I had met and he told them. They were most curious about the jeep, how it ran and whether I had had any breakdowns or thefts. What was my impression of Mexico?

Carlos told them I wanted to meet and talk with as many people out in the country as I could and that I was interested in both the history and agriculture of the Yucatán. He told them about our visits to Edzná and Uxmal and my lecture from the "professor" at the museum. Everyone had a good laugh at the "sacrificial scene" — except Alfredo who remained serious throughout. *"Sí, mataban a mucha gente. mataban a mucha gente,"* he said. They killed many.[17]

Abruptly, Carlos said, almost as if by design: "And he wants to know what you think about the money Mexico owes to the gringo banks!" He then threw out the question I'd pestered him with earlier: "Why, with all the money we have from oil, did we have to borrow another 90 billion dollars from the foreigners?"

His voice carried well, and at this a hush fell over the place. Men turned their heads from tables across the room. Even some of the *borrachos* at the bar cocked their ears, waiting for the response.

"I do not think the money was for the people but for the *caciques*. Since they used it for themselves, why should the people have to pay it back? It is very hard for us to live anyway, without having to pay for this." Alfredo was no longer taciturn.

"I hear that [former President José] López Portillo put it all in the banks of Switzerland," Felipe said. *"Ladrones... son todos ladrones.* Thieves. All of them are thieves. Now they tell us times are hard, and we must sacrifice to make them good again!"

"Prices are already higher now for seed and fertilizer and for gasoline than they have ever been," said another, who had left his table and come to stand behind Carlos.

"One is not able to earn enough to buy everything that is needed. That is why we have to borrow every year — just to eat."

Alfredo agreed: "Everybody borrows more and more each year. Farmers, businessmen. Even the government, who has much money, borrows."

"Someone will have to pay very soon for all of it," laughed Felipe.

"Yes!" exclaimed Carlos. "And who do you think will have to pay?"

He stood and faced the group, many of whom now left their tables at the far end and crowded silently around to listen. Others on the porch pressed in behind them. Someone unplugged the jukebox. The joint had gone quiet except for Carlos' voice.

"I asked you: Who do you think will have to pay all of the debt in the end? The *caciques*?, the bankers? Oh, no, my friends. Their money is already in Miami, in *dólares*.

"We — all of us — here, all of our friends and families — we will be the ones who will have to pay the debt. And how, you ask, can they make me pay it?

I will tell you: *Inflación!* Inflation! That is how they will make you pay it, and you cannot say no — they will take it from what you earn because the money you are paid for your crops will buy less and less, and they will use the difference to pay the gringos — and steal a little more while they do it."

Murmurs of agreement swept the room, but at the wave of a hand the men were silent again. All eyes were fixed on the speaker and, thus emboldened, Carlos proceeded to harangue the *cantina* for half an hour.

He had a measured and resonant delivery which rose and fell at just the appropriate moments for emphasis, or silence to let a point thrust home. I had no idea if I were witness to a mere expurgation or something more severe.

Finally, after explaining how they were all being led like *cabrones* to economic slaughter, he offered no solution other than to stick together and make the co-op produce even more than the year before. He then mentioned the reason for his coming that night: to get from them the formal proposal for expenditure of the funds to be borrowed and the signatures of the responsible parties. He left the papers with them as we said good night.

"Most of my clients can speak Spanish," he said, "but not many can read and write it very well. I try to teach them. That is not my job but I will do it if they ask me. Not many Maya wish even to speak Spanish. Alfredo will be able to prepare the documents and I will double–check them later."

"How can a Mexican function without being fluent in Spanish?" I asked him.

"Our people are sufficient in their way," he said. "For most of them it was never necessary to speak Spanish to survive. But that is no longer true. To have power today, to have a good life, it is necessary to speak Spanish. I could not do what I must do without Spanish." Carlos, too, was part Mayan and spoke the Yucatecan dialect fluently.[18] But increasingly, he told me, he tries to work with the farmers in Spanish.

I asked him, as we walked, about the reports of Guatemalan insurgents in Chiapas and how many of them were said to be Mayan, from both sides of the border. He had heard of them — it was frequently discussed — but he knew of no one from Yucatán who was involved.

"Everyone here is very loyal. We love Mexico. We want to work and care for our families. But we are very tired of corruption and arrogance and stupidity on the part of the bureaucracy. I want to work to change that."

I asked him if he ever thought about running for the national or state congress. Though he worked in the state of Campeche, Maxcanú was in Yucatán. He wanted to live in Mérida, Yucatán's capital, but always with the option to return to his hometown. It seemed to me that he was as good a bet as any to win a seat from Maxcanú. At least he knew everyone in town, and everyone he met in my presence thought highly of him. He surely got on well with the PRI since his position was a patronage one.

"I want to lead the farmers to a better life first," he said. "Then I want to do many things for *mi pueblo*, for Maxcanú. After I have done those things, then I will try to help all of Yucatán." Spoken like a good politician, I thought.

When we reached the house, his wife had arrived from Mérida with the children — a girl about four and a six–month–old boy. She was at once solid yet petite. Handsome brown eyes — friendly, curious. Very much, indeed, like her husband.

Fifteen of us spent the night in hammocks slung in the common room. His parents had their own private quarters. Some of the smaller children bundled up in two's and three's. Carlos and his wife and baby shared one, and two younger brothers and their wives did the same. I struggled restlessly not having used a hammock since Africa, nine years before. I finally gave up and threw my sleeping bag on the cement floor. There was no plumbing. A single hose from the kitchen connected to a street main. The facilities were simply a cautious trip to the garden.

Had alien navigators in the 12th century sought Earth's best local knowledge, they would have landed not at the abbey of Abelard but at Chichén Itzá. There in the low jungle of Mexico's Yucatán, among the ruins of monumental temples and playing courts, are the remains of a structure so outwardly similar to Mount Palomar that bright students readily identify it as an observatory. Forty–one feet at its zenith, this half–crumbled dome was built with such precision that its openings, from the center, align almost perfectly with the setting sun at the vernal equinox, the setting moon at its greatest northern and southern declinations, and due south.[19] Were its destroyed hemisphere intact, the other cardinal points and the autumnal equinox would surely be delineated.

To facilitate these calculations, and those of the complex calendar extrapolated from them, the ancient Mayans devised a mathematical system based on 20, vigesimal, compared to our decimal. Their system included a zero, placing them with the Babylonians and Hindus as history's only peoples to discover this concept which Europe did not receive until the late Middle Ages. Copernicus, Galileo and Kepler, in their rollback of European mysticism *after* the voyages of Columbus, did not calculate the year as exactly as did the Mayans and their Toltec successors. Even our Gregorian calendar is less precise.[20]

Yet, while the European observers were "heretics" whose work triggered the unraveling of theocracy, the Mayan astronomers were themselves the priests and used their knowledge to consolidate clerical power. Thus, the irony that Native American science led not to enlightenment but shamanism.

Built near the largest regional well or *cenote*, actually a seepage through a rare crack in the peninsula's limestone, Chichén was a Classic Mayan complex. It carried on for at least another three centuries after the collapse of Tikal and other Lowland Maya cities in the tenth. The majority view holds that between 918 and 987, the Putun Maya, a tribe of coastal traders, took advantage of the collapse and, in alliance with the Toltecs from Central Mexico, captured Chichén.

The Putun were also known as the Itzá, thus the name, Chichén, well of the, Itzá. Later Mayan chronicles indicated that the leader of this invasion force was the legendary Quetzalcóatl — given here the Mayan name, Kukulcán. El Castillo, the Great Pyramid, was built by him as his monument. Other conflicting chronicles state that the place was not captured once but three different times, with the Itzá twice expelled to Champotón, the village near Edzná where I had picked up Carlos.

It is certain that the Toltecs were the enforcers in the end, either as allies or suzerains of the Itzá. It is further certain that they brought with them the blueprints from their monumental constructions at Tula, also known as Tollán. This legendary site, 50 miles north of Mexico City, had already radiated its influence into the Valley of Mexico. The Aztecs borrowed heavily from Toltec martial and architectural techniques in their ascendancy 300 years later. They also adopted its fateful myth: the return of the invincible Quetzalcóatl, the bearded warrior–god. The psychological advantage of this myth, as much as cavalry and arms, brought Cortés victory against overwhelming odds.

The Toltec and their Itzá allies did not impose an empire in the Yucatán. They let the surviving Yucatec Maya continue to rule their own towns without interference as long as they paid tribute to Chichén. This samurailike arrangement was buttressed by the razzle–dazzle of Mayan metaphysics, which the Itzá–Toltec co–opted.

The result was that, while there was little cultural innovation, trade flourished as never before. Canoes and rafts plied beyond the Gulf of Honduras, probably to Panama and possibly to Colombia and Venezuela.

Returning for a moment to the inconsistency between Mayan science and sorcery, it might be said that geography almost assured it. Mesoamerica's vulnerability to the hurricane vagaries of the Caribbean on the north and the Pacific storms on the south subjects its inhabitants to generally predictable but specifically erratic seasons. Observation of the sun, moon and planets was perfected as it was realized that certain of their positions presaged the rains. But since these could be mere sprinklings or vexing inundations, a complex system of deities and heavens was concocted to be sold as a package along with the calendar: It wasn't enough to predict — there must be gods to appease.

Perhaps just as inevitable as was their creation, the gods of the Mayas demanded human sacrifice. As in all such atrocities, those least likely to offer effective resistance — children of the less well connected, young women and captives — became the victims. Recent academic apologists for this savagery have attempted to diminish their numbers and to suggest that most of those slaughtered were captured soldiers and losers, indeed, some now say "winners," of games. But the evidence from the *cenotes* — there were many, Chichén's was just the biggest — and skull gardens belie this revisionism.[21]

Whether because of their relatively high–tech astrometeorology, fertile soil, or placated gods, Mayan horticulture was successful. They became the hemisphere's most productive farmers, surpassing even the Incas in husbandry — though not in storage and distribution. Tombs opened at Chichén, Palenque, Tikal and throughout Belize contain evidence of beans, squash, chilies, fruits, berries, cotton, tobacco, henequen, cacao, rubber, shells of numerous crustaceans, dried seaweed and other marine life.[22] When considered with their millennium of unsurpassed architecture, ceramics and commerce, the Mayas clearly earned the sobriquet bestowed upon them by Sylvanus Morely: "The Greeks of the New World."

Carlos and I arrived about 4 p.m. and took a room at the modest Hotel Piste, four miles from Chichén. There was broken glass about the entryway; flies swarmed over discarded watermelon rinds and the pigs sawing through them. An aged air conditioner settled mosquitoes at the expense of a draft of mildew.

After a short nap we drove to the ruins to catch the 7 p.m. sound–and–light show. A kennel of Greyhounds was disgorging Italian and French tourists. Someone hawked jaguar dolls and teddy bears. There were sarape and belt peddlers and ice cream and corn dog stands.

The flood–lit pyramid, El Castillo, was awesome. Other imposing ruins loomed. We sat on folding chairs next to two Louisiana matrons with binoculars and a bird guidebook with which they addressed the Babel of throatings in the adjacent undergrowth.

The lights dimmed, then expired. Incipient scratches from hidden speakers suggested that a prerecorded program would ensue, with no decibel to be spared. Escape was out of the question: Dum Dum Dum Dum … Dum Dum Dum … Drums! More Drums! Louder still. Then came what was someone's idea of a primeval chant punctuated by a scream and a percussive explosion. This was repeated twice more then faded into the background to be replaced by a voiceover in Gatling–gun Spanish. Spotlights in multiple colors shone first on one structure, then another. At intervals the drums and voices and screams would return to the foreground then fade again, as an entertaining, if vastly simplified, history of Chichén Itzá was presented.

Most vividly narrated was a game in the Ball Court, the object of which was apparently to hurl a grapefruit–sized sphere through a stone hoop. No hands or feet were permitted to touch the ball. The players wore thick padding on their backs, knees and shoulders. Elaborate headgear both protected and adorned.

Not visible at night, but referred to in the narration, was a restored stone relief of two players near midcourt. The etched scene indicates that some of the participants, winners? losers?, forfeited their lives. The player on the left is shown holding a sacrificial knife in one hand and the severed head of the player kneeling on the right in the other. The blood from the latter's neck is gushing upward into seven distinct spouts to become the roots of trees. The current interpretation is that the game determined who would become the victim — "honoree?" — to be thus dispatched to the gods with a message of goodwill or an entreaty. Formerly, it was simply thought that the penalty for losing the match was losing your head. One thing is certain, archeological wisdom changes with each new crop of graduate students that arrives. During my three months in Yucatán and Central America, a quarter of the gringos I met in the bush were working on Maya digs.

The show ended with a simulation of the famed "undulations" of El Castillo's guardian serpents. These were sculpted slithering down the north side of the temple, heads at the bottom, mouths open, fangs ready. In what is without question one of the most convincing priestly hokums of all time, the snakes, at the precise moment of the vernal and autumnal equinoxes, appear to writhe. This mirage undoubtedly imbued the proletariat with a compliant reverence for the regime.

93

Following the show, Carlos led me away from the disbanding audience into the central complex, partially lit by the now restored floodlights. The ruins close up are formidable, indeed, even to a veteran traveler. One can imagine the awe, the fear, that Chichén must have instilled in a visiting merchant or emissary — or captive. As we walked toward the *cenote*, a guard sternly ordered us out. No roaming about at night.

Next morning, we were among the first visitors. Carlos had been here a number of times — several with a high school history class he had taught. His Spanish was easy to follow, unlike the staccato bursts of the recording the night before.

"The ceremonies of sacrifice would begin there," Carlos said, pointing to the top of the great pyramid. "The priests would build fires and dance and chant, sometimes for days." He called my attention to a narrow opening near the bottom where, in one of the great discoveries of Mayan archeology, a Carnegie expedition found another, complete temple from an earlier time. In an inner chamber was a *chacmool,* a reclining god, its knees and elbows drawn up, as if it were relaxing in a meadow or on a riverbank. There was an altar depression in its stomach. Its head faced to the right so that it appeared to stare directly at you as you approached, surely a most terrible sight to sacrificial victims dragged before it. The Carnegie group also found a "jaguar throne" with eyes, fangs and spots made of jade. Carlos insisted that we brave its oppressive humidity to enter this sanctum. It was well worth the effort.

My friend next illustrated how the priests supposedly took their drowning victims to the *cenote*. There was a 65–foot drop from the rim of the pit to the surface of the water, itself more than 65 feet deep. The well is some 160 feet wide.

If it was a very bad year, with no rain at all, people would come to Chichén from many distant places to make their own personal offerings to the gods. Artifacts from as far away as Nicaragua and Panama have been found; one necklace from Ecuador has been identified.[23]

Although many victims were young women, there is no evidence of a cult of "virgin sacrifice." Many victims were unbound. It was customary to throw them in at dawn, wait until noon, and then call down to them. If they responded they were pulled out and asked to relay any messages the gods had given them.

According to the early Spanish bishop, Diego de Landa[24], as late as the mid–16th century these rituals were still being performed. Wrote Landa:

> Into this well they have the
> custom of throwing men alive as

a sacrifice to the gods in times
of drought, and they believed they
did not die though they never saw
them again.

The Spanish mayor of Valladolid, some ten miles away, wrote
after a visit to Chichén in 1579:

> The lords and principal personages
> of the land had the custom, after
> sixty days of fasting, of arriving
> by daybreak at the mouth of the
> cenote and throwing into it Indian
> women belonging to each of the[m],
> at the same time telling these
> women to ask for their masters a
> year favorable to hi[m]. The women,
> being thrown in unbound, fell
> into the water with great force
> and noise. When they tried to
> raise their heads [they were bea–
> ten with] heavy blows.[25]

Landa noted that the people tossed into the *cenote* all manner of
artifacts, including those made of precious stones. He predicted that
gold would be found if the pit were ever excavated.

In the 1890s this was done, by Edward Herbert Thompson, the
American consul in Mérida and an acclaimed antiquarian of his day.
Laboriously persevering over many years, first to persuade the
Peabody Museum at Harvard to grubstake the effort, then to
transport all manner of heavy dredge and pumping equipment to the
site, Thompson at last hit pay dirt. He retrieved from the well,
"dozens of artifacts made of copper and gold, including tiny bells,
rings, a golden bowl and cups, effigies, sections of a mask [and]
human bones and skulls ..."[26] Thompson and the Peabody were
limited in their recoveries by turn–of–the–century technology, but in
decades since, other groups, including Florida treasure hunters with
professional divers, have fairly well picked the site clean of artifacts,
most of which have remained in the custody of the National Museum
of Anthropology — unlike those retrieved by Thompson, which he
removed to the United States, setting off a major furor. In fairness, he
could have done little else, since there was no Mexican institution
competent or honest enough at the time to preserve them.

Because of the large number of human remains recovered, it was
at first thought that they were the residue of Itzá–Toltec rituals,

particularly in view of the latter's tradition of massive sacrifices to their Mexican gods. However, so many specimens have since been identified as Classic Mayan that there can be no doubt that human sacrifice also played a central part in Mayan idolatry for centuries.

Certainly the Itzá–Toltec continued the *cenote* drownings, doubtlessly with the eager connivance of the local Maya. In these ritual sacrifices, as well in the broader culture of the place, it is still an open question as to who assimilated whom. Who were the ultimate "conquerors" and who the "vassals."

Whatever the answer, Chichén continued to prosper until late in the 13th century when, like its Lowland predecessors, it suddenly declined and its inhabitants disappeared into the forest.

Neighboring Mayapán assumed a dominant role for the next 200 years until, crippled by an inconclusive rebellion, it too was abandoned to the jungle. That was 1441, a mere 61 years before the "Great Navigator," off the Yucatán on his fourth and final voyage, hove in sight of a galley–length trading canoe bearing women, children, cacao, cotton, copper, axes and swords set with obsidian — and the world changed forever.[27]

Some farmers moonlighting as roofers in Mérida offered Carlos a ride to Maxcanú. We said *adiós* and vowed to meet up again. I had learned from him a great deal about Mexico.

El Castillo, the principal Chichén Itzá pyramid.

7

NIZUC

*'We could have been killed. I'll never
try another unknown river at night.'*

"Ahoy! Ahoy there ashore! Where are we? *¿Dónde estamos...
¿Dónde estamos?*

I'd just lit the Coleman lantern and banked the fire. A steady
10–knot easterly coughed gusts to 25. The sky was clear.

Cupping my eyes toward the sea, I saw nothing. Suddenly a
ghost of a sail fell off, luffed madly, then dropped. It was a small
catamaran. Two figures hustled about the deck. One called out:

"Ahoy! *¿Está allí Club Med?* Is Club Med up there?" He switched
to English and pointed upstream.

I shouted into the wind: "No! Back there! Behind you! *¡Está
atrás! ... ¡más allá!*"

I waved my arms and pointed up the coast. The French
resort–fortress, quarantined from Mexicans and nonguest foreigners,
lay five miles north.

But the boat sped into the mouth of the small river and out of
sight.

Shrugging, I resumed mixing a salsa for the *mero bocinete*, a
tasty red fish donated to my pot by Señora Fulvia, the proprietress of
Restaurante Nizuc. Except for my tent, her grill–shack, now shut,
was the only structure on the two–acre island.

I was opening a can of applesauce when the reports came in
rapid succession followed by a sizzling, like meat in hot grease.

The power lines! They must have struck them at the washed–out
bridge. For some reason the wires had not been re–routed along the
new highway, a quarter–mile inland.

I grabbled a flashlight and ran for the planked footway that
joined the sandbar to the mainland. Slipping, I sloshed through muck
to the bank and ran up to the road.

"Help! Help!"

From the lip of the dead bridge I made out two figures thrashing
in the water. The lowest of three sagging wires had caught the ship's
mast. Sparks still popped from the contact. Silhouetted in the
fireworks, the swimmers neared the bank, the one closest tugging his
mate. In a moment, both were aground.

"Are you okay?" I called.

"Yeah, I think so."

9

"What about your friend?"

The second fellow staggered into some weeds and threw up.

"I'm okay. You all right, Phil?" The first one asked.

"Yeah, man," he replied, quaking. "Pete, that tide musta been stronger than we thought. Drove us right into those lines before we knew it. I just did manage to jump before we fried."

"Yeah. I got it even though I was already in the water. Knocked me silly."

"Man, it hit me through the fiberglass if you can believe that!"

There was another round of sparks, then silence. The circuit breaker — surely there was one — had been slow to respond.

The wind nudged the boat toward shore. When it reached shallow water I helped them pull the mast under the wires with the loose halyard. We then worked the 18–foot craft downstream until we could secure her in the island's marshy lee.

A crew from the utility arrived after 40 minutes. The power was off all the way down Cancun's tourist strip they said. In short order, though, they radioed the substation to kick it back on.

The men said they'd taken five days to sail the 400 miles down from Key West. They'd landed the day before at Club Med where the finicky French, whose uniformed goons immediately evict interlopers, "allowed"$_{28}$ them to remain but denied them the use of their facilities. They'd located a public dock upriver but overshot the estuary in the dark.

"We could have been killed," Phil said. "I'll never try another unknown river at night."

I tripled the salad and opened another couple of cans of applesauce. The fish was more than enough for us all. My guests ate sparingly.

"I was completely paralyzed," Peter said. "My muscles were pulsating like one of those lab frogs that still twitches after you cut off its head."

We sat around the fire until late. The 31–foot mast had been damaged by arc burns at the top of the shrouds, one of which was severed. These had evidently taken the brunt of the current. Phil thought the damage was minor and quickly repairable.

They'd averaged four–and–a–half knots from the Keys. The wind was steady and they'd capsized only once. "She righted right away, no problem," one said.

Navigation was seat–of–the–britches. "We only used wind and currents," said Peter, who was 23 but looked nineteen.

"Yep, and we made it with just a couple of minor corrections," Phil added.

100

They worked summers with Outward Bound: canoe trips, hiking, the lot. Winters they waited tables at a D.C. restaurant. Phil, who was 27, skippered Caribbean cruises when he could get the work.

After a while they decided to walk out to the highway and hitch to town. Next morning I went in to buy supplies and when I returned the cat was gone. Señora Fulvia said they'd towed it upriver with a *lancha*. A note on the tent thanked me for my help.

Nizuc provided me a time for rest. After a long drive from Chichén Itzá, I found the little island quite by accident. A congested market road emptied into the neon caldera of Cancun. It was like Fort Lauderdale in March. Bronzed teenagers frolicked in open rental Jeeps. Pairs of sultry young women in T–shirts and invisible bikinis drew ride offers from the jeeps and hisses from local machos. Families from Nebraska and Tennessee, smacking cotton candy and bleach–tasting ice cream, strolled amongst postcard vendors and pickpockets. A column of buses belched in locked traffic. Peasants in open trucks and tourists stared at each other.

Flagship of Mexico's go–go resorts, Cancun is a temple to the ego of Luis Echeverría Alvarez. He believed that progress required that a nation of peasants first become a nation of waiters. When not busy accommodating Mexican foreign policy to that of Cuba and the so–called nonaligned group, part of a failed campaign to become U.N. secretary general, he was initiating his "new economics."[29]

The result was the conversion of pristine wilderness into a tarmac strip of Las Vegan proportions. Virtually overnight, Cancun, a desolate stretch of mosquito coast, had became Acapulco East. But looked at another way, a former jungle and mangrove swamp was now a thriving commercial center, a veritable successor to its ancient neighbors, Palenque, Chichén Itzá and the other Mayan cities.

A freeway led out along the Caribbean past opulent hotels with hosts of courtiers and private militias. This became a two–lane highway through half–begun ventures separated by long stretches of sand. Some obscure tracks led toward the water. I followed them to the washout and found the walkway to the island. A one–night camp became a week's haven.

Nizuc was deserted except from around 11 to 3:30, lunchtime. Señora Fulvia, two old women and the boy who helped her would show up with armloads of food, trundling the food across the rickety planks. By noon the shack exuded the appetizing aroma of grilled fish and frying plantain.

I made camp in a grove of palms a hundred feet from the shed. The first day I was treated like an intruder but by the third we had become friends. The señora saw that I was left with goodly portions of mero, *tikinxic,* or the house specialty, *ceviche* — made with huge Yucatán snails, and shrimp netted just out from the island.

The shack was primarily a working person's lunch counter but it was also an "in" place where cognoscenti could escape the tourists. Patrons included owners of bars and restaurants, sales people, and a coterie of semipermanent European and American hangers out.

I remained on "my" end of the island for the most part, writing up the journal and a few letters. I also tried out some of Señora Fulvia's suggestions on an old grill she left out for my use. I chatted up the clientele, some of whom lingered over beer well after closing time.

Four Mexican tow parachutists and their French instructor tarried thus one afternoon with more tequila than I thought it possible to drink and still fly. But they finished the last bottle and lifted away, Ozlike, behind the motorboat that the Frenchman gunned to top speed.

Once, twelve market vendors from Mérida came late and ordered a full dinner of ceviche and mero, which Señora Fulvia cheerfully prepared. Her labor that day was not concluded until six.

Nights I was not completely alone. A family of fat *mapaches,* raccoons, would wander in around midnight and feast on scraps left in drums. The first night I plowed out of the tent at what I thought was a human prowler. Eight pairs of beady eyes stared back at me in the sudden light from the flash, then disappeared. I set wire trips on the camera the next night and caught them. Unfortunately that film was exposed by US postal agents.

The last morning I broke camp before sunup, taking care to wash and scald–rinse pots and mess gear — a practice I tried to follow throughout the trip. Three fishermen were wading in the shallow marsh to the west, scooping bait fish into a long seine. One of them I recognized as a relative of Señora Fulvia's who had come by one day for lunch. I offered them coffee *colado* which they gratefully accepted.

It looked like a slow, easy trek on south with two or three nights on the beach, the first at Puerto Morelos about 25 miles down. From there I could opt out to Cozumel by ferry or continue straight on to Chetumal, the last town in Mexico.

In case I needed more than the few days remaining on my vehicle permit to make Belize I drove to the immigration office in town to get an extension. My permit had arbitrarily been set at 30 days instead of the usual 180 at Matamoros. A fellow in front of me at the time had asked that his be changed from 60 days to nine months and this was quickly done by substituting the latter time in longhand and rubber–stamping the appropriate seal. By the time I noticed my own discrepancy the official had disappeared down the long line of weekend traffic and a cop was waving me on.

A clerk at immigration referred me to the airport *aduana*, 12 miles on the other side of town. There I waited while the boss jested with a wrinkly–faced fellow with glazed eyes. When he at length spoke to me, he said that I must see his *jefe* in the main office, a quarter–mile away.

After misdirections, I arrived to find three French and two Germans ahead of me with the same problem. A perturbed woman took our names and advised that the *jefe* would see us shortly. The wrinkly–faced man appeared to tell us that it was "impossible" to extend our permits that day, that we must return tomorrow — but since that was a Saturday, it would be Monday before anything could be done.

How could a procedure that took only seconds at the border be so complex here? I asked him.

The *jefe* was not moved by this question. Indeed he seemed to take offense at it, plopping down petulantly behind his desk that was heaped with peanut hulls. Reaching into a drawer he pulled out a bag of them and began adding to the pile, expertly cracking the shells with his hand a split second before popping the mast into his mouth.

The hulls, I saw, would soon dribble onto the floor. I became so engrossed in the dexterity of the man's wrist, and in the growing residue of his indulgence, that I gave no thought to his piggishness and even for a moment forgot why I was there. Most intriguing, was his ability to continue talking and shuffling papers without losing a single goober. Just as an avalanche was imminent, a rotund fellow, thirtyish, enveloped in a jumbo Hawaiian shirt, approached the chief's desk with exaggerated deference. The latter tilted his head back, chin raised — as a primitive satrap might acknowledge a slave's proffered ministrations. Whereupon, the subaltern scraped a portion of the hulls into his hands and carried them to a trash can by the door. Returning twice, he repeated the process until the desk was clean.

This done the *jefe* handed the scraper my car papers and ordered him to "*prepararlos.*" The lackey seated himself at a small black typewriter with a very long carriage and pecked at it for half an hour, glancing occasionally out at the room at nothing in particular.

"You know I zing you have won ze argument. But it will cost you somezing," one of the French said.

"What do you mean?" I asked quietly, realizing as I did exactly what it was she was saying.

"Oh, you know. Dash. *Mordida*. You must offer to pay a peenalty or jees hand heem 10 or 20 dollars when you check ze papers. It will be quicker for us all if we go along with it, *n'est–ce pas?*"

It wasn't the place to explain to her my resolve not to pay another petty bribe — except perhaps to avoid violence or false arrest.

For the third time in as many weeks, I had been stopped by small town cops. The last time near Chichén. They'd asked for my driver's license then told me I was speeding and that they would have to keep it until I appeared in court the next week. "Of course," they then said, "you can pay us here now." The fine had been only six dollars — the amount I happened to have in my shirt pocket.

The pecking continued for another 20 minutes. Finally, the fellow shucked out the last page and stapled the completed forms to my *permiso*. Handing it to me, he ordered me to take it to the "man in the green jacket." I had no way of knowing who he meant and saw no one so dressed. Still, I took the papers and walked back into the other office, past the desk of the *jefe* — the top of which had again disappeared beneath a flow of hulls, and into the general area where colorfully dressed young women chewed gum behind typewriters without paper.

I held up the papers — which surely they recognized as routine — yet none of them so much as acknowledged my presence. I felt stupid asking for "the man in green," so I asked, "Where is the chief of car permissions?" But no one answered.

Then I saw the *jefe* returning from another office, his jaw swollen with peanuts. He was wearing his official green jacket. Taking the papers, he studied them, looked around the room for a long moment, then went to the glass–enclosed booth near the door. He sat on a stool, his mouth level with but a foot or so away from a speaking hole, so that to hear I had to stoop at a ridiculous angle. Not wanting to believe what I heard, I asked him to repeat it:

"No puedo hacerlo hoy. Debe regresar el lunes. Mañana es sábado." Can't do it today. Come back Monday.

In 40 minutes the underling had only managed to hack out a form letter, with eight carbons, from *me* to the *jefe* of *migración* — the office I had figured all along had final say over tourist car permits which was why I went there in the first place — begging him for another 10 days to drive to Belize. After almost an entire day wasted I had to face the entire bureaucratic maze again.

Out of curiosity I asked one final question: Is there really no way one could get this done here, today, right now?

I should have known the answer:

"Only emergencies. And there is a *multa*."

"How much, the fine?"

"Twenty dollars," came the reply.

I felt the bills in my shirt pocket, then decided: no, the hell with it. I've got six days left and would rather pay a bigger fine at the border than reward this sluggard for his shakedown charade. So I just moved on.

As it turned out I had a day to spare.

CAY CAULKER

*'I want my children to be human peoples, not
artificial peoples.'*

Mom's Triangle Inn
And Tropical Restaurant
Belize City

TODAY
Hot Fish or
Hamburger
Rice and Beans
Fried Potatoes
Milk Bread
Coconut Pudding
Coffee
8.50 Bz

—

SAM MORRISON
Please Contact Home or Mrs. Michall Gleason
YOUR MOTHER IS MOVING TO SILVER CITY, NEW MEX

—

US Citizens looking to Immigrate to Belize. Would
like to find someone that would write to us, giving
information and suggestions. I will be making trip to Belize
sometime within the year to look at the country. Also into
the possibility of buying Agricultural Land or starting a
business. Please Write, we would appreciate hearing from
you. Thank you for any help you can give.
    Bill Paulman
    General Delivery
    Willow, Alaska
    99688 USA

60 ACRES SALE
20x30 Cement Building
Fenced Cross Fenced
18x20 barn w. loft
Water System
15,000 US
                    Owner Jacob Lapp
                    Cossadaca, N.Y., USA
          Contact SALVADOR MESH, AGENT
                    San Antonio
                    Cayo Dist

—

FOR SAIL
35' TRIMARAN SLOOP $25,000US
This great Liveaboard Cruiser is completely equipped and ready
to go anywhere. Contact John Woods at Cay Caulker on Board
"HUAN" or you will find me somewhere around Belize.

Messages: _____

—

Hi Janet & Peter!
        We found your message 4 days after you left! We
spent 1 week in Mérida/Yucatán, Casa de Huespedes Calle
62 M. 507 — if you go there on your way back ... it's really
cheap. It would be fun if this Message would bring love.
Wish'd you come back. We don't know if we'll Make the
whole trip by land. Everything sounds so terrible the more
south we travel. All the best to you.
        TAKE IT EASY MAN — WE LIKE BELIZE!
        — ULY & TOOSTEN

CAY CAULKER
Getting from here to there is Half The fun
When You Ride With ...
"CHOCOLATE"
My Boat, the SOLEDAD, Is A 26' Skiff
Has two Motors for Safety And Has A
Sunshade And Large Comfortable Padded Seats.
Belize City to CAY CAULKER is
21 mi, So you might As Well Relax
And Ride In Safety and Comfort.
$12.00 Bz. One Way
Ask for me at MOM'S Restaurant Or [photo of boat]
Private Charters to Other Cays
Sportfishing Also Available.

—

"They cut the umbilical cord with their machete, then the baby
dies from tetanus. They don't call me — or if they do, it's not until the
infection has spread and it is too late. Sometimes the mother dies, too,
but always the baby. Yes, it is macho, the macho thing to do. Boil the
blade in water or heat it in the fire. That would be enough. I have told
them this. But they either forget or they refuse to do it. I keep on but
sometimes my job seems like Sisyphus's — you know, the one who
offended the gods and had to push the rock up the mountain. It
always rolled back down. I once thought it was that they just had
difficulty learning. It isn't that they *can't* learn. They just refuse to
apply it.

"Diarrhea is pandemic from parasites. Intestinal. Every kind
you can think of. It's heartbreaking to see newborns with it.
Sometimes they don't give them water, only breast milk, so they don't
get the diarrhea until three or four, when they're weaned. Still, many
babies have it anyway. Contamination is everywhere. Sanitation is
nonexistent.

"Look, see this ditch. It is raw sewage. It flows right into the
river over there where many of them draw their drinking water. And
the mosquitoes. You should see them swarm! Just now they are down,
a pest at night; not so much in the day. But after a rain, they fill the
air. Malaria is a killer, too. The Sickle Cell helps, but it isn't true that
it prevents it altogether."

Sister Claire, RN, looked about 50 but could have been in her
late 30s. Prim, a bit hard–faced, but brimming with pragmatic
concern, a kind of gritty resignation, if that is the right word. I mean
to say that she had long ago matriculated through naïveté, shock,

109

despair, and ennui. She had reached a state of benign detachment, leaving in her arsenal only the twin disciplines of her order and profession, in the application of which she served neither from devotion nor sentimentality but from the sheer purposefulness of a craftswoman at her wheel.

I met her in the market.

"You'll find fresh vegetables here a luxury," she said. "The blacks eat them hardly at all and grow next to none. What we get come from the Mennonite farms."

She had just returned from Orange Walk. Yes, I told her, I had passed through — two days before. There was a church in the Gothic style but built of wood with a corrugated iron roof and shutters, concrete base. It was surrounded by an eight–foot mesh fence, double–capped with barbwire. Up the street was the colonial administration building, now a school, identically constructed. Every square foot contained a kinetic black child; shrieks of expending energy above a restive roar.

"I know it well," the sister said. "Illiterate children teaching illiterate children. The only learning is in the Mennonite schools but even they are poor excuses."

I thought of the children of Cornelio Dikk, the Mennonite farmer who had brought a basket of eggs into the small East Indian store where I was eating beans and rice garnished with ground coconut and sugar and a chunk of something chicken. The Indian waved him away: "*Ya lo comprado.*" Already bought some. He wore that unmistakable Mennonite expression of guarded earnestness — an outer compliance but practiced wariness within. His hat was semicowboy, the same sub–Stetson felt worn by nonwranglers in rural America before Ford, Coors, Caterpillar, Mack and Rose's Feed became haberdashers.

Later on the way out of town, I saw him squatting under a tree, thumb listlessly extended. His place was 12 bad miles off the highway. I feared for a spring once. We passed buggies, horses prancing, whose occupants waved without smiling. Boys in overalls and calicoed girls scuffed and gabbled home from school. Cattle lowed and birds sang in fine meadows.

We chatted in Spanish, he speaking no English and I no German. He withheld at first, but gradually expanded. He raised the same, he said, as his neighbors: corn, sorghum, some poultry from which he sells the eggs, wheat and a few cattle. Sugar cane is the main crop, but at the time prices were so low on the international market that many Belizeans had switched to marijuana. The Mexican federal prison in Chetumal was full of gringos who tried to transport the weed to Brownsville. But Mennonites have no truck with pot.

Washing the rig at cattle ford near Spanish Lookout, Belize.

The farms we passed were equipped in the old–fashioned way, much as an outsider might expect. Later I would be surprised at the modernity of the ones at Spanish Lookout, near San Ignacio, with their top–of–the–line Internationals and John Deeres, combines, bulldozers, front–end loaders and shops to repair them.

Most Orange Walk Mennonites eschew electricity and plumbing. The Dikks had neither. But I wondered whether this was due to piety or poverty. Dikk, for example, had an ancient tractor, a Ford he said, though I didn't see a nameplate. It was like those in films of the Dust Bowl 30s. It had been at work recently although he was unable to get it to turn over for me, perhaps because of my Nikon. Photographs, I soon learned, were out of the question.

Mennonites, even those driving buggies, will shyly dip their hats over their faces at the sight of a camera. His wife came into the little shed where we were talking and pretended to sort through a bucket of screws and bolts, all the while keeping watch on the camera.

She had long, thin arms and wore a black velvet nunlike habit over pale skin. She looked 55 to 60 but was only 38. They had ten children, five boys and five girls, three of whom now approached cautiously up the little path from the road, schoolbooks in tow. We had passed them on the way in but Dikk had said nothing.

The nun interrupted my reverie: "Medicine here is for the rich or not at all," she said. "Good young doctors can make bundles in the islands, Jamaica or Trinidad or the Bahamas — not to mention the States." She worked out of Belize City she said but traveled the country teaching at schools and hospitals and missions of other faiths when she was asked. Maternity care was her specialty, with an emphasis on diet and sanitation. And sterilized machetes.

I recalled the office of a practitioner I had passed the day before:

SPINAL LIFE CLINIC
Dr. Allen
SPINE DOCTOR
Specialist to Nervous and
Chronic Dis–Ease

"Basically a chiropractor," she said. They're not altogether bad for people with aches and pains. But for preventive medicine, they're useless."

She settled on a fair head of lettuce and a bunch of plump carrots from the counter of an old woman she addressed as Sarah. "If you're needing veg you'd better pick up a few of these," she said, lifting the carrots. "Lettuce, too. I'd grab a head if I were you. Might not see the likes of this for another week. Till Saturday at least." It was Monday so thus admonished I obeyed.

Some men were unloading sacks of flour and potatoes from a Mennonite delivery truck. Sister Claire said *adiós* and made her way through chandeliers of plantain.

A long, delicate hand reached in front of my face. It held, of all things, a business card:

Fresh Herbs Roots & BARKS
Professional Herbalists
Richard and Ofelia Williams
Belize Herb Center
Stall No. 48 & 49 Central Market
Belize City, Belize, C.A.

Displayed on a long table were banded sprigs and castor oil sized jars of promising tonics:

LOVE OIL
Aceite del Amor
Rub on your person and read
Psalm 47 seven times daily for
seven days to gain love and respect
from neighbors. Use with the sixth
chapter of Song of Solomon for love
of mate.

FIRE OF LOVE
Fuego del Amor
Put one drop behind each ear; make
a cross on forehead; put a drop on
each pulse, one on the navel, one
on each ankle.

The merchant smiled, revealing missing front teeth. His braided hair jiggled as he laughed: "You, especially, my friend, need the Fire of Love."

Giant overturned turtles, still quick, quivered in final humiliation on the wharf next to the elixirs. Skiffs drew alongside to disgorge their catches under the bargain–sly eyes of large women with parasols and shopping bags, whose children taunted the reptiles. One poked at them with a stick. The animals' eyes bulged toward the sea, between whose undulant breasts they had scudded safely for four hundred years to sand and eggs; she who now abandoned them.

I returned across the Belize River, here about a hundred feet wide, on the narrow pedestrian ramp of the "royal" bridge, a vintage British army field span. Traffic was two–way, but vehicles larger than pickups had difficulty. Fuming Bluebirds, commercial lorries and troop Bedfords snailed across.

It was in Belize that I first began to be aware of the large number of amputees, many double ones, in Central America. Empty–sleeved beggars were commonplace. Men with missing legs hobbled with crutches or canes; luckier ones went about in crude wheel chairs or crouched on platforms with rollers. To a lesser extent women suffered these handicaps but they were rarely seen in public.

A great many stumps appeared cleanly cut, not lumpy or twisted as might be expected from congenital deformity, collision or occupational trauma.

"Machete. It is the machete. A sharp one can fell a good sapling with a single blow. An arm or leg is nothing to it," Alexander Bennett told me later. "When they fight, one of them always goes for his machete, and then you can have even the heads rolling."

The pedestrian walkway was pressed with early morning shoppers and people going to work. Government agencies employ a quarter of those who have jobs. Nineteen, for example, were retained behind the ridiculously ornate facade of the "RESEARCH DEPARTMENT, Central Bank of Belize." Above the entryway was the royal seal of George V, lavished with gold trim. Within, amidst a hubbub of coffee and gossip, a woman poked at a typewriter.

Most Belizeans are unemployed. Loitering, reggae and burglary are the principal pastimes for young men and boys. As in the rest of Latin America half the population is under age 15. High fences with concertinas of barbwire attest to the pervasive fear of theft. Every warehouse had two guards listening to reggae radio and minding guard dogs that were quick to alarm. Mom's diner had two who roamed the rear enclosure where for a dollar extra, you could park your car. When anyone walked past along Handyside street the dogs would erupt.

With a territory the size of Massachusetts or El Salvador, each with roughly 6 million inhabitants, Belize has only about 150,000 people: some 100,000 blacks, 30,000 mestizos of whom more than 15,000 are refugees from Guatemala and El Salvador, 10,000 full–blooded Mayan Indians — mostly in the forests and mountains of the south — and 10,000 whites. Half of the latter are the industrious Mennonites and the rest American and European residents of varying degrees of longevity. There are perhaps a thousand East Indians and Chinese, mostly small merchants.

Belize became a colony almost by accident. The British desperately needed timber for shipbuilding and fuel, having clear cut Jamaica and the outer islands. The lower Yucatán offered a bountiful source. So in the 1850s they moved in, shoving aside the few remaining descendants of the once–powerful coastal Maya.[30] The territory was claimed by Guatemala but it had never established a presence and, militarily it was powerless against the Brits.

In the 1960s, with Belize's imminent independence, Guatemala declared its "sovereign right and duty" to reincorporate this "violated province of la Patria." The result was a shaky delay of independence until 1981, giving Belize the distinction of being the last noninsular colony of the British Empire. By then, British troops, including a battalion of Royal Marines, had taken up defensive positions. In the mid–1970s there were a few minor skirmishes but after Argentina's ill–fated 1982 attempt to beard the Lion in the Falklands, the "Guats" have been quiet.

Guatemala probably has a valid claim; the territory was included when it seceded from Mexico. But after 140 years, the language, race, culture and economy of Belize is so different from those of its neighbor that accession would overburden Guatemala and re–subjugate black Belizeans.[31]

In spite of Mother Britain's iron skirts, special status as one of international aiddom's favorite orphans, and the Caribbean's richest fishing coasts, farmland, and forests, all but a few thousand of the inhabitants live in poverty in or just outside of Belize City or one of the small towns like Stann Creek or Orange Walk.

"We are an 'Aid Country,' " Bennett said. "Our people all come here to Belize City because the foreign aid projects are here, the tourists are here. This is where the money is and the free food that is given out. I sometimes think one can get too much good will. We need to become more self–sufficient. But who will go to work in the forests or farm the high country as long as he can get by for nothing in town? It is a shame for us to admit that less than 5,000 Mennonite farmers raise the food that feeds the whole country. That and the aid food. Without them we would all perish. We must start learning how to feed ourselves. There is so much good land that is wasted."

The roughly 5,000 non–Mennonite white population includes missionaries; timber growers and brokers; Coca–Cola managers and foremen — Coke bought up a half million acres of the country's richest forest land to grow Minute Maid oranges; a regiment of international agency and foreign aid representatives, including the largest per capita Peace Corps contingent in the world, 150 — more than one for each 1,000 Belizeans; not a few minor fugitives from justice, mostly American; and a peculiar sort of perpetual tourist some locals refer to as "Cay Lizards" — vagabonds. These hang out in the little string of coral atolls in the Gulf of Honduras that cap the world's second longest barrier reef.

The islands are an annual destination of some 20,000 scuba divers, mostly from the upper Midwest. The center of these activities is Cay Caulker, an odd mix of industrious black fishermen and sailboat makers and a daily changing population of vacationing Caucasians searching for paradise. Adding to the latter is a trickle of yachties and overlanders who only stopped for a few days but took a fancy to the uncomplicated lifestyle and remained.

Katherine Lee had stayed on now more than sixteen years. Few could remember when "Mom," as she became known, wasn't a part of Belize. "Sure, I know Mom Lee. Everybody knows her," Sister Claire had said. "She's quite a character, isn't she? Feeds, sleeps and stepmothers half the gringos that come through."

I had wound up at Mom's Triangle Inn, myself, after being stunned by the rates at the pretentious Fort George Hotel and its kitty–corner sibling, The Villa: Single, $75, "none presently available"; "Inside" Double, no view, $130. A once crimson but now rust–pink Plymouth Barracuda had succumbed in front of an establishment smelling of hamburgers, onions and hot pastry. Mark, its young German driver, "From Los Angeles in twenty–one days," allowed that this was "where any reasonable person would stay." It was indeed, at a mere $15 a night.

Mom had sailed to Belize in 1970 — with her son, Jim, on his catamaran. They had set out from Newport Beach, California, following the west coast of Mexico and Central America to the Panama Canal. A rough storm had hit near the Bay Islands of Honduras, forcing them to limp into Belize for repairs. A hostelry needed a manager and she took the job, eventually acquiring it herself and renaming it Mom's, with a restaurant.

When the place burned in '84 she relocated to the defunct Triangle Hotel, whence the present name. Hemingway's borrowed admonition notwithstanding, Mom's was a great place to eat.

Don Hazelwood and Jenny Worthen had driven 4,000 miles in an old Chevy camper from Portland, Oregon — she for the "adventure" but Don "for a midlife career change." Selling cars and insurance had carried him to 40; now he resolved to "move" tropical woods. One morning, he and I were finishing breakfast as Mom held court at her table with a local lawyer and four sultry Michigan secretaries, each wearing an identical oversized baseball cap stuffed with auburn–tinted hair. They might have been quadruplets. The place was filling with gringo brunchers, among whom Chocolate's crew were hustling passengers. His poster didn't give departure times, but something suggested that it was whenever the boat was full. This was subjective, there being no Coast Guard regulations governing capacity. Twelve people could be crammed into the skiff, sometimes fifteen. Most had only backpacks and sleeping bags, although the quadruplets had what looked like enough suitcases for a private run.

The converse of a long wait was a quick departure — without you if you weren't there, previous assurances to the contrary notwithstanding. One paid only on arrival. Chocolate was also the booze–route man for the island and several nearby cays. A dozen cases of Belikin beer and a hundred thirsty sailors' rations of Tropical rum, "charcoal colored," were being loaded when I passed the wharf earlier.

Down on the market side of the bridge, young blacks with reggae radios cadged tourists for the cay skiffs. There was a commission of $2.00Bz, $1.00US. Even passengers already committed were pompously ushered to the boat by these fellows, as if they were *their* recruits! The three crew members who solicited Mom's patrons for Chocolate were on a straight salary, but it was a good one and they were expendable, so they worked at it.

Chocolate, himself, was upstairs watching a soap opera with Sue Williams, Mom's daughter and heir apparent, on Chicago satellite TV — dish pirated by a local entrepreneur who collects door–to–door for the service. If someone fell behind, service was cut to all and the name of the deadbeat posted. Arrearages were few.

In what surely must be one of TV's weirdest warps, the entire population of Belize is Chicago–media primed: "Cubbies," "Bulls" and "Bears" fans. The rare Belizean migrant to the United States seeks out Chicago, whose colony of Carib exiles is one of the largest. Marshall Field, Bayshore Drive and Sheridan Road are as familiar to Belizeans as to residents of the Windy City.

A tall black man, about 50, in bush jacket and matching panama stood in the front door of the cafe.

"Mr. Hazelwood?"

"Over there," Mom nodded toward the table where Don and I were sitting.

The fellow came and stood by the table, towering above us like one of the great trees that were his trade.

"Mr. Don Hazelwood? Name's Elston Wade."

They shook hands, Don standing halfway. I was introduced.

"Please sit down." Fresh coffee was ordered and I went to the head. When I returned Wade was lecturing:

"... Brazil wood. Lot's of things are called that. Santa María and Cristóbal: Same thing. Blond mahogany. What you want are woods that are sturdier, longer lasting and cheaper than what's available up in the States."

The so–called Caribbean Basin Initiative was designed by the Reagan administration to strengthen regional economies against Communist subversion. It lowered or eliminated tariffs on most basin imports, wood included.

With a concurrent surge in demand for tropical woods, it was hardly surprising that a good many of the gringos in Belize City were there trying to line up wood export deals. Wade was more legitimate than most local brokers in that he had his own mill and placed bulk

117

orders for others. Don had been given his name by a satisfied customer in Portland.

"Let me give you an example," Wade continued. "Teak is a big item for decking and cabinet work. But we have samwood and qualmwood that is superior and far, far cheaper. And cabbage bark — now for a solid deck, you can't beat cabbage. Far superior to teak. Or Billy Webb; that's even harder and more durable. There is no better wood for shipbuilding than Santa María." He produced a briefcase full of chip samples.

"Of course, we have a high–quality pine and cedar from up in the mountains and a wood called mayflower: absolutely the best for cabinets and furniture. But you come see. Come out to my mill, and I will show you." Wade would deliver all wood at 50 cents Belize a foot in town or 45 at the mill. He gave Don directions. "When could you come take a look, man?"

"Thursday," Don said. He was waiting for instructions from Portland. Types, sizes, amounts. The message was coming by telex. It was overdue, but it should come Wednesday at the latest.

"Beg pardon... Excuse me. I don't mean to butt in, but I couldn't help overhearing you talk about woods." The heavy Australian accent belonged to the fellow at the next table who was precariously leaning our way on the back of his chair. "The name's Barclay. Cian Barclay ... that's c–i–a–n, not s–h–a–w–n, like in the States. They lose the Irish spelling there in favor of the phonetic, if you know what I mean? A bit confusing at times, you know. Heh heh. Mind if I pull up a chair?"

We introduced around.

"I do deals in what–have–you," the Australian said. "Primarily we find venture capital for entirely new projects. We're taking a long hard look at Belize. There's great value here. Great value."

"In what, for instance?" Don asked.

"Oh, in woods for sure. Speciality woods. Mahogany, Santa María, Cristóbal, you name it." He named virtually all of the woods Wade had mentioned, but without Wade's detail. His headquarters was, he said, in Mexico City. He presented his card: XportMport Group, Inc., 999 Reforma. An address in Mobile was also listed.

"A hell of a place to do business, Mexico. If you can get it on there, you can do it anywhere. Half our overhead is *mordida*, if you know what I mean."

"Do a bit of coke, would you?" The voice was also Australian. It belonged to a fellow I had seen over at the Villa bar the night before. Part of the crew filming *Mosquito Coast*. There had been a dozen of them, mostly Aussies and French. The French, as always, kept to themselves and I saw nary a one in Mom's the two weeks I was in and out.

The question about cocaine seemed oddly provocative.

"Absolutely not!" Cian was indignant at the suggestion. You could tell he meant it. Drugs were far from his line.

"Just joking, mate."

"Ron" introduced himself. The two Aussies bantered in a scorpionlike danceabout, pregnant with enmity.

"Over here, mates!" Some of Ron's companions from the Fort George strolled in.

They drew up chairs, greeting Wade, who nodded reservedly. I could tell that the film people were disdainful of this "Yank dive," as one of them put it to Ron. From time to time one of their number would have to stay at Mom's as a last resort, but they preferred the more ostentatious Villa or Fort George, particularly since their lodging was not their expense.

"How do you like filming in Belize?" I asked them, making conversation.

"You've got to be joking to ask that question," the one named Alex replied sarcastically. "This place is a bloody cesspool. Shame on you Yanks for stirring up your bloody little war down in *Nicker–agua*. Otherwise we'd be doing this one in Honduras where it happened."

He was referring to Mosquitia, the northeasterly coastal area of Honduras, which was the actual setting of the novel. Ostensibly, Belize was chosen because of the fear of getting caught in a Contra Sandinista cross fire along the Coco river border. It was common banter to put the blame for this on US support of the Contras. An official with the outfit told me, however, that Belize was selected because it was easier to get to and, for them, cheaper than transporting the whole cast and crew into the Honduran jungles. This, in spite of the fact that Belize has the highest prices in Central America. The currency exchanges at a constant two to one to the dollar; consumer prices are slightly above those in Miami.[32]

Ron said that the lead actor, Harrison Ford, refused to stay "on land," even at the Fort George. A yacht had been sailed down to house him. You could see it anchored well out from the seawall just down from the George. "Too close in, and the little bastards'll row out and steal you blind," Ron said.

"What made you mention drugs?" Don asked Ron in a tone of genuine curiosity.

"There's scads of it here. Pot is like bubble gum. The kids grow up on it. Half the farms upcountry are sown with it. You can't get the bloody locals at Gracy Mountain, the filming location, moving until they've had their afternoon smoke."

Someone mentioned the stench. It was particularly bad that morning. I wondered if Sister Claire, as accustomed as she was to it, could tell a difference.

119

"Sydney decided to stay at the hotel until time to go. It was too much for him."

"I've been in China, Vietnam. But this is the pits," another allowed.

The "smell of Belize" was a pervasive sickly sweet odor that, while at times stifling, was generally tolerable. But you could never escape it. It hung in the air as a given constant and some claimed that during an inversion you could smell it as far out as the cays. The municipality took pride in a new sewage and water system installed in the 1970s but the many creeks that lace the town were used for every human convenience and disposal. That explained the remark by Sister Claire that the river was an open sewer. The best respite from its vapors was at Mom's, whose smoking grill mostly repelled them.

Elston Wade hadn't said much since the interruption. He stood up abruptly, shook hands with Don, and walked out. Don said he'd try to get out to the mill Thursday.

We drove out in the jeep some 30 miles. Patches of shanties with names like Burrel Boom whizzed past. We gained Bermudian Landing about noon. This was a narrow crossing of the Belize river by cable ferry. Wade had said his mill was a mile down on the other side.

The ferry's four crew, alternating in pairs, cranked a handle that pinched a heavily greased cable through a set of gears. The men shared a jug of rum, chased occasionally with the river's velvet–green swirl. As we reached the far bank one of the men began shouting and pointing upstream.

"Eesnake... Eeebigsnake, man! You dunno how beeg she is! She's eatin' the other one." A gargantuan black tail had half swallowed a stubbier competitor. The two reptiles writhed and thrashed about like cinematic titans. Trickily juxtaposed close–ups of the event would have served as a gratuitous insert for a space western. The snakes were the day's highlight. Wade's mill was not to be found. No one we asked had ever heard of him.

Alexander Bennett and I had lived in the same residence hall in London in the early '70s. He was doing postgraduate work in education, I in law. He left with high hopes and fresh ideas on promoting literacy back in Belize.

He had become known as a progressive administrator and gadfly. His wife ran the top kindergarten in the City. I went out for a short visit. He lived near the town soccer field in a comfortable duplex well protected by an attack mongrel. His buoyant idealism had abated, replaced, as in the case of Sister Claire, with an unexpectant resolve — not cynicism, mind you, but far from the boxer's bravado with which he had once accepted every challenge.

120

Ferry crossing, Bermudian Landing, Belize.

"That's absurd," Bennett said when I told him the World Almanac reported the literacy rate here was 80 percent. "It would not be half that. Most students drop or fail the sixth standard, eighth grade. I suppose they can read signs, comics or some headlines perhaps, but functional literacy here is not greater than 25 percent, if that." He had resolved, he said, that while it was a worthy goal to try to get everyone to read, Third World schools should concentrate on students who show ability and on practical courses, such as agriculture.

Peace Corps Associate Director Louis Lindo, a native, put it this way: "Belize is a very young nation. Sixty–four percent of its people are under twenty; 54% are under fifteen. The solution is first, teachers, *then* teaching." Lindo, whose trade was forestry, with two years' schooling in Cyprus and four in Scotland, said that the Peace Corps was putting its main effort into teacher training. The goal was to have every child attending a certified, by US standards, school. "To do that, at least half the teachers have to be certified," he said.

"Most schooling here and elsewhere in Central America is done by the churches, primarily the Catholic, but also by a few missionary Protestant denominations. The denominations treat education almost entirely as a means of spreading the faith. This results in a bias toward academic rather than technical training. Belize needs a skilled work force — farmers who know modern production techniques, foresters. Belize has tremendous potential as a wood exporter."

He, himself, had been a sawmill operator for five years. "There is a great variety and consistency to our timber. We could be one of the world's primary exporters, not only of exotic lumber but of finished wood products as well."

The Peace Corps ran a a program called REAP, Relevant Education for Agricultural Production, which included basic home economics: vegetable gardening, pest control, hygiene — keep pigs fenced and downstream from dwellings. I asked Lindo if I could interview some of his volunteers. Sure, he said, if I kept their names confidential.

Each was in his or her mid–20s and recently graduated in business, agriculture or English.

"You have people out there who've only completed primary school teaching at the secondary level," one said. "It's pathetic. In one school not a single member of the senior class could pass a standard US 8th–grade exam — not one!"

Another, a young woman, ran a modified 4–H program for youngsters in her district. Poultry and vegetables were emphasized. She had some success with her chickens: some pupils were already marketing fryers and eggs before the class was over.

"But public education here is a joke," the English major told me. "Except in Belmopan, that is. There, the kids of government officials and bureaucrats do extremely well. It's the home influence. Always the home."

Large snake ingesting a smaller one, Bermudian Landing, Belize.

"But that doesn't solve much of the problem, does it?" the business major said. "Almost all of those kids are mestizos. We have to find a way to get the black children motivated." It was a familiar problem. Although the Mestizo population is less than 20 percent of the total, it provides most government officials and civil servants. In spite of their freshness and personal optimism, none of the three felt that Belize would ever achieve political or economic self–sufficiency.

"We have to face the truth," one said at last. "Some people, some cultures, are just not capable of becoming modern societies. Some countries, like this one, will always be backward and dependent."

That was hard to accept and even that volunteer, I thought, did not really believe it. But it was an accurate measure of the frustration felt, not only by them, but by the dozen or so of their companions with whom I later spoke.

Cay Caulker. Sand Fly Island. There are no sand flies where there are few people. At Half Moon Cay, for example. The flies are a human pestilence, nurtured in filth and grime. Like a monster waking from its sleep, the flies jump to life at sunset. You can hear the screams of the new tourists caught without insect repellent on the beach and in the rickety wooden toilets built out over the water, the waste deposited directly into the sea.

Caulker, also spelled Colker ... Callker ... Calker, is refuge for countless species of waders, pelicans and migratory fowl — ornithological as well as human. The latter include glazed–eyed layabouts and dopeheads, some affecting the style "Italian pirate" — hair curled full but short, thin gold Hollywood neck chain, shirt unbuttoned to just above the navel and, in one ear only, a small gold or jadeite earring.

Gamussa was the uncrowned king of Caulker. Diver, fisherman, sailor, carpenter, guide, philosopher — each was performed with an aplomb and serendipity that astounded even senior magicians of the sea.

Among these was Bobby, his closest friend and rival, whose 32–foot sloop, *Sea Hawk*, had carried them both through danger from the furthest banks. "Gamussa de best man for de reef," Bobby said. "Nobody better."

With dangling braids, hoisted trident, bellows lungs and impish grin, this black Poseidon could submerge for more than four minutes at a time. Using a waterproofed manual the size of a small telephone directory, he could spot for you scores of species from among hundreds endemic to the Belize reef that is considered, along with the Great Barrier Reef of Australia, the world's richest in marine life.

Twice we drifted and snorkeled for long days, tailing fish of every shade and color. There were angel fish, snapper, huge grouper, sea urchins, starfish, men–of–war and conchs with resplendent shells, to name only a very few. Regularly we were shadowed by great manta rays, one approaching to within a few feet near a ledge where we had pursued a nurse shark.

My guide was not only competent but reliable in a place where reliability was tempted with rum. When not diving he was fond of hammocking in the shade of his porch or sanding one of the purple–jibbed sloops of his mentor, Nelson Young. Young was a septuagenarian wooden–boat craftsman, whose sturdy Santa María sloops beat distant waters, from Hatteras to Huron.

In spite of the abundance of fish the mainstay of the local economy had been lobster. Thousands were trapped each month and flown to the States. Then the bounty disappeared. Stacks of traps lay rotting on the piers.

"Dey kill it demselves, man, you know," Gamussa said. "Dey want to take all de females, even the ones with eggs. Every one of dem tossed in de bucket. Dats three, five thousand little lobsters we don have next year, you know."

Gamussa, diver and fisherman, Cay Caulker, Belize.

The fishermen were becoming reef–trip guides, waiters and T–shirt salesmen. The "top job" was "DJ" at Martínez's, which had usurped vespers:

Thud Thud Boom–Boom ...
Thud Thud Boom–Boom ...

The disco's bombardier wore a cat T–shirt from Chocolate's wife's emporium: "Life's a Beach." It was 7:30; time to quake the island. A woman up at the *Asambleas del Dios*, Assembly of God, church complained that the place was corrupting local youth.

"But you fight de TV! Always fighting!," somebody scolded her. Chicago TV was dished here, too.

"I want my children to be human peoples, not artificial peoples. Who dey have now to look up to?" she replied. The owner had said he would keep the sound low and shut early. Nothing on Sunday. But that promise had not been kept. "My house is so close to dis place. I have four children. We cannot go to sleep until so late! Why they do dis to us?" This was a recurring lament from the Rio Grande to the Río de la Plata from those overwhelmed by the mechanical screeches and moronic babblings of the electric celebrities.

Gamussa referred to Mollie as his "good woman." They had met the year before when she had come down on vacation and taken an instant fancy to each other. They lived in his sturdy beach shanty on the north end of the cay. Mollie's tale was a strange one. A self–described "poet and original flower child," she started up a record company in California with her husband. "When he died last year I turned it over to my father. He runs it now. I just couldn't go back to it, after what happened; not without my man." I let it pass, but a few days later, we were drinking mai tais after a long day on the reef and she asked how I had driven to Belize.

"Good thing you stayed away from Oaxaca. That's where we were attacked." Then came the story. She and her husband had driven to Mexico on a short vacation. One night they pulled onto the shoulder of the highway to take a nap. A track led into some woods but she ignored it. "If I had just driven down there he would still be alive." They fell asleep in the back. Three Mexicans woke them up, pounding on the door.

" 'What do you want?'

" 'We want to *chingar* a gringa.'

"He told them to go to hell then said, 'Let's get out of here.' He climbed over into the driver's seat and started the engine and one of the men pulled a .38 revolver and shot him three times — in the temple, the throat and the chest. He was dead instantly. I could see it.

126

There was blood everywhere, all over me. They grabbed me and pulled me from the car, bashing me on the head."

She was taken 20 miles or so, during which time they stopped for tequila and cigarettes.

"They were very drunk. One of them I couldn't see. They let him off to watch. The other two took me into some woods where they raped me. They sodomized me. Why did they have to do that? I hate them for that. That really hurt me.

"I got a good look at the driver. He was well–dressed, tall, thin, with a white face and pock marks all over it. I'll never forget him. He didn't look at all like a Mexican. Sometimes when I close my eyes I can see that face. The other one was squatty, typical. I gave their description to the police later."

They let her out just off the highway. The squatty one pointed the gun at her as they drove off.

"I ran and hid behind an abandoned shack until they were gone. I wanted to flag the first car, but every time one came by I hid. I was afraid it was them again. Finally two buses came together and one of them took me back to the car. My husband's body was still there. I drove to the last town, to a clinic there to get my head fixed and get him declared dead. I had bled a lot but the wound was not serious. There was a small mortuary and they took his body and prepared it. I buried him right there the next day. Or maybe it was the day after. Yeah, that's when it was.

"I had to drive to Mexico City to get a death certificate from the US Embassy. They were bastards. I was stopped by the cops there for "wrong turn" and they drove me all over town until I snuck a $20 bill out of my wad of about $500 and handed it to them and said this is all I have, I'm going to the embassy to borrow money and they took it and then drove me — one of them driving the patrol car and the other one with me — to within a block of the embassy.

"The embassy people were terribly unfriendly and unsympathetic. 'Formal' is not the right word. They were hostile. Told me what did I expect sleeping out like that on the side of the road. I think they suspected that somehow I had lured the men to attack us. They wouldn't do the certificate right away. They had to go and make their own investigation.

"My car broke down just across the border from Laredo and I had to hitch on to Austin. The *Dallas Morning News* called later that week and said they'd arrested the guy that drove the car. He was a veterinarian. A new nice car, nothing big or fancy, but nice, you know, a Fiat or Vega."

She had heard nothing further from the Mexican authorities or the embassy.

"I don't want to go up there and testify. I might never come back. What good would it do? My husband's time had just come."

Gamussa put down his rum and said nothing, his eyes fixed on a full moon that had pushed itself out of the sea like a great red eye.

A young Dutch woman served breakfast in her tidy hut down an obscure path into the forest. Her petite hand–lettered signs were on a fence post and a palm and in the grass among yellow flowers. They were inconspicuous, so that you did not see them at first, but only after you had been wandering the paths for a time. Little arrows on them pointed the way.

I had been told about the place by two "locals," Americans who had lived on the cay for some months. They had just returned from a "vacation" in Guatemala.

How odd it was, the incessant goings and comings of people to and from the island. True, there were the foreigners, the searchers for paradise, who came and went in the shuttles, so that population was constantly shifting and changing, even in a single day. But there were the natives as well who, in spite of their good–natured deprecation of our urban conditioning and our regularly congratulating them on their luck at residing in Shangri–La, appeared to think of themselves as being in parentheses between town visits, like children with once–monthly passes to the fair. They returned laden with things of the market that they would compare: polyester shirts and dresses, trail bikes, VCRs, portable radios — some of considerable size — and a variety of minor electrical appliances.

The three piers at which these arrivals and departures occurred were at discrete distances from each other. It was as if there was some unspoken understanding that those establishments in–between — some even more substantial than "Ignacio's" or "Antonio's," which had piers — would not build them, themselves, since to do so would overburden the already imposed–upon shore.

There was something therapeutic about those distances — the color, perhaps, of the planking, which changed ever so subtly from dark blue to turquoise and back again as day wore on into midday and then into evening. The earliest times were the most vivid, of course, because of the shadows. And the thirty minutes or so just before dusk. But in the midafternoon there were also thoughtful colors, which wrinkled gently over the water with the voices of the foreigners who would cluster on the dock ends to sun bathe, drink beer and smoke.

You could walk halfway between the piers and not hear the voices, that is except for an occasional scream, which was oddly muffled.

With darkness my last night on the cay came music — hymns from the *Asambleas del Dios* congregation, struggling against the disco's mournful amplifications:

> He leadeth me
>> *Thud Thud Boom–Boom*
>> *Thud Thud Boom–Boom*
> He leadeth me
> By His own hand
>> *Thud Thud Boom–Boom*
> He leadeth ...
>> *Thud Thud Boom–Boom*
> Me ...

Tapir or "mountain cow," Belize.

9

ATITLÁN

Women screamed and clutched their children.
One woman held up an infant, but no one would
take it.

Returning from a walk, I found the following note slipped under my door:

> SANDY — We heard from the Swiss
> Embassy that you asked for us. We are
> gladly well, but these two people who were
> shot are friends of ours with whom we
> traveled for three months. We are staying
> probably in the camping El Real, 30 km
> from guat City toward Santiago Atitlán.
> Please leave a message at the reception
> Colonial when we could meet you.
> Nicaragua border seems to be closed since
> some days. Kind regards. Emil and
> Liliana.

We had met on the beach behind the ruins of Tulum, sharing a campfire and dinner. In one of those baffling chains of coincidences, we ran into each other several times after that and began quipping about who was following whom. At Tikal, the citadel of Maya civilization, we had just missed seeing each other again. They left a note on the jeep the afternoon I became lost in El Mundo Perdido, a forest of overgrown tombs that stretches into the vast wilderness of Petén. This is Guatemala's dark jungle province that borders Mexico's equally remote state of Chiapas.

I had been photographing birds at a pyramid which was to be opened soon. Debris and overburden had been cleared and chalk marks made over the entrance, or what was assumed to be the entrance. For over an hour I wandered, mocked by canopies of birds. Just as a night in the woods seemed imminent, I stumbled onto a path.

Back at the village I found the taciturn innkeepers at beer. They would not have noticed my absence for another two days. Their concern would have been for the rent and if the police would let them keep my belongings.

I tarried further, poking through the ruins and listening in on the discussions of some archaeologists excavating a tomb that had given up the remains of a 5–year–old child. Her bones implied Mayan diet, disease and mortality.[33]

Driving progress was slower than expected one afternoon and darkness closed in. Guerrillas operated in southeast Petén as did bandits. They raided and ambushed, and then slipped over the border into Chiapas to hide and train. They were easily concealed among the tens of thousands of Guatemalan refugees and the Mexican army was not eager to pursue them.[34]

I camped in a copse well away from the road but on the edge of a clearing. Close by, a creek joined a fast stream. Coffee brewed, I fried potatoes and foil–baked in the coals a small rooster I had bought that morning from an old woman. He had crowed a lot and once escaped the twine loops binding his feet, spreading feathers and scat in my gear as he flapped about.

That night the voices of the forest were soothing. An owl declaimed and two whippoorwill–sounding respondents whooped in reply. Later something waddled across the creek, hissing at an annoyance. A gnawing and scratching ensued near the fire. Shining the light I surprised two raccoons.

I woke up to human singing and the strains of a guitar. Nearby, in the creek, a baptism had begun. Three fellows wearing red sashes strummed guitars for some 40 faithful. The preacher was in the water directing "What a Friend We Have in Jesus" in Spanish. Five persons presented themselves for submersion. There were other hymns and a chant in a language I did not recognize. First, the women took the lead, the men doing a delayed chorus, then vice versa. They sang a cappella, sirenlike. Surely they saw my camp but no one approached. Within an hour they were gone.

I passed several days at Catamaran Island on the Río Dulce, just down from Modesto Méndez. This was a Guatemalan boating retreat run by an American, Kevin Lucas, from Pensacola, Florida.

The habitués included most of the main politicians and military leaders and a guy named Federico Kong, the owner of "Revlon Products of Central America." Kong was fond of sending helicopter loads of friends and clients from Guatemala City to be pampered and entertained in the hostelry's sumptuous quarters.

The staff of 20 waiters and boatmen spoke of Kong with an almost obsequious deference. The magnate kept a fleet of motorboats which were maintained by Clyde Crocker of Paris, Texas, who lived aboard his own 40–foot ketch, *Christine*. A 27–year Air Force veteran, Crocker had taken up sailing after retiring. When he hove in here, "I knew I'd found home."

Mother and daughters paddling down the Río Dulce
to market in Lívingston, Guatemala.

He bought 10 hectares on the river, built his own pier and
started a house. He accumulated a small flock of waterfowl that
quacked, honked and splashed under the dock.

Cruising yachtsmen had adopted Catamaran Island as a
stopover on their journeys through the Caribbean. Just then there
were nine boats either slipped or anchored out. Motoring the Dulce is
relatively easy below Lago de Izabal.

Though it can be done, sailing the river is not recommended;
anything beyond a storm jib or staysail is risky, except for a splendid
open stretch below Camelias. There are channel markers every

quarter–mile, approximately, between the island and the mouth of the river at Lívingston, a five–hour ride in a 35–horse *kayuka,* dugout.

I hired a boatman, Enrique, and we headed downriver early one morning in his *kayuka.*

Through the mist scores of other craft were discernable. Some were carefully carved, others merely logs with notches for sitting. There were women with children and produce en route to market and fishermen casting nets. Children with spears stalked fish in the mouths of streams; others poled dugouts through reeds searching for turtles.

Enrique's brother, Carlos, and his wife, Rosalia, waited for us in the doorway of their hut. This was a cane and palm thatch dwelling built on a bluff. We stopped to drop off supplies: two new machetes, a carton of Hilton cigarettes — *"la da más"*— , a jug of Orange Crush, a 10–pound sack of "enriched" Gold Medal Flour — *Harina de Trigo Enriquecida,* two cans of Maggi *Consume de Pollo* and two large familiar cylindrical boxes — *MOSH QUAKER.* A daughter was sent for money and returned clutching a ghetto blaster tuned to a distant rock station. She claimed she listened at night to Mexican radio, the Voice of America and Radio Havana. As we were leaving, she asked if she could show me something. We walked past hammocks and baskets to the rear of the hut.

"Look!" she said proudly.

A shaft of sunlight flooded a life–sized poster of Michael Jackson.

Lívingston's 10,000 inhabitants were three–quarters Carib blacks, most of whom lived in a sprawling shantytown stretching northward along sand banks above the Caribbean. A narrow Indian barrio wound upriver into banana groves and corn patches and eventually into the forest itself. The other inhabitants, largely Mestizo and East Indian shopkeepers, inhabited the town center.

A crude porcelain bust of *"Madre"* was raised on a concrete slab beneath the city hall. The sculpted white woman bore little resemblance to the mothers of Lívingston. There was about it the suggestion of celebrity, as if some buxom film personage of the early 1960s had been the model.

A mud street ran from the wharf up a hill to the town, where it was briefly cobbled. There was a scrambling of bars, eateries, soft drink stands and East Indian sundries shops. One sold only rum, and at six it became the principal gathering place of the Caribs who poured from pastel shanties of green, purple and pink as long afternoon shadows fell across gardens of crimson and gold.

"Madre," a bust of the ideal mother in front of the town hall in Lívingston.

"They quite know how to paint the houses for the afternoon light, don't they?" an English traveler observed. It was true. But each moment of the day had its own distinctive light and colors that were joyous to the soul. Early in the morning, there was a rich olive or jungle green, which dominated; later, around eight or nine, the greens surrendered to brilliant yellows, giving you in the lingering coolness, the confidence that you really could, after all, get done everything you had set out to do before sundown. But by eleven, the torpor would arrest even the most resolute — until five–thirty or six. But by then it was time for rum.

One of the sailors up at Catamaran Island said, "A 10–minute job takes all day and a half hour job takes a week, if you're lucky."

I learned of the shooting the following weekend in Puerto Barrios from Roger Gamble, the deputy US ambassador. He was having breakfast with friends in the dining room of the charmingly dilapidated old banana company Hotel del Norte where I had spent the night. I overheard them talking about the incident and intruded to ask further.

"It happened over near Santiago Atitlán, just south of the lake. A Swiss couple. Evidently, they were ambushed by a group of the URNG. It might have been bandits, but I doubt it. The word is they didn't rob them." I asked if he knew the names of the victims. He did not. I told him about the Swiss I had met. He didn't think they were the ones.

"They hadn't time to get that far unless they drove straight through without even stopping in the city," he said. "How are you traveling?" I told him.

"I would strongly urge you to reconsider driving through Guatemala. Certainly, I would avoid Santiago Atitlán. This is the second attack out there in less than a month. A Dutch couple were shot about three weeks ago over in the same area. We have a travel advisory at the Embassy of places to stay out of. I'd check it if I were you." There had been at least 20 such incidents in the past year. "And that's just gringos; they shoot Guatemalans every day."

"Now Blanche, you know by now that unless you're absolutely sure she's going to be productive you've got to move her, get rid of her. We can do training up to a point but these girls have to meet us halfway. You heard how that shop in Honduras sounded. Your shop can sound like that. Did that tall slender girl show back up? When are you gonna put her to work? What time do you start sewin'? At seven? We'll be there before then."

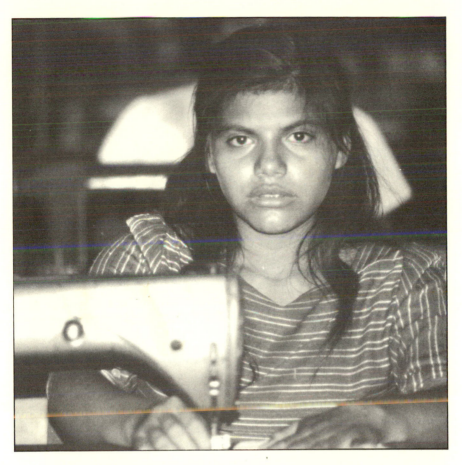

Sewing machine operator in Gator of Florida textile plant, duty free zone, Puerto Barrios, Guatemala.

The accent was North Florida drawl. The caller hung up and returned to the table next to the deputy ambassador. They had mumbled "morning" when he came down earlier. I caught a smirk of condescension on the face of a British freight agent at another table. I walked over and introduced myself. We chatted and he invited me out to look at his operation in the Duty Free Zone at Santo Tomás, Barrios' bustling port of entry and warehouse district.

Forty–five women, some as young as 16, sat at rows of sewing machines. Two supervisors corrected and encouraged them. The machines were 1940s Singers and other vintage models. The women were anxious: only a few would be hired. Bee metaphors are hackneyed but appropriate. In the bland florescent lights, the hum of nervous energy strummed from the line. No one left her machine, except two zipper sewers who smartly delivered bundles of trousers to an inspection table.

"I've been in this business 35 years. I can walk into a shop and just listen and tell you if that is a *surging* shop. When they're surging, you can count the profits. I can hear it now. They're still slow, but this is going to be a *surging* shop. Yessiree!"

J.W. Harold, 55, was the factory representative from Gator of Florida. "Not the little green one," he hastened to add, pointing with a hint of sarcasm at his left breast pocket. "We had it first but they beat us out of it." He was vague about his exact title but his job was starting up and supervising garment factories around the Caribbean, places that used to be referred to by American progressives as "runaway sweat shops."

"I've set up plants in Haiti, Jamaica, Honduras, you name it. Our policy is to move in and set it up and get it going. We train local management and then let them run it. In two years we hope to have 240 regular employees here. We've got 250 over in Puerto Cortés, in Honduras. Frances here is my plant manager over there. You want to see how they can *really* surge, you got to see that plant."

Frances nodded, all the while keeping a close eye on the applicants and two supervisor–trainees, one of whom was Blanche of the breakfast phone call.

"We pay these women by piecework. The reason this is slow this morning is they don't have the piece rate yet. When they do you come back and you'll see *surging* — that's 800 pair of pants in eight hours. We pay them the minimum wage at first. Once they become permanent employees they get small raises based on how long they're with us but big money if they really produce. If they *surge*, they get the surge rate — that varies but it can be up to fifty percent more. Of course we're real strict on sloppy work. Have to be. Especially when we're doing work for the majors, Sears, Penneys and other big chains. We did $30 million with Sears last year. They send their own inspectors down here to check up on us because we're sewing their labels in — right here, not back in the States like we used to. Used to, they had do it themselves; no more."

Pay was in cash, "a little envelope full of quetzales[35] at the end of the week. The minimum wage we have to pay is 108 per month. If she makes 400 units a day, which is half surge, average, then she'll take home 160 per month — cash, all hers; no withholding. If she does 600 per day, she'll take home another 40 quetzales, or 200 a month."

There were no retirement benefits, paid vacations, health insurance, worker's compensation, plant–safety checks, child–labor law enforcement, or employee counseling.

J.W. Harold, manager, Gator of Florida textile plant, duty free zone, Puerto Barrios, Guatemala.

"You sound like some guy from the garment association," he said when I made those observations. Gator was not a member.

"Look, these people make five times what they could anywhere else. And once they're hired they're yours. You can't just fire one without going through a lot of red tape and rigmarole. They don't have a union but they've got cousins and uncles who work for the government. If they think they've been mistreated they can cause real trouble.

"These people will work if they have the opportunity. They're not lazy. What you hear to the contrary is bull. Let me tell you, I've managed plants all over the States and down here. There are no better workers than Central Americans, particularly the women."

The Swiss Embassy receptionist wouldn't give out any information but around 10 a.m. a consulate official called. No, she said, the victims were not my friends. But she had heard from another couple who might be the ones I had mentioned. They were coming in later that day. She took the name of my hotel and said she would tell them I had phoned.

What was the condition of the others?

"The husband is not good. His stomach was all but destroyed. He has not regained consciousness. The wife will have no permanent injuries. She is doing much better."

Would it be permissible to visit her?

"It would cheer her immensely. Just try not to stay too long. Check with the nurse on duty first."

I went out to the Hospital Herradera Llerande at the medical school campus. A nurse led me to the young woman's room.

"A visitor, Señora."

Ursula Giterio was sitting up in bed. Some books and magazines were on a table nearby, one opened to a crossword puzzle. "Do come in," she said. She spoke with a heavy but pleasant accent. I tried some French. "Oh, do speak English," she politely admonished. "I prefer it."

I told her about Emil and Liliana, and that it had been several weeks since I had seen them. "Yes. Those are our friends. We have traveled together. They are supposed to be here soon."

A doctor and nurse had been talking in hushed voices outside her husband's door as we passed. The doctor looked solemn, defeated. I asked if there was anything I could do for either of them. She said thanks but the consulate were taking care of things. Relatives had been notified, and two were on the way. Marco would have to be returned to Switzerland but his condition was too grave for him to be moved just then.

"How long have you been traveling? I asked.

"Almost 19 months."

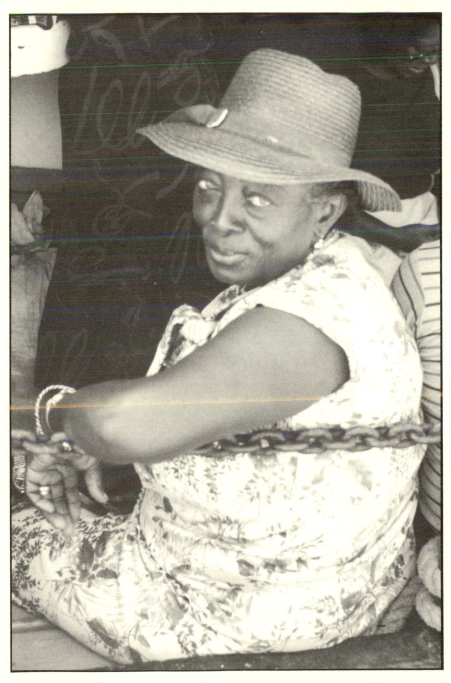

Ferry passenger, Puerto Barrios, Guatemala

They had begun in Africa, following more or less my own route in 1977: Sahara, Congo, Kenya–Tanzania, all the way down to Cape Town. They shipped to New York and drove across Canada to Alaska, returning by ferry to Seattle. They met Emil and Liliana in California, and the two couples had stayed together through southern Mexico where they had separated with the idea of meeting up again here.

The shooting happened early in the afternoon just south of the volcano at San Lucas Tolimán. The road was suddenly blocked by a Toyota pickup. There were three men with guns. Marco gunned the van around on the shoulder but the pickup overtook them and they were forced over at gunpoint.

"We offered them money, the car, everything we had, but they didn't want that." They beat her husband with the butts of their rifles and made him kneel on the side of the road. She pled with them to spare their lives, but they laughed and opened up, hitting her in the arm and abdomen and her husband in the stomach. The assailants then sped away.

The next thing she remembered was waking up here in the hospital. There had been no arrests and none was expected. No group had claimed credit for the ambush.

I wrote down the number of the hotel and told her to call if there was anything I could do. Also, would she please tell Emil and Liliana where I was if she saw them.

"Bee bee bee bee bee bee bee bee ..."
The monotonous beggar's bleat rose above the rattle of traffic on Tercera Calle near the Hotel Pan American.

Buses with names like Dios Es Amor, God is Love, Dolores, Chávez, and Fantástico — the names painted in gold sparkle below rainbow fringe — cracked the air with backfires. These machines, made by Bluebird, Wayne, Ward, Ford, and other US firms, contribute significantly to the ambient particulates of the city's hovering smog.

There are tens of thousands of such buses in Mexico and Central America. All are built on the standard school or church bus shell sold in the States. Since they are made "for export" they are exempt from US Department of Transportation standards for passenger capacity, seat width and spacing, cushion comfort and pyro–toxicity, exit access, body strength, roof–crush, interior crashworthiness and catalytic conversion.

Mufflers appear to be optional. Highly rust prone in the humidity of lower elevations, they soon suffer dysfunction. Replacing them is not a high priority. Some drivers remove them intentionally. A merely rumbling engine does not announce one's presence strongly

142

enough in a culture where noise is a virtue. Horns on these beasts do not "toot" or "honk," but rather shriek at locomotive decibel. Their use is not spared.

"Bee bee bee bee bee ..."

The beggar was having a good afternoon. Many made a special effort to push through the crowd to drop a coin or bank note into his cup. He appeared to have paramount possessory interest in this corner. Other mendicants practiced at less auspicious stations further along but none with his resonance or success. Shopkeepers seemed not to mind his presence. A young girl brought him fresh rolls from the bakery next door; the owner paused to visit. Old men, with palettes of lottery tickets, and a money changer surreptitiously peeling a wad of cash, came up to chat and transact business.

The beggar gave 2.8 quetzales to the dollar, two–tenths better than the smelly little *cambio* alcoves where you were tugged by pestilent urchins: "Hey! Hey! Hey, you! Hey Meester, what you want? What you need? You need change dollar? Thees way ..." There was no difference in their prices. Once in a while, the kids might tell you 2.8 or even 3, but when you got in the place the guy on the other side of the speak–hole always said two–six. The 2.6 was for cash; if you had travelers checks, you were lucky to get 2.4 and sometimes it was only two.

Avoiding the *cambio* hustlers I dropped a coin in the beggar's hat — his cup was full — and returned to the Hotel Pan American to have coffee and read the *Miami Herald*. A well dressed American woman, about 60, with blue–tinted hair was playing "Brahms' Lullaby" on the lobby piano.

Beginning in Belize I had noticed that business people, Peace Corps volunteers and other US residents had been receiving, mostly unsolicited, copies of various "news digests" dealing with the war in Nicaragua and other regional conflicts. Among the more well distributed were *Central America Report* and *Mesoamerica*.[36] Their bent was decidedly anti–US and pro–Marxist.

Resident journalists for the major American media were also recipients and even used the publications as sources, sometimes cited, sometimes not, for their own reports. It turned out that the editor of *Central America Report* was the official representative of a major US television network who also ran pro–Sandinista "educational seminars" out of his office. A listed distributor for these sheets was something called "Inforpress" in downtown Guatemala City. I decided to drop by for a visit.

There was no sign about the entryway, which looked like every other on the unkempt block. Inside, however, was a different story. My knock was answered with the buzz of a lock–release switch.

143

Pushing in, I found myself transported from the dusty bustle of a Latin city into a world of quiet European efficiency.

A moderately stout matron, about 55, with lowered bifocals looked up from a desk neatly stacked with outgoing mail. One batch was of a back issue with the cover photograph of an American soldier, rifle across his lap, and the caption: WAR IS PEACE: US Policy in Central America. Paper–clipped to each was an introductory letter to new "subscribers."

"Vat can ve do for you?" She hadn't hesitated to address me in English.

I asked if this were the office of *Central American Report*.

"Vat information do you vant?"

I told her I was just traveling through collecting information for a book on the region.

"Ve are very busy as you can see."

Two young men had been pushing a metal trolley back and forth between the library and what looked like a mailing room. People were back there typing and stuffing envelopes.

"You are a reporter, yes?"

"A writer. Freelancing," I said.

"Oh, vun of those. You vill have to come back some other time."

A phone rang somewhere far to the rear, and she ushered me firmly toward the door, then ran back to the phone. Just as she turned away one of the trolley boys came back through.

"How many subscribers do you have?" I asked, in Spanish now.

"Oh, more than 15,000 now," he replied. Friendly fellow. "We'll have more than 30,000 in a few weeks."

"Who are they?"

"Mostly Americans. Students, businessmen, many professors. The majority in the United States, but many in Latin America."

"What about Peace Corps volunteers?"

"Oh, them too. They are our best *clientes*."

What did he mean by that?

"*¡Muy Pagados!*" Paid up, he said enthusiastically. They paid for their subscriptions and sent in new names all the time. They and the Stateside students. The *periodistas* and *profesores* didn't pay that much but they got theirs anyway, every issue, right on time just like the others.

"How many of all your *clientes* are *pagados*," I asked him.

"*Menos que diez por...*" Less than 10 percent.

"I taut I told you you must leave. You do not have de liberty to talk vit dees man. Tomás! Sigues!" She brusquely ordered the boy away. I opened the door to leave but she gave me a rude nudge, nevertheless.

Schoolmates, Puerto Barrios, Guatemala.

Emil and Liliana came by the hotel my last night there. They had spent most of the past few days with Ursula out at the hospital. She would be released soon, but there was no word about her husband. It didn't look good for him.[37]

Emil said they had decided to ship around Nicaragua, since everyone they had talked to either said the border was closed or that there were Contra ambushes and artillery barrages near the Honduran frontier. I told them that I had heard it was safe.

They would follow the Swiss Embassy's advice, Liliana said, and ship — probably from Puerto Cortés or Tela in Honduras. "After what has happened to our friends, we really must be careful," she said.

I decided, notwithstanding the ambush, to push on up to Lake Atitlán. They had been hit on a back road; if I stuck pretty much to the main route, I'd be all right, I figured. Besides, it was worth the risk to see the volcanic center, igneous and political, of Guatemala. We said our goodbyes and pressed on our separate ways.

Situated beneath two massive but recently inactive volcanoes, Lake Atitlán fills the crater of a third. Its mountains and forests gave Mayan holdouts almost 200 years' respite from the Spanish who, under Cortés lieutenant Pedro de Alvarado, are credited with Guatemala's conquest in 1530.[38]

Once again, Santiago Atitlán was a redoubt of rebellion — this time a nest of guerrilla activity by the URGN and, in the ensuing anarchy, of random banditry and vigilante reprisal. The ambush of the Swiss couple, the recent beheading of a Canadian priest and the disappearance of two American freelance journalists gave foreigners no expectation of immunity.

Provided one could reach it safely, I was told, the village of Panajachel offered seminormalcy, challenged only by the occasional bank robbery or hit–and–run killing.

The place was also a *Pasqua,* Easter, vacation mecca for local gentry and for a number of foreigners. Many made an annual pilgrimage to the town, doing day trips out to neighboring villages with markets as exotic as Hong Kong's: Sololá, Huehuetenango, Chichicastenango.

A hundred or so *extranjeros*, mostly aging American hippies and other cultural fugitives, actually lived in Panajachel, prompting some to refer to it, somewhat disparagingly, as "Gringotenango." But there were also artists who found refuge from the threat and hypocrisy of *"El Mundo Plástico,"* as one referred to Europe and the States.

Statue of banana worker, Puerto Barrios, Guatemala.

Paul Thompson had come down from L.A. to do a background piece on guerrillas in the region. He had tried to dig into the matter of the freelance reporters who had left Panajachel the previous October to travel through the back country until they found the URGN.

The barman at *El Último Refugio* — where the mystery was a subject of conjecture — said he figured they had been shot on sight by the insurgents. Someone else said they were being held hostage; still another, that they had "gone native" to get a better story, which everyone agreed would be "sold to the New York Times." Presumably, the authors would be enriched beyond the standard $150 fee for such submissions.

There was also talk of three coffee plantation owners and their families who had been shot the week before — all from well–placed ambushes. The wounded were pistoled with coups de grace. One was caught in midspan of a bridge at 7:30 in the morning. His Mercedes was riddled with shot, killing him, his wife, two grandchildren and a young hired hand. He was making the payroll rounds of his plantations.

"The bastards are out there, I can tell you that." A wiry young fellow came over to where we were sitting at the bar. His name was Johnson and his left forearm was in a cast. He said he had been attacked the week before on the way back down from the States.

"Four guys in a BMW. Drove up alongside me just this side of the Mexican border. They had pistols. Wearin' masks. I put it to the floor, but they were too fast. Shot my VW all to hell. Lucky all I got out of it was a busted hand. If they'd been worth a damn, I'd be one dead gringo."

We ordered another round of "Old Friend," Guatemala's imitation bourbon. Paul offered one to Johnson, but he waved him away. "Orange juice. That's all I do," he said.

Indian women squatted along the sides of streets peddling blankets and souvenirs to passersby, mostly upper–class Guatemalans in their twenties and thirties who looked like suburban Californians — white, tanned, immaculately coiffured. They came in boisterous entourages of Jeep Cherokees and Chevy vans, some towing brightly painted speed boats, others lashed with sailboards, kayaks and rubber dinghies.

An eddy of peasants huddled against the flow of tourists at the Café El Patio to stare at the color television screen there. Paul called it "The CNN Cafe" because it was regularly tuned to that channel.

Out back was a large dish antenna. The volume was decibeled
to assure penetration for some distance:

> But she brushes so well ...

> We didn't get to be the biggest copying
> company by making cameras ...

> Share a little bit of yourself at the
> Church of Jesus Christ of Latter Day
> Saints. The Mormons ...

> Double pleasure's waiting. Doublegood
> doublegood Doublemint gum ...

> Bad news at the dentist? Only Reach
> has reaching bristles to get between teeth
> and along gums ...

> New Legatrin, the medicine that says
> good night to night leg cramps ...

> And now here's Sandy Kenyon with
> the Hollywood Minute ...

The day before Good Friday I took a ferry across to San Pedro. It
was a village isolated from the commercialism of Panajachel but the
road around the lake had been graded and the streets were full of big
semis driven home for Easter. There was good light for taking
pictures and in the late afternoon I was able discretely to photograph
the inhabitants going about their daily lives. I took a room in the
guest house behind the Catholic church, an auspicious place from
which to view the Good Friday candlelight procession which began in
the courtyard. It wound through the hilly passageways of the village,
eventually entering the church at the end opposite the rectory.
Throughout the night, there was strenuous singing within and by
private carolers in the street below. The guitars and tambourines of
three separate evangelical congregations rose on the night air long
after the Catholics had retired.

Next morning I set out to climb San Pedro Volcano, reaching a
point several hundred feet above the tree line before turning back. I
had underestimated the time required to get to the summit, about
eight hours, and the ferry left at four. The foothills were carpeted
with coffee plants and, beyond them, a rich growth of low forest rife
with butterflies and hummingbirds.

By Saturday noon, thousands of Indians had settled to the east of Panajachel, sprawling across the mouth of the wide arroyo that delineates the town limits before ending in the lake. They arrived standing in 5–ton trucks, 40 or more to a truck, so that another body could not have been stuffed into any of them. And they arrived in school buses so full that some passengers would succumb to the heat or lack of air, it was said, though I did not see this. They built fires and began to cook their *comidas* and the air was heady with the pungency of gastronomical antiquity.

Evangelicals attended upon the bullhorned declamations of preachers in white shirts and black ties. Bibles were waved and struck upon the knees then waved again, sweat streaking down faces and saturating shirts. The wrath to come was conjured so vividly that minions conducted swooned auditors away to be slapped and fanned until they regained consciousness. Others were led to the lake where they held hands and were baptized. A Catholic priest performed Mass with candles and statuary. But most of the people simply expended themselves in secular revelry. Some waded into the lake, a few out quite a ways. None swam. *Kayukas* darted back and forth.

There was a surge from the back of the crowd, young men tearing ahead, knocking others aside. One shouted and pointed to a person struggling in the water. Nearby was an overturned canoe. Two figures fought the water closer to shore. No one gave them a hand. A *kayuka* came alongside their companion but he slipped beneath the surface. The crowd pressed toward the water. At first the reaction was playful but it turned from glee to annoyance to concern and finally to terror as more and more people were forced into the lake. Women screamed and clutched their children. One woman held up an infant but no one would take it. The pleas of the people to be let back onto the land could only be heard by the helpless ones on the edge. When my turn came, I plunged in, floated out a ways beyond the melee, half tiptoeing, half breaststroking as the depth receded then returned. The water, cold at first, was oddly refreshing. Finally, I sloshed ashore at the boat landing and settled back to watch the riot.

As quickly as it had stampeded to the water, the mob now lunged at the landing: a police skiff was delivering the body ashore. A sergeant's whistle summoned a squad of soldiers who forced a path. A pathetic bundle was shouldered by four of them to a truck and driven away.

The excitement dissipated, the crowd mulled its boredom. Then it turned toward the festival platform, where a rock band was tuning up with strains of "I Want to Hold Your Hand." From a billboard high above us, the Marlboro Man cheerfully lit his cigarette.

Easter pilgrims at Lake Atitlán, Panajachel, Guatemala.

10

UTILA

*'It's absurd for the United States to help these
people develop a product with one hand, then
take away their market with the other.'*

There is a cave on the Honduran island of Utila in which the
English buccaneer Henry Morgan is said to have hidden more
Spanish gold than all that yet recovered from sunken galleons.

John Emerson Jackson, 86, told me so. Rocking in his front
porch swing, voice steady, deep hazel eyes mirroring vagrant clouds
above Ellen Jackson's trellised roses, he would have made credulous
the Missouri antic, Tom Sawyer:

> Aye, when I was a boy
> we climbed all down in that
> cave looking for ol' Henry's
> gold. Never found a
> doubloon — only bat guano
> and a dead monkey. Just
> because we didn't find it
> don't mean it ain't there. We
> know it was there. You
> could feel it. That cave goes
> on for miles and miles
> under the island. Even goes
> beneath the sea. Someday,
> somebody will keep crawlin'
> til they find that gold.

The island is one of the *Islas de la Bahía,* Bay Islands, three
chunks of land lying 40 to 60 miles out in the Gulf of Honduras. They
were discovered by Columbus in 1502 on his last voyage.

For 250 years, Utila, the westernmost and second largest of the
three, served as lair and way station for English plunderers of the
spoils of New Spain. Chief among its celebrated guests, legend holds,
were Morgan and Francis Drake who are said to have looted from the
viceroys half of what they had pillaged from Mexico and Peru. The
privateers needed a place to stow their loot before returning to
England. The cave was the perfect cache and Utila was well away
from main sea lanes.

In 1831, white settlers began arriving from other Caribbean colonies. Some blacks came, mostly from St. Vincent and Jamaica. Legally the latter were freemen, the British navy by then enforcing abolition. However, one could not easily shift jobs on a small island, much less leave for greener parts without money for passage.

Early arrivals were mostly fishermen and, it is now boasted, rebels who chafed under the formal regimen of colonial rule. Some locals even claim their ancestors lived here during the days of the great sea dogs, raising the inference of direct descendancy from the kleptomaniacal Morgan who did not refrain from the looting of an occasional London–bound merchantman. But that seems unlikely: colonial records reflect no permanent settlement prior to the early 1700s.

Although officially Hondurans, white Bay Islanders consider themselves English. They harbor a ritual disdain for the mother country who "abandoned us to the Spanish," the local word for mainland Hondurans, in 1859 as part of a settlement of Caribbean claims.

Eight miles long and two to five wide, Utila and its larger sister islands of Roatán and Guanaja to the northeast are coral afterthoughts trailing the continental plate, much like the neighboring Belize cays, but older by a few millennia. Only a third of the main island is inhabited. The rest is low and marshy and subject to total flooding during the monster hurricanes that sweep through, on average, every 10 years.

Some 750 Utilans actually reside on a cluster of tiny satellite cays west of the marsh: Diamond, Jewell, Pigeon and Suck Suck. So small are they that the houses of the inhabitants, built 10 to 15 feet off the ground, and the plank walks between them cover virtually all the surfaces of the islets.

Cay society is strict: Church services daily, no liquor allowed, long skirts for women. Trips to Utila town are limited to perhaps once a fortnight. Visits to the mainland are much rarer.

Pests, among them chiggers, the ubiquitous sand fly and mosquitoes, thrive here. Swarms of these insects curse the interior so that few Utilans without plots to tend venture there.

Population figures are inexact, but they hover around 2,500. Fewer than half are present at any time. The missing, mostly heads of young families, are away in the US Merchant Marine, which has long since replaced fishing as Utila's chief livelihood.

A number of these seamen, like Dempsey Thompson, saw action on tankers and Liberty Ships in World War II. Thompson was on a refrigerator ship at Guadalcanal, Leyte, the Solomon Islands and Okinawa. A younger fellow, "Sam," called at Saigon during the Vietnam War.

Others, mainly women, work in clerical and service jobs in Louisiana, Florida and Texas. Green–card permits are expedited with the aid of a small but well–placed network of former Bay Islanders, including young women who "married well." An American husband is, for some parents, the pinnacle of daughterly expectation. Those who can afford to do so send their children to college in the States, with small denominational institutions, principally Methodist, preferred.

Except for a wrinkling of hillocks back of the town, the island's single prominence is "Pumpkin Hill," an anomaly of more recent volcanic origin. The entrance to the cave opens just to the south of the hill, in a small upthrust that is probably an auxiliary vent or flow from the same disturbance.

At Pumpkin's foot are maybe a hundred acres of meadowland choked with wild hay and prickly scrub. To the north is one of the island's few sandy beaches, wedged between two long stretches of jagged coral known locally as iron shore or razor rock.

A few hundred feet out, the sea bed drops off a thousand feet. According to divers, this depression contains one of the most spectacular sea life displays in the Caribbean. It is also perilous. Big Tom, a 20–foot great white shark, lurks there. An island legend, the fish has trashed many a net and attacked small craft.

In addition to Morgan's cave and its doughty "lost colony" of English settlers, Utila was also known for a strange, delicious fruit, a papaya called "Red Mammy." Native to the island, the melon had become a sought after delicacy as far away as the United States — from which it was formally banned under medfly quarantine regulations.

Red Mammies, smaller and more succulent than their pink mainland cousins, had won their reputation in large part as the result of a cooperative organized by intrepid Peace Corps Volunteer Tim Gast. Find Gast, I was told by a fellow volunteer at Copán, and "You'll see why the Peace Corps is cost–effective." Only the Marine Corps, I thought, was more self–conscious about taxpayer dollars. It turned out that the two services had even more in common: stifling of innovation by Washington bureaucrats.

Leaving the jeep with American teachers at the port of La Ceiba, I boarded the trader boat, *Florida*. The chugger sagged with lumber, piping, crates of oranges and 33 Utilans returning from Ceiba market or from "'Guci" and "San Pedro," as they referred to Tegucigalpa, the capital, and San Pedro Sula, the second city. The stern skipper personally collected fares. I pushed forward through tarred ropes and produce.

Utila town was a thin line of whitewashed houses ending on a wide lagoon that severed habitable land from the marsh. An airstrip, hidden from view on the eastern tip, was sought just then by a rumbling DC–3 of *Lineas Aéreas Nacionales.*

The plane circled, then bore in at treetop level, its engines whining above the put–put of the *Florida's* reluctant diesel. The now–ingratiating captain, breath heavy with garlic and beer, pointed out Pumpkin Hill to two young Swedes, muttering something about it being a hazard to aircraft.

On the pier, a crowd of residents awaited family and mail. Three children raced ahead of an employee to catch the mooring line. A very large woman blocked egress amidships. Passengers respectfully circumvented her.

"You got de meats and de tatos for me dere, Cap'n?" she demanded.

"Got 'em all you ask, Big Mama," he replied.

Ena Elizabeth Cooper Muñoz ran Utila's only restaurant, Big Mama's Cook Shop. She cooked when it suited her and the fare might vary from that chalked on the menu board. If you didn't like it — well, you could go somewhere and build a fire and fix your own. She told that to chronic complainers: "Feexyurohn den, bugowd."

Big Mama's big lungs could scold half the island in one yell. Some Frenchmen there to put in an air navigational beacon only half jested that they could hear her from the rise where the station's dish opened like an inverted mushroom. "She is incredible, that woman. A voice like a cannon," one exclaimed.

He had argued with her over her french fries and undertaken to show her "how one can make the fried potatoes with less grease and better taste." Big Mama was not about to have her cuisine corrupted by Cordon Bleu.

The Frenchmen then arranged to have their meals cooked privately in a local home. That had proved cumbersome so they were back now with Big Mama, nibbling forlornly at a table by the door.

Chicken was Mama's top dish. She wrung their necks out back around 10 each morning. They were then plucked in scalding water and deep–fat fried. A dozen or so ranged even into the dining room, pecking up anything that hit the floor.

"On bouffe pas bien ici," one does not eat well here, one of the Frenchmen allowed with a shrug as he watched two big roosters fight over a fry fallen from a neighboring table. But his palate was too sensitive. Most travelers gave Big Mama's fixins higher praise.

I took a room at Trudy's Hotel. This was done only after prospecting the length of the waterfront for quieter lodgings. A portable radio dominated Trudy's. It belonged to one of the crewmen of the DC–3, a lanky, morose fellow with a drooping mustache.

The crew left early the next morning, though not without one last riotous broadcast. It began at the far end of the pensión. Muffled thuds, mingled with yelps and moans for "muh bay–bee," told that they were awake. At length, a door opened and the decibels escaped into the hallway, augmented now by whistles, bells and buzzers, like a celebration of Pac–Man's progress.

The hotel was a popular R&R destination for Peace Corps volunteers, especially women. Trudy's cooking was superb. If you wanted to have breakfast or supper — no lunch was served — you had to reserve in advance. Only guests were allowed on the premises. Each was politely but firmly advised that "no foolishness" would be tolerated, as if there were anything at all foolish on Utila.

Except, perhaps, at the Reef Room, a less than reputable establishment with lodgings for a half dozen young mainland women. Their patrons were some 20 Honduran soldiers billeted nearby.

Of course there was the Bucket of Blood, a raucous disco at the far end of town adjacent to the Monkey Tail Inn, but even respectable folks were known to quaff there. One of the first things you learned on Utila was that some reporter from the *New York Times* had included the Bucket on his list of "The World's Ten Best Bars."

One of the next things you learned was that monkeys once lived on the island. Mr. Jackson said they were a unique species of "longtails." Tim Gast said they had probably been the same variety of *ateles,* spider monkey, common on the mainland. In any event, all had been shot for sport by the 1920s. The forest was haunted by their silence.

One morning, early, I struck out for Morgan's cave. Mr. Jackson had given general directions but when I stopped at his store for sandwiches, Dempsey Thompson drew a map, on the back of which he wrote the following:

"Go toward Pumpkin Hill and when you have first seen it across an open meadow, walk on for another 50 paces or so and then look behind you, and you will see the ridge high and to your right rear and the place covered by a fig tree with roots clinging down the hillside. That's where she lies."

Dempsey, 56, and his wife, Hester, were the parents of eight daughters, one of whom became Miss Honduras and married a Houston sporting goods dealer. Her clippings papered the walls of Dempsey's Grocery and General Mdse. Two younger sisters shyly attended to customers. One brought coffee for her father and me. I promised to return and look at the scrapbooks.

Two young American women at the hotel accompanied me to the cave. They had arrived on the weekly Cessna shuttle via Roatán the evening before. I advised trousers and plenty of mosquito repellent.

157

One was a Peace Corps volunteer in Intibucá province. She knew little about fish farming, but that was her first billet, helping some villagers start up such a project. The co–op so prospered that she had been assigned to begin another.

Between jobs she'd received a surprise visit from two Michigan classmates who were hopscotching through Latin America. A week on Utila seemed a great idea. That day the second friend had gone snorkeling with the Swedes.

We passed small pastures, closes really, but few had cattle. There were occasional pens of wallowing pigs. Communal grazing was the rule with the burden on each landowner to fence out ranging animals. Lately disputes had arisen as stock trampled corn stalks, papaya groves and banana plants.

Some tracks led up to the French navigation station where you could scan the whole town, from the steeples of the churches to fishing skiffs bobbing past the wharves. A handsome ketch with an American ensign was striding into the bay. Shards of twisted metal, the remains of a small aircraft, glistened in the sun at the end of the runway. Behind us, to the northeast, lay Pumpkin Hill.

When the trail ended in the meadow beneath Pumpkin, I remembered the "50 paces or so," but missed the fig tree.

"There it is," one of the women finally said. "Over there behind those bushes."

It was decided that I would do the honors. Scrambling up on the roots of the tree, I gained an outcrop before an opening barely larger than a foxhole. A yellowed rope tied to a limb paid out into the cavern.

My companions called for me to be careful.

"I'm only going in a short ways," I shouted.

Grasping the rope, I slid down to a space ample enough to stand and surveyed the interior. It was dank and smelled of mildew. There were footprints in the dirt, and guano. From somewhere came a high–pitched tone, a cheep, soft at first, then louder, then gone.

The prints led to a narrows barely wide enough for a person of average build. I was about to try it when I caught a reflection to one side.

Walking over I found some rocks in a circle with two boulders placed opposite. On a ledge was a dented lantern and a can of kerosene. A pile of scraps and bones lay to one side along with several bottles of rum, one of which had caused the reflection. The rope, which had held the promise of a long guided tour, ended in a matted clump. The end was tied to a pail.

Returning to the passage I squeezed through. The sound of the moment before returned.

Shining the light forward I beheld one of nature's unnerving spectacles: Flying bats, hundreds, perhaps thousands of them. I had anticipated a few but their numbers were staggering. Several approached closely, cheeping as they passed. I quickly decided to abort my spelunking and moved to retreat, in my haste hitting the flashlight on the wall. It blinked momentarily, went out, fell and rolled some distance, ending in a dim glow. I groped toward it.

"Don't go out completely on me," I pleaded. I realized I had lost my bearings.

The bats became bolder. One swept near my face.

I grabbed the dying flash and crept along the damp wall. I had just found the opening when my foot pressed something soft: a human hand! It jerked away. A stubby—bearded face resolved itself. Before I could apologize, the specter spoke:

"Hey, man, you got any rum, man? You don need be scared 'dem bats, man."

It was one of the young Carib men from the town. I thought I recognized him but wasn't sure. Perhaps from the boat or the Bucket of Blood. He was less than sober.

Finally begging his pardon, I delivered the disappointing news that there was no rum in my kit, asking in the next breath if he lived in here.

"No, man. We just come here sometimes to cook a pig and have a little fun time, man."

I inquired further but he was in no mood for a long conversation. So apologizing again, I resumed my retreat.

"Don' tell nobody you seen me here, okay, my friend?"

I assured him that I would not.

"Were there any bats in that cave?" one of the women asked impatiently as I rejoined them.

"You're not kidding!" I replied, describing the swarm. "Bats and a very strange bird."

"That'll be 85 cents, lemp for the bananas," the grocer said, "plus another four lemp for the oranges and soda." I paid the tab with a 10—lempira note and pocketed the change. The lempira at the time was 2.6 to the dollar.

"You want to find Teem's house? I take you there." His delivery boy had heard me ask for the Peace Corps volunteer. I agreed, and we set out.

Tim Gast lived on the west end of town, near the old Methodist Church and primary school. The place looked like it would be hard pressed to survive a spunky gust, much less a hurricane. The floor sagged and the foundation seemed a bit displeased with the perpendicular. Plumbing was one—way — out to the back hillside from the sink and bath. Water was hauled up from the next–door neighbor's cistern.

Shaky steps led to an oversized porch whose longevity was even more doubtful. From here was conducted much of the business of UTICOL, Utila Cooperative, *Limitada*, the fledgling enterprise committed to bringing to the world the joys of Red Mammy — and greenbacks to Utila.

"We started this project with only 12 acres of papayas and zero dinero," Gast said as he leaned back in a creaky old rocker and propped his feet on the porch rail.

Marcia, his Brazilian wife — a lanky dark–haired beauty who shared his zeal for the islanders and their papayas — brought out a plate of cookies and a pitcher of herbal tea. They had met in graduate school at the University of New Mexico a few years before. She put the tea on the floor to steep and settled with the cookies into a chair next to her husband, slouching her long legs over the rail next to his. They might have been Ozark hill folk pondering the weather.

"With normal rainfall, one acre will produce twenty tons of commercially marketable papaya in one 'lifetime' of cultivation. After three years, though, the plants wear out so they continue to produce, but not commercially. You really can't market 2– to 3–pounders, and that's what you get after three years. It's best to clear the land off and start over again with new plants."

"How long does that take?" I asked.

"Not long. We can plow an acre under and replant and have papayas ready for market in just over eight months.

"The average market weight is six pounds, although we get them as large as twelve and even twenty."

The majority of the co–op members were blacks, Gast said.

"There's a lot of animosity here towards the blacks, but in my view they make the best farmers. They're willing to stick with the project even after a bad year and to work together with other members. That's the main thing. There are some really good white farmers, but many tend to be either too ornery or too proud to work as part of a co–op."

Gast had prepared the project proposal in July of the previous year with a colleague, Richard Bowman. It was presented to an advisory committee of Honduran nationals, which served as a kind of screening group and a liaison between locals and the agency.

"Unfortunately, it included a number of mainlanders with traditional grudges against bay islanders, especially Utilans."

We talked about the strife, the result of the islanders' condescending attitude toward their fellow countrymen and the latter's envy of islander industry and independence.

160

There was also the problem of resource allocation. There were a number of mainland US Agency for International Development, A.I.D., projects with greater committee support — two were urban housing in Tegucigalpa and land–title registration in El Paraíso. The upshot was that they recommended against the papaya project, and it was only through personal intercession that he and Bowman were able to persuade A.I.D. to go along. Forty thousand dollars, 109,000 lempiras, had been allocated and to date about a third had been spent.

"I hope we can get the project off its feet with this initial outlay," Gast said, "but we've really been hurt by the refusal of the US Agriculture Department to make an exception for our product under the medfly quarantine restrictions.

A request for an exemption had been referred to a "certified regional expert" but so far he had refused to come out and do the required testing. There had been several letters exchanged but nothing had come of it. Both fresh and dried fruit were produced but each fell under the quarantine designed to protect American crops from the dreaded Mediterranean fruit fly.

"Would you like to walk one of the fields?" Gast asked. I said that I would.

The president of the co–op, a 25–year old black farmer, went with us. The patch was some 10 acres; its papayas were almost picking size.

"About another week, now, and they'll be ready," the farmer said.

"Where do you market them?" I asked.

"Over on the mainland, mostly Ceiba, Tela and San Pedro," he replied. "We send a few to the capital and Roatán, but mostly just on the coast."

"It would be simple to ship them to Miami or Tampa," Gast said. "There are two or three boats a month from the islands."

The *Hyber Seven* and *Hyber Intrepid*, which ply out of Ceiba and Roatán, were two of these. Refrigerator ships, one of them made a trip to Florida every fortnight laden with lobster, year round, and shrimp, June to December.

"No reason they couldn't add a container of Mammies," Gast said. "Just the damned medfly restrictions. Man, there's never even been a medfly that I know of in Honduras, much less out here. Even if they wanted to be extra cautious, they could have an inspector come out and spot–check our crop at random. We would gladly pay his travel expenses."

The papayas, he said, were the island's only chance for export earnings.

"It's absurd for the United States to help these people develop a product with one hand, then take away their market with the other."[39]

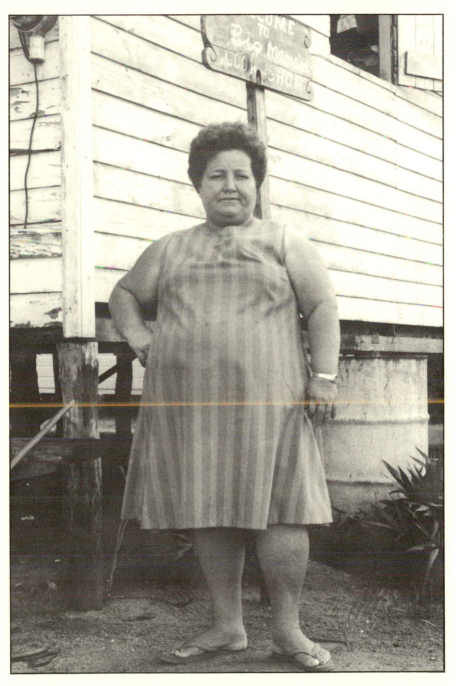

"Big Mama" in front of her eatery, Utila Island, Honduras.

11

TEGUCIGALPA

'The threat to Central America isn't Communism.
It's deforestation. Honduras is literally becoming
a desert.'

I headed inland from La Ceiba. It was now the 21st week of the journey. Time was slipping by. The Nicaraguan civil war was in one of its slack periods — a good time to take a look at its effects close–up and, if possible, talk to some of the participants. Many were in Honduras.

One night I camped in some scrub on the banks of Lake Yojoa, roughly halfway to Tegucigalpa. An old man came at dawn and called out:

"Pescado fresco ... ¿quieres?" Fresh fish! Would you like?

Sleepily, I struggled out of the tent, examined the catch and bought all four for 10 lempiras — more than they were worth. But fried up in olive oil with chopped potatoes, onions and scrambled eggs and garnished with garlic and hot chilies, they made a wildcatter's breakfast. That was just what I needed.

The fellow hung around while I built the fire and got things going. The jeep attracted his attention, and the gear. He'd never seen an Oasis 4–quart canteen before. I took a pull and handed it to him. He sipped, suspiciously.

"Whiskey, no?" he asked. "No, no whiskey," I replied. He shrugged good–naturedly and grinned. I considered offering him a swig of Old Grand–Dad, but the fifth was buried in the spare part box.

When his eyes locked on the skillet, I insisted he join me.

"¡Sí! ¡Cómo no!" he replied.

Even when we each had eaten our fill, enough was left for supper.

A pot of cowboy coffee, from beans bought in Tela market, warmed the moment. When, as here, there was no plug for the grinder, a fist full of beans in a rag would be pulverized with the hatchet nub. We drank it all and then some, the grounds doing double duty.

"Es bueno, éste. Es café natural del país."

"Better than Nescafe, isn't it?" He slapped a knee and grinned in agreement.

Francisco, a rare reverse migrant, had come out here from Tegucigalpa some 15 years before. An uncle had a small patch and no one to help. Francisco and his family pitched in and when the uncle died, he left the land to him. In addition to his wife and 13 children, a brother and his two sons lived on the place. They fished to make extra money, selling mostly to motorists on the side of the road and to a resort kitchen down the lake. He liked being out on the water. *"Muy tranquilo,"* he said repeatedly. I agreed that it was indeed very peaceful.

Would I like to go out fishing?

"How much?" I asked.

"No, you don't have to pay money. We'll go out until noon — *mediodía."*

Never one to turn down a fishing trip, especially a free one, I doused the fire, stowed the pans and drove the jeep into some brush. Francisco insisted there was no trouble with *ladrones.* "Only the people of the lake come here. They do not steal. Besides, they would see my pail." He left his bucket on the hood.

The boat was flat–bottomed with an old 15–horse Johnson outboard and two worn paddles. I got in first and he pushed off, handing me a throw line baited with a fat bream. The water was blue, deep green–blue. The sun, breaking through a smoky haze, sparkled on it. A breeze brought an alpine freshness which might have put us in Tirol or Idaho — until upwards of noon when the smoke gathered again, hiding the sun, but greenhousing its heat. By then it was apparent that his luck for the day had ended in breakfast. We drifted toward shore, nudged by the breeze.

"Would you like to meet my friend, Enrique?" he asked as we sloshed up the bank. "He likes books, too."

Enrique Campos was the manager at some isolated cabins and a restaurant known as the Hotel Agua Azul, a weekend hideout for 'Guci big shots and diplomats. Just then it was empty, so he rented me a room for half price, $18.00. Enrique was Nicaraguan. He had stuck around until '82, then decided the Sandinistas weren't going to give back his farm — or pay for it. So he split.

"Oh, I still have family there, in Managua, and we write. But they have their own lives, and I have mine."

We were in the Azul's kitchen, an old ranch–style cookery with high ceilings and friendly kettles steaming on a cast iron stove. There was a staff of 11 to feed, even when there were no guests.

We talked at one end of a thick–planked mess table. The chef sat at the other writing up a list for the weekly shopping trip to the capital. He had just promised Francisco 20 lempira for three buckets of fish the following Friday when a full house was expected.

Ceremonial stone head, Copán, Honduras.

The fisherman and a son sat out back having a beer. He had refused a tip, hands raised: *"Somos amigos."*

Enrique had managed to leave Nicaragua with enough money to travel a while but hadn't wanted to become a vagabond. "And I have no interest in politics" — implying that while he wished the opposition to the Sandinistas well, he had had enough of "fighting, always fighting."

He had discovered, he said, reading.

All the writers he had heard about but never read. We climbed the hill behind the kitchen to his house. It was filled with books — from a moldy set of the Greek and Latin poets to modern French and American novelists. Camus, Sartre, Céline, Steinbeck, Hemingway, Styron. Many were worn, dog–eared and underlined. From the porch there was a full view of the lake. An old typewriter sat on a table.

When I told him that my contact with Latin American literature was limited, he wrote out a small bibliography. The Uruguayan Juan Carlos Onetti was included, along with the Argentine Eduardo Galeano. He handed me his copy of "Afternoon of a Death Foretold" by Gabriel García Marquez and was pleased that I had at least read that. We discussed the plot and the dreamlike inevitability of it all. Enrique must have written seriously, himself, I thought, so intense and poignant were his reconstructions. But he said not. The typewriter was "only for notes to myself and for letters."

"Have you read Camus?" he asked after a long pause in our conversation.

I said that I had.

"I would like to have met him," he said softly.

Tegucigalpa. Jimmy "Las Brisas," a Canadian expatriate who ran a restaurant by that name in Tela, had recommended the Hotel Real but it was closed. A clerk at the posh Rondo, $60 a night, steered me to the Grenada, at eight bucks a bargain certain. The room was clean, most street noise muffled and the fan worked. Mosquitoes flocked — they hatched in a stagnant drain out back — but my licorice–smelling Zebra brand Chinese coils made them tolerable. The inevitable disco thumped and shrieked from a side street but sleep could be had from two to seven, which was sufficient. I parked the jeep at a DIPPSA national gasoline station next to a movie house up the street. They had all–night security: *"No hay problemas."*

The Grenada's guests included Palestinian merchants from La Ceiba. Honduras has the largest Arab population in the Caribbean, most of them descendants of Ottoman refugees in the early 1900s, but a few who have fled the current conflict with Israel.

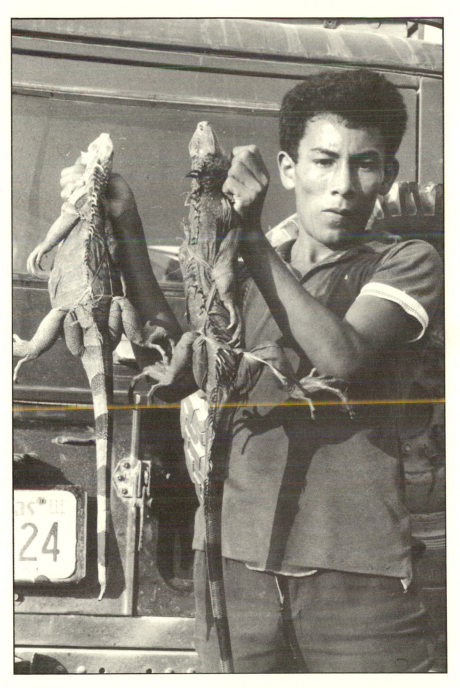

Iguanas for sale near Tela, Honduras.

There were students from small towns looking for jobs or admission to college, Peace Corps volunteers and missionary folk in transit or up for "consultations." Most were friendly and helpful with tips on good cheap restaurants, the best place to change dollars — cash only for the real rate — and directions about town.

A Chinese community thrived in the capital. Many had come from Hong Kong since Britain had agreed to return the colony to China. One family, now 14–strong, had fled the mainland in 1949.

"After 1997, the date of cession, there will be reprisals, confiscations, repatriation. It is naive to think otherwise." Mr. Chang, the father, was adamant.

He and the other adults had made modest progress with Spanish. But the children — between 8 and 20 years of age — could have been born here, so proficient had they become in a single year. Honduran school chums joined them in the family *tienda* to kibitz and check homework between customers — all under the proud eye of grandmother Chang, who was well into her 80s. Already, the store was the busiest in the neighborhood.

I noticed the old hawker the first time I walked down Avenida Séptima. Drawn, arthritic, yet aggressive, he moved like a spider as soon as he spotted a customer in the passing crowd.

"Lotería ... Lotería ... Aquí saca los billetes ... Hay aquí más suerte." Get your lottery tickets. The luckiest numbers right here.

He would wince and feel the small of his back, shift his weight, and even sit from time to time on nearby steps. But he never seemed to miss a sale. The clients varied, from ragged crones to smartly dressed men with briefcases. The one thing they had in common was the old ticket vendor — and his luck, but I knew nothing of that.

"A good Peace Corps volunteer works himself out of a job. Just like Bud Welborne. He's got the Miskito Indians into business — "

"It's Florida on the phone, Mr. Stevens." His secretary stood in the door.

"Excuse me."

"Hello, Stevens here. What? This country is covered with smoke! You can't land here."

"Pete" Stevens was the director of the largest, 300–plus, Peace Corps contingent in the world. He cradled the phone with his chin, winking at me conspiratorially. A binder with "Unclassified" taped on the spine lay open on the desk.

"What's that you say? Well, that's impossible..."

He held a sheet of paper up to the phone, as if it could read.

"Well, you tell 'em they're out of their minds if they think we can have all that done by the first. The fifteenth, just maybe, but the first?" He rolled his eyes and shrugged. "Come down, and I'll show you. But bring your Smokey Bear mask. You can't breathe without it." He hung up and called the secretary back in.

"Get the preliminary report on that Mosquitia project for me — oh, and tell Bud there's a writer here I'd like him to talk to."

"Reports! This is a special investigation of — well, it's classified, intradepartmentally, anyway. We're the *Peace* Corps, though with all the paperwork, sometimes I think I'm back in the *Old* Corps!" He had served four years in the Marines after World War II, mostly in Japan. Later, he earned a degree in industrial management at MIT, then spent the next fifteen years consulting in Latin America — from breweries in Ecuador to export–import in Peru. He joined the Peace Corps in '71, serving stints as director in Guatemala, Venezuela and Columbia. He "lay out" for six years with a private development outfit with jobs in Mexico and Honduras.

"If you lay out for as long as you stayed in, you can come in again. When my time was up they asked if I'd like to run the operation down here. I said sure.

"Now, let's see, where were we? Oh, yeah. Self–sufficiency and conservation. You need both in these places, but you have to have self–sufficiency first. Give the people a stake in preserving their land, their environment.

"Take these damned forest fires. You've mentioned the smoke. Is it always this bad? Stick around. Sometimes you'd think the town was on fire. We haven't had a blue sky here since — anyway, not this year that I recall."

I asked about the war in Nicaragua. Had Peace Corps volunteers been placed in danger? "So far, no. I try to keep them out of border areas, except in Mosquitia. The Coco River is no border at all. Bud Welborne can tell you what it's like to live as close to the front line as we get."

The Contras, he said, would never be strong enough to threaten the Sandinistas as long as they were denied matériel by the US Congress. He was ambivalent about it, himself, he said.

"The fact is that the Sandinistas are incompetent. If the Soviets cut them off, they'd fall of their own weight.

"The threat to Central America isn't Communism. It's deforestation. Honduras is literally becoming a desert. Parts of it already look like Egypt."

I asked what conservation effort the Peace Corps had made.

"Can't touch it! We have one or two small forest–management schemes, but conservation as we know it in the States is out–of–bounds. Too political. The government owns most of the land, and you'd think they'd at least try to contain the burning and cutting. But there's just too long a tradition of shifting agriculture. That's what they call it. But now they don't shift, they squat. And then you have the big cattle ranches. They overgraze and compact the land. But you can't touch them either. Hamburger export is big business here. Somebody said that every time you go to McDonalds you kill an acre of rain forest. That may be overstating it a bit, but it's in the ballpark.

"We've got foresters available for Honduran assignment, so has A.I.D. We've tried to get a major reforestation project, but I've spent enough time in Latin America to know that that's a dead end. At least for now."

Aside from peasant stubbornness and the clout of the large ranchers, much of the problem was the Honduran bureaucracy.

"*Mordida*, of course, is always around in any Latin government. But here that's much less of a problem than in, say, Mexico. The main difficulty here with getting anything done is that the wheels of the bureaucracy just grind slow. And the top politicians like to keep it that way. The president here has to make every final decision. Even something as simple as a shrimp export permit requires his personal approval."

He then talked about various projects that were under way. The emphasis, he said, was on "bootstrap agriculture;" subsistence crops, rotation, mulching, fish farms. Personal and community hygiene efforts had been stepped up; deeper, more sturdy wells, sewage disposal, and immunization, for example.

He mentioned Tim Gast and his "Red Mammy" papayas. "That's the kind of commercial breakthrough you dream about in our business. If they could only get that USDA medfly waiver, they'd be fat." The waiver snafu was an example of the US government working at cross–purposes with itself, he complained.

"Here you have everything you need: a superb product, cheap transport, the fortnightly Roatán freighters to Florida, and now, thanks to Tim there, a local co–op setup to make it all go. And then, wham! — this stupid medfly thing. There's more medfly danger from Mexico than from here, yet they're exempt."

Bud Welborne came to our meeting with notes and reports at the ready. He had the enthusiasm of a midshipman and the bottom–line eye of a banker. After two years in one of the Peace Corps' toughest, and most dangerous jobs, he was mustering out. The next day was his last. Vernon, Texas would take some getting used to after the jungles of Mosquitia.

He had been, he said, "a business consultant" for *Mopawi*. That was the name the Miskito Indians gave the cooperative he godfathered for them. It means "continual development."

"It's strictly a Miskito–run project," he asserted. "I made it plain from the beginning that my role was merely advisory. There are 17 directors — 16 Miskitos and a Moravian missionary."[40] Their aim was higher prices for their products while paying less for necessities.

Mopawi contracted with the Honduran government to supply its food distribution agency with fish caught by co–op members at prices higher than those offered by buyers for the few large merchants who had previously controlled the market. The co–op then bulk–purchased food staples, clothing and hardware, which it sold to members at bargain prices. The project was seeded by low interest loans from the Moravians and the Canadian government's aid–development bureau. The speculators were forced to meet the higher price for the fish or be shut out of the market altogether. Consumers now pay less, since supply is diversified, with the government agency playing a moderating role. So great had been the price spread in the controlled market that even with the new competition merchants do well.

"Here was an example of producers taking advantage of market–price distortion by speculators to get a better price for their product at no cost to the consumer. They did it by organizing themselves."

Since there was no full–term high school in Mosquitia, the co–op funded 12 three–year scholarships for Miskito students. Vocational schools in Tegucigalpa and the John F. Kennedy Secondary School in La Ceiba were favored. Agriculture, mechanics and carpentry, in addition to business and accounting, were required courses.

Mopawi also supported a variety of self–help projects, such as the development of wooden plank sailboats for use on the Coco River. A traditional means of transportation that had fallen into disuse, the boats made use of a drop keel for navigation close to shore and in shallows. According to a quarterly report Welborne helped prepare, "The available number of sufficiently large trees for dugouts is decreasing dramatically. Plank boats using local materials and sails are a good alternative to fuel, which is expensive and often irregular in supply." A Netherlands aid agency helped with this project.

Mopawi had turned such a good profit that, in two years, it had become the largest taxpayer in Mosquitia.

Welborne shrugged off Stevens' praise of his efforts: "The people have done it all, themselves. I've just been a good observer."

I asked him what effect the war had on the Miskitos.

"The young men from some villages were very active supporters of the Contras for awhile. They felt the Sandinistas had sold them out. The Sandinistas had certainly forced many of them to relocate away from the border. A lot of the ones on our side of the river were definitely refugees from that. But the Contras had blasted their villages and killed their families and forced them to fight with them. There were some Contra volunteers, though. They formed their own fighting units, called *Misuras*, and would go off for weeks at a time. A good many were killed. Then, gradually, the survivors began coming home — some of them on leave, but many deserters who would sell their guns. I think they started thinking, 'Hey, no matter who wins, we'll still be losers.'" Welborne agreed with that assessment: "Many of those guys were compelled to join up. Some forced recruitment still goes on, but now it's more persuasion. The Contra recruiters come and ask, 'Do you want to help your people; if you do, then come and fight with us,' but not many go now."

When I returned to the hotel one night, the clerk nodded me aside and presented a message on crumpled wrapping paper: a name, "Arana," and a phone number.

"You must call tonight," he whispered. *"Es muy importante."*

The phone was at the far end of the desk on the wall. As I called, he stared curiously, shifting his eyes when I looked up.

"Can you meet with us tomorrow morning at 10 o'clock?"

"Where?"

"We will take care of that. Can you be at the Texaco station at the statue of Columbus near the airport at 9:30?"

"Sure. Can I bring a camera?"

"No. No cameras are permitted. You must come alone. A car will pick you up. Now tell me what you look like."

When I arrived there was no one at the station except the attendant. A blue Datsun pulled from the edge of the lot. The driver asked, "Are you Mr. McMath?" He demanded my passport, studied the photo, then motioned for me to get in. A woman had been waiting for a bus a half block away, but as we prepared to enter traffic she ran up and jumped in the back seat. She held an ugly little automatic under a shopping bag. We meandered melodramatically for several blocks through adjacent side streets. The woman watched for followers. Finally, she looked at the driver in the rear view mirror and said, *"No hay nadie."*

We regained the highway and came to a division of upscale homes, fenced and guarded. The car stopped at one built into the side of a hill. A guard with a .38 Special under his belt opened the gate. Two attentive but relaxed Dobermans heeled behind him. Another car was just leaving; the occupants ignored us. We took its place.

I was directed through a side door and found myself at the bottom of a short flight of stairs dominated by a rotund but agile gent who descended to greet me.

"You are Mr. McMath? I'm Frank Arana, the person you spoke with on the phone."

We shook hands.

"Mr. Rodríguez and the others are waiting for you, but first the guards must check your person. Just a routine precaution."

Two unarmed functionaries frisked me, a perfunctory gesture, I thought, since I wore only a shirt and trousers. They flipped through my Honduran school tablet. Arana then ushered me into a room where four men sat at a table. Maps and charts covered the walls. One of the men stood and Arana introduced us. He was Inadlecio Rodríguez Alaniz, one of the members of the FDN Directorate.

Arana asked if I would be comfortable in Spanish, and I said yes, slowly. Fine, he said. He would translate if necessary.

"... So you see, that unless we can get the weapons, particularly artillery and antiaircraft missiles, we cannot beat the communists. Only two things can happen, then. Either we will be destroyed or, worse, we will be forced to accept a false peace with the Sandinistas.

"I have no doubt that when they see us abandoned by the Americans, they will tell us we can come home with no reprisals. They may even agree to certain of our terms, such as for a free press, freedom for political prisoners, elections and the rest. But as soon as we are disarmed they will break these promises."

He said that most of his men had also fought against Somoza, many in the ranks of the Sandinistas, themselves. They longed for home. "After 10 years of fighting, who would not?"

Many Americans, I said, thought the Contras had been on the other side, Somoza henchmen and colonels.

"There are no *somocistas* with us. True, we do have some former officers, but they had no special privileges or political positions under Somoza. The great majority of our soldiers were not even old enough to fight at that time. It has been seven years, you know, since Somoza was overthrown. These young men were only 12 or 13 years old then. Of our senior officers, 17 percent were in the *guardia* under Somoza but only one was a full colonel or above. Why is it that the American media exaggerate the importance of these fighters, yet say nothing about the Cubans fighting with the Sandinistas?"

"What evidence do you have of that, of the Cubans?" I asked.

"The Sandinistas have admitted this. They have awarded citations to them at public ceremonies. Just the other day they decorated two they called 'Heroes of the Angolan Revolution.'"

Arana broke in to say that the year before they had killed 13 Cuban soldiers.

"They did not have Cuban uniforms or identification, but we could tell from examining their bodies."

"What do you mean?" I asked him.

"Dental work, the same kind as the Cuban army. And tattoos: 'Fidel,' and like that."

"But have you ever captured any Cubans, to know it?" I asked.

They had not. Still, they were adamant that they had killed the ones they said they had killed.

The US Congress was at that time bitterly debating yet another Contra aid renewal measure.

Arana said: "The important thing now is that the Sandinistas are using the Soviet helicopter tanks, Hind gunships, which can shoot a thousand times as many bullets as we can on the ground. They are killing more of our men than their infantry. The small hand–held Stinger missiles can knock them down. Without them, it is impossible to move effectively during the day. But with only a few hundred of these Stingers, we can keep them out of the sky. We really must have these small missiles and also artillery and tanks to give our soldiers cover in the attack. The Sandinistas have over 300 Soviet M–55 tanks; we have none."

I said that many Americans, even those who sympathized with them, were concerned that money previously given was unaccounted for, that it had been diverted to private purposes or used on the black market. The *Miami Herald* had just published a story which said that congressional investigators could account for very little of it, that no records had been kept.

"Look, we must buy as many things as we can with that money, make it stretch as far as possible. So we use the black market. We can get two, sometimes three times lempiras and other currencies there for each dollar than at the official exchange rate. Also, what government can sell us munitions? There are US aid laws against such things. We are not recognized as an official entity by the Honduran government or even the government of the United States. And for our own diplomatic purposes we cannot use banks in those countries." Canceled checks could be traced.

"We explained all of this to the *Herald* reporter, but he still printed the story as if we were stealing the money and gave nothing of our side of it. He even refused to come and look at our books."

There were two sets of records, he said, one kept within the FDN, itself, and another, parallel set, kept by an outside accountant.

"They both show in detail exactly how we have spent the money, except that ours show specifically the names of suppliers from whom we have made purchases and the outside books merely confirm each transaction without naming the parties. We offered to let the reporter see a summary of them, but he never came to look."

Had the *Herald* man taken a peek, he might have seen the tip of the Iran–Contra iceberg seven months before the US press was scooped on the story by a Lebanese weekly. But maybe not. Certainly, the totals, if accurate, would have shown more receipts than US government funding and reported private donations. And turning over a few rocks around Contra headquarters might have flushed some of the same operatives who later led other investigators to the White House. But that is all hindsight.

176

My hosts complained that the American press had said little or nothing about the "500 millions of dollars" of arms reportedly delivered by the Soviets to the Sandinistas while "quibbling" [Arana's interjected word] over the 30–odd million they had spent, most of it from private donations.

"We have the greatest respect for freedom of the press," Rodríguez said. "That is one of the freedoms we are fighting for here. But I sometimes think that your press is working for the other side. Surely that cannot be. But why do you persecute us so?" He recited a list of recent reports of alleged negligence and misconduct by the Contras and by Americans training in Honduras. Among them were Contra destruction of forests and cropland along the border, the forced dislocation of civilians from those areas, the killing of women and children in cross fire, and, by US advisors, the accidental dropping of chemical agents on farms, trampling of crops, the raping of school teachers and the spread of AIDS to women in Comayagua.

"I must be honest: We have made mistakes. We have surely killed innocent people who got into the line of fire or who were mistaken for Sandinista troops. We have destroyed crops — on occasion intentionally. This is not our policy, but it was done, and when we know who did it, those persons have been disciplined. But this is war, man. We cannot absolutely control everything that happens in the heat of combat or afterward. Nevertheless, we do everything we possibly can to avoid those things. We teach our soldiers the Geneva Convention, and the need to protect and care for prisoners and civilians. We know only too well how much we are hurt by such incidents."

"And it is the right thing to do," Arana interjected, again in English. "We do not want to become the very evil that we are fighting against."

"How do you view Mexico?" I asked, changing the subject.

"Mexico is no example for a free society, for a democratic people. That country is ruled by a closed, dictatorial party which is so far from the Mexican Revolution that it is ludicrous to call it 'revolutionary.' And look at how the Mexican government gives in to the communists — always supporting them diplomatically, sending oil to the Sandinistas, letting the Soviets operate their subversion and espionage right out of Mexico City, itself. And in Chiapas, it is stupid for them to think they can pacify the Cubans by giving the Guatemalan communists military freedom in Chiapas. They are only kidding themselves. One day they will see that it was they who were the big chicken all along, the ultimate target. And many people in the United States who now oppose us will see it too — only then it will be too late. No, Mexico is not a model for democracy."

"While we are on the subject," Arana interjected, "we should say that the United States has not always been a steadfast model for us either. Before 1945, you had two State Departments: the one that dealt with the rest of the world, and the United Fruit Company that dealt with Central America. Of course, it could not have been done without the connivance of men of power here, men who put their own greed, their own ambition, above their country."

His voice quivered as he delivered this unexpected lecture on American arrogance and duplicity.

"Somoza and all the other dictators were products of this policy. As long as the bananas got to Miami and the Reds stayed out, you could not care less what happened to the people of Nicaragua. Well, in 1979, just when democratic forces had almost kicked him out — without any help from the United States, although we begged President Carter for it — our revolution was stolen by the Sandinistas — with guns Carter gave them."[41]

There were then two French journalists in Tegucigalpa who had been assigned by a Paris weekly to obtain pictures of US forces on maneuver as part of an exposé on Central America.

Air Force Captain Arthur Skop, the US Information Service officer at the American consulate, suggested that I hitch a ride with them out to Palmerola, the joint US–Honduran training base. The Frenchmen were on a strict but automatic per diem, it turned out, and were happy to have someone to share the gas: the more expenses they saved the more of the per diem they pocketed.

In pursuit of this windfall, two tedious hours were passed picking through the bays of a number of service stations in an attempt to locate a tool with which they could disconnect the odometer on their Suzuki rental van. At first, I suspected some mechanical problem but as the purpose of our delay became evident, I offered to spring for half the mileage so we could get on with the trip. They persisted, however, until it was clear that the device was inoperable — doubtless made so by the rental agency after long experience with such shenanigans.

It was dark when we finally left Tegucigalpa and the highway was not posted for distances, curves, exits and hazards — of which there were many in the form of pot holes, poor shouldering, sudden construction sites and landslides. An apparent detour became a track that ended in a settlement infested with hostile dogs and taciturn villagers. These meanderings occurred at speeds which those familiar with Gallic *autopistes* will appreciate.

The driver, a frail, agitated fellow with a severe case of acne, had brought along a personal pair of black–leather driving gloves, which he delicately removed to study his map. His taller companion animated a discussion about their already missing one deadline and how they might best peddle to other publications the photographs that were not run with the story. It was agreed that great care must be used to avoid detection, since dismissal was the penalty for moonlighting work–product.

We found a small pensión in Comayagua, the colonial and early republican capital. It was a forlorn city, the paucity of goods in its open market and the hangdog demeanor of the vendors bespeaking a communal resignation. Scores of children slept on sidewalks and in the plaza. Among them were several amputees, one missing both arms — cleanly severed just below the shoulder. Their begging was subdued, not aggressive as in Tegucigalpa. There were occasional *cantinas* with hand–lettered signs in English. "American spoken here. Nice girls," said one.

Next morning we were delayed at the Palmerola main gate by a crowd of women with children who had come for medical examinations at the base dispensary. Most would be sent to the local hospital, though some, such as those with eye disease and chronic dysentery, were treated here. There was a more orderly queue of men waiting to apply for base maintenance jobs.

Two MPs and a number of Honduran soldiers were on duty. The Americans vetted the letters from Captain Skop while one of the Hondurans surveyed the van's underside with a mirror attached to a pole. Another looked under the hood and went through our belongings.

A pleasant young woman in Air Force blue stepped forward from a jeep as we were passed. "I'm Staff Sergeant Martin, your escort." The Frenchmen uncased their cameras and started to shoot the scene at the gate but there was a whistle from one of the MPs: "Put those jobbies away, or we'll confiscate them."

"You'll have to wait until we get to designated areas for photographs," Sgt. Martin said politely.

"These choppers are the best in our business. They carry 32 men each and all their gear. No waiting around. Their passengers are ready to fight on arrival. It's only an hour and ten minutes from here to Danlí — that's a two–and–a–half hour round trip, with unloading."

The athletic major's name was Gary Steimele "The 159th Aviation Battalion, Fort Campbell, Kentucky, at your service! You call, we haul!".

The five CH–47 Delta Chinooks were among the helicopters used, he said, to rush Honduran soldiers out to confront the recent Sandinista "invasion."

They had been flown down in C5–A Galaxy transports. Steimele refused to say just how many there were, but insisted there were "more than enough to carry all the troops they [the Hondurans] can field and a hell of a lot more."

"Did any US combat troops accompany them?" I asked?

"Now you know better than to ask that question," he said. "No, seriously, none at all. We're here strictly in a support capacity. The only shooting we can do is in self defense."

We were encouraged to take pictures of three of the machines as they took off on a "local training mission." The small Frenchman had some difficulty with his camera, and the major obliged with a short delay until he could get ready. Then Steimele gave "thumbs up" to the lead aircraft and we filmed away in the furious wash. One of the ground crew lost his baseball cap, which the major caught on the fly.

Back at the legal officers' hut, we stood around drinking coffee and talking about troop behavior. One of the Frenchmen asked what disciplinary steps had been taken against soldiers involved in assaulting civilians.

"None of my troops have done anything like that," a Captain Hayne said. His office hadn't had "a single disciplinary case involving soldiers and civilians."

"What about the rape of the school teacher and the AIDS epidemic?" the other Frenchman asked, referring to an article on those allegations in the *Miami Herald*.

"You know, that guy never came out here to check his facts," Sgt. Martin said. "We would've let him see the hospital admissions and other records. But he never came out. We talked to him twice and asked him to do that, but he never came."

Another was less generous: "I wish I could meet up with the jerk who wrote that bull about us. I could ring his lying neck. What kind of guy would smear his country's soldiers just to make himself look like some kind of hero to his pals in the media?" Sgt. Martin interjected that there was "an ongoing investigation" of the AIDS allegations but that no case of the disease had been uncovered.

"We've put out the word every way we know how — through pamphlets, radio and whatnot, and so have the Honduran health officials, for women who suspect they might have been exposed to go to their local clinics to be tested. So far, over 500 have done so and only eight have indicated preliminary–positive, requiring further testing, and to date none of them has been shown to have the virus." As a result of the allegations, liberty had been cut. Weekend passes were rare, and overnighters restricted to "safe" areas, like San Pedro Sula and the capital. Group bus tours were encouraged.

We were driven to the dispensary. Although from the outside it looked like just another hooch, it was a metropolitan hospital in miniature. An operating and recovery room contained "every instrument, anesthetic and drug needed for routine or combat surgery," a nurse said. "We can set legs or brains. Most of our work is military routine — dysentery, jungle fevers — but we also do civilian emergencies like car wrecks and traumatic amputations. It's incredible what these people can do to each other with those things," she said, referring to machetes.

Children were treated for severe infections, including gangrene from neglected injuries. "And dysentery. It's really epidemic among the very young kids," Dr. Sid Lawerence, a lieutenant colonel, said. "Dehydration from that kills so many." But the kids were not immune from gratuitous peril. A little boy with a gunshot wound to the head had just been resuscitated in the emergency trauma room at the rear of the hut.

Nurses and aides were regular Army and served on six–month rotation; the doctor–reservists, from three to six months at a time.

I asked again about the AIDS "epidemic." They were adamant that it was nonexistent.

"We've looked at our civilian and military medical records going back as far as we can and seen nothing of the kind," Nurse Practitioner Captain Ray Lariosa said. "In fact, not a single case of AIDS has been diagnosed here or been confirmed in tests out of this facility. No Honduran physician has referred or reported such a case to us, and they report everything imaginable. If you ask me, I think that's just another sensational media scare. Why they write things like that is beyond me. There's no way a reserve doctor with a private civilian practice and professional standing would be a party to a cover–up, especially on something as deadly serious as AIDS."

"There are no infantry people here — this is a transportation unit, military stevedores, if you want. But they're ready for trouble if it comes their way, right men?"

"Yes, sir!" came the roar.

In the collective response of the "men" of the 368th Transportation Company were three female voices, women soldiers — one a corporal who proceeded to scold several male privates who were taking their time unloading munitions crates.

Their commander, Captain Robert Guarino, West Point '82, ordered the unit to form up for inspection. The Frenchmen were beside themselves straining for *femmes à la guerre* photo angles.

"Where are their rifles?" I asked.

"The only people who are permitted to carry weapons here are Military Police on duty. Everyone else's are in the armory. Of course, we can get to them PDQ if we have to."

"What about a surprise terrorist attack, sappers, on the base?"

"We think we can handle it. Every one of these people is qualified with his or her rifle every six months. They know their immediate action drills."

These "stevedores" were responsible for unloading military transport vessels at Puerto Cortés, a hundred miles to the northwest. Weapons were hauled in a separate truck, the captain said, not carried by the soldiers in the trucks with the freight. That sounded awfully risky, and I told him so.

"Honduras is a friendly country. We're here as guests. There's no need for us to be armed at all times."

I asked if they put out sentries or set up a perimeter defense.

"There's no perimeter defense by our troops, other than MPs. The Hondurans do that. It's their base, you know."

US troops at Palmerola Base, near Comayagua, Honduras.

12

MANAGUA I

*'I can't understand the American media. With all
their concern for freedom of the press, only a very,
very few have supported us. They say we are
subversive, so what should we expect. There is a
war here, so we should not complain if we are
censored. And anyway, they say, it is the fault of
the United States.'*

I entered Nicaragua in the 24th week of my journey at what was
called El Espino, but all that remained were the ruins of a customs
house, its walls charred with soot and pocked with shrapnel. After the
amiability of the Honduran guards and the antic bargaining of a
money changer, the silence was hollow, portentous.

Beyond the ruins, the emptiness expanded. Scanty brush clung
to a scarred earth. The personless, colorless space brought memories
of Slavic frontiers, with broad sterile swaths between boundaries and
the outposts of those charged with their oversight. Why? Perhaps it
was administrative convenience. But most countries' border stations
adjoined each other — good fences minded by good or at least
tolerable neighbors, proud flags whipping in diplomatic tandem.
Maybe Honduras was intolerable because of her begrudged hosting of
the Contras in Coco River jungles.

The same emptiness expanded before friendly Costa Rica's
border as well, at Peñas Blancas, where there had been no hostilities
for years — since the Sandinistas had launched their own, there
always futile, attacks against the Somoza guard. True, far to the east,
along the San Juan River, some disgruntled Sandinistas under
ex–Comandante Eden Pastora gathered; but their forays were
sporadic, inept. The terrain was not conducive to assault. It was too
easily defended by a handful of troops. Perhaps the berths were
buffers against a larger intrusion. But Costa Rica had no army and
Honduras' was less than a tenth the size of the Sandinistas' — now,
per capita, the largest army in the hemisphere, save that of Cuba; per
capita, quadruple Mexico's. There must be other reasons, I thought,
having less to do with arrival than departure.

The two young American women I met on Utila came to
Tegucigalpa in time to ask if they could "hitch on down." We got to the
border at four.

A self–proclaimed *somocista*, the money man ladled the inflated
Sandinista *córdobas* from a bulging satchel at 1,600 to the dollar. This

was 400 less than the best black market rate in Managua, but double the official exchange of 800.

"Only 1,000 in Managua," he lied. "Best rate here with me."

I followed the old travelers' rule–of–thumb: change a hundred bucks at the border and bet on a better rate in the capital. Besides, arriving with more than that risks confiscation, or worse. Currency speculation is a serious offense.

The only traffic along this formerly busy stretch of the Pan American Highway was a freightless northbound flatbed. According to the captain of the guard, food shortages in Nicaragua drew a few Honduran drummers. Elder Nicaraguans straggled the other way, clutching their belongings. Young people were conscripted for the Sandinista army and labor battalions. Deserters do not use official crossings. The post was a lonely one.

He said we were the first Americans to drive across in a long while. Years earlier, right after the Sandinistas had taken power, many had come — in minivans and church buses and clunkers with California, Massachusetts and Minnesota tags. But it was dangerous now, with the civil war, so other than a trickle of overlanders — usually Swiss — most arrivals were backpackers who traveled *por dedo*, hitchhiking. They got rides to San Marcos de Colón, the last Honduran town, then walked up to the border.

"They are young — *jóvenes*. They say they are going to work in the revolution. *'Solidaridad,'* they say." He laughed. "*Hay mucha solidaridad.*" There is much solidarity. He asked why so many Americans wanted to work for communism. I told him I didn't think they saw the Sandinistas as communists but as reformers who thumbed their noses at Washington. He shook his head. "*No es verdad, señor,*" he said, eyeing me suspiciously.

As we prepared to leave, he offered a word of warning:

"Do not drive early in the morning or late in the afternoon."

It was five miles to the Nicaraguan outpost. Behind a customs shed a plankway led to an old house trailer. There was a single window, curtained with thin linen so that you could be observed but could not see within. This was *migración*. You placed your passport in the window and a hand took it. Nothing was said. Pages were turned. Previous entry and exit stamps being studied, perhaps; or perhaps a comparison of one's face with the photograph, or the name with those on some precautionary list. You sensed that more than one observer was behind the cloth.

Entrants were required to exchange $60 at a fantasy rate of 70 *córdobas,* tantamount to an entry tax of $58, and to display another $300.

We were directed to follow a pickup full of soldiers. They waved their rifles and gestured to us in a friendly way. My passengers reciprocated. One, who could not have been 17, kept giving us her "thumbs up" long after the others had crouched with bandannas to battle the dust.

Somoto was a poor but busy little town with parched dirt streets, except near the plaza where they were laid with rough stone and brick. There was a single small *huéspedes* with no name, which charged 600 córdobas a night, provided there were three to a room. I threw my sleeping bag on the floor, and the women took the beds. The jeep was ordered left in an enclosure a mile away.

The main street had been cordoned off for a *fiesta*. The barricades were barbwired in double concertina — one of many gratuitous uses by the Sandinistas of military devices for the gentlest of occasions. Doubtless the commander of the local garrison was contributing to the event. There was a rock–marimba band, and the dance was joined by both civilians and soldiers. Among the latter were the "thumbs up" girl from our escort and her sergeant — both now in mufti. She grinned and gave the signal again, raising both thumbs at the back of his neck.

This was a benefit for the *secundaria*, high school. My friends and I each gave a thousand córdobas, to the effusion of those soliciting — an example of the wild disparity in currency values: our offering was a mere fifty cents at the black market rate, yet it was more than a day's wage for many of them.

Not everyone came to the party. Soldiers, this was apparently a recruit depot, drilled and shouted disjointed cadences in the post yard. Their rifles were held askew and their marching was disorderly. Four sergeants berated them. In the fuchsia twilight, there was fear in their faces.

After dark, radio noise and raucous laughter spilled from the barracks. The only menace was in the red–and–black posters affixed to the post's fence and the plaza's trees. On one, a distressed young woman cradling a child was approached by troops, whether friendly or alien was not clear. The caption read: "You can never betray them." Another extolled the virtue of soldiering and proclaimed that Nicaragua was not for sale and would not be surrendered: *"¡Ni se vende! ¡Ni se rinde!"* There were portraits of César Augusto Sandino, and the words of defiance from his telegram to Captain Gilbert Hatfield, USMC, in Ocotal on July 14, 1927: *Patria libre o morir* — A Free Fatherland or Die! The Marines grew wary of this "butcher," as they called Sandino: captured Leathernecks were found mutilated and skinned alive from the waist up. No tears were shed by the Americans when Sandino was shot by a national guard firing squad on February 21, 1934, paving the way for the ascendancy of his arch rival, Anastasio Somoza García, the first of the Somoza dynasty.

Twice during the night, short outgoing barrages shucked from nearby batteries. "Only practice," a sergeant said in the morning. But the old hotel man said Contra patrols sometimes entered the area. He said the rounds were fired randomly at their suspected assembly points. Since there was a curfew no civilians were endangered, he said, although he looked down when he said it.

Article:	Opposition leaders depart Managua
Solution:	DO NOT PUBLISH
Article:	Cardinal delivers mass
Solution:	DO NOT PUBLISH
Article:	US deportation of Nicaraguan refugees suspended
Solution:	DO NOT PUBLISH
Article:	Ten bishops criticize the "Church of Liberation Theology"
Solution:	DO NOT PUBLISH
Article:	Colombian maneuvers on San Andreas Island
Solution:	SUPPRESS PARAGRAPHS 6, 7, 8, 9, 12
Article:	Breakdown of the vote against terrorism in the United Nations
Solution:	DO NOT PUBLISH
Article:	Photograph of leaders of the Social Democrat Youth Movement
Solution:	DO NOT PUBLISH

— Seven of 32 articles struck or altered from the April 18, 1986, edition of *La Prensa* by order of Captain Nelba Blanton, the Sandinista censor.

Jaime Chamorro Cardenal, managing editor, obeyed but posted stillborn copy on *La Mural de Censura*, a bulletin board outside *La Prensa's* ramshackle offices in Managua.

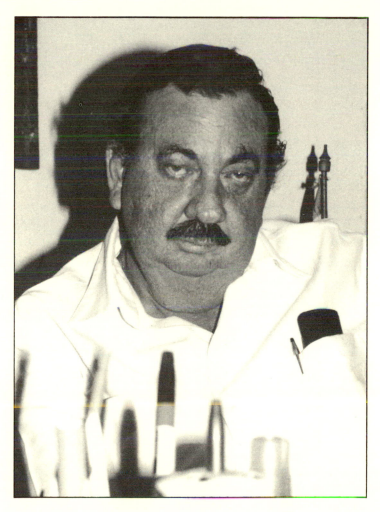

Jaime Chamorro, managing editor of *La Prensa*, Managua.

Once the editors would leave blank spaces or run photos of movie starlets where copy had been cut. The dateline would carry a caveat: "Published Under Government Supervision," "Published Under the Law of Emergency," etc. Such was now forbidden. Even passing censored articles to foreign writers was a grave offense, for recipient as well as donor — as I was soon to learn.

Although the "wall" was itself a violation, few saw it so it posed little threat to public sentiment. Only employees and others with special permission could legally enter the compound. Most of the latter were foreign political tourists with government guides. To protect against vandalism by foes the paper placed a guard at the gate. He phoned inside for clearance. I had no appointment but Americans of whatever stripe were welcome. Sandinista agents monitored all comings and goings from the parking lot alongside North Highway. The street had been renamed, on maps at least as there were no street signs in Managua, in honor of Jaime Chamorro's late older brother and the paper's editor, Pedro Juaquín Chamorro Cardenal.

It had been the ambush–murder of Pedro Juaquín by four unknown, presumed *somocista*, assailants in January 1978, that removed the opposition's sole consensus leader. The result was the co–optation of the 1979 revolution by the Sandinistas as Somoza collapsed and moderates quarreled among themselves.

"He was the only one who could have brought everyone together before the Sandinistas took control," González, the owner of a welding shop, later told me. "Chamorro was our strongest leader. But many did not support him."

Jaime Chamorro stapled the previous day's censorship casualties to the board.

"Just keeping the record straight," he smiled. "Perhaps we could call it 'The Wall of Truth.' We also send copies to San José." *La Nacional*, the Costa Rican daily, ran a Saturday supplement for *La Prensa*. Included was copy censored by the Sandinistas and exile chitchat. It was edited by Pedro Juaquín Chamorro Barrios, the martyr's oldest son.

"Used to, a great many came to read them," the editor said quietly, referring to the wall. "Now few do. It is the police and the *turbas,* Sandinista mobs. Everyone is afraid."

We returned to his office, a small room with an oversized air conditioner. It so lowered the temperature that he would turn it off until the smoke fróm his potato–sized *Joya de Nicaragua* necessitated its revival. As he savored the stogie, we were joined by Violeta Chamorro, his brother's widow. Tall, lissome, graying, she was 57 but looked 40 in spite of webbed cheeks and purple sacks under sleepless eyes. She exuded that quiet verve forged on the anvil of absolute adversity. She had worked side–by–side with her husband as he fought Somoza and American meddling for a quarter of a century. She succeeded to the editorship upon his death — although daily management fell now to Jaime. For a time after the dictator fled, the Chamorro matriarch served on the five–member coalition directorate. She resigned in 1980 when it became obvious that the junta was merely a rubber stamp for the Sandinistas.[42] Their three members bloc–voted the party line.

190

Ironically, Violeta's youngest son, Carlos, now edited the Sandinista organ, *Barricada*, and another brother–in–law, Xavier, published *El Nuevo Diario*, a staunchly pro–government but less stodgy daily begun in 1980 when the family split over support of the regime.

When Jaime and Violeta struck an independent course, Xavier and most of *La Prensa's* employees walked out and formed the new paper. Some of the workers privately told her that they had no choice. "The intimidation was too much for them," she said. "They grieved over it, but the block committees are very persuasive." She referred to the Sandinista neighborhood organizations that intimidated residents who worked for opponents of the regime.

Why was it, I wondered, that one family had become so indispensable? Was this not the same old Latin American pattern reasserting itself yet again, even in what was ostensibly a "People's Revolution." All but two of the Sandinista *comandantes*, themselves, were from upper–middle–class Nicaraguan families.

"The only reason they have not closed us down is for the propaganda it gives them," Violeta continued. "They need to be able to say to the tourists and reporters, 'See, it is a lie that we do not have freedom of the press.' "

From the avenue came the megaphoned bark of a drill sergeant followed by a high–octave roar. A chant ensued: megaphone — *roar*; megaphone — *roar*. Another double column of children in youth–brigade khaki were strutting past, shepherded by "Che"–bereted *militantes*. I had encountered these cohorts throughout the morning. Right–of–way was ceded to them. It was the week of "May Day." The children were returning from Sandinista training camps. Older ones, 14 or thereabouts, toted M16s and AK–47s. Straggling tots, some barely six, brought up the rear with wooden stocks painted with red stars, hammers and sickles.

"What is it they are shouting?" I asked.

"Yankee Dogs. They shall not pass!," Jaime replied.

This was a variation on one of the Sandinista's most imposing rallying cries, a "roll call" of those killed in battle. After each name someone in the troop or audience answered, *"¡Presente!"* When a number had thus replied, all shouted in unison, *"¡No Pasarán!"* They shall not pass — the "they" being, presumably, the Americans and their proxies. This also appeared in graffiti scrawled in red and black paint with ostensible spontaneity on walls throughout Managua, including the houses of government opponents such as the Chamorros. Sometimes, Jaime said, the children were orchestrated to shout "traitors" and "gringo lackeys," and worse when they passed *La Prensa*.

"Guilty of Treason." The two were said to be CIA agents.

"When they no longer need us to support their propaganda myth of 'political pluralism,' they will shut us down. Even censored, we are for them very dangerous."

The paper was harassed in other ways. There had recently been a revival of *turba* threats against employees and their families. Occasionally, there was a "spontaneous" gathering of these young toughs in the parking lot, some darting inside to spray–paint slogans.

The *turbas* were also conducting an "educational campaign" with *La Prensa*'s street vendors and route kids. Many of the neighborhood carriers had quit and few shops outside of tourist places like the Hotel Continental, then packed with foreign reporters, network film crews and "solidarity cadres," would sell it. Still, according to Jaime Chamorro their paid circulation exceeded that of the two other papers combined.

He had brought his and Violeta's lunch to the office in a little picnic basket. There was a jar filled with Coca–Cola and some orange juice in a bottle that had once contained a very good *Rioja*. He offered me a sandwich but I declined, having eaten a late breakfast. On the wall was a copy of an El Greco portrait of a knight in armor.

"I saw it when I was a child," he said. "I liked it then and still do, for the same reason. It tells me that perseverance in the face of hardship will win in the end. A kind of hero to me, I guess."

"I can't understand the American media," Violeta persisted. "With all their concern for freedom of the press, only a very, very few have supported us. They even say we are subversive so what can we expect. There is a war here, so we should not complain if we are censored. And anyway, they say, it is really the fault of the United States."

Even old friends in the newspaper business, she said, insisted on keeping their financial contributions private. When one publisher, who had made a small donation to a fund for *La Prensa*, was asked how he could then write an editorial praising Sandinista toughness with local opponents, he had replied: "The Sandinistas have to do what they are doing. You should support them, yourselves."

Jaime gave interviews and attended publishers' meetings and academic gatherings in the States and Europe whenever he could, always using the opportunity to lambaste the Sandinistas and solicit support for his paper. At the time, however, he was taking great care not to appear in the same forum or even meet with Contra officials. Violeta took the same precautions. They feared that the government would use such contacts as a pretext to deny them re–entry into the country or close the paper. Prosecution for treason was always possible. But in addition there was a certain pride, indeed a sense of superiority of sacrifice, among those who had elected to remain in Nicaragua and oppose the Sandinistas on the home turf. Contra and other exile efforts were acknowledged, but you had the sense that "the real heroes" were those who stayed behind.

Jaime relit his cigar.

"Let's go take a look at today's effort," he said.

Violeta led the way and we followed, Jaime trailing great puffs of smoke. He paused outside a door partly ajar. Within, a voice declaimed in English.

"Stand here," he said. "I want to see their expressions when they see us."

He opened the door, uncovering a political tour group. Their Sandinista guide looked first at Jaime, then at my camera. He started but said nothing, not even a greeting. Finally one of the Americans offered a "hello," and Jaime nodded and shut the door.

"You are the first foreign visitor in some time who has come here unescorted," he said. "We like them to know we still have people just drop in. Don't worry, they won't hassle you."

We continued to the pressroom, passing the sports desk where Christina, Violeta's youngest daughter, was pasting up wire service baseball summaries.

"The Sandinistas control all of the newsprint and paper," Violeta said.

The paper was limited to six 8–page editions per week, down from seven editions with an average of 35 pages each prior to 1981. The formerly bountiful Sunday edition had been scrapped, though Saturday's was datelined *Sábado y Domingo*. "Some week days we cannot go to press because the censor is late drafting the order or so much has been cut there is too little to print," Jaime said.

Few advertisers remained, he said. Those businesses who could afford ads were intimidated not to patronize *La Prensa*. Yet a glance through Saturday's April 26 edition showed a full page of classifieds for everything from help wanted to refrigerators and hair salons, 1/6–page ads for the local Mazda dealer and the National Bank, 15 solicitations from physicians and surgeons and over 30 movie house bills.

"You can't publish a newspaper with classifieds and professional notices alone. True, some advertisers stick with us out of loyalty. Others risk rebuke from necessity, particularly if they are trying to sell something like a TV or car. We do have the most readers, after all. The bank? We have to carry government ads."

The paper was about ready. Violeta changed a headline and moved a local story inside to make more room for wire service reports. *La Prensa* at the time received AP, UPI and Agence France–Presse. Jaime nodded his approval. Christina came in with some fresh coffee and the baseball roundup. *Béisbol* was no less important in Nicaragua than in Pittsburgh or Peoria. Virtually every town of any size had a club which competed in the Nicaraguan national league. Nicaraguans followed the US major leagues avidly.

"Why," I asked, "do the Sandinistas really care what you say about them? They have the guns."

"Read these," Jaime said, handing me two articles. The first was a speech by Tomás Borge, minister of the interior, to students at the Nicaraguan School of Journalism. The other was the introduction by Sandinista journalist Ana Corina Fernández to her "Course for Censors of the Sandinista Television System." She taught it at the Humanities Department at the University of Nicaragua.

Borge's message, "The Necessity of a New Model of Communication in Nicaragua," declared:

> "We must help our message get beyond our borders, enhancing its credibility, because a special problem we have is the [Capitalist] media have such great power that it is able to distort reality. [To combat this] we must build an extraordinary communications force, not only within but outside Nicaragua, [and] I'm speaking not only of radio but ... all other media."[43]

Lectured Fernández:

> "Both [capitalism and socialism] use the power of mass communications to influence their populations' values and opinions.
>
> The information received in this manner determines social attitudes. These attitudes are gradually reinforced [to the extent of] thought control ...
>
> This course consists of ... methods of analysis by censors ... that will permit you to [do this efficiently].[44]

When I left, Jaime gave me clippings of two op–ed pieces he'd recently done for the *Washington Post* and the *Miami Herald*[45], and asked his secretary to Xerox all articles censored during the past month, together with the censor's orders.

I was puzzled by these modest, disarmingly ordinary–looking people. Were they really besieged champions of freedom or simply political "outs" grinding personal axes? As one minor Hollywood personage put it to me later in the lobby of the Hotel Continental while waiting for her cadre's Inturista bus: "They ain't castable. They don't look the part."

Jaime, particularly — who was said to have corrupted Violeta's once stalwart support for the revolution — was referred to with derision. But both their names, and that of *La Prensa*, tumbled twisted from the mouths of the youthful foreigners who carried on their "dialectic" far into the night in the mosquitoed courtyard of the Huéspedes Santos. I had found a room there for $5 a night — US dollars only, cash upfront, 40 times the 100–córdoba rate charged locals. The Chamorros were, at the least, "terribly misguided" and, in the view of Doris, a comely Berkeley sophomore, "traitors to the revolution who should suffer the consequences." She and a friend, Kim, had been "working with the peasantry" near Estelí and were about to enroll in a special Spanish course. I ought to "check it out."

One of a number of groups operating in Managua at the time for the instruction of foreigners, the *"Casa de Nicaraguense de Español,"* was a self–described private language and political seminar that ran from four to eight weeks. Terms were flexible. The majority of students were middle–aged women, many from Marin County, California and others from Canada and the Midwest. Spanish was taught from eight to eleven followed by a catered lunch on the patio. Crockery was picnic in style, but the fare was elegant. Lunch the day I visited consisted of pasta, roast beef, chicken, spiced ham and meatballs, salad beans *vinaigrette*, freshly baked bread and, for dessert, a choice of three petite pastries, one a tasty chocolate meringue.

The Casa's importance to the Sandinistas was indicated by its location in one of the confiscated *somocista* estates on the prestigious South Highway. Feuding over these haciendas threatened Sandinista unity. New regime fondness for such ostentations of the old was one reason cited by Eden Pastora, *Comandante Cero*, for his departure into exile and opposition.

Afternoons there were educational tours, usually a visit to a ministry; cultural events, "Revolutionary Art of Struggling Peoples" was a current exhibit; or a chat with Sister Mary Hartman, Order of St. Agnes, director of the Sandinista Commission for the Promotion and Protection of Human Rights.

"What we have here is a government which, I'm not saying they're Christian, but which has the same ideas as those of the Gospel — feed the hungry, clothe the poor, visit those in prison. So they have the same commitment as us." Sister Mary espoused the views of the "popular church" or "Liberation Theology" — an interpretation of the scriptures which permits, indeed requires, political involvement to relieve injustice and oppression.

196

Liberation Theology began in the 1960s among young Catholic priests from middle–class backgrounds educated mostly in elite European and American colleges and swept up by that decade's giddy wave of "situation ethics" and "direct action."

At a 1968 conference in Medellín, Colombia, reluctant bishops agreed that the church should concern itself with social justice. The Liberationists seized upon that as legitimizing political action by the clergy. The individual priest would judge his own cause and method of involvement, even to the extent of holding political office. Preference should be given to the poor in the administration of sacraments — even to the exclusion of the middle class. Finally, violence — even torture and killing — might be "forgivably necessary" in the pursuit of social justice such as in wars of national liberation. A corollary to all this among the more radical was that little difference existed between Christianity and Marxism. They were seen as essentially the same. "My kingdom is not of this world," notwithstanding.

A number of priests supported the Sandinistas, making available their churches as meeting places and safe houses and becoming party activists. Two of these, brothers Ernesto and Fernando Cardenal, became ministers of culture and education, respectively. Father Uriel Molina, a Franciscan, set up Valdiviso Center, a bookstore mecca for solidarity cadre and political tourists. Ostensibly an ecumenical foundation, the center, "[B]egan to hold conferences and publish and sell books, newsletters, and other literature. It became the intellectual headquarters for visiting priests, ministers, academics and others in the Liberation Theology camp. These visitors, returning home to the United States or Europe or elsewhere in Latin America, would write or speak in praise of the Sandinista Front and its Christian supporters ..."[46]

The most prominently displayed volume at the time was a fawning interview with Fidel Castro by a Dominican "Friar Betto," in which the differences between Christianity and communism were seen as minor. A poster display for the book in English spoke of the two as "essentially compatible faiths."[47]

Sister Mary, who reserved her age but looked 50, had joined the Order of St. Agnes after her freshman year at the University of Pennsylvania. She came to Nicaragua in the mid–1960s and was assigned to mission work among the Miskito Indians. In Managua she met Molina, who sent her to visit local prisons. She met several top Sandinistas, including Tomás Borge, just before their escape in August 1978 during the seizure of the national palace.

In 1980, when the new government was looking for clerical participation, the Sandinistas named her to the human rights commission. It was, they liked to say, the first such body formed by any nation. Critics charged that this commission was actually a propaganda front to counteract the work of the Permanent Commission on Human Rights. The latter held the Sandinistas to the same standards — and public scrutiny — as it had Somoza. It revealed numerous cases of false imprisonment, maltreatment, mutilation, executions and disappearance. The Permanent Commission's work was treated as reliable by Western intelligence services but was deprecated as partisan by US peace groups and other Sandinista sympathizers who had earlier used its findings against Somoza. The Permanent Commission was eventually denied access to prisoners but continued to publish information abroad gleaned from prisoners' families and friends and confidential prison sources.

The Sandinista commission spent most of its time with press inquiries and conducting tours of *Granjas de Régimen Abierto*, "Open Farms," where former low–level Somoza guardsmen worked in fields adjacent to barracks. The commission did not conduct tours of El Chipote or Zona Franca, maximum security prisons in Managua which housed political prisoners.

It was remarkable that a Catholic order would permit a member to participate in such a partisan activity. The Order of St. Agnes not only did so but contributed substantial sums to the commission's coffers and solicited other charitable groups to do the same.[48]

Some of the more than 40 people — mostly mothers with children and old men — with whom I spoke in Sister Mary's waiting room had no idea whether their relatives were even alive. Two women, with nine tots between them, had come to ask about their husbands, arrested two weeks previously. The men had been put in the back of a truck and driven away.

"We go to the police and to the army but no one will tell us anything," one said. A neighbor, who was a Sandinista block leader, suggested that they come here.

They were clad in their very best poor clothing. They had learned to be patient or perhaps it was a part of their natures. Some had been here so many times that they were familiar by name to the receptionist and the other uniformed functionaries who wandered in and out carrying files. One woman wanted to know if her spouse had received the little cloth–bound packet of food and toiletries wives were permitted to leave here for forwarding. Had he sent a message, a letter? She asked if there was a visitor's day set. If so, it would be necessary to plan for the uncertain riding of buses that would get them to the prison before the designated hour. Tardiness, regardless of the cause, was not tolerated.

Not long before, one bus was held up by a tank column. The machines crunched back and forth on the road then cut through the countryside. When the bus arrived at the prison it was after hours and no visits were permitted. The warden told them that things would go well for the prisoners if the families would join a demonstration in León against the United States air raid on Libya. Signs and banners and posters of Fidel Castro and Mu'ammar Qaddafi and the *comandantes* were given to the passengers as they disembarked. A second bus from another prison was already there. Its passengers had at least been able to see their men, but their visit was cut short so they, too, could participate in the demonstration.

After the march began, a caravan of Inturista buses dusted past carrying the media. Party officials and workers let off for the occasion swelled the procession. When they reached the plaza, the media were set up to film the event, which was reported locally as, "a spontaneous outpouring of solidarity for the heroic Libyan people," and as a "Sandinista demonstration" by the foreign press. Similar "protests" occurred throughout the country.

The wife of the welder, González, who related these events had been on that second bus, the one whose passengers had seen their relatives. She had gone to visit her father who was still confined as an "unrehabilitated *somocista*." The Gonzálezes were under an order restricting their political activity. They could neither hold nor attend meetings. They would not elaborate further nor say what party they had supported — although I took it to be Somoza's former Nationalist Liberal Party to which she said her father had belonged.

Their home was modest but comfortable. The garage adjoined it, and each of them worked there. They had six children. Their hands were calloused and their faces hard but not unkind. Their eyes were steady as they spoke. No one arranged for me to talk with them. My rear mirror took a limb, and when I tried to bend it back in place it broke in two. I needed a small welding job and a gas station mechanic sent me to the *soldaría* of González.

"There are no political prisoners in this country, in the sense that there are in, for example, Chile and South Africa," Sister Mary told me calmly, her hands folded on a clean desk. "The only ones like that are those guilty of counterrevolutionary activities. We are making great progress in rehabilitating them. But rehabilitation is voluntary. No force is used."

A group from the Santos had gone the day before on one of her tours where they saw men forking hay, watering crops and loading produce. They were allowed to talk with any of the inmates, and each one they spoke to said he was well treated.

"Unfortunately, the next visit won't be for another week," she said.

199

The receptionist announced that an interior ministry deputy was there to see her. The sister thanked me for coming. We shook hands. She gave me a passel of booklets.

That Sunday, I went to the Hotel Continental for dinner. Two couples from Madison, Wisconsin were sitting at the bar sharing impressions. They asked for mine. We got on and they bought me a cold Victoria, one of the two local brews. This was generous since there was no beer anywhere else in Managua — only rum — and the hotel was rationing the beer two per customer.

Two troop buses pulled up to the lobby curb. An Inturista director went to the desk to announce that transportation was ready for those who wished to attend church services. My companions started toward the door. "See you there. Come and worship in solidarity with us," one said.

Papaya vendor, central market, Managua.

13

MANAGUA II

The parade was a recapitulation of the land through which I had passed the previous week. It was a compressed collage of the promise, chagrin, defiance, and escape entailed in the settling of a new order and of the ennui that inevitably attends the realization that government, whether conventional or revolutionary, is finally quiescent.

Buses and vans were jammed into the narrow streets of the Barrio Riguero within four blocks of Santa María de los Angeles. The cab driver shrugged and raised his hands. I nodded and bailed out. He backed away, looking for a turnaround.

The air vibrated with the twangs and throbs of electric guitars and a bass.

The church was modern: low–built but spacious, octagonal in shape. Tracts explaining Liberation Theology were distributed by an usher. One referred to "the healing ministry of Sandinismo." A guest registry was open on a table. "Welcome to the Church of the People," a young woman exclaimed as she greeted new arrivals. "Would you care to sign?" I did so, adding my own to what were surely a hundred pages of American names and addresses. The band, five–pieces, played on a raised platform. A purple–draped podium and assorted paraphernalia adorned the dais. The musicians appeared practiced, relaxed. The music was rhythmic, harmonious, stirring. It was clear that the performance was routine with them.

The congregation consisted almost entirely of thin, intelligent–looking white people in sandals or low leather shoes without socks. Many were standing and swaying in time with the music which had taken a folk bent. Some carried portable tape recorders which they occasionally tested and modulated. Others darted about with cameras, video equipment, lights and tripods. Flashes popped.

The circumference of the inner wall was painted with murals, not of Christian saints and beatitudes but of Sandinista heroes and allegory. In one, the commanding figure of Sandino, holding the blue and white national flag, stood facing unseen pursuers of fleeing people. Opposite, Carlos Fonseca, founding guru of the FSLN, declaimed in front of the familiar red–and–black Sandinista ensign.

In another panel Sandinistas with musical instruments faced a squad of Somoza guardsmen whose bodies were those of roosters and snakes. In yet another two Sandinista warriors contemplated abstractions of dismembered torsos. These paintings, and a feverish fresco at the rear of the chapel, reflected a blend of Sistine piety and Weimar "heroic realism" imitative of Soviet and German poster art of the 1920s and '30s and its Diego Rivera Mexican adaptations. Fatigue–clad figures in the fresco were ambiguous. One Oakland worshiper insisted with hushed reverence to have discerned the likenesses of the *Comandantes* Ortega and Borge.

Borge kept two offices in the Ministry of the Interior: a principal one from which he directed the business of the Secret Police and other agencies of human control, and another in which he received foreign tourists and journalists. In the former, were portraits of Marx, Lenin and Sandino. The walls of the latter were graced with an array of crucifixes, prints of Christ and a collection of icons — gifts from American religious delegations.

Father Molina, the Valdiviso priest, was absent tonight but an articulate associate took the pulpit. His subject was David against Goliath, the poor of the Earth against the United States. He extolled the Liberation Church:

> How many times have the capitalist
> nations sought divine intervention in their
> wars of greed and oppression? Why can't
> the oppressed ask for the same help in their
> wars of liberation?
> And if priests and chaplains went into
> battle with the imperialists to help them
> enslave the masses, why cannot holy men
> do the same to throw off that same yoke of
> bondage? Who can say that the church does
> not have the moral obligation to wage war
> itself, shed its own blood, to throw off
> economic and political oppression?

He said nothing of the faith's traditional severance of matters spiritual and material. It was, I believe, implicit in the minds of most of the congregation that that separation had been a false one, that the two were ineluctably intertwined, and that the relegation of the latter in the past had served merely to hobble the poor in acquiescence to penury and servitude. That to be rendered to Caesar and to God was now the same.

Window in Santa María de Los Angeles church, Barrio Riguero, Managua.

At the end, we all stood and held hands and prayers were given by parishioners and visitors alike for the success of the *comandantes* and for the United States, that its leaders might see the light and recant, and for us all that we might go forth from that place and spread the word about the Sandinista millennium and work with our congressmen to keep guns from the Contras. Following the benediction the band returned and struck up "We Shall Overcome," which was sung fortissimo. There were no black people among us.

Outside I was asked to disembark from the troop bus which was reserved for "special cadre," according to the driver. The group from Philadelphia let me ride in their van but charged me five dollars — double the cab fare out.

Managua, situated on the lake by that name, was once one of Central America's more attractive cities. It was leveled in 1972 by an earthquake and the fires that followed. Somoza–Debayle and his henchmen are said to have embezzled and Swiss banked most of the hundred–plus million dollars contributed by western nations and private donors for relief and reconstruction. Fourteen years later it remained unrebuilt.

Great open spaces stretched through formerly thriving commercial and government districts. Meadows of weeds exposed an occasional concrete slab with protruding rods and rusted clumps of paleo–Somoza refuse.

The riven National Cathedral stood an open hulk — rather, I thought, like those bombed–out shells in East Berlin, an ad hoc monument to a haunting past, its Venetian facade draped on high occasions with Marxist bunting and admonitions. This week's message read: "Our Power is Consolidated with Work and Defense: Long Live the First of May!"

The nearby National Palace withstood the shock and now served his successors as it had Somoza: 67 of its 96 congressional delegates were Sandinistas; all but a handful of others were pliant lackeys. All heads of ministries and their principal lieutenants were party members. Somoza had exercised no firmer grip on power.

Heroes of the Sandinista pantheon loomed suddenly from massive billboards. Smaller scenes of struggle and defiance appeared on ballpark–type fence sections, some twenty of which ran for two blocks toward the lake from the Hotel Continental. These were favorite subjects for tourist cameras; one student faithfully brushed copies in watercolor for friends back in Iowa. A three–story olive–bronze statue of a soldier brandishing his rifle dominated the principal interchange. Revolutionary murals covered the walls of houses and lot fences. Many of these dated from the summer of 1984, the fifth anniversary of "The Triumph."

I searched in vain for the old Pensión Pan Americana, where I had lodged a few days when hitchhiking to South America back in early 1970. I later learned that it had been destroyed in the earthquake. There was a guidebook list of places to stay but they were either full or shut. A cabby recommended two small hotels not far from the town center: La Mesa and the Santos. These were very basic consisting of unventilated rooms and a common area. Neither served meals though the Santos, a two–story walk–up affair about a central patio, had a makeshift bar for soda and beer. Dining was catch–can but there were two small eateries within four blocks that catered primarily to government functionaries and foreigners.

At the suggestion of Sally, a helpful wire service reporter, I went out to the office of "Witnesses for Peace." Patricia Manning was the assistant director. Volunteers, she said, "commit" for two weeks to live in a village subject to Contra attack. Assignments were coordinated by a staff of six who committed for eight months. They liaised with Sandinista army intelligence, who suggested appropriate localities. It had all begun back in '83 when a group of "peace persons" had come down on an "inspection tour," she said.

"Everywhere we went the killing and maiming stopped so we decided to establish a presence in as many villages as we could find volunteers." Participants came from "all over the United States and some from Canada." No one had yet been hurt. "We've been very fortunate. But the word seems to get out that a witness is present so no attacks come."

They felt that the project was so successful that they wanted to expand it. A decision had been made to that effect the week before in Washington where staff and former volunteers had gone to lobby Congress against voting further aid to the Contras. I asked where they might witness next and she quickly replied, "Chile."

Had they considered Afghanistan, Ethiopia, Cambodia? Could they not be just as effective interposing themselves between the rebels in El Salvador, for example, and the villagers there? Or Guatemala? Surely the Marxists guerrillas in those countries would respect villages protected by friends of their allies, the Sandinistas?

"Those theaters are not of practical concern to us," she replied tersely. "What we are doing is opposing the aggressive policies of our own government. Others in other countries can and should do the same."

I asked about the "kidnapping" the previous summer. Some forty "witnesses" had set out down the San Juan River amid great fanfare in effect daring the Contras to impede them.

"We sought to use our bodies to reopen the river for peaceful uses by the Nicaraguan people," she said.

It was later suggested by some that the enterprise was a propaganda stunt organized with the Sandinistas who helicoptered troops disguised as Contras to the river, set up an "ambush" and when the "Peace Barge" floated by, fired upon and "captured" it.

The passengers were detained for about a day, with the press — a number had gone along — filming and scribbling away. Then, abruptly, they were released. Contra leaders denied having anything to do with the incident, and no one familiar with their units and personnel was able to identify any from photographs.

"I was on the radio the whole time, just in there," Manning said defensively. "I can tell you it was not a charade. We were scared to death."

Hershell and Probst had been reporting from Central America for major American dailies for more than two and three years, respectively. Baker was a free–lancer who had sold articles in Europe, though American papers were his main customers. He had done a few stories with TV network news — but without credit. "They use my stuff but adapt it for video," he said. All three considered Managua their headquarters.

I met them at the Comedor Sara, the least Spartan of the diners, where you could get fresh but overly salted lake fish, fries and salad for just 1,500 *córdoba*. A shrieking parrot performed for children who tossed it scraps. When the only table vacant was next to the bird an attractive Nicaraguan woman sitting with the journalists offered me a place. I could tell the gesture was hers alone. Reporters invariably develop an air of condescension toward other Westerners and I found this particularly true in Nicaragua. These fellows were no exception: a sullen smugness blanketed what had been an animated discussion before I intruded. Still, once we had introduced they deiced: what route had I taken? Had I seen any US forces? Contras? Fighting?

Hershell, a hollow–faced man in his early 40s, was not impressed with the US claim that its maneuvers in Honduras were defensive, that there were no plans to invade Nicaragua. "How many times have we heard that one? Then, pow! You have Lebanon. Grenada. I don't think Reagan will rest until he's crushed Nicaragua. It'll be the Marines again; it's just a question of when."

"I think they'll wait until they get a really good excuse, then they'll come in," Probst said. He didn't believe the recent border clashes along the Coco River were good enough. "But when they really want one, they'll find it, even if they have to stage it, like the Gulf of Tonkin."

"It's a crying shame what we're doing to Central America," Hershell said. "Just look at the AIDS epidemic in Honduras. When will we learn to leave these people alone? Revolution is inevitable in these places. All we do by opposing it is make it more violent when it does come. And in the meantime we spread our own diseases — physical and materialistic — to these people."

Hershell had done follow–up stories on the AIDS and chemical warfare allegations concerning US troops in Honduras. Just then, he said, he was trying to pursue earlier reports of the Pentagon clandestinely supplying the Contras by leaving them with weapons after maneuvers. "Whole caches of rifles and rockets,"[49] he said several times. He was "hopping up to 'Guci" the next week to finish the piece. That sounded like old news to me, but Hershell claimed to have an inside source that would pin it down in detail, as well as implicating the Honduran military in equipment sales kickbacks with previously appropriated US funds. I asked him why he didn't catch the next flight out. Why wait another five days?

"It's May Day here, Thursday. I'm covering that. It's an active week what with all the solidarity delegations and the Congress. People here from all over, Europe, the US. There's a chance Daniel may agree to sign the Contadora Pact." He referred to an effort by several Central American presidents, meeting on tiny Contadora Island just off Panama City, to bring an end to fighting in the region.

"He missed it last year," the young woman, Rosalita, "but to you, Rita," said. "I made him promise to be here this time." She laughed and squeezed Hershell's arm. He smiled thinly. She was a "policy reporter," whatever that meant, for *Barricada*. When I pressed her for specifics she playfully changed the subject. Other diners greeted her respectfully as they came and went.

A British reporter I met later said that Nicaragua had become "a cult beat" for some American journalists. "It's the glamour of the thing, partly, but also it's good for the c.v. And you don't really have the danger you had, say, in Vietnam or Biafra and places like that. The key is consistent production." It was understood, he said, that the way to maintain a constant flow of copy was to "stay on the good side of the Sandinistas."

The friendly reporter I mentioned earlier, Sally, had talked candidly about what happened to journalists who stayed here too long — anywhere, for that matter. "You get involved," she said, "And that's bad. You lose even the pretense of objectivity. I think they make a deliberate effort to get to you anyway, but after a year, two years, you're really vulnerable." It wasn't really blackmail or other direct intimidation. "It's more subtle than that. It's the feeling that, gee, here are people I know. They're my friends. So you've become one of them — not officially, of course. But it's awfully hard to keep objective when you see these people everyday, especially if you're sleeping with them. That'll color your judgment, especially if you already are sympathetic to 'the cause.'"

I had asked her whether she knew of anyone who regularly was used to plant stories — propaganda, disinformation. "Oh, I won't say anybody deliberately writes stuff they know is false, but some US reporters here get little favors from the Sandinistas. It may be a minor scoop, like the capture of some Contra agent, or just advance word — a leak — about a change of position. Or they'll give them preference on flights out to the bush to interview villagers. Little

209

favors, but they can help a lot when you're desperate for a story. Most reporters here are straight–arrow, if biased. There's no question the general drift is pro–Sandinista and anti–US, but they don't buy everything the Sandinistas put out. Still, the temptation's there, professionally, I mean, to come up with dirt on the Contras, the CIA — there's an instant readership in the United States ready to believe anything bad you can write about US policy down here. And editors are hungry for it. So you can be sure some whole–cloth stuff gets printed."

Dinner came, a huge plate of fish and salad with a mound of lightly done french fries. I stood a round of rum and coke for my "hosts." Hershell said he would try to make the next morning's CUSCLIN demo at the US Embassy and give me a quick insider's tour of town afterward.

I walked a circuitous route back to the Santos. A lone lamp bathed the shadows in just enough light to read a plaque honoring one of those who had died in the uprising against Somoza. His name was José Jerez Díaz, "Mario." The plaque gave the dates of his birth and death, at age 20, and contained the words: "Martyr of the Revolution: It is not important if we fall; others follow." A moving paraphrase of the tribute to the French Resistance.

When I reached the hotel all was quiet. The jeep, which was parked along the curb just outside the gate, was intact. Thievery was considered quite uncomradely and the Sandinistas were relentless in punishing it with hard labor of indeterminate duration. The lights were already out and the entry gate locked. My calling woke the husband of the manager, who let me in. I added my poncho liner to the single sheet on the sloped cot and lit a mosquito coil. Its smoke hovered efficiently; a hint of a breeze stirred the air; I fell asleep.

I was awakened by voices of accusation and surprise.

There was a scuffle and profanity and a woman's query in English: "What are you trying to do, you bastard?" Another woman cried: *"policía! policía!"* There was the hee–haw trill of a siren, a hurried closing of doors and the garbled squelch of an official radio. I crept down the stairway to see what was going on.

In the courtyard, now lit by military flashlights, were a half dozen MPs, the manager, her husband and the Sandinista Party organizer who had been with Kim, one of the Berkeley cadre, earlier in the evening. He had been discovered as an unpaid guest, just how was later disputed. The señora said he was trying to sneak out; Doris said that the husband had been lurking outside Kim's room. The young man's right eye was cut, and he cupped the palm of a hand over it.

"Where is the *muchacha*?" one of the policemen asked.

"In my room," the manager replied.

"We must speak with her."

The señora left and returned momentarily with Kim, who was clad in a sheet. During the melee she had run naked from the room. The sergeant insisted on taking everyone to the station. On hearing this, Kim grasped the shoulder of the señora. Suddenly, there was a commotion in the street.

"Alto! alto!"

The driver, who had remained with the paddy, shoved an unkempt gent through the gate. The latter staggered, almost falling, his face puffy, eyes red. "This *hombre*," the policeman used the word mockingly, "tried to break into the jeep parked out there." The sergeant demanded that the owner state whether anything was missing.

"Go get the gringo with the red beard," the señora said to her husband. Incredibly, this farce had now led to my own participation.

I slipped up the stairs and was in the room when the knock came. My concern was that they would inspect the rig and find the articles from *La Prensa* that were still in the brown envelope with the paper's return address. Though they watched my once–over, they made no effort to look, themselves. The sergeant accepted my finding that nothing was amiss. It was with difficulty, though, that I persuaded him that I did not wish to carry a complaint against the *tipejo*. He would still charge the culprit with petty mischief he said. At length the entourage departed with the failed yegg and the interloper roughly handcuffed. To her relief, Kim was exempted from their train. She said nothing to her consort as he was led away.

Next morning, the ruckus was the talk of the hotel. It was generally conceded that the manager's husband was guilty of voyeurism or, at least, "excessive force." Kim, however, did not appear to tell her side of the story.

In time, concern shifted to more serious matters.

Miriam, a just–graduated anthropology major from UCLA, commented on how effective Sandinista education seemed to be, "Especially with the younger kids. Their reading and math are superior to elementary kids in Southern California." She and her friend, Debbie, had been working with a Solidarity Brigade that was building a new school in a small village near León. When I asked if the kids were still being taught to count using illustrations of Soviet hand grenades and AK–47 rifles she stared coldly and said, "That was an isolated incident.

CUSCLIN May Day flyer, Managua.

"But so what if they do? They will one day have to defend themselves against imperialist aggression. American children counted from pictures of guns and tanks in World War II."

Debbie agreed but hoped that the Sandinistas would live up to their "commitment to teach peace, not war." She was clearly uncomfortable with such training aids.

"Were you able to find bread?" Horst, a West German carpenter, asked. I had told him and his friend, Hermann, that I would buy an extra baguette for them if there was any, but there wasn't — disappointing the people in a long line at the principal bakery, the *Panadería Plaza de España*.

Bread shortages, unheard of during Somoza, had become commonplace. The family of González, the welder, said they had an aunt who lived near a bakery and would buy for them. She was able to do so only once or twice a week. Even packaged bread was sold out in the *supermercados*.

I mentioned this to Horst, expressing surprise at the scarcity of goods on the shelves. Built in the early 1970s on the model of their American counterparts, the supermarkets now resembled depleted warehouses. The three I visited each contained hundreds of feet of vacant shelving. In none was there any produce, canned meat, flour, baking soda, cooking oil, beer, even sardines were absent.

Plentiful were canned Bulgarian, BULGAR brand, white beans. These took up two complete aisles in the Plaza de España store. Each store also had a full shelf of rum and vodka — made in Nicaragua, the latter's logo spelled in Spanish with ersatz Cyrillic characters.

In an effort to camouflage the empty space, clusters of non–food items such as combs, sisal rope, toy soldiers, rat poison, insecticide and sunglasses had been spread about. With what surely was unintended irony, near the checkout counter was an unshelved pallet of Russian vinegar.

"What do you expect? The fascist Reagan embargo is responsible for those shortages. The starvation policy of imperialism. You've seen its results firsthand." Don, a recent Harvard political science graduate, had joined the conversation.

I suggested that many of the shortages were due to the massive military buildup. Half the male population between 18 and 45, according to the government, was in an active or reserve unit. "That's got to include a lot of farmers, don't you think?"

"A liberated people have every right to arm themselves and defend their revolution."

Others turned from their own conversations or looked up from their reading. Doris, who had been engrossed in Castro's speeches, set them aside.

"... They are at war with the largest military power on earth. They have no choice. They tried to get by with a small army but the United States armed the Contra mercenaries and now threatens to send in its own troops."

Echoes of his words rang from the periphery: "have no choice ... gringo bombs ... but what do you expect? ... yeah."

"But we did help them for two years," I replied. "More aid than all other countries combined. We only cut it off when they wouldn't stop running guns to the Salvadoran guerrillas."

"Compared to our ability that aid was peanuts," Don retorted. "We should have done far more especially since we propped up the Somozas for 40 years. And don't they have a right to support their friends? The United States sure as hell does. And those 'friends' are the enemies of freedom of the oppressed peoples they control. They are all US puppets."

There was a chorus of concurring murmurs. I felt like a Philistine beset by Pharisees.

"I hate to interrupt this fruitful discussion," someone said, "But does anybody want to share a taxi to the Embassy?" It had slipped my mind. Today was Thursday, the day of the weekly demonstration by American citizens in front of the US Embassy. Since it was May Day a big crowd was expected. It started at 8 a.m.; it was 7:45.

A large crowd had already gathered at the Embassy gate. Their mood was merry, buoyant. Leaders of the Committee of US Citizens Living and Working in Nicaragua, CUSCLIN, were clearly delighted at the turnout.

They huddled with their chairman, a seventyish fellow in a wide Panama hat, who said his name was "Camillus Dufresne from St. Louis, Missouri." After a few minutes they emerged to announce that the demo would start "as soon as all May Day cadre have arrived."

Inturista's ubiquitous buses soon parked up the street, their passengers trebling our number. Some 40 constabulary with automatic weapons patrolled the area, detouring traffic a block either side of the mission — except for troop trucks which were flagged through ceremoniously.

The soldiers were waving and cheering and exchanging cries of "solidarity" with CUSCLIN regulars, among whom I recognized Manning and two of her colleagues from Witnesses For Peace. Hershell, the reporter from the Sara the night before, didn't show.

Several Nicaraguan embassy employees looked out nonchalantly through the iron fence. No diplomatic staff were in evidence. The deputy information officer told me later that zoom video and photographs were surreptitiously taken of these events to identify participants.

214

Those demonstrators nearer the gate began to walk counterclockwise. Others took the cue and there were chants of "USA OUT OF NICARAGUA," "AMÉRICA SÍ, CONTRA NO" and "REAGAN TERRORISTA — SOY SANDINISTA." After 20 minutes or so the marchers were motioned to gather in front of a microphone set up by one of the policemen.

Two persons had brought guitars, and the crowd sang along. There were familiar protest ballads and one in Spanish that was a tribute to Sandinista martyrs. A woman read a poem she had written. It extolled the sacrifice of the Nicaraguan people and promised that "victory will be theirs."

Many of the participants had cameras and once it seemed as if there were more photographers than participants.

A prayer was followed by testimonials: first by regulars then by visitors. Some spoke firsthand of the progress being made to increase literacy, crop yields, care for the aged and infirm and the like, and how it was all hampered by US support of the Contras and the trade embargo.

Others told of Nicaraguans who had been crippled or killed by the Contras. One woman from New Jersey said that she was "a veteran of the 60s" and had, "served in Selma, at Columbia and the Pentagon" and that "the cause we witness for here is even more important than those." All present, she said, had a duty to write their congressmen demanding that no further funds be voted for the Contras and for a lifting of the embargo.

Finally, the proceedings ended with a singing of "America."

A table was set up to collect names and addresses. One group was attending the "International Workers Congress," then under way. The Sandinistas claimed that representatives from over 50 nations had come.

The US contingent, their leader said, was marching in the May Day parade with a Sandinista union. He called his delegates over to make sure everyone knew where to meet.

In addition to Dufresne, among those present were Jim Goff of the "Ecumenical Center for Theological Reflection" in Orinda, California; María de Zuniga who said she was "a public health worker with 18 years in Nicaragua"; and David Sweet, a professor of Latin American history at UC Santa Cruz, who said he had helped set up Witnesses for Peace. The group, he insisted, was "not necessarily pro–Sandinista. We are against violence of any kind, anywhere in the world, and we are prepared to place our lives in jeopardy to prevent it."

By 10 a.m. it was 90 degrees in the shade at the Santos. I parked the jeep and walked over to the Continental to meet Sally for a cup of coffee before she flew to Costa Rica on an assignment. I wanted to thank her for her help. The lobby was bubbling with anticipation.

A Sandinista *capitana* in starched fatigues was recruiting unassigned guests to march in a "friendship brigade." She had been at the Santos earlier and signed up some of the women there, impressing them with tales of organizing in the countryside.

Network TV crews were moving their equipment. Some had already set up along the route but returned in relays to the bar.

A reporter from the *New York Times* was interviewing delegates.

Sandinista cameramen filmed away while clusters of tourists were instructed on where best to observe the parade. Some were marching. Others had begged off due to the heat. The reliable Inturista buses arrived and an agent announced that those who were joining such and such brigade could now board for its assembly point. There was movement toward the doors.

Sally was on time but rushed.

"I have to pick up my ticket this morning or lose my seat," she said. There were as many standbys as booked passengers. She had been jumped to the top of the list by a friend who worked at the Aeronica ticket office. "That was a big favor," she winked. Hope it doesn't cost me my objectivity!"

She was doing a story on an upcoming meeting in Esquipulas, Guatemala of Central American chiefs of state. Many thought that was where Ortega would sign the Contadora treaty.

"There's always another treaty, another 'process,' another meeting," she said. "Just like American presidents, these guys find it easier to play with foreign problems than solve domestic ones. And at these conferences they get treated like royalty, not politicos."

She was not hopeful that peace was nigh. "These people are dreadfully poor. They crowd into the cities. They watch TV. They see all the things they can't have. The governments are corrupt to one extent or another. Maybe change can be forced peacefully, democratically. But probably not. It's sad to say but maybe some form of Marxism is their only way out."

She saw a friend from one of the wire services. They were catching the same plane. He was also standby. They decided to share a cab. "See you in Lima, maybe," she called as they pulled away. She had asked for reassignment to South America and had requested Peru.

The taxi had barely disappeared when the buzz of departing cadre was interrupted by sirens followed by a great rumbling. A column of 20 Soviet T–55 battle tanks lunged down the Avenida Bolívar toward the parade terminus at the National Cathedral. Its formation was paced, disciplined. The Nicaraguan crews and the infantrymen in personnel carriers accompanying them sat with the reserve of elite warriors. The street was sacrificed to their entry, its asphalt buckling beneath them.

The parade was a recapitulation of the land through which I had passed the previous week. It was a compressed collage of the promise, chagrin, defiance and escape entailed in the settling of a new order and of the ennui that inevitably attends the realization that government, whether conventional or revolutionary, is finally quiescent. There were cynics marching as well, and of them are made counterrevolutionaries — and, sometimes, democrats.

The contingents required four hours to fill the plaza. The Sandinistas estimated their numbers at more than 100,000 and there were at least half that — remarkable on a day when the heat would have balked the grittiest Mississippi cotton farmer. There were brigades from the country's major cities — Granada, León, Estelí — and those representing unions, peasants cooperatives, fishermen, Sumo and Miskito Indians, and artists. A delegation of black residents of Bluefields on the Caribbean coast marched past. In one company was a full rank of CUSCLIN regulars. In another, from a Managua barrio, were many of the women from the Santos. In yet another were Sister Mary Hartman and her staff from the human rights commission. From a shaded area near the plaza, nonmarching Americans from the Hotel Continental cheered their compatriots.

On my own way down I met a young woman in a wheel chair. She was late joining her unit and was having a hard time throttling the wheels through the crowd. A friend had promised to push her but he was leading their march and must have been detained. She'd decided to wheel the three miles on her own, something she did regularly at less congested times. The red and black FSLN banner she insisted on holding aloft left her with but one hand for the chair. Would I help? Sure, I said, and off we went.

Pushing the contraption was more difficult than it looked. It was remarkable that she had made it this far so quickly. When we gained the Avenida Bolívar she directed me toward a clump of trees where she would await her unit. A cart vendor selling pop poured two into baggies with pinches of ice, retaining the bottles. Thus refreshed, we continued our exchange between her greetings to passing comrades.

Her name was "Chábe — Elizabeth, in English," and she was a neighborhood organizer and "student activist." She was majoring in "the history of revolution." She gave talks "to workers and peasants who can't read well enough yet." She hastened to praise the official literacy campaign.

Her friend, the leader, wanted to become a doctor "but he must first work with the people," meaning, I took it, that the party came first. He had just been selected for study in East Germany.

Others had been chosen for schooling in the Soviet Union and other Warsaw Pact countries. Her own preference would be Hungary. She had a friend there, a teacher she had met during his aid tour in Nicaragua.

Her unit was preceded by a wide banner — *"Arriba los Pobres del Mundo, de Pie los Esclavos sin Pan,"* Rise up, you poor of the world, On your feet, you slaves without bread — and trailed by another — *"Reagan Terrorista."* She motioned for me to roll her into the front file, just behind the right banner–picket carrier. She referred to me as we arrived as her "gringo amigo," the phrase rippling good–naturedly through the ranks. At first no one spelled me and I feared I had thus involuntarily joined the parade. Soon a tall, good–looking fellow took the handles and I became a spectator once again.

There were speeches by East Bloc diplomats, PLO and Libyan representatives and delegates to the Workers' Congress. Some were quite winded so the keynote of President Ortega was considerably delayed.

In the torpor, pop and coconut milk vendors thrived. Visiting cadre made periodic trips to the Continental's oasis, many remaining to watch the proceedings on television.

Speakers referred to *"Los Martires de Chicago,"* the union leaders prosecuted as the result of their alleged provoking of the "Haymarket Riot" of May 4, 1886.[50]

Ortega's speech was an hour's philippic which laid Nicaragua's malaise at the door of the United States. By his fielding of the Contras and his trade embargo, Reagan had wrecked the nation's economy. Of the $360 million in planned exports, Ortega said, only $270 million had been traded. At the same time international lending agencies had been effectively blocked by the United States from making loans to Nicaragua.

"As long as this Yankee aggression continues," he said, "we will never sign the Act of Contadora."

Ortega called upon the country's workers and peasants to produce more. Harder work, he said, would defeat American economic aggression.

The audience was attentive at first but soon those on the rim began to spin away. It was not so much Ortega's delivery — nor a surfeit, generally, of oratorical tedium. Rather it was simply the heat: it had grown so exacting that even those few who could find shade were fanning themselves with a distracted urgency. Toward the end I joined the exodus to the arctic sanctuary of the big hotel.

218

Sandinista loyalist on her way to the May Day parade, Managua.

Celebrations, official and spontaneous, continued far into the cooling night. Bars knew no curfew and official discos, improvised beneath scrap wood pavilions on vacant lots, pealed American rock to twisting cadre. Beer, hoarded by the government for the occasion, was plentiful. Exuberant celebrants roamed the streets chanting slogans and singing of glories past and those to come. Squads of police and soldiers patrolled, but with orders of admonition rather than arrest: Let the people have their fiesta; after all, they are celebrating us. Still in all, there was a vague suggestion of unease — as if some sensed a method to their revelry.

As I walked back to the Santos, there was a crowd bunched in the adjacent avenue at its corner with our street. Someone had fallen. A girl's feet, her shoes missing, were visible. There was a great deal of blood. A Sandinista ensign lay to one side. A jeep halted and soldiers pushed through. People came running from a disco. They shoved closer to stare. An ambulance arrived and the girl's body was covered and placed on a stretcher. Her braids fled as she was lifted but an attendant caught them and folded them back. She had been struck, someone said, by a car with flags on the hood. It did not stop.

My arrest came at noon a quarter–mile from Costa Rica, in the emptiness of which I have spoken earlier. I cleared customs and immigration smoothly. Vehicle inspection was cursory.

They were waiting around a curve, some twenty of them. They waved me down with their rifles.

I was alone at the time. My hitchhikers had returned to Managua. One had her purse snatched. The US Embassy issued her a temporary passport and a letter attesting to the theft. She also had a copy of the police report. Nevertheless, a visa was required before she could leave the country. It could be got only in the capital. I took the two of them back up Lake Nicaragua toward Granada until we found a farmer driving his family to the city in an old Pontiac. I agreed to wait for them until seven on the Costa Rica side. If they didn't make it by then, maybe we'd meet up in San José. Now I was the one who might not show up.

It was unclear whether the men had been waiting for me in particular or whether such searches were routine. A surly plainclothesman with a poorly sutured gash from nose to temple ordered me to stand down. He was flanked by two troopers with submachine guns, the Czech kind of which Third World police are fond. Other men were already opening the back hatch and climbing to the rack. I called for them to be careful lest the roof not support them. I offered to take down the things, myself.

No sooner had I spoken than I was shoved from behind and told to follow a lieutenant. After some distance he turned and asked my purpose in the country and whether I had *"contrabanda."* I could hear my belongings slapped, rattled, unzipped and spread on the gravel. I assured him that I was merely a writer collecting material for a book. At first he seemed to accept this explanation but after looking into the distance his eyes came back and he asked softly if I was not in reality *"un agente contrarevolucionario?"* I insisted that I was not. He demanded my passport which I produced, thinking that it was good that I'd kept it out for to go into the jeep's safe at that time would have exposed to them several thousand dollars in travelers checks and half again that in cash. Not much for a smuggler but about right for a spy.

I remembered the *La Prensa* articles and censorship orders at the instant the scarfaced fellow called: "Lieutenant, come and look at this. He is carrying government documents." He held the sheaf of orders with the national seal and "Ministry of the Interior" on the letterhead. They had been tossed into a box with weights of Sandinista tracts, books and newspapers and my notes from the time since Tegucigalpa. The latter were mostly in improvised shorthand. I had taken the precaution of mailing earlier journals ahead to Costa Rica.

"Where did you get these documents?" he asked.

"At *La Prensa*," I said.

"Where are you taking them?"

I explained again that I was a writer. I had picked up all I could on the country for a book. As he could see, the bulk of the material was Sandinista propaganda. I told him visitors were encouraged to talk to everyone and take what we wanted no matter the source. When "our group" had visited the paper I'd asked "the guide" for copies of recently censored material and no one had objected. This was a small chance to take but by putting the onus on the Sandinista guide, perhaps the editor, Jaime Chamorro, would be saved a hassle. To be frank he probably wouldn't have given a damn if I'd flat out told them he had forked the documents over.

They tossed the gear haphazardly into the jeep and told me to drive back to the post. I was put in a room with two young women who stabbed unartfully at the keys of typewriters. Another came and went, building the tower of forms from which they were working faster than they reduced it. One of the gunners sat facing me and another stood outside the door. The lieutenant came after an hour and led me to an office in which a major sat with the scarfaced one. Through a window I could see that the jeep had been emptied a second time and its contents were being inventoried.

I was told to sit and the questions previously put were answered again. A woman to whom deference was shown but who wore no insignia entered but said nothing.

221

Didn't I know that it was an offense to possess censored material and government orders? I said that I didn't and that in any event the guide must have known the articles were censored since I'd asked for them while he was there — which was technically correct, although I was not with his group, and he was three rooms away at the time. The phone rang and the major's tone changed from menacing to obsequious.

"Sí, mi Comandante! Cómo no, mi Comandante. Inmediatamente, mi Comandante."

At the first *Comandante*, the lieutenant stood to attention and the others sat upright. I was asked if I had any evidence of my status, and I said none other than letters from my publisher at the time and the editor of the *Arkansas Gazette* attesting to my bona fides. These were in the sliding Moroccan pouch of papers I had taken from the safe earlier along with the passport, and I handed them up. They were in English but their formal appearance was impressive and he described them to the party on the other end. Seeing the pouch reminded me again of the safe and I wondered why they had not told me to open it. My only conclusion was simply that they hadn't seen it bolted beneath the driver's seat. The major hung up the phone.

"Your case has been referred to Managua for decision," he said. I was returned to the same room as before but the typists and their papers and machines were gone. A single table and two chairs remained. The guards took up their former positions and the door was closed.

The time seemed to race, then plod. Through the walls I could hear voices and, I thought, recognize those of the scarface and the major. Only occasional words were understandable: *contra ... contrabandista ... confiscación ... interogación especial.* Special interrogation by the Sandinista secret police was not a pleasant prospect. I thought of habeas corpus and bail and the presumption of innocence — rights most Americans take for granted. I thought of my freedom being dependent upon the judicial system superintended by Tomás Borge and Sister Mary Hartman. Then I remembered the letter I had been shown the day before by a lawyer in one of the tour groups at the Continental.

It was from Robert G. Post, a professor of constitutional law at the University of California at Berkeley. He was invited to speak to the National Assembly of Nicaragua. They wanted to learn, he said, about the United States Constitution. Professor Post was so impressed with what he saw that he wrote about it to the local paper when he returned to Berkeley. Said the letter, in part:

It is hard to question the [Nicaraguan
government's] dedication to the material welfare

of its population, its commitment to eradicate their poverty, to improve their education, or to maintain their health ...

[Sandinista] pronouncements may be merely propaganda, hypocritically concealing a relentless but hidden drive for total domination.

Hypocrisy can be difficult to detect. The time I spent in Nicaragua certainly was insufficient to reach a firm and comprehensive judgment on the question. But I did have the distinct and overpowering impression that the potential does exist in Nicaragua for the kind of pluralism that Americans, committed to our Constitution, would recognize as political freedom.

[E]very one I talked with ... expressed distaste for the political repression and monolithic nature of the Cuban state. The Cubans are "yes men," one ... judge told me. "We ... are more independent than that."

All this could be hypocrisy, but I doubt it. The difficulty is that tolerance and pluralism are difficult to maintain in times of war. The Reagan administration's policy of ... military aid and economic pressure is producing anger and intolerance.

... Our present policy will almost assuredly undermine whatever chance Nicaragua may have to enjoy a true democratic pluralism.[51]

His letter was photocopied and circulated by the "Bay Area Lawyers Committee on Central America" to all sitting federal and superior state court judges in the United States. It was accompanied by a cover letter, on university stationery, from Post, who encouraged their own participation in a "Judge's Tour of Nicaragua" set up by the Lawyers Committee.[52]

After four hours, my detainers somehow became convinced of my solidarity — or at least my innocuousness. The major announced that the documents would be confiscated and that I was free to go. The woman who had remained silent and expressionless pushed the remainder of the material toward me across the table.

"*Son muy mal informados,*" the major said, holding up two articles by Jaime Chamorro. They were very badly informed. "*Muy mal informados,*" he repeated twice more. From the back of the room one of the others added: "*No es un buen hombre, éste. Lucha contra la revolución.*" Jaime Chamorro was not a good man. He fought against the Revolution.

I tried re–packing my things into some kind of order but was too tired to worry with it. Besides, it was best to split before my custodians or "*mi Comandante,*" whoever that was, changed their minds.

How I relished the tediousness and delay of the Costa Rican border post with its sleepy officials and comically inefficient but expensive, $5, *fumigación.* The rusty nozzle of the pesticide hose barely dripped a concoction so watery that it surely would eradicate nothing save the shekels from my pocket. Passed in an hour and with no sign of my former passengers, I drove to the first settlement, the Pacific bluff hamlet of La Cruz fifteen miles to the south. A rodeo was in progress at the outskirts and onlookers in bleachers surrounded by pickups cheered and waved their hats at young men on broncos. The main cafe served a good sirloin for less than four dollars and for two dollars I found a tidy room. A squall marched in at midnight, easing my sleep with the first rain in weeks.

The women made it across next day and we hiked to the remote jungle beach of Naranjo in the Parque Nacional Santa Rosa. Magnificent rolling shoulders of high green surf pounded the sand. Three rangers on horseback met us on the trail. Jaguar were common in the park, they said. You could hear them scream early in the morning and late in the afternoon.

Mural on a government discotheque, Managua.

14

SAN JOSÉ

*Costa Rica society collected there for gossip and
coffee. There were beautiful women, students,
exiles, businessmen, contract workers and
tourists — for all of whom the Gran Hotel was
both respite and rendezvous. Concert strains from
the rococo National Theater next door escaped
into the plaza.*

San José relaxes at 3,800 feet in temperatures between 60 and
75 degrees. Although 1 million people swell its environs, it is calm by
Latin standards, with friendly cops, street scrubbing equipment and
litter baskets. That said, the impression should not be left of a
sanitized and somnambulistic metropolis: Most trash escapes, a TV
blasts from every shop and conveyances with detached mufflers tax
one's health and sanity.

Shortly after my arrival, Costa Rica inaugurated its ninth
elected president since 1948, Oscar Arias Sánchez. I went to the
national soccer stadium for the event. Most hemisphere chiefs of state
attended, of whom León Febres–Cordero Ribadeneyra of Ecuador, a
reformer who had just survived an attempted coup, received the
strongest ovation. George Bush, then vice president, represented the
United States to reserved applause. The crowd booed Claudia
Chamorro Barrios, Violeta's Sandinista daughter and the Nicaraguan
ambassador. A border clash the previous weekend had left two Costa
Rican guardsmen dead. And there was growing disgust for the regime
that, someone said, had "sent thousands of refugees to take *Tico* jobs."
Police were courteous, not abrupt; solicitous, not intimidating. Festive
blue–and–white bunting of the PLN, National Liberation Party,
decked the stadium. Stalwarts waved flags, children balloons.

One contrasted the spontaneous revelry of these partisans with
the orchestrated rancor of the Sandinistas. What caused the
difference? What was it that kept Costa Rica's experiment in
reasonableness from spreading to its neighbors? Robust since 1890
with but three brief interruptions, one would have thought that its
democracy — rather than a hoary totalitarianism — would be the
nemesis of the ossified oligarchies of the isthmus. Some pointed to the
large European population and the small numbers of Indians and
Mestizos. The inference was that the latter were "culturally
incapable" of democracy, given their strong traditions of machismo

and one-man rule. Others argued that history and geography were in Costa Rica's favor.

Deserting the bloated Mexican Empire with its neighbors in 1823, Costa Rica had, by 1839, cut away from the defunct United Provinces of Central America and asserted its present identity. Contrary to its name, which means Rich Coast, the country was thought to have no great agricultural or mineral potential. Its settlers were small farmers and entrepreneurs. There were never large plantations or mines, thus no concentration of land in the hands of a few *caciques* with dependent masses of illiterate peasants.

The country's topography is conducive to individual farming. Fertile valleys lie between thick forests, some of the last virgin stands outside the Amazon. Cattle ranching developed but on a scale much smaller than the grand estates of Nicaragua, Honduras and Guatemala. Coffee became a major export as did bananas from the northeast Caribbean coast and later from the Pacific southwest near Golfito. Placer gold deposits were found and exploited. But these interests were unable to capture the government as they did in the rest of Latin America. The result was the growth of a substantial middle class who demanded public services and had the political power to get them.

Whatever the reason for its stability Costa Rica is the most civilized Central American nation by Western standards. It has the region's highest per capita income and many times more telephones, television sets and other appliances than any other nation in the region. There are more miles of paved roads than in Nicaragua, Guatemala, El Salvador and Belize combined. Greater than its economic success is an environmental and cultural flowering unique to Latin America. A system of 19 national parks protects one of the hemisphere's richest repositories of wildlife and natural beauty. Its secondary schools and universities are by reputation unequaled in the Hispanic world; dance, art and theater are not only generously endowed but popularly supported.

Raising dust in the jeep seven miles west of the Parrita River, I saw in the distance a stretch of ocean undisturbed save for a cloister of stucco enveloped by palm groves. Knots of Angus grazed in deep pastures. Las Cabañas de Los Angeles were run by a retired San José hardware merchant named Sigifredo Sánchez — a stout, sad-faced sort for whom a guest was rather an audience than a client.

He graciously let me camp under his trees, refused payment, and insisted that I join him for a *comida* whenever his appetite struck.

Small gardens of wildflowers brushed the place with a joyful air. In one a bust of a young American woman — said to have drowned here in the early 1970s — smiled anticipatively toward the sea. Bananas, papaya, mango and avocado from the orchard were daily courtesies of the house. There were two species of lemon, *dulce* and *ácido*, for the sweet or sour palette, and succulent grapefruit. The beach, blown free of mosquitoes by a soft but constant wind, yielded sand dollars the size of saucers. And how rhythmic were its ivory–smiling waves. Singly, they broke, not in errant followings, scudding to within inches of the trees before receding on the ebb. A good dog came and nuzzled my leg as I returned from a swim. When I bent to pet her she purred and rolled over like a cat. She slept under the jeep, protecting it. So good to have a friend, she said, even for a moment. Coffee–colored patches on white fur; coffee snout.

I managed some writing but mostly read and listened to Siggi and two vacationing ranchers and their wives pronounce on Costa Rican politics and how the country was being "ruined by socialism." Taxes,[53] they said, were absurdly high and there was little incentive to go into business or reinvest. One was sending his money to the States "as soon as it's made." His wife said it was "getting time to go to Miami." Still, their market for export beef, mostly to buyers for American burger chains, apparently remained strong since they had recently increased their herds. These people, from the mountainous border province of Alajuela, had no love for the Sandinistas, who they said were training insurgents to stir rebellion in Costa Rica. According to one, Costa Rican rebels had formed a company–sized unit called *Los Ticos*. They had trained near Granada then gained battle experience by helping the Sandinistas patrol the San Juan River border. Some had been killed or captured by Eden Pastora's troops.

But most people here would never accept a totalitarian system, they said, under whatever guise — although Former President Figures, a democratic socialist who was now a confidant of Castro's and a court favorite of the *comandantes*, was advocating a Sandinista transplant for Costa Rica. If it came, it would have to be imposed by force. One of the farmers was something of an amateur tactician and opined that the country's many good secondary roads would make swift passage for the Sandinista's Soviet tanks. "Ticos," he said, were "too independent and easygoing" to form an army but would surely resist in small groups "until the United States comes to help us."

Siggi, who had been uncharacteristically silent, said that was all wrong.

Costa Ricans were "not independent, only quarrelsome; not easygoing, merely slothful." The Sandinistas, he retorted, could make short shrift of them. "But remember, my friends," he said, "elections are easier. Tyrants prefer to take power by using the system, itself, by calling themselves something nice, like reformers or patriots. Like the

229

cabrón Figueres. It will all be over before you know it. And the Americans! Hah! Do not wait for them. They will not bother with us, whatever happens."

Such windy pessimism was, I found, contrary to the general buoyancy of the population, for most of whom politics, even those of their tempestuous neighbor, were a remote concern.

From there I drove south to Playa Manuel Antonio, a wilderness beach along a rain forest teeming with fauna. Giant iguanas, tree lizards, butterflies, sloths, two species of monkeys, over a hundred of birds and a great variety of crustaceans thrive there. Among the crustaceans is a large red "tree crab" that ranges into high forest on, the headland between two half–moon bays washed by a gently rolling surf. Visitors stay at the Cabañas Ramírez, a mile from the entrance, or in one of three lesser accommodations. The road dead–ends at the shallow lagoon which borders the park. You wade it to get to the entrance. The nearest settlement is the town of Quepos, population about 7,000, five hilly miles up the coast.

The smaller of the two bays, the one just past the lagoon, offers superb anchorage for canal–bound yachts. Transpacific cruisers make this their last stop for supplies, purchased in Quepos, before striking for the Marquesas.

I took a small *cabaña* at the Ramírez for $4.00, worth it for the hot shower, but slept most nights just inside the tree line of the first bay. A troop of white–faced monkeys swung past at dawn. You could swim out a quarter–mile or more and back–float to shore on the swells — taking care to right yourself for the final catapult to the beach.

Back in San José, I phoned 34–28–32, the number given on the dateline of *Mesoamerica*. A pleasant female voice answered in Spanish then shifted to English with no trace of an accent. Word processors clacked softly in the background. I asked for the editor.

"Mr. Morris is in Managua but is expected back tomorrow," she said. "Are you with the network?"

"Just a writer traveling through," I told her. "I'd like to get his impressions on the situation down here." She would ask him to call first thing next morning.

After months of camping and cheap hotels it was time for a touch of luxury. So I checked into the Gran Hotel de Costa Rica on the central plaza. Turn–of–the–century in style, its great lobby was comfortably furnished for reading and quiet conversation. Its food was tasty and reasonably priced and service extended onto the patio. Costa Rica society collected there for gossip and coffee.

Fred B. Morris, ABC–TV resident agent and editor of *Mesoamerica*, at his office in San José, Costa Rica.

There were beautiful women, students, exiles, businessmen, contract workers and tourists — for all of whom the Gran Hotel was both respite and rendezvous. Concert strains from the rococo National Theater next door escaped into the plaza.

The bibliophile assistant manager provided me with a small interior suite for the price of a single room, about $35. There, for eight days, I caught up on my journal and answered mail that had accumulated since February at the American Express office around the corner. The housekeeper brought in an old wooden work table and saw to it that I was kept supplied with coffee. In the small bricked parking area before the main entry, the jeep became an object of curiosity under the watchful eyes of the bellmen, who proclaimed its peripatetic history and the scope of the present undertaking.

Fred B. Morris phoned back that night and we agreed to meet downstairs for breakfast at 7:30. With peppery gray hair and scratchy goatee, he had an elfin countenance suggestive of the wily exile, street–schooled in Latin ways. Engaging but wary, he was inconspicuously dressed save for an exquisite gold chain and medallion behind an untucked Tico shirt, open above the third button. Fluent in local argot and savvy to the fluid political mixes of the isthmus, Morris was in ostensible camaraderie with some of its primary and many of its secondary personages. He was particularly established in Costa Rica and the "New Nicaragua," grasping through these connections intermittent opportunities, among them sales of construction chemicals and waterproofed roofing. But Morris had other pursuits less capitalistic in nature, of which the pro–Sandinista Institute for Central American Studies and its monthly organ, *Mesoamerica*, were of especial interest in view of his position as resident agent for the powerful American television network, ABC.

His first stint in Latin America, he recounted, had been in the late 60s and early 70s as a Methodist missionary in Brazil. He had previously done some reporting, so he became a part–time correspondent with *Time* magazine. An article critical of the then–military regime, to which he contributed but didn't write, was his undoing. "They arrested me and tortured me for a month," he said. "Head–thumping, 24–hour interrogation, solitary confinement, the lot. I thought I'd never see daylight again." Finally, he was released and expelled from the country and told never to return. "I did a first–person piece for *Time* when I got back. Really stirred things up for awhile."

He became a minor celebrity on the Northeastern lecture circuit, tried teaching, then decided he would "give Costa Rica a try." Soon he was "on the inside" with a few key contractors and purchasing agents. He formed a construction firm, M.Y.C. Services, and Adecon, an adhesives distributor. M.Y.C. Services handled the chemicals and

Adecon the roofing. He married a native Nicaraguan who, though a naturalized Costa Rican, retained extensive family and political ties in Managua.

Morris had friends "at the top" in ABC and when he was offered the resident agent's job, "I took it without hesitation."

The Central American Research Institute was begun in 1980 as a nonprofit group by "some people interested in promoting honest scholarship and a free exchange of ideas on Central American problems and in demilitarizing the region." He would not say who the other founders were, but in November 1982, "I took it over, and we've tried to make it self–sufficient." To do that he started the "study seminars."

"It's still nonprofit, though, legally — and on the books," He said with a chuckle. "But we ought to go into the black this year. We've quadrupled our enrollment." Courses were scheduled as far out as May of the following year for every month except December. Participants came from all over. "We just had a Presbyterian group down from the Midwest, 26 of them. Clergymen and their wives, a few laymen. Next week we have a mixed group from Philadelphia and San Francisco. Academics, a few professionals — lawyers, judges, that kind of thing." For many, such sessions were tax deductible as "continuing education" — foreign affairs being "essential" to their occupations. Spouses and children sometimes came along. The price of the sessions at the time was $835 per person, students $775, including round trip airfare from Miami, lodging in a hostel and meals.

Morris was a frequent traveler, speaking regularly in the States to peace meetings, conventions, and such. The following month he was to address a Methodist conference and student groups at several colleges.

Seminar clients and "interns" were recruited at such events. The interns were mostly graduate students: Iowa, Indiana, Northern Illinois, occasionally from the West Coast. They volunteered for anywhere from a few months to a year, some longer. Several were doing advanced degree work. Others had simply "taken a break to come see for themselves what's going on." A few had fellowships, including US government grants. Those short on cash could teach English to Costa Ricans.

Their "Research Analysis" appeared each month in *Mesoamerica*. Some topics from the May 1986 edition: "Human Rights Abuses by Contras"; "Disregard for Civilian Population"; "Contra Lawlessness — Theft of Property"; and "Contra Instigated Arrest, Detention and Torture."

Seminars were intensive, Morris said. "The first three days we give them a complete course on the history of Central America and the present conflict. We don't try to give 'equal time' to everybody though occasionally we've had a Contra exile over. But they get enough of that in the States. What we want them to get here are firsthand facts, not polemics. Then we drive them up to Nicaragua for the next six days. We take them around to the important historical sites, but the emphasis is on meeting people, not only leaders, but working cadre — teachers, peasants, anybody who has time to talk to us, and you'd be surprised how many do. We bring in a Miskito Indian leader or one of the Moravian bishops out there on the Atlantic coast; we take them out to talk to Witnesses for Peace, the Nicaraguan Commission on Human Rights, Ministry of Culture. We even take them to *La Prensa*, the anti–government newspaper. They can talk to anybody they like, even the editors if they're around and will talk to them. They're usually up in the States making anti–Sandinista speeches."

I nodded, thinking of the Sandinista guide with his badge, his nervousness when Jaime Chamorro unexpectedly opened the door. I wondered if it was one of Morris' groups, but I decided not to mention my own visit or the run–in at the border. With his Brazilian jail experience Morris might sympathize — but maybe not.

"I've made 25 trips to Nicaragua with these groups in the last three years," Morris said. He stayed with his wife's family in Managua: "They're good people. Middle class, Sandinistas. Active in the party, but objective, intelligent people."

I asked how he felt, as a journalist, about Sandinista censorship of *La Prensa*. "You know, to quote Omar Cabezas,[54] 'I feel pretty good about it.' That's what he said the other day at one of our seminars in Managua. I put the question to him myself. He said he felt that way because at least the paper could publish something. It was war — the country was at war against the world's most powerful nation. He pointed out that during World War II, the United States closed down 22 newspapers and imprisoned their editors before any US soldiers had been killed.[55] But we've had 12,000 people killed; that's equivalent to 1.2 million Americans in a country 100 times the size of Nicaragua. So we've decided to censor certain military and economic propaganda that's being used against us. Most of it isn't even news, just propaganda.

"*La Prensa* wrote a story saying there was a shortage of rice. So what happens? You guessed it: Everybody runs out and buys up all the rice in the markets, so by God there *is* a shortage, a very severe one. But there wasn't until they wrote that story. They created the shortage, themselves. A self–fulfilling prophesy. So now, when they have a story dealing with things like that, shortages of food, material, they better have their facts and sources damned straight up front. They can't use 'Freedom of the Press' for rumor mongering.

234

"There is actually more freedom of expression in Nicaragua than here in Costa Rica, where all the papers are owned by the elites. They say the same thing day after day. In Nicaragua you have *La Prensa*, *Barricada* and *El Nuevo Diario*. Each one is different. I don't like censorship, but if I'd been the *comandantes* I would've closed the damned *La Prensa* down years ago."

Mesoamerica's masthead informed readers that the Institute was dedicated to the cause of peace and justice and was supported by contributions from religious organizations, foundations and individuals, as well as by subscriptions. Rates were $30 for twelve issues, $20 for students.

What was the circulation, I asked him.

"We mail out over 5,000 a month. Research libraries, think tanks, activist groups, churches. Every member of Congress and key staff people get courtesy copies. We also send copies to Peace Corps and foreign service people — anyone on the local working level in Latin America. People in a position to influence policy. Many Central American US Embassy personnel, for example. All media people who come through or who report regularly on the region get copies. We get a lot of names from regular subscribers. Overall, about half is paid circulation, half courtesy."

I told him I had seen bundles of *Mesoamerica* at Inforpress in Guatemala City. What was his connection with them? "We exchange issues. Sometimes we send out *Central America Report* and other publications that they distribute, ourselves. But Inforpress is primarily a sophisticated clipping service. They send us articles and commentary from all over Central America. This is a way to cross–check our own information. We tend to be very skeptical of anything phoned or sent in unsolicited. We like to double–check. Their sources are usually quite reliable."

The maître d' eyed our table impatiently so we adjourned through the breakfast queue to the lobby. Before we parted, Morris invited me to visit the institute the next day.

Morris' office was a substantial townhouse in the polished suburb of Santa Ana. Secretaries and "interns" bustled back and forth. Two word processors with color monitors were being used to prepare copy for the next issue of *Mesoamerica* and to expand a mailing list.

"Mr. Morris has stepped out for a few moments," the receptionist said. Perhaps I would like to have a cup of coffee and browse. She gestured toward a floor–to–ceiling stack of shelves housing more than a hundred tracts, brochures, broadsides and "digests."

Some of the anti–US / pro–Sandinista publications
distributed during the Nicaraguan conflict.

Their names evoked urgency, authority, even romance: *Honduras Update, Central America Report, Central American Bulletin, Newsletter of the Regional Center for Socio–Economic Research, Humanista, Envío.* I had seen them for months, individually and in reverential displays, in Peace Corps houses, small hotel lobbies, Sandinista bookstores, a reporter's satchel — but never all arranged in such disseminating orderliness.

"WAR IS PEACE — US Policy in Central America," said the March *Central America Report* over a *Life*–sized photo of a grim–faced GI cradling his rifle. Another number headlined: "ORDERS TO KILL — The Manufacture of Murderers." Inside was yet another exposé on US training of the Contras. *Informador Guerrillero*, with a logo portrait of Che Guevara, carried news of the Guatemalan insurgents and alleged atrocities there by government forces.

In a nearby corner were several stacks of current numbers of *Central America Bulletin, Central America Report* and *Mesoamerica* already collated for mailing. One box was addressed to The Honorable Christopher Dodd, US Senate Office Building, Washington, D.C. 20002.

"How long does it take a shipment like this to get to the States?" I asked the secretary.

"It depends. Three to ten days by regular mail. Those go up overnight by APO." As any traveler knows who's ever tried to avoid delays and theft by using this system, it is usually closed to outsiders. An employee who lets you use it risks loss of the privilege and a reprimand.

After half an hour, Morris walked in. He apologized for being late. "Some people think there are 10 days in a week," he sighed. The secretary poured me a fourth cup of coffee and Morris showed me to his office. It was spacious but not extravagant. Computer copy and news clippings cascaded from "In" and "Out" trays onto the floor. Layouts of the periodical's pages covered the desk. I did not feel that I was in the office of a roofing contractor. I said so.

"Well, I honestly must admit that the publication, the institute, takes most of my time these days," he replied.

Did he not find himself in a conflict of interest, being a journalist and at the same time an advocate for one side?

"Not in the least. I am quite capable of separating these two functions. News and opinion are easily distinguishable by a professional journalist. Besides, what I do on my own time is my business."

His network duties, he said, were of the "ear–to–the–ground and logistical variety," but he also covered stories himself, such as the trial that month of a libel suit by one Hull, an American farmer in northern Costa Rica, against two US journalists who had reported that he was a CIA operative. He had lost the case.

Morris' primary function seemed to be as access broker to the Sandinistas. And although he did not assign or oversee ABC reporters, his influence was substantial.

"I've carefully developed impeccable sources. That's not something you can do overnight; it takes years. It's based on mutual trust and respect, especially in Nicaragua, given the long history of mistrust and disrespect between Americans and Nicaraguans. So my network gets first shot at a helluva lot of quality stuff on the top foreign story of the time. They don't blow it by misreporting the facts and slander, if you know what I mean."

I asked him what he thought US policy toward the Sandinistas should be.

"We will have to accept them sooner or later, why not now? The Contras are sure as hell not going to overthrow them. Sandinismo is consolidated. The only way to undo it is to nuke them. You have to remember, 50 percent of the population is under 15. The average age is 17. All they have heard, seen now is the glory of the Sandinistas for seven years. Their total memory is one of Sandinista patriotism and triumph.

"And you don't think those hardscrabble Nicaraguan farmers support the revolution? Most of them now own their own tractors — at least their co–ops do. They may be Soviet–made, not the John Deeres they would prefer, but they're a hell of an improvement over hand and animal labor. And the land belongs to them.

"And the Sandinistas are responsive. Somoza never bothered to go out and meet the people. In Nicaragua every Thursday there's a televised meeting called 'Face–to–Face with the People.' The president and the cabinet sit down at a village or town meeting. Some guy asks where are the street lights you promised for five years and they have to have an answer."

Leaning back in his chair and crossing his arms, he summed up his feelings: "Look, what the hell difference does it make to the United States if cocoa, bananas, coffee are raised by communist peasants or capitalist peasants? The only way these countries will ever see progress is with a massive redistribution of the wealth, and that means the land. And like it or not, that can only come through socialist revolution. Marxism, if you will."

Two days later I drove from the hotel up to the national guard headquarters in Cartago. It was raining in the old mountain capital and the morning was cool. People puddled about under umbrellas.

The plaza was surrounded by guardsmen in military ponchos, rifles at the ready — an unusual display in a country that abjures even the suggestion of force. But no chance could be taken with their famous prisoner.

The greatest warrior of the Sandinistas was now their basest traitor: Eden Pastora, "Commander Zero." Having taken up arms against his former comrades four years before, he had suddenly renounced further fighting and asked for political asylum. Many Ticos argued against it, contending that for four years he had violated their country's neutrality with embarrassing impunity.

Pastora's daring capture of the national palace in the summer of 1978 had rescued the FSLN from malaise and given a jolt to the flagging revolt against Somoza. The following year, *El Cero*, alone of all the *comandantes*, saw sustained action. While the Ortega brothers and the rest were parading through Managua, Pastora was locked in combat with the last of Somoza's guard. When he finally arrived, days later, the tumult of his reception paled their own.

His confinement room was Spartan but comfortable. Two cots were separated by a beige Formica dresser with matching telephone. There was a card table and folding chairs. Hospital–green walls bore a poster profile of Christ, resolute, a photo calendar of the pope and Cardinal Obando y Bravo, and an altar miniature of family snapshots beneath a crucifix.

Pastora had a medium build — stocky, with the faintest suggestion of a paunch. He looked 10 years younger than his official 49. He was articulate, friendly, curious — but not loquacious. He could have easily passed for a successful fisherman who now owned his own guide service, an up–and–coming Rotarian fund–drive chairman or chamber of commerce president.

Delegations of exiles hoping to meet with Pastora came and went throughout the morning. They waited, sometimes for hours, at the sentry box. After being announced, they were made to stand in view of the window. If an audience was granted, they joined the queue. Some twenty were there by 10 a.m., when I arrived. It had been reported in *La Nación* that *El Cero* had been moved to Cartago after his surrender to Costa Rican authorities — as much for his own protection as for administrative convenience. A few of his former troops were still encamped along the San Juan river border with Nicaragua. He had urged them to follow his example.

The officer of the day, an old captain, would knock quietly and ask *mi Comandante* if so–and–so should be admitted. Pulling back a tattered drape, Pastora would study the applicant from the window and invariably say yes. Upon admission, one signed the duty log at the end of the hallway.

The phone rang. It was the guard desk with an updated list of calls. The rules required that calls not be put through but returned.

An orderly brought a tray of sandwiches and a pitcher of coffee.

"*¡Sí!*" Pastora nodded at the captain as he inspected yet another group. He shrugged his shoulders and smiled to indicate he didn't really know who they were or the purpose of their visit. He was obviously lifted by this unrelenting stream of supporters. He would see anyone, he said, who wanted to see him.

Such accessibility was part of the legend which exploded onto the world following the capture of the palace and the freeing of Sandinista prisoners held by Somoza. His improvised code name for that operation was *Comandante Cero* — Commander Zero. The moniker stuck like a badge of honor.

Much of his appeal was his disdain of ceremony, an endearing contrast to the airs and bombast of the other *comandantes*. Their orotundity had earned them and their followers the pejorative nickname *piricuacos* from Costa Ricans — after a kind of olive–plumed "mockingbird" which bobs, flutters and screeches about, making a nuisance of itself.

Fear of his popular appeal plus his "reformist" ideology — he was considered a mere social democrat, unable to comprehend or participate in class struggle — caused the other *comandantes* to ostracize him. He was given the figurehead job of deputy defense minister and denied appointment to the directorate.

Four petitioners, three men and a woman, business or professional people it seemed, were admitted and *El Cero* shook hands around. He gestured towards me: "*Un amigo norteamericano. Escritor.*" They smiled, guardedly. He offered them some of the food, which they declined, seating themselves at the table.

Was it true, they wanted to know, that he had quit the fight against the Sandinistas? No, he told them, only for the time being he will not continue military engagements.

It had been reported that the majority of his lieutenants and their men had disbanded or left for Honduras to join the Contras. He said this was because the CIA, whom he had spurned since his April 1982 pronouncement of defection, bribed them to do so.

But some said they left Pastora because he was all talk and no fight. He could not raise money independently of the Americans, they said. Yet he refused to cooperate with them. The result was no money, no supplies, not even medicine for the wounded.

Supplies, he admitted, had been drying up. Many of the men had to forage for food in the forests along the San Juan River. They were reported to have helped themselves to crops and animals on both sides of the border. There were complaints. The Costa Rican government had served notice that it would move to cut off all supplies if the marauding did not cease. Mostly, though, Pastora simply ran out of volunteers because the Contras had better gear, a larger presence, fed well and even paid their troops a modest stipend.

"But I am lucky. My best men are still with me. And the others will return when they see that the Contras cannot win."

Pastora did seem to lead a charmed life. In late May 1984 a bomb had exploded during a press conference at his jungle command post. He escaped with shrapnel wounds in both legs and minor facial burns. A total of seven people were killed. The evidence, including the nature of the device and its timing, pointed to the Sandinista secret police of Tomás Borge. Ironically, Pastora had not only liberated Borge during the 1978 palace seizure but twice rescued him in combat. The American press — several of whom were injured, one fatally — were reluctant to blame the Sandinistas.

"CIA scenarios" for the attack became a virtual obsession with TV network and PBS news bureaus over the next few years — some based upon the supposed presence at the scene of a phantom photographer traveling with a Danish passport. Pastora accepted that it was probably the Sandinistas but did not rule out other authors. Candidates included renegades from his own resistance faction, the Revolutionary Democratic Alliance. Its civilian leadership had just agreed, over *El Cero*'s objections, to link up with the Contras in Honduras.

"*¿Quién sabe? Tengo muchos enemigos.*" I have many enemies, he said when I ask who else it might have been.

Two former sergeants and an aide were admitted. The aide handed Pastora a typed statement which he had previously dictated and now read aloud. It was an explanation to his followers and to the exile community of why he had lain down arms and asked for asylum. The statement suggested that *El Cero* did not intend to go back to commercial fishing, his former occupation. It spoke of "the larger contest ahead," and held that while arms may be set aside temporarily, the cease fire was but a tactical respite: "We shall continue to organize our political forces."

"We want to pledge to you our continued support," one of the civilians responded when he had finished. They embraced him. Pastora asked that they give their current addresses to one of his sergeants. He picked up the phone and requested a half hour without interruption to complete our interview. He conferred briefly with the aide then lay back against some pillows on one of the cots. I sat on the other. One of the sergeants poured coffee but seeing that it was cold ordered some fresh from the orderly.

"Won't you lose any support you have left inside Nicaragua by quitting?" I asked him.

"Not at all. But I do not quit, as you say. We will continue the fight by other means — education and organization — inside the country and in other parts.

"Our support in Nicaragua remains strong. They are many, many thousands, and many more than have the FDN. They are in León, Estelí, Managua." He named a dozen or so other towns and villages where he claimed clandestine support. "It is not possible to count them all, they are so many."

Why had he turned down American aid? Did he not want all the help he could get?

"We did not reject all their help. In the beginning, in 1983, during early operations against the Sandinistas, the Americans helped us. But I would not be dictated to by the CIA. They wanted to give orders to us, just like they did to the *somocistas*. Nicaragua must have its own destiny. I fight for a truly *nacionalista* revolution — just like Sandino, himself, not a return to *somocismo*. The great majority of Nicaraguans want to assert our nationalism, not to be dominated by the Soviets or the Americans. We want to have good relations with both of them but we don't want either violating our national sovereignty. If the Contras come to power as the *cabrones* of the CIA, then they cannot call themselves true nationalists, true revolutionaries — just as the government in Managua cannot call themselves, in truth, 'Sandinistas' because they have become the *cabrones* of the Soviet Union and Cuba."

Still, he wanted it clear that his, too, was a socialist cause. "I am a socialist. I also believe in small businesses and private ownership — but by everyone, not just a few. I believe in democracy, a multiparty system. I could never be a communist any more than I could be a monopolist, a *somocista*. Sandino rejected both and so do I. So do most of my countrymen."

I knew that he had long claimed close ties to Sandino. He even revived the moribund "Sandino Revolutionary Front," displaying its banner during the announcement of his break with the Sandinistas in April 1982.

Which Latin American country did he think would be the next to have a "revolution" — or would there be another one at all?"

El próximo será México." Mexico would be the next, he replied.

"Mexico is a volcano — *una caldera*." He heaved his arms upward in mimed eruption.

"The people of Mexico have suffered in some ways more than other Latin Americans. They actually *had* their revolution but it was betrayed by the leaders. They took for themselves the land that belonged to the peasants. In fact, much of the land still belongs to the same families who owned it before the revolution. Mexicans who managed to escape poverty now see themselves destroyed by inflation. Man, the Mexicans know how to fight each other! If you think there is war in Nicaragua wait until you see what the Mexicans can do!"

Comandante Cero, Commander Zero, Eden Pastora.

He turned down the cigarette offered by the aide who stood to indicate that my time was up. Two young men, teenagers really, came into the room and embraced him. "My sons," he said after a long moment. We shook hands.

Pastora sought to close on a forceful note, gesturing rapidly: "I will continue this fight no matter what, because I am the only one who can unite the people. I do not have millions of dollars but I have the people. I'm not part of an international movement, I'm part of the people. The people know this. That is why I am the one they will follow."

The orderly, hoisting a tray of steaming chicken, rice and beans entered as I left. From the corporal of the guard I learned that *El Cero* had signed autographs for the entire detachment.

"*Es un gran hombre,*" he said. "*Es el Liberador de Nicaragua.*" A great man; the liberator of his country.[56]

Outside, the town was sheeted with rain whipped in the cross currents of an uncertain wind.

A drift log being washed ashore at Playa Manuel Antonio National Park, Costa Rica.

15

COLÓN

I could not fend off the four of them, especially if
they were armed. It was a dark moment, indeed.

After the rambunctious congeniality of Costa Rica, the
militarismo of Panama was chilling. Suddenly there were grim men
with automatic weapons, a bristling closeness of guns and oil and
leather. Before every bank and public building and inside hundreds of
tawdry casinos that swilled pensions and wages, the men with the
guns stood.

The nation's walls groaned with the inscrutably smiling,
acne–scarred face of General Manuel Antonio Noriega Morena —
commander of the guns, dictator, successor to General Omar Torrijos
Herrera, who, in 1977, delivered the Panama Canal to the national
patrimony from the timorous clutches of the Carter administration,
then died mysteriously in a plane crash.

Sometimes there was also a portrait of the country's president,
Eric Arturo Delvalle. It was displayed hesitantly, not with fervor, not
in a position of primacy or honor or of any particular status whatever
— to one side, as if hung there upon some sly afterthought; an official
photograph has been received, and it must be put up, and so this
placement — an implicit recognition of the subject's titular status, a
mere caricature of the Caesar to whose smile he aspired.

It was said among the people in David and on the beach at
Río Mar and in Colón and in the capital that Noriega was a smuggler
of arms and of drugs, a looter, a skimmer, a briber and a taker of
bribes, a thief — and a supervisor of others who smuggled, looted,
skimmed, bribed, and stole; and that he was a murderer who had
killed, himself, and who commanded others to kill.

But it depended upon with whom one talked as to whether these
things were said with a smirk or with a weary shaking of the head
and a glance over the shoulder. For the men with the guns, and for
the poor of the barrios of San Miguelito, it was the former; for
teachers, shop keepers, constitutional lawyers and persons of the
cloth, it was the latter.

The strongman had, through years of careful organization and
demagoguery, built an ironclad political machine. Its base was the
country's forgotten majority of dispossessed, from whom he had risen.
Its muscle was the army and police, over which he asserted absolute
control. The lifeblood of the apparatus flowed from Panamanian
banks, among the world's richest and least regulated. Not only

commercial and shipping receipts, but deposits from foreign investors and multinational corporations seeking high interest and havens from taxes and scrutiny at home.

The largest depositors by far were the Colombian cocaine cartels who used Panama's banks to launder billions in currency. Kickbacks and rake–offs from these operations as well as bribes paid directly into his accounts, here and in Switzerland, gave Noriega personal control over an almost bottomless cash till.

This, plus the ruthlessness with which he responded to the slightest public criticism, enabled him to become entrenched as one of the region's most feared tyrants. For those who supported him — from his personal detachments of barrio thugs, "dignity battalions," to members of the rubber–stamp congress and the puppet president, Delvalle — there was job security.

Noriega conducted a duplicitous foreign policy, clandestinely aiding both Contras and Sandinistas in the Nicaraguan civil war and funneling Cuban arms to insurgents in South America. Simultaneously, he relayed selective information on these goings–on to the CIA and hosted that agency's training and staging operations. In addition to its banks, the drug lords had free run of Panama's airports for refueling, product storage and arms shipments.

United States intelligence, both military and CIA, had by mid–1986 become aware of Noriega's duplicity. No effort was made to impede him either for fear of losing a source of intelligence, instigating a crisis over the canal or stirring anti–American sentiment in yet another volatile country.

Perhaps the full extent of Noriega's involvement remained unknown to top Reagan administration officials. For whatever reason Washington remained satisfied, even enthusiastic. Military officials continued to liaison with him and he was courted by a steady stream of dignitaries, from assistant secretaries of state to the then vice president, George Bush.

Federal prosecutors were not so amenable. Within 20 months, Noriega would be indicted by Florida grand juries on drug conspiracy charges. In December 1989 he was deposed and captured in a massive US military intervention. But at the time of my visit he was firmly in power.

Panama has bridged the history of the Americas for twice as long as the United States has been a nation. When, in 1531, the Spaniards faced the challenge of Peru — finding the "mysterious empire," conquering it and carrying home its gold — they had to heave their armor, cannon, powder, iron tools, saddlery and provisions across the malarial isthmus of Panama, construct new ships, then sail south into unfathomed waters.

Policeman, La Chorrera, Panama.

Later, the stolen treasures of the Incas were laboriously unloaded, packed over the "Trail of the Crosses" to Portobelo on the Caribbean and hoisted aboard yet other vessels for the annual *flota* via Havana to Seville.

As early as 1534, King Charles I of Spain had commanded a survey for a canal in hopes of cutting his losses of men, treasure and shipping time. Yet 318 years later, overland transit remained a nightmare. Witness, this young US Army captain en route to California with a party of gold rushers:

> [T]he rain would pour down in streams, followed in not many minutes by a blazing, tropical summer's sun. These alternative changes, from rain to sunshine, were continuous in the afternoons. I wondered how any person could live many months in [Panama].

> I, as regimental quartermaster, had charge of [the] transportation. The unusual number of passengers [and] the large amount of freight ... created an unprecedented demand for mules. Some of the passengers paid as high as 40 dollars for the use of a mule to ride 25 miles, when [it] would not [otherwise] have sold for ten.

> Meanwhile, the cholera had broken out, and men were dying every hour. About one–third of the people with me died [and] one–seventh of those who left New York ... now lie buried on the Isthmus of Panama.

> — Ulysses S. Grant[57]

Cape Horn was not rounded until 1616 — by the Dutch explorer Willem Schouten. And although Magellan discovered in 1521 the strait in Tierra del Fuego that bears his name, that passage was unfamiliar to the conquistadors, for whom the long intervening Pacific coastline remained an enigma:

> The Spanish mariner groped his way along these unknown coasts, landing at every convenient headland, as if fearful lest some fruitful region or precious mine might be overlooked should a single break occur in the line of survey. Yet, it should be remembered that, while the true point of Pizarro's destination is obvious to us, familiar with the topography of these countries, he was wandering in

the dark, feeling his way along inch by inch ...
without chart[s] to guide him, without knowledge of
the seas or of the bearings of the coast, and even with
no better defined idea of the object at which he aimed
than that of a land, teeming with gold, that lay
somewhere [to] the south.

— William H. Prescott[58]

Even in later times, both southern routes took far longer than
isthmian portage and the horn was fraught with hellish winds, ice
and towering seas. Thus, early on, it was necessary to maintain fleets
in both the Caribbean and the Pacific, making Spain's the first
two—ocean navy. Until the 18th century, most Pacific vessels were
caravels fitted out by the conquistadors — Balboa set the first keel,
their privateer successors, and merchant syndicates. The syndicates
financed the Panama–Lima trade and after 1565 the transpacific
route of the Manila galleons.

Panama became a separate colony with Portobelo its capital.
During the next two centuries the town was the trading hub of the
Caribbean. Merchants of Madrid's most aggressive competitors,
Britain and Holland, were for long periods excluded — though not
goods plundered from them.

The feuding this engendered eventually triggered the War of
Jenkins' Ear, cut from his head, he told Parliament, by a Spanish
boarding party. The result was the sack of Portobelo by the British
navy in 1739. Soon afterward the Powers adopted an open—trading
policy. Portobelo was reduced to a minor dependency of Bogota,
joining that nation when it declared independence in 1822.

Relations were never harmonious with the central government.
Open rebellion flared in 1903 when the Colombian senate rejected a
canal proposal submitted by US President Theodore Roosevelt. On
November 3rd of that year, with Roosevelt as midwife, the province
seceded to become the Republic of Panama.

Within days, the United States concluded an even more
favorable pact. Among its provisions were grants to Washington of
exclusive bases and the right to intervene militarily to restore order,
which it did repeatedly over the next 40 years.

Work on a canal had first begun in 1880 by a French company
headed by Dr. Ferdinand de Lesseps, who had built the Suez Canal.
Panama was to be his crowning glory. A cartoon of a colossal
de Lesseps bestriding the isthmus was a fin de siècle metaphor of
French grandeur.

His mistake was insisting on a sea—level trench like the one he
had dug in Egypt. The mountain passes were too high and the granite

251

too hard. Dysentery, cholera and malaria decimated his work force. More than half of the Frenchmen who came to Panama died there.

By 1889 the company was bankrupt. Reorganized, it struggled along until the United States bought it out in 1899 for $40 million. Interestingly, the Americans used a lock–and–dam plan rejected twenty years earlier by de Lesseps. The US Army Corps of Engineers directed the project and the US government backed the entire cost. The anopheles mosquito, found by American physicians in Cuba to be malaria's infectious agent, was eradicated.

These advantages plus superior planning enabled the United States to complete the largest single engineering feat in history up to that time. The canal opened for business on August 15, 1914.

At 29,762 square miles, today's Panama is slightly larger than West Virginia. The shortest direct air distance from north to south, Caribbean to Pacific, is 30 miles. The canal, which meanders slightly, is 51 miles long.

Fresh water is used to lift ships through with 50 million gallons flushed out to sea each time a ship transits. But the water level of the Gatun drainage area, which supplies the canal, is falling steadily, a cause not of canal traffic but of the destruction of the isthmus watershed by slash–and–burn agriculture.

Panama was once covered by one of the world's largest rain forests. The only virgin stands that remain today are in Bocas del Toro province on the Caribbean and in still relatively unsettled Darién to the East. The central forest contiguous to the canal has shrunk to a preserve some six miles square north of Balboa.

An ambitious reforestation project, begun by the US Agency for International Development, made some progress until the mid–1980s, but recently it has suffered losses of acreage due to fire and encroachment. Its long–term success is doubtful.

The results of several years of interim Panamanian control of the canal were evident.

Buildings, docks, warehouses, roads, streets, postal services and, most conspicuously, the Panama Railroad — renamed *El Ferrocarril de Panamá* — were dilapidated. Streets were poorly maintained, with potholes and washouts common; warehouses, their windows and doors broken, were at the mercy of thieves; the old Canal Zone Yacht Club, rather a sanctuary for passing sailors and homesick GIs than a watering hole for the rich, was decaying; post offices were overstaffed and inefficient — fifteen employees sat defiantly idle behind the windows at the small central office in Balboa. Three harried clerks waited on long lines of patrons.

Beer ad, La Chorrera, Panama.

But the concern most often expressed by US workers and military personnel was that the Panamanians would simply be unable to keep machinery on–line and the channel from silting up. Indeed, the Panamanian government was negotiating with a Japanese consortium to operate the facility after the year 2000, with channel–widening and/or construction of a new sea–level ditch a part of the deal.

The canal has lost the military significance it held in a bygone age. And even its value to trade has greatly diminished, with faster, cheaper rail and interstate highway competition in the United States.

Yet for a great many traders it is still important, if not crucial. In 1984, for example, *163 million tons*[59] of freight moved through efficiently with an average of less than thirty hours for each ship to travel from deep water to deep water — 39 percent of it between the US East Coast and Asia.[60]

And total tonnage is again increasing as larger ships, many of them standard "Panamax" hulls, go into use. Panamax vessels are built just under the canal's dimensions. At 106 feet in the beam, 950 feet from bow to stern, and with a draft of 39.5 feet, they will carry half of all freight by the year 2000, according to officials.

In a typical year, fewer than 30 naval vessels transit. But perhaps low military usage during peacetime is a poor indicator of strategic value.

"When the bridges on the Mississippi from St. Paul to New Orleans are destroyed and our railroads and interstates mangled and cratered, that's when we'll need the canal. We won't need it until we *have* to have it and then it'll be too late, pardner. Then we can all say, 'Thanks a lot, Jimmy Carter!'"

The speaker was a retired US Army Corps of Engineers colonel, called "Colonel Sam" by the others. As he concluded, there were mock groans of alarm.

"But Colonel Sam if things ever came to that you don't really think the Russians, or whoever, would just leave this ditch running, do you? Why, they'd bomb it shut too." The skeptic was an Air Force major, Willard, a B–52 veteran over Vietnam.

"Bombing the canal would be a piece of cake," he said. "One good hit in the right place and you'd have to resurrect Teddy Roosevelt to get it going again."

"But you're talking nuclear," Tom, an ex–canal supervisor, said. "If things stayed conventional we could defend it and funnel troops and gear through pretty damned quick."

Painted bus, Panama City.

"Conventional? Where the hell would they be coming from, Colombia?" Willard retorted. "Besides, you wouldn't need an A–bomb to knock this thing out. A few thousand–pounders in the right place would cave in enough silt to close it for the duration. Knock out the gates and control sheds. Especially if you planned on using it later yourself, you sure as hell wouldn't want to destroy it."

This high–level strategy session took place at dusk one night in the old yacht club bar overlooking the Pacific entrance to the canal. The channel was lightly congested with backed–up freighters and a cruise liner hung with a city of lights. About every 40 minutes or so a ship, just lifted through from the Caribbean, would steam under the Balboa bridge and one of the backups would head inland. Club slips held several score of motor launches, most of them belonging to Panamanian big shots, and a half dozen yachts, several of the latter in transit. Of the sixty patrons of the bar there that night, nine were gringos, the rest but four, Panamanians, civilians it seemed with little or no connection to the canal. The four were British yachtsmen delivering a sleek ketch from Australia to Liverpool. It was tied at the end of the main pier. The Brits chided the colonel for his "jingo" pronouncements and laughed at the strategic importance he attached to the canal.

"Best you bloody Yanks be out of here. Leave the bloody canal to the Panamanians. The Age of Imperialism is past, don't you think? Come to think of it, you had best be getting home from Nicaragua too."

An American presence in the isthmus seemed assured for some time to come, whatever the deployment of the US Southern Command when its lease on the Zone runs out in 1999. Despite its troubles, Panama is such an appealing place to live that many US servicemen and civil servants come back here to live after they retire.

The Brits were friendly in the end and they and the colonel bought each other rounds.

If the canal is a world crossroads, the overland route into South America is still a maze of jungle trails. Even when Panama was a province of Colombia, intrastate commerce was always coastal. The reason is the formidable Darién whose forests and mountains are a major expeditionary event in themselves. Overlanders lacking the tackle and time required to do this, must ship to either Buenaventura in Colombia or Guayaquil in Ecuador.

When I inquired of forwarders and agents, the earliest ship to Buenaventura was a month away but the SS *Ruth Lykes* would leave for Guayaquil Monday. So at the conclusion of the sixth month of my journey I booked the jeep on the *Lykes* and myself on a plane to Quito.

256

Lime and tomato vendor, La Chorrera, Panama.

Quito was high and cool and resplendent in its history and architecture. Unlike the sweltering isthmus, through which the greater plunderers and their bishops sped posthaste, colonial Ecuador had known power and culture. The conquerors turned this northern capital of the Inca into a Hispanic citadel of commerce, learning and art rivaled only by Lima to the south.

Climbing through Quito one swirls into this glorious past — though always escorted by the ubiquitous horseman of poverty.

An old woman, a barrel strapped to her back, bore up a hill, stopping at garbage bins and trash piles. I followed, watching. Deftly, she collected an odd shoe, pop bottles, a bolt, a strand of wire. The street led to an *avenida* in which a tire had been set ablaze by protesting students. The demonstrators, one carrying a Che Guevara poster, were chanting in front of a university building for the release of some detained comrades. Police, supported by two mobile water cannon, stampeded them in our direction. The old woman made no move to avoid them. I hung in her lee. At the top of the street she stopped to pick through the rubble. The police regrouped and merchants unshuttered shops. One of them smothered the tire with a bucketful of crumpled plaster. As I overtook her, the woman retrieved a pair of sunglasses, the fancy reflector kind favored by teenagers and detectives. She started to flip them into the barrel, thought better of it, and lifted them to her face. It was then that I saw that she was a girl.

American tour groups en route to the Galápagos Islands thronged Quito's air terminal. Twenty thousand people a year now visit the archipelago, about 800 miles out to sea. There, the young Charles Darwin collected many of the bird and other specimen that later provided evidence for his theory of natural selection. At the time, however, he was principally concerned with describing the islands' geology which, considering he was only there three weeks, he did remarkably well.

I had gone out for two weeks myself once, back in 1970. I met an American expatriate who ran a sort of hardware store, a makeshift dispensary of whatever tools and sundries he could scrounge from occasional ships and from salvage shops in Guayaquil. I rode with him up to his "farm," four mule–hours through giant cactus, some thirty feet high, to the crest of a long–extinct volcano. Scrawny chickens pecked out a living among fallen fruit in a sparse orchard and potato patch. For a week, I followed the trammeled swaths of the giant tortoises that inhabit the place.

Whalers and privateers had taken the reptiles live as a supply of fresh meat, eventually extinguishing three of their 15 species altogether.

Garbage scavenger, Quito, Ecuador.

The islands were now a national preserve. According to researchers I met in Guayaquil, the government restricted the number of tourists to the capacity of several licensed cruise ships and small hotels. Fragile areas such as the turtle beaches were off–limits. Once a favorite layover for cruising yachts, stops were now limited to 72 hours in the Academy Bay anchorage at Santa Cruz Island. A few thoughtless sailors had despoiled the precincts and stole rare species from unprotected shores.

Clearing the jeep from the Port of Guayaquil required an exercise in patience, perseverance and posturing which would dissuade any who have survived the ordeal from doing so ever again without the services of a freight expediter.

At the beginning, no official would sign or stamp a required document — there were 24 separate pieces of paper! — before his counterpart in another department had done so.

These were not in the same building but spread throughout the complex of docks and warehouses. Some would be out to lunch, on break or simply absent for no apparent reason. Others had shut themselves up against the mobs of agents and hustlers and some few hapless owners, like me, who shoved and shouted at their doors. At length a kindly old customs captain took pity on me and wrote out the precise steps to be followed. He then signed and stamped a manifest which permitted subalterns to proceed. Still there were desperate moments, including a mile–long sprint to garner the last stamp before quitting time.

Guayaquil was unexpectedly cool and dry. I had remembered it as a sweltering place but that had been in March. This was June. The semifinals of the world soccer championship erupted from every television screen in town. Even the humblest vendor had his own or a shared color set to watch. The chief sponsors were, as in Mexico, cigarette and beer manufacturers and the local *banco*. The commercials for the bank had an excited fellow shouting simply *"El Banco es el Banco es el Banco."* The cigarette brands had local names but were all made under Stateside license — R.J. Reynolds, Liggett, the rest. The same commercial I had seen in Mexico with the dozen or so girls cavorting on the beach who surround two bronzed guys and everybody lights up was shown repeatedly.

I crossed the wide confluence of the Guayas and Daule Rivers above the Gulf of Guayaquil and entered Peru's great northern desert at Tumbes. The road followed the ancient highway of the Incas. This was Pizarro's conquest route of 1532.

Beer drinker, Trujillo, northern Peru.

One evening in those limitless spaces, I camped on a flat above a lift of dunes — out of sight of the highway I thought. I set two tasty redfish smoking on the grill. These had been bought that afternoon from a fisherman I watched ride in with the tide on a tiny balsa raft.

Such fishing, a technique used for thousands of years, requires expert seamanship. Rather more like surfboards than canoes, these craft are sailed well beyond sight of land. Yet the fisherman can return to the same place on a coastline with virtually no feature by which to navigate.

I wondered how far out one of them had gone and still returned. I saw some boats that were much larger, made of two or three dugouts lashed together and with canopies. Might Thor Heyerdahl have been right? Might not some of these fishermen's ancestors have sailed — or been swept — to the Pacific islands? Or back to Asia, itself?

Such was my reverie when returning from an after–dinner walk I saw a truck pull over and douse its lights. Four figures got out and headed up the slope toward my fire which I now realized was reflected by a rock outcrop. They paused occasionally as if searching for tracks, then resumed their ascent. I could not fend off the four of them, especially if they were armed. It was a dark moment, indeed.

On occasions like this, thankfully rare but harrowing when they came, I remembered the trusty government .45 I had packed as a circuit–riding Marine lawyer in Vietnam. Though I'd fired it only twice — without prejudice — having it handy eased the mind. But I had decided long ago, on the 1970 jaunt through this hemisphere and, subsequently, in Africa, that the hassles with police and customs agents outweighed the advantage. You never know you need it until they have the drop on you, anyway, I reasoned. And I had managed to talk my way out of every scrape thus far.

This looked like the exception; or maybe these guys were merely curious, just out to see who was up here. Strike up a conversation. Ask a favor. Maybe they'd had engine trouble and needed a hand.

Not likely, any of these. Nobody goes off on social calls in the middle of the desert, least of all at night. And Peruvians are among the world's best baling–wire mechanics. In any event someone could be flagged down. Traffic was light but steady. No, these guys were up to no good.

When they were almost to my camp an odd thing happened that abruptly ended the episode and prevented me from ever knowing the purpose of their visit.

Twin boys, near Tumbes, northern Peru.

A van, followed by two large *camiones*, approached slowly from the south and stopped facing my visitors' truck. A figure alighted, signaled back to the others, and soon an impressive contingent was marching toward the truck whose horn bleated with alarm. Its headlamps flashed furiously.

"Maricones. Hijos de Puta ..." Shouted one of the climbers in the first words I had heard them speak.

"Vámonos," cried another.

They scrambled back down the dune, stumbling and rolling comically in their haste. The truck started and drove away, bathing the latecomers in its lights, but they made no effort to stop it. When it had gone, they returned to their own vehicles and drove away. Although my foursome had had time to accost their visitors, they emerged only after the highway was empty. Within half an hour, their truck cautiously returned, collected them, and resumed its journey.

I waited until they had gone, stowed my gear unceremoniously, and skedaddled. I found a new site many miles distant. Sleep was fitful.

Late the next afternoon I made Sullana where I checked into the rather upscale Hotel la Siesta. In the lobby after dinner I was handed a business card, "NorPeru Expeditions," by a young man who said he was a guide and taxidermist for the outfitter. He urged that I should go into the nearby mountains with them to hunt the spectacled bear. The hotel manager, he said, had just returned from one of their expeditions and his party had bagged a big one. I thanked him but it was not a time for killing the spectacled bear.

Author and jeep in the north Peruvian desert, near Sullana.

16

MIRAFLORES

*One could have been in London's Knightsbridge
or Paris' Fauberg St. Honoré, so full of fashion
and folly were the shops.*

The *Malecón Cisneros* weaves along the ocean promontory of
Miraflores, Lima's palisade of privilege. Narrow patches of brown
grass occasionally interpose themselves between the one–way
thoroughfare and the precipice. To the east are the mansions and
townhouses of Peru's extracted wealth and its more favored retainers,
foreign executives and diplomats. The southern winter's fog cloaks
the beach in its pall, closing visibility at times to within a few
hundred feet and yielding only grudgingly to the forlorn strobes of *El
Faro de Miraflores*.

Alan Davis had the penthouse condominium of a thin
nine–story, red–brick highrise just south and across from the
lighthouse park. There nannies strolled toddlers and soccer balls were
kicked about by screaming secondary scholars and junior bankers.
Tolerated intruders into this rosy–cheeked sanctuary were cart
peddlers of tomatoes, oranges, tangerines, melons and papayas. A
knife sharpener touted his whetstone. Their cadenced trills brought
fists to windows and activated elevators. María, the maid, would hear
them and rap the double–paned glass with her coarse knuckles,
snatch her shopping basket and stand at the steel door.

Access to the redoubt was by elevator alone, the fire escape's
stairwell being barred below and the exit to it from the apartment
triple–bolted and shackled. The lift was a heavy, creeping car, some
five feet square and six high, operated by two keys employed
simultaneously; a third gained entry to the building. Precise
combination turns of the first permitted rapid access to the flat.
Hesitation was hazardous: The doors yawned, then snapped like
industrial pincers.

There was a sanctity about the keys. It was decided that only
two sets would be kept — one for Alan and one for the handsome
young live–in maid, who considered herself *"Una hija del campo"* — a
child of the country. That is, she disdained the sophistry of Lima, to
which she and a quarter of Peru's daughters had migrated, she from
Cajamarca, during the past 20 years in search of jobs and fulfillment.
They had swollen the city's numbers to 7 million, a third of the
country's population.

Except for the few lucky ones such as herself, they had found instead disappointment. María had already worked for a succession of wealthy families and diplomats when the Agency for International Development personnel office hired her as Alan's maid. Her monthly salary was 1,200 *intis*, just over a hundred dollars. In addition she received lodging, a narrow room behind the kitchen, and meals. She had weekends off to visit relatives and two afternoons to attend a sewing class for which Alan paid the tuition.

"I would get you copies made, but it's not a good idea to have an extra set lying around. Besides, I don't have time and I'd rather she didn't learn how to do that."

So I would check with María and try to harmonize my returns with her probable presence. There were few misses and I was not terribly inconvenienced. At night and on weekends I kept the keys. But Alan was ever insistent on knowing where they were and so one of us was always asking: *"Tienes las llaves?"* — and the other would laugh and produce the keys. One could not be too careful. There were rumors of loyal servants compromised by petulance, poverty and fear: Terrorists had cold ways of reaching into the dwellings of their victims. Extreme caution was but simple prudence.

Unannounced visitors were suspect. No one; not even other Americans known to visit regularly; not even Barry Row, the hearty gym trainer and his gregarious Venezuelan wife, Olga; not even mission staff; was to be admitted without advance clearance from Alan. This could be obtained by calling his office but telephone service in Lima was not always dependable. And his duties as assistant director for food distribution frequently took him out of town, where it was worse.

The name of an expected repairman or guest would sometimes be left on a pad. Yet the phone would ring, and a voice would say there was an urgent delivery, an unscheduled inspection; or say nothing but you knew someone was there. Perhaps there was a wrong number; perhaps the connection was faulty.

From the intercom on the porch other voices would call up. María was obedient and refused to push the buttons which would open the door, bring the elevator, open the door. She once even excluded Monique, Alan's aristocratic Peruvian fiancée, and a friend who popped by to look at his collection of modern art. Later it was decided that Monique, alone, could come up but she was not given the keys.

Alan varied his 10–mile commute to the AID office on the Avenida de España, two blocks from the Embassy and across from the ominous reflective–glass tower of PIP, the Peruvian Secret Police.

Some mornings he drove to work and parked in a "bombproof" lot reliably attended more or less, around the corner. Otherwise, he was called for by an Embassy chauffeur at 7:30, although the time could shift within a half hour either side. The schedule was arranged the night before, with alterations and delays signaled via the emergency CB radios kept by all mission staff.

The conveyance was likewise changed daily. At times it would be a white Datsun pickup, at others a car–pool van or a station wagon. And, of course, the route was staggered — sometimes wending for miles out of the way.

On days when he was fetched, Alan would stand at the window with his coffee and cigarette, scanning the Malecón for the aberrant and descending only when the vehicle pulled to the curb. The same watchfulness was observed when he drove to the Miraflores bowling alley for diplomatic league play each Tuesday night, or to the condo of Bill Johnson, the Embassy cryptologist, who hosted a Thursday poker game in a neighboring battlement more elegantly appointed and impenetrable than his own.

By such precautions my friend adhered not merely to official procedure but to the adamant custom of the enclave. He balked at toting his revolver, kept loaded at bedside, or accepting a bodyguard. In these and many other little ways, Miraflores cleft its inhabitants from Peru as irrevocably as the Pacific sundered them from China.

But for me Alan's flat, in its luxury, provided a much needed respite from the fatigue of driving and the nuisance of my own incessant vigilance against pilferage. Its cleanliness and order were a reprieve from the dirt and disarray of life on the road.

This was not the first time my host had extended me the courtesy of shelter in a foreign land.

In 1977, I arrived unexpectedly in a Sahara sandstorm driving the very same jeep. He was in his second year as a Peace Corps teacher of English and, practically speaking, the United States consul in Tânout, an oasis in Niger. The place was ruled by an ailing chief's regent–son, with whom he had become fast friends. The son treated Alan's enclosure as an adjunct chancery and conducted there much of the town's official business. Disputes over goats, water rights and market locations were adjudicated as Alan looked on inscrutably. I tarried at Tânout for nearly a week, sharing his raj before resuming my trek across Africa.

An accumulation of artifacts from those days and subsequent years of foreign service decorated the apartment: Fulani masks, Masai spears, Incan pottery. The view seaward was relaxing in spite of the fog, which, when it receded, revealed an expanse of uninterrupted beach. There was a bountiful library, including several recent archeological texts with photographs.

I spent lots of time browsing with my feet propped up, concentrating at length on a battered paperback edition of William H.

Prescott's classic, *History of the Conquest of Peru*, and John Heming's *Conquest of the Incas*.

Mornings I walked three blocks to a kiosk for *El Comercio*, the *Le Monde* of South American papers and a relief from the forests of sleazy tabloids that vied for the most gruesome photographs of murder and accident victims. My reading was supplemented with long visits to Lima's stupendous cathedrals, colonial buildings and museums, particularly the *Museo Nacional de Antropología y Arqueología* in Pueblo Libre.

Alan assigned me the guest room; the jeep was looked after by the building's custodian, Señor Antonio Velázquez and his family of eight. They occupied a one–room servant's quarters that opened onto a small plaza. There was a garage with room for one vehicle where the rig found a temporary home.

The Velázquezes were friendly, diligent. The señora patched garments and the eldest son, Julio, ran errands. He and his brothers also helped Antonio watch the building. One of them would remain near the entrance until curfew, deferentially admitting tenants but stopping others. It was a tedious business but one never knew when "they" might come. Just who they were was vague, uncertain. Yet they were always on one's mind in Lima — if unspoken. The most feared, without doubt, were the *Sendero Luminoso*, self–styled Maoist guerrillas whose atrocities included mutilation and beheading. The *Movimiento Nacional Tupac Amaru* was another they, but less feared. An urban–based guerrilla group that officially eschewed random butchery, it pulled bloody heists that left hundreds of orphans.

Neither contained many of the Indian peasants who make up half of Peru's population and the great majority of its chronically dispossessed. *Sendero* propaganda, nevertheless, claimed an aboriginal nativity at the *Universidad Nacional de San Cristóbal de Huamanga* in Ayacucho, the official center for the study of Indian history and culture. By 1970 *Senderista* professors and their student disciples had co–opted the school's faculty and politics, dictating tenure and curriculum in what became a dialectical Babel.

American and European leftists flocked to this new Marxist mecca. *Quechua*, the principal Indian dialect, became the *lingua franca* for all instruction and "dialogue." Emphasis was upon a "return to the land" to organize and there was open recruitment of "village cadre." Fighting off both revisionist and conservative foes, the *Senderistas* maintained this revolutionary preserve until suddenly, in 1978, they went underground.

Moche ceremonial figure,
National Museum of Anthropology and Archeology, Pueblo Libre, Lima.

Abimael Guzman Reynosa, a/k/a "Comrade Gonzalo," an ex–professor of philosophy who referred to himself as the "Mao of Latin America" and "The Fourth Sword of Communism," was supreme leader, a tyrant who resembled in practice the Cambodian butcher Pol Pot.

Sendero began its campaign of violence in 1980 with firebombings to disrupt Peru's first elections in twelve years. Although the effort failed it began a pattern of terror against peasant leaders — principally mayors, magistrates and election officials.

Most victims were Indians, thus the spectacle of middle class revolutionaries executing the leaders of the very people for whom the revolution was supposedly fought. Some victims were literally carved alive in front of their families. Others — young soldiers, horticulturists, power linemen, veterinarians, surveyors and engineers — were summarily shot.

Senderista assassins masqueraded as electricians, florists, plumbers and even priests.

A senior admiral was gunned down in Callao by young terrorists in parochial garb, two of them women. Many *Senderistas* were barely adolescents, children being preferred recruits because they were more easily indoctrinated and less susceptible to police infiltration.

Tourists had been immune from *Sendero* attacks but the week before I arrived a bomb exploded on the Machu Picchu train, killing seven. Reprisal, *Sendero* said, for the massacre of more than 300 of its partisans in prison riots at El Sexto, Lurigancho and the island fortress, El Frontón. The ostensible reason for the assaults was to save employee–hostages but earlier rebellions had been resolved peacefully and fewer hostages were held than before. Most of those prisoners killed were shot in the back as they lay prone after surrendering.

The massacre had provoked an outrage, even among conservatives. Some opponents of President García claimed that the threat of a coup forced him to give in to military demands that the "Communist vermin be exterminated." Others said that he, himself, simply seized the *raison d'être* presented by the situation to liquidate them.

Even in confinement, the rebels had maintained discipline, barricading their cellblocks into "autonomous republics," displaying Marxist paraphernalia, chanting slogans and keeping to a rigid schedule of "revolutionary instruction." Prison guards were baited with threats and insults. It was not surprising that the order to quell the disturbances was ruthlessly obeyed.

272

Pre–Incan trophy head from northern Peru,
National Museum of Anthropology and Archeology, Pueblo Libre, Lima.

García's hand was forced, in the view of many. The riots
coincided with the first meeting in Lima of the Socialist International.
A show of strength was thought required to save face in front of so
many foreign guests. Some said that this was precisely the outcome
intended by the *Sendero* high command, who thereby compelled
García to create fresh martyrs for their cause.

In spite of a sometimes vicious rivalry between them — *Sendero*
disrupted *Tupac Amaru* demonstrations and *Tupac Amaru* reputedly
detained *Senderistas* — they shared some of the same suppliers.
Weapons captured from each were traced to caches shipped to the
M–19 Colombian guerrillas via Nicaragua. Rifles of North Korean
manufacture were found on *Senderistas* but North Korea was among
the government's own vendors. Those weapons presumably were
stolen or taken in combat. A Bulgarian freighter tried to unload
Soviet weapons at a remote desert beach in July 1986. Thwarted, the
ship raced back to Panama where it and its cargo were seized by

General Noriega. Mysteriously, they were later released. Its consignees were never identified.

International alignment of both groups was conjectural. Although Maoist, the *Senderistas* ridiculed current Chinese leadership as revisionist and bombed their embassy. They castigated the Soviet Union for not doing enough to help "struggling peoples." *Tupac Amaru* insisted on its own independence. What was certain was that there was enough injustice and oppression in Peru to motivate revolutionaries of every stripe — left, right and all shades in between — without outside agitation.

Armed attacks by *Sendero* had been concentrated in the remoter regions of Huancavelica, Ayacucho, Apurímac and Cuzco. They did occasionally manage to blow up power lines in the desert north of Lima, causing the city's monotonous *apagones* — power outages.

Now there was a sudden, concerted "move to the city." Recruitment and assassination in Lima accelerated. Police and premises guardsmen were primary targets. The guardsmen were so cautious as to carry their pistols cocked in–hand, whether the place guarded was a bank, pastry shop, theater or automobile dealership. Once when I pulled over to ask directions at a bank, two of the guards dropped to their knees, rifles at the ready, while a third held his pistol on me with both quaking hands. They did not relax until I had driven away.

Each morning's papers reported at least a half dozen ambush–murders, some accompanied by a robbery or kidnapping, others by a note pinned to the victim's chest proclaiming "Death in the name of the people to those who serve their oppressors."

Such incidents became so frequent and brazen that the government, fearing a putsch, had imposed a curfew from one to five a.m. There were no exceptions. Police escorts were required for emergencies. Enforcement was severe: summary detention and a heavy fine — not to mention the risk of being shot by nervous troopers. These impositions on the capital's Epicurean social life resulted in demands for its abatement and that was ordered at year's end.

One Calvo, a fiftyish Peruvian entrepreneur, athletic uniforms, reported that he had been the victim of an attempted abduction. He gave his account one night after dinner at Olga and Barry Row's.

"I was getting in my car to go to work and this jogger sticks a pistol through the window and orders me to open the door." Calvo complied but "grabbed him in a hammer lock and dragged him to the ground. His pal tried to shoot me but I kept the first one between us. When he got close I knocked the gun out of his hand and took off up the street." The assailants stole the car and later shot and killed

Calvo's nephew who overtook them at a light. The car was recovered but the men escaped.

Calvo was edgy these days. He arrived for dinner with two bodyguards. They moved about during dinner, peering out of windows and casing the house.

"Were they *Senderistas?*" someone asked.

"Who knows? They were incompetent, whoever they were!" Calvo jested. He had received calls from someone who said he was one of the would–be abductors, threatening to try again. "But I'm ready for the bastards." He gestured at the toughs.

Fewer than one in 10 kidnappings was reported, one of the papers said. Most victims' families simply followed instructions and paid the ransom demanded. This was rarely, for the rich, an enormous amount — usually around $10,000 or $20,000. Calling the police might prove useless, or worse: one gang just exposed had as members 25 PIP police officers! Some underlings had been arrested but the leaders had fled to Colombia.

"You know, I think most of what goes down is just old fashioned robbery — has nothing to do with politics," Barry said. "Those guys that hit you weren't political — they were just after a fast ten thousand."

"Ten? Hah! You sell me cheap, my friend," Calvo joked. "With my new line of CALVO," the label he'd begun putting on his gear in spite of a threatened suit by Calvin Klein, "I may soon be the richest man in Peru!"

"Or they could be old friends from the States!" Olga joked.

Calvo, it turned out, had participated in projects that caused his visa to be revoked. He was vague about these but did say that they had to do with his management of a chain of Baltimore massage parlors. "But that visa revocation means nothing. I just fly to Montreal, hitch to Vermont, then catch the DC Amtrak."

In *"El Centro de Miraflores,"* particularly on the *Avenida Larco,* one could have been in London's Knightsbridge or Paris' Fauberg St. Honoré, so full of fashion and folly were the shops, from the latest "designer" wardrobes to gargantuan pastries. In one bakery, four birthday cakes were being readied. One was occupied by a division of toy soldiers, another by a family of porcelain dolls. Each confection stood more than three feet high. There were ovens of tarts and cookies.

Along sidewalks, vendors of "native" earrings, bracelets, necklaces and leather work displayed their wares on blankets while hustlers accosted passersby with ersatz Moche ceramics. In the shaded, triangular central park, artists set up easels of schlock but also original work of energy and daring. Many students supported themselves by selling here, some to regular patrons, others to lunchtime browsers and to tourists. In a grove, the confident bronze head of John F. Kennedy gazed skyward.

When their team won the final game of the world soccer cup in Mexico City, resident Argentines poured into the streets. Thousands of *Limeños* accompanied them, singing and waving Peruvian flags alongside those of their sister republic. It was as if the victory had been a joint endeavor in spite of the early and ignominious elimination of their own *equipo*.

I wandered Lima's sprawling *mercados*, finding everything from saddlers and weavers to potters and tool makers.

In a plaza next to the Palace of Justice stood scores of notaries at portable desks with typewriters and cabinets full of rubber stamps, ribbons, legal forms and petitions — one for every stage of every proceeding. In walk–ups were nests of *abogados*, lawyers, some of whom advertised from windows with giant placards. Each of the notaries had a kind of contingency struck with one or more of the lawyers, and they were most skilled at smelling out the handsomer suits. When, for a moment, it was thought that I might be a prospective client, I was rushed by a half dozen of them in a barnyard flurry. I thought it amusing that, although the system might be Byzantine in comparison to our own, some fuctional arrangements were the same. I did not know at the time the full insidious extent of its workings.

Entering the plaza was a narrow street of small restaurants and cafes catering to lawyers, judges, clerks and their employees. A group of Indian minstrels — with flutes, mandolins, drums and cymbals — performed inside them and in the plaza.

In a neighboring district, I ventured into an open market, stopping for a shine. While on the stand, I was approached by an apparently friendly kid, about 12, who affected an interest in baseball but was fascinated with my $25 Casio watch. He disappeared but as I prepared to leave I was bowled over by an older brat who grabbed the watch, scratching my wrist with his fingernails. Fortunately the band held long enough for me to shove him against a wall. He dropped the loot, whimpering and pointing where it lay. When I let him go he sauntered away, confident that neither the merchants nor their customers would lift a hand. Their vacuous, resigned expressions told more than the event itself.

The plain of Lima is not entirely flat but pimpled here and there with rock–dunes and outcrops which, in Western cities, would probably be neighborhood parks but here are squatter barrios — compressed, forbidding domains where no stranger dare venture. These *pueblos jóvenes* — "young towns" — of straw, corrugated iron and transparent plastic, seemed literally about to explode, so saturated with aimless human energy were they, so choked with smoke and stench. Only in Mexico City had I seen such warrens of despair.

Traffic was no less congested, deafening and asphyxiating than in other Latin cities. There were few stoplights which, in any event, were merely advisory. Intersections were governed by horns, the more obnoxious gaining right-of-way. Cars were vintage and battered, the most common being Volkswagen "bugs," Fords and Chevys from the 50s and 60s. The wealthy even preferred these clunkers. Upscale models invited theft and attracted kidnappers. There were almost no Mercedes or BMWs and the few spied were escorted. Even a heap would be scavenged mercilessly if left unattended. On a side street near the Malecón, I saw a '53 Buick disappear in four days — from the first smashed window to the last tire — until all that remained was the chassis on rims.

In the Cathedral of San Francisco were catacombs containing the bones of thousands of parishioners buried there between the 16th and 19th centuries. Bodies were covered with lime to hasten decomposition then stuffed inside, one on top of the other. When a vault was filled another would be opened. While it was common knowledge that the church had been used for such purposes, the great number of burials was unknown until an archeological excavation in the 1960s. All the dead which could be gotten at without disturbing the building's foundations had been disinterred, their bones separated anatomically and stacked in open vats. Someone had gratuitously arranged their skulls in concentric circles at the bottom of a broad, shallow pit lighted for public viewing.

Beneath the ornate Church of the Inquisition several blocks away, the Holy Office's "confession" chamber had been restored. All manner of mechanical devices for compelling discovery, from screws and racks to scalding water and hot blinding irons, were being applied to mannequin victims by mannequin inquisitors. A notice from the year 1680 warned villagers against striking prisoners being herded to trial.

Below the chamber were cells just large enough to hold a human being, some with barely room to sit. Standing would have been impossible. Into this agony of blackness and silence, except for screams from the room above, those convicted of lesser heresy were condemned to lie for up to ten years. More serious offenders had the flesh flogged from their bones or were cooked alive at the stake.

Torture and mayhem were not the exclusive province of the Spanish. Much of the pottery on exhibit at the Museum of Archeology depicted the inviscation, castration and mutilation of prisoners and their shrunken heads brandished as trophies.

Miraflores cafes fill with businessmen and fashionably dressed women in the early afternoon and again around five. Waiters in full dress are alternately solicitous and scolding as they tend patrons and evict urchins. As in most large cities the same beggars, usually working in family relays, make small fortunes in this business, allotting territories and ejecting interlopers — be they other professional panhandlers or the truly destitute.

The grandest of the grand cafes is the *Monte Bianca*, officially an "ice cream parlor" but also a superb *brasserie*, with Lima's most European luncheon menu and a connoisseur's selection of wine and coffee. I went there one Sunday afternoon to meet a fellow named Ron Babb, to whom I had been referred by the rector of Miraflores' Episcopal Church of the Good Shepherd. A hollow–faced young man with deep–set eyes approached my booth.

"Are you Mr. McMath?"

I said that I was.

"Are you alone?"

"Yes."

He looked around, warily, to satisfy himself that this was the case and sat down. A waiter came and he ordered a chocolate shake with two extra scoops of vanilla and a large espresso. Folding his hands, he stared at me for a long moment that suggested distraction or even menace. Later I felt that it connoted rather a girding–up for the darkness into which, on my account, he was once again about to descend.

"I suppose I should start with the arrest? Or how would you like me to do it?

"However you feel the most comfortable telling it," I replied.

He smiled thinly, locking his eyes on mine until at length, reconnoitering the cafe a final time, he told his story — measuredly, almost woodenly, but with that serene candor that only survival can compel:

"Such a thing was for other people. It could never happen to me. And evil — that was something for religious fanatics. I never gave it a thought. Do you believe in evil? I don't mean just bad things, bad people. I mean absolute, deliberate wickedness — the Devil?"

Mummy, ca. 1300 B.C., from the Paracas penninsula, south coastal Peru.
Researchers claim that what appears to be an expression of terror is merely
incidental to the hands having slipped from the eyes after burial.
National Museum of Anthropology and Archeology, Pueblo Libre, Lima.

17

LURIGANCHO

*'He will ... dwell in the
parched places of the desert,
in a salt land where no man
lives.'*

"... a thin, very weak slop of rice and beans. They bring it in open barrels in the back of a truck from an army base. It's always cold and dirty. You have to come into the yard to get it with your own bowl or plate but some guys don't have anything so they use a plastic sack or newspaper even. You can hear them coming so people crowd in front of the gate and there is fighting because it's not enough that they bring so you have to be one of the first to get it.

"There's no running water. The pipes are broken so every morning for half an hour they throw a hose over the fence and you have to bring a bucket and fight again because the water runs slowly and there is little time. It is not fit to drink, only for bathing, but if you are thirsty you will drink it.

"There is a toilet out in the yard beside the *pabellón,* cellblock. It has planks around it but basically it's just a hole in the ground. The sewer is the worst — just an open cesspool. The stink, the smell, it never goes away. Flies breed in it. Cockroaches and rats. Sometimes the Peruvians kill the big rats and eat them.

"All day long there is noise. Shouting, cursing, crying. Radios on different stations, all turned up real loud. But you get used to it. You go out into the yard. That's what most people do. They spend their days out there reading, talking, doing nothing. You can do some sports, a kind of handball, for instance. The gringos mostly just get high — cocaine, paste, marijuana, cheap booze. The place has its own pushers; they have a hierarchy. The warden and his staff — they bring it in.

"You get arrested for having cocaine; you have a feeling of guilt, of self–despisement. You say, 'I never want to see the stuff again.' Then you get the feeling that you are here unjustly. Why do they punish me if they do the same thing? If the stuff is legal for them, even for me — and they are selling it to me? The prisoners say this to their judges but the judges ignore it.

"They can't understand — especially the very young ones, especially the Americans — they can't understand why *they* are the ones who must endure such suffering. Most will say, 'I'm innocent, I was set up,' which is true, at least being set up. But not innocent, not innocent, not really. They knew what they were doing: the drugs for big money, really big money. A hundred thousand dollars for one trip, maybe more. That's what it was for me, the money.

"The American Embassy does more than the others. Most never come at all. But the Americans send someone twice a month. They bring mail and messages and paperbacks. Food packages. They relay messages to the outside. The Italians go once a year and drop off some magazines. They tell them it serves you right to be here. The French do the same. I think though that the French are surprised at the number of their nationals here — 15 of them at one time, half as many as the Americans. They don't want that extra burden. It's not part of their job. They're not trained to deal with it.

"The prisoners don't understand this. Being a prisoner is a shock, the worst situation you can get yourself into in your life. Being in a foreign prison is even worse, especially in a place like this. No friends, no family to support you. Nothing. No one. So their Embassy is the only place they can turn and when it does not respond, does nothing, they become despondent.

"I was arrested here in Miraflores. It was an operation set up by the American drug agency. The Peruvians just came in on it later, at the last minute, to make the arrest. I'm convinced of that. It was the Americans. They had suspected what I was doing for a long time, but they could never catch me in the United States.

"I had a friend who was a pilot for a small airline in Puerto Rico. He asked if I would like to help him with some 'gun business' for a general who had taken power in Bolivia. I said sure, why not? We flew a shipment of firearms down to La Paz. There was a big committee — army and police people — who met us at the terminal. The leader was a German, ex–major of police. We knew some of the same people back there [Ron's father was German, his mother British], and we hit it off. He introduced us to our contacts. The deal was, we would bring down guns and take back cocaine.

"My friend and I wanted to start our own airline which we did do eventually, in a way. We bought a charter company in Puerto Rico, Air Service Inc., and we opened an office in Miami. There were no planes. It was just a front for the smuggling operation.

"Then the general was overthrown, and all the people who worked for him got kicked out. The major showed up in Miami and said he had this great plan: we could continue smuggling — out of Peru. He had the official contacts if we would supply the people with the stuff. We had worked with several suppliers there before but never in a big way.

"So I flew down to Lima and met him. We rented an apartment, near Avenida Larco, here in Miraflores. He suggested the one to get. I checked around and found that one of our previous contacts could supply all we needed. I introduced him to the major and he said this was just the fellow we'd been looking for. 'I like his style,' he told me.

"When the first batch arrived at the apartment, I was with a girl friend. The major called and said come on over. It was all there, four kilos. Plastic bags. He said, 'I'm going out to get some drinks.' He had just left when the police kicked down the door and stormed in with machine guns. They took me to the police station. There was our contact and a bunch of other people I'd never seen before, all supposedly part of the cocaine ring.

"This major was never serious about doing business. He had somehow turned informant. I trusted him because he had been the ramrod for the Bolivian business. He was the last one you would think would become an informant.

"The first thing I said when they questioned me was that they should look for the major. They said he doesn't exist. The apartment was rented in his name, not mine. His name was in a file with the things they had confiscated but they always said, 'He does not exist, he does not exist.' I read about him later in a newspaper. He was arrested in Germany and put in prison. Frankfurt, in '83. Jorhim was his name.

"They took me to a room alone and hit me like a punching bag in the stomach and back and kidneys. It was not really an interrogation, just beating for the sake of beating. Then they did photographs and fingerprints and left me alone for the rest of the night.

"The next day I was moved to another station. You've seen Peruvian colonial houses? There's a little servant's room behind the kitchen. Used to, the station had been a house like that and the servant's room was already full of prisoners, mostly just criminals but some political, too. The smell was terrible and it was dark, black — like going down into hell. I thought I would suffocate.

"You could hear the screams of people being interrogated. They would take some of them from this room. Their friends would cry and mumble when they screamed. They were praying they would not be next. They brought them back bloody and sweaty and when they could talk, they said what they had done to them. They would burn cigarettes on their skin and kick them in the groin. Also they would tie their arms behind them and pull them up on a rope by a pulley. One guy they pushed under water in a tub until he almost drowned.

"There was no inventory of my belongings. Everything just disappeared, my gold ring, my watch, my wallet and money. Different ones took different things.

"A day or two after my arrest, a Peruvian lawyer — his name was Montenegro — came to my cell, out of the blue. The PIP, Special Police, had called him. He told me that I could go free if I could get him $100,000 to pay the "necessary authorities." I said that sounds good but I don't have it, no way to raise that kind of money. I later found out he did the same thing to other foreigners, taking their money and doing nothing. He was arrested once for fraud but nothing came of it.

"A few days later they took me over to his office and let me make a collect call to the States. They thought I would call for money but I called my lawyer up there, a guy in San Antonio named Taylor. He came down about a month later. He was shocked at the legal system here. There is no logic at all, nowhere to start. Nothing. You're arrested and that's it; you become part of the web, part of the world that does not exist for ordinary people. You are caught in it and you cannot escape. A lawyer can do nothing.

"They took me to prison. No one knew where I was. It took Taylor a week to find me. After two months, they took us, I was arraigned with the Peruvians, to the Palace of Justice to appear before a judge, but he didn't wear a robe, just a plain suit. A prosecutor read the investigation report and the judge said he would send the case to a higher court. I asked if I could have bail. He laughed and said absolutely not. Then they took us to Lurigancho.

"You don't have your own cell unless you buy space from somebody who has one or you get to be his boyfriend. I didn't have any money so I was put in with 20 others. I couldn't buy food but because I was a gringo they figured eventually I would get money so they took care of me. They had their own kerosene stove for cooking and some prisoners ran little restaurants in the common area.

"The only thing the administration does is check you in and assign you to a cellblock. After that you are on your own. That's it. You can walk about in there wherever you want to go, but the Peruvians have gangs and they are always stabbing and killing each other. You try to stay away from the gang members, but it is not always possible.

"After a few months I started getting some money through the British Embassy. My parents would send a little something each month. All I needed was about $300. Food was $200 and the rest for clothes, some basic furniture and some newspapers. A vendor walks through the blocks every day. I would buy *El Comercio* and *La República*.

"Market women are allowed in twice a week. They bring fruit and vegetables and spread their goods out on blankets and sell them to the prisoners, to the ones who can afford to buy. Some of these women bring jugs of clean water. They charge you extra for the jugs — about 2 dollars — but next time you just pay her to fill the jug, about 10 cents.

"I got a cell with two other foreigners — a Frenchman and an American. They were complete drug addicts, wasted. Most of the gringos were. This young German guy was put in with us right after I came. He had a wife and three children and a music business in Berlin — intelligent, very sensitive. He had been arrested for having only a few ounces, enough, he said, for his own use, not to sell. I believed him. Gradually the guy fell apart. The monotony, the violence, the filth, the thoughts of his family. He started using cocaine all the time. Before long he became homosexual with the dealers. They would use him and pass him around to their friends. He was a very good looking fellow, about 30, but he looked like an old woman after awhile. I couldn't take it, it was pitiful, and a bloody nuisance — always they are in the cell doing it — so I would throw them out. Finally, he moved in with one of them.

"There are over 5,000 men confined in Lurigancho. Maybe 80 to 90 gringos — maybe a third of them Americans. Most were in for cocaine. Some were tourists who took a chance, maybe on the spur of the moment. But the majority came down here to get the stuff. The Peruvians are common criminals primarily but some are also political. Probably 70 percent are waiting for trial — some for as long as four years or more.

"Some of the gringos have girlfriends. These are usually just street girls who go there looking for a foreigner, someone, anyone to get them out of here. A foreigner is the ultimate, the greatest luck for a woman. Tourists are OK, but they leave. Not prisoners, at least not for a very long time. Time enough to make babies. And when the kid is born it comes in, too. The women hope the gringos will take them home when they go. Some do; most don't.

"Visiting days for women are Wednesdays and Saturdays, but a little money to the guards gets them in on other days. They go right into the cells.

"If you want to receive a phone call you have to write a formal request and the wait can be up to a month. It takes about 15 minutes for them to get you from the cellblock to the warden's office where the only phone, is so you must coordinate the call with your presence. Otherwise, the person will call and you won't be there. Of course, you must pay for this privilege and it is very expensive. Castro Castro, the former warden, would charge gringos $50.00 cash for this, sometimes $100.00.

"Castro Castro extorted money even from prisoners who were officially released. To leave the prison you had to have his stamp on your documents. He wouldn't do it until you paid him. The price varied but always it would go up, so that when you paid what he asked — say, $500 — he would say, 'Well, that is fine but there are further formalities' or something like that until you came up with another $500. One prisoner, a Jamaican, was kept over almost a year like this.

285

"Sometimes you can pay a guard to go to the Embassy and get your mail or a package. Or your girlfriend or a market woman can do it. I had an account at the British Embassy. I'd give one of the guards a check for 20 pounds and he would go there and cash it and bring me the money and my mail or whatever. I'd pay him his expenses and a dollar. Of course he and the other guards opened the mail and if there were any valuables in the package, a radio for instance or even a cake, they would take it unless you paid them something. Since the package is already open, if there is no letter or note telling what was in it, you never know.

"Sooner or later most of the gringos get a visit from their family or girlfriend from home, usually the girlfriend. She is overwhelmed by it all. The last time she saw him was at home and he was cool and on top of things and having lots of money. They are shocked to see him in such a place. Usually they stick around for a month or two, then leave and never come back. They go to the Embassy, to court even, but they learn there is nothing they can do, that it is hopeless, so they leave. They have their own lives to live and many of them are very beautiful women.

"Gringos are useless to them on bail and besides you can sneak out of the country. Inside they are a constant source of bribe money for the prison officials and judges and lawyers. And they are easy examples for the Peruvians to the American government that they are really doing something about drugs — and for the American politicians to show the people there. It is all so phony and useless. These guys are the pathetic ones, the helpless ones, the small fry. The big drug runners are the top brass of the army, government ministers, businessmen, the elite. They ship planeloads of cocaine through Colombia to the States and Europe.

"Anyway, I told my girl not to come and she didn't. We kept on writing for a year but one day she wrote and said simply, 'It is finished. I can't wait any longer.'

"The first reaction to this letter is to be pissed off. Then comes the pain, the guilt. You say, if only I could talk to her. But there is no way except that she will call you, which she won't because there is nothing to say. And even if she would you have to go through the request and the payoffs to the guards and to Castro Castro and then she might not call after all and you keep thinking that she has someone else now who is making love to her.

"There's a hospital there but there's nothing inside. The beds don't have sheets. There are doctors, four of them. They are paid very little. It is poor work and they are poor doctors. Prisoners go there for rat bites, knife wounds — almost everyone carries a weapon, a blade of some kind. Most of their work is sewing up knife wounds. There is

286

also hepatitis and tuberculosis. One of my cell mates got TB. He died from it, wasted away for two years.

"The Peruvian who was my contact also died, of cancer of the intestine. He was a businessman; a transportation business. I went to see him every day until about six months before he died when they took him to another place, they said, for treatment, but they did nothing for him but let him rot. He came to court the last time in a wheelchair. He could hardly sit up; he smelled terrible. I don't think he knew what was going on. A week later he died.

"You have to pay constant little bribes to get your case even scheduled for a hearing. First you have to have somebody out there who will do this, and they must be paid. Then they must pay something to the clerks to 'find' your file and call it to the attention of the official who schedules the cases. He won't do that unless he's paid, and then the clerk of the head judge must be paid and then the judge — all of this just to get a trial set. I was lucky since my Peruvian codefendants had their wives and girlfriends constantly going every day to harass them. But if you are alone your case just sits in some office for years, so you have to pay somebody. You hire a lawyer. The lawyer comes to visit and says you have to pay the money I told you. This can come to $10,000 or $15,000 — whatever they think you can raise — and it has to be sent to the lawyer. He is supposed to see that it gets to the officials but sometimes he takes it all for himself, and you never see him again. Even if he pays some of it to get your case moving you must always pay more. To get your confidence, the lawyer will say that he is friends with the judge from when they were children or in law school or something, but in most cases this is just a story.

"Once the trial begins it is very disorganized. They don't start with one case and take it to its conclusion. They read from the documents of one for, say, ten or 15 minutes, then go to another, frequently repeating the same things. During the six months of my trial I must have gone up there 30 different times. Each time is hell. The guards beat and kick you and spit on you. You are kept in what is really a zoo cage, sometimes for more than a day, without food or water. They don't have people there to feed the prisoners and the guards only come to take you to the court or back to prison.

"The judges weren't really interested in the witnesses. A witness doesn't change anything; they are just lying or stupid. So they go by what's in the file — the police report, what the prosecutor says.

"When I finally got to testify they asked things like what could you buy with credit cards in Europe, how much airline tickets cost, what was my girlfriend doing now in Miami. Idle curiosity. I finally got this lawyer, paid him $300 to call witnesses to show that the major — not me — rented the apartment, that I had other business than dope, but none of them came.

"He did argue that I should not be punished any more because the main criminals — he actually named the major for the first time — had been permitted to escape, had not even been charged. The prosecutor said I was the ringleader, not the major. And that me and my accomplices, I had never seen them before except for the guy who was our contact, should get 15 years. They gave us all 10.

"Peruvian society is based on exploitation. Everyone is always looking to use, to screw someone else and to keep from being screwed themselves. It is a constant preoccupation with them. The Peruvians hate each other. They are suspicious, jealous, without trust. Even one's closest friends. A foreigner, a gringo, sees this, and he can't handle it. The intentional cruelty, the meanness. The system of justice reflects the society. It's deliberately devised to be as complicated and frustrating as possible. The endless nothingness, the torture of wasted time, wasted lives — that is all part of the pain to be inflicted by the rulers on the ruled; by the upper class, through their administrators, on the lower class, but cleverly so they are always above it, and it can't touch them. There is something animal about it. It is not human. The deliberate cruelty of it, the intentional injustice. And always watching, never trusting, looking for ways to inflict pain. This is simply impossible for an American or European to accept. So they give up, go to drugs, go insane. You will see for yourself."

We joined a line which ran along the prison wall, doubled back, then headed out towards a shantytown. There was fog and dust, wind–clawed from the scarred earth. Vendors sold oranges and taffy twists. Children played and cadged. The prison was at the base of a half–dune mesa. Its compounds were double–enclosed and bounded by fences rolled atop with barbwire and skirted by barriers of heavy, razor–edged obstacles between elevated guard towers. The enclosure was perhaps 200 yards wide by 500 long.

The barracks of a 200–strong detachment of the *Guardia Republicana*, the Peruvian elite guard, adjoined one end. Some 80 civilian employees, many of them hardscrabble types barely distinguishable from the prisoners, saw to the daily routine. Only a few were armed — those posted with shotguns at the principal gates and on the roofs of the cellblocks. Towers and perimeter were manned by machine gunners of the *Guardia*, soldiers as surlily disdainful of the keepers as the kept — and as wary. The lackluster *empleados* were known to run in the face of an attack by the Pampa Rats, gang members who rampage through neighboring blocks looking for drugs, money, revenge and "young meat" — youthful prisoners to rape. A blocking phalanx of them carry shields of mattresses abreast, which absorb shotgun pellets as if they were pebbles. Others in the rear hurl rocks, glass and Molotov cocktails. The *empleados* sometimes let hit teams of Rats into the cells of those behind on drug payments or who otherwise become an object of special attention. Young gringo "virgins" have thus been harshly initiated into the realities of prison life.

There was a casual air in the queue that morning. My group were 12 — nine members of the congregation of the Episcopal Church of the Good Shepherd, Gary Harris, Ron Babb and myself, the only first–time visitor.

Gary and Ron were unlikely partners. Gary was a slender black Jamaican raised in Cockney East London and Ron a preppy Anglo–German with only the slightest hint of a Prussian accent. They had met after six months there in solitary confinement — the result of a presumed escape attempt though each denied complicity in which the *Guardia* had been bribed not to shoot at gringos climbing the fences. Such a scheme had succeeded the year before. Each said he had converted to Christianity during the ordeal. They shared their experiences and resolved to dedicate themselves to helping their fellow inmates "see the light." This they began to do by holding group discussions and prayers. When they were released the following year, they formally organized Foreign Prisoners Fellowship. The Church of the Good Shepherd agreed to sponsor them, providing an office and a modest operating fund. They expanded their efforts to include the 30–odd Europeans and North Americans in Los Chorillos women's prison.

"We are *missioners*, not missionaries," Gary insisted. "Our mission is to give the lads someone to talk to while they're trying to shake off from drugs and hate. We try to teach from our own experience but we leave formal training and Baptism to the Church."

They also eschew lawyering — although at first they undertook to perform the myriad of filings and copyings of documents required to get dead cases moving.

"After awhile everybody wanted us to help with their case," Ron said. "Now we have to turn them down. We contact lawyers and family and the like and relay messages. We don't have the money and staff to do the detail work ourselves."

Just finding money to live on was a problem. As convicted criminals they were forbidden work permits. Yet a condition of parole was that they work. They had to show evidence of employment to their parole officer with whom they had to check in once a month. Fortunately the fellowship counted as work.

It was the check–in requirement — daily reporting the first month, weekly the second, then monthly after that — that they knew defined the ultimate parameter of their dilemma: when to try to escape Peru.

"You have thirty days from the last time you sign in until you're back in prison if they find you," Ron said. "All the embassies know this — they know the only way for us is to escape. And they want us out as soon as possible. We are an embarrassment and extra work for them. So they give us new passports, without a visa, of course. It's up to us to get a visa — impossible legally since we are felons. What most do is try to make it to a remote border post — the Amazon is best, down the river from Iquitos. Or down the Madre de Dios from Puerto Maldonado into Bolivia. You try to take back roads with no police checks or you tell the ones who ask for your *papeles* that you lost your old passport, the one with the visa, and you hope they'll believe you. The same with *migración* at the border. So far it has worked — they'd just received a card from an escapee who had made Rio — but it's more dangerous now. They have special instructions to look for us, for foreign parolees trying to escape."

Aside from fear of capture there was the feeling of guilt for abandoning their comrades and the fellowship. Soon both would have to make the choice. Freedom was always uncertain. Already parole had been canceled for 60 Peruvians who had been "erroneously released" according to a new administrator. The decision was pending appeal. What if it were upheld and extended to include them as well? "I could never go back," Ron said. "I spent too many years in that place."

The group was asked by Gary to form a circle. He read a divine admonition, which might have been written with Lurigancho in mind:

> [Y]our wealth and all your
> treasures I will give away to
> plunder. I will enslave you
> to your enemies in a land
> you do not know, for you
> have kindled my anger, and
> it will burn forever. Cursed
> is the one who trusts in
> man, who depends on flesh
> for his strength and whose
> heart turns away from the
> Lord. He will ... dwell in the
> parched places of the desert,
> in a salt land where no one
> lives.

He stared off into the distance for a moment, then leavened Jeremiah's harshness with the promise of Isaiah:

> ... But they that wait upon the Lord shall renew
> their strength; they shall mount up with wings
> as eagles; they shall run, and not be weary, and
> they shall walk, and not faint.

He then prayed that our coming would alleviate the suffering of those within and enable them to see the "divine purpose of their ordeal." Forgiveness and salvation were also asked, not only for the prisoners but for their custodians and tormentors.

A guard summoned us gruffly to the admissions desk. Our identity papers were placed in wall slots and numbered discs, one for each slot, were given in receipt. These were entered in a log. Another guard rubber–stamped our left arms just above the wrist with a half inch purple ink square. We were next directed to a room with long tables where our parcels were searched by three matrons. Anything remotely sharp or ballistic was confiscated. This done, still another employee painted the number of our disc in red crayon inside the stamped square, whereupon we were shut in separate closets to be strip–searched for concealed weapons. A warder then rubber stamped a red triangle inside the square. After him there were three gates, the last opening into the *pabellones*.

The first thing I noticed was the stench. It was so overpowering I almost retched. Inmates waved at us from between the bars of cellblocks, their arms like the tentacles of some bizarre aquatic plant. Gary and Ron were quickly recognized and voices called out to them:

"¡Hola Gary! ¡Hola Ron! ¿Cómo estás? ¡Hola! ¡Qué Tal, Cabrito! ¿Tienes muchachas? ¿Tienes muchachas? ... ¿Putas?"

As we approached *Pabellón 7* there was a surge of white faces from the sea of brown: blond hair and red, fair but peaked skin, eyes aglow–green yet feral. And then black skin too and warm black smiles. Hands reached out to clasp ours, to grasp our shoulders and stare into our faces. Mouths spoke:

"Why are you so late? We thought you weren't coming."

"Il y a du courier pour moi?"

"Did you talk to Miriam?"

"Did my old lady get the letter? What did she say?"

"Do I have a trial date, old sod?"

"C'est pas vrai! Elle m'a écrit?"

"It's good to see your ugly face, mate.

"Patrick is bad again. You must see him, talk to him. He might not make it this time."

We entered the block through a narrow metal door that opened into a cramped but busy commons. Some men sat eating at short tables. Food steamed in kettles on gas stoves: inmate "restaurants." Other prisoners gave way to our little entourage. Several called out to Gary and Ron, who bade them join us. Two did, a Chilean and a Puerto Rican, clutching their Bibles like deacons. We entered a courtyard where other prisoners lounged in the dirt or tossed balls. Some stared silently, among them the one called Patrick whom Gary hailed but without response. Ron ushered us toward a small "visitors room" — a dank, bunkerlike enclave occupied by a table and crude benches and cutoff barrels for seats. Banter and news ensued with mail and messages passed to a lucky few and to some not so lucky. Ron and Gary walked back to Patrick and huddled with him, trying to cheer him up.

A handsome 31–year–old South African amputee, George, had still not received a verdict although his trial had been "in progress" for almost a year. Since he had been confined going on four, he was hoping for early release, even if found guilty.

His story was a most unusual one.

"I was a motocross fanatic by the time I was 12. By the time I was 18 I'd won more races than anyone my age and most older fellows. When I was 21, I won the South African national championship. The accident was right after that."

He and his girlfriend were headed along the Garden Route to Cape Town when a truck struck them broadside. They "flew through the air for a hundred feet." His shoulder struck a road sign in such a way that it cleanly severed his right arm.

"I woke up and the first thing I thought was, 'Oh, my God! He's killed her' — she was lying in a clump and jerking. So I get up to go over to her and I suddenly feel off–balance and look down and see my arm is gone. Then I see it lying in the road, about 40 feet away. I start walking toward it, but the driver reverses over it — he's trying to get away, duck out. When I pick it up it's all crushed."

The young woman was not badly hurt. She tried to flag down passing traffic. "We must have looked weird, me holding up my arm and her waving and shouting like a mad woman!" Finally, they were taken to a Cape Town hospital, stopping on the way to pack the arm in ice.

"I actually walked into the emergency room and handed them the arm, then passed out."

Efforts to reattach the limb failed. It was too damaged. But within a year George was back cycling as "The One–Armed Wonder." A winning record brought invitations to compete in Europe. An Amsterdam surgeon who read about him donated a prosthesis.

"It was more than an artificial arm — it was a *super* arm. I could do anything I could do before, only faster. It had tiny computerized parts. I could hit, pull, punch like a fighter or pick up a tea cup."

Racing "didn't pay the best, but I made enough to get by and bring in the birds." He moved in with an English flight attendant who "got me into the Amsterdam fast track." He started using cocaine, then selling it. "I made fantastic sums — up to $300,000 a year after I started bringing in my own stuff."

"I was able to follow the sun," he wrote in a fellowship testimonial. "I visited many countries on a great international roller coaster ride. Then, one day — BANG!"

He smuggled mostly from Peru, secreting the contraband in "a special latex sock." One day an accomplice suggested that he use the hollow of the prosthesis instead. "It would hold twice as much and it was the perfect cover." The last run had gone as usual — until he checked in for his flight to Paris. Lackadaisical customs agents had been replaced by US–trained narcotics inspectors.

"They took me to a back room. One of them took a long knife and said, 'Do you think it will hurt?' and he stuck it — stabbed it — right into the plastic arm. There was no blood; but the fine cocaine powder poured onto the floor like water — 630 grams of it! Everything I had — all my baggage, my wallet, my jewelry — was stolen by them right away. I tried to pay them to let me go. I offered the customs chief $1,800 from a wad of $3,000 I had in my money belt. He just smiled and took all of it."

Like Ron Babb the previous year, he was taken through a series of police stations and put in El Sexto. Then he was moved here, where he had been for 37 months.

"The toughest thing for me was when my father, who was dying of cancer, came to see me. It was our last meeting. He came with my mother. It was dreadful. I can never forget the expression on his face, his sorrow, hers; the two of them seeing me in this place."

While we were talking, Ron came in and told George his case had been "postponed indefinitely." On hearing this, he stalked out of the bunker, catching his empty sleeve on a nail. He stood in the courtyard rigidly, alone, staring into the muddy sky.

"Shut up and stand up!" Gary had concluded his tête–à–tête with Patrick, who was now gabbing effusively with another prisoner. Harris held his Bible high over the table and rapped for silence:

"Enough of the bull and whine, you sinners and outlaws! It's the Lord's work we are now about." Harris' voice was unexpectedly commanding, his cockney stammer and a slight lisp curiously endowing him with an authority far greater than priestly unction.

"Quiet, Patrick!" There was only half a laugh between them. Patrick and the other miscreants fell silent.

293

"All right, now we will start by singing hymn No. 4, 'Amazing Grace.' Everybody got a book to look at?" There was some shifting around as everyone found a hymnal to share. We then sang all four verses.

"... *was blind but now I see.*"

"Okay, mates. Sit down. Anybody know what dis is?"

Gary held up an American $5 bill.

"Aw! C'mon! George! You ought to know the answer to that one. Whatssis?"

George shrugged vacantly, then smiled for the first time since getting the bad news.

"The evil of Satan."

"At's right! All agree widat? Dis 'ere's the cause of most of the sorrow of the world, ain't it?"

Gary then delivered a stem—winding sermon that would have evoked a chorus of amens from the most devout Southern Baptist congregation. He lambasted "Demon Coke" and "Demon Gold" and "Demon Selfishness — the final cause of your suffering" — and then laid into "Old Satan, himself, the King of Hell."

"Think, now! You feel sorry for yourself for having to pass through this dope—dumb hell. But think of the people, the children, the little babies in their mothers' wombs, who you were carrying this stuff to so's you could be rich."

The fellowship is based, one learns, upon the premise of guilt—admission as a prerequisite to "rescue." Although used in the traditional sense of Christian redemption, the word also has an immediate secular meaning best put by Ron.

"What it means is that you can't really be part of the group, get the full hand of fellowship — be rescued from physical addiction to dope and mental collapse — until you cut the bull and admit that you're not here because of bad luck or being set up or because of anything but your own criminal conduct. You broke the law by becoming a dope smuggler. You did it for money, for greed. It made no difference to you that dope kills people, turns them into monsters. You knew it did that but you didn't give a damn. You have to admit that to yourself, to God, then to the other members of the fellowship. Then it can help you."

While the Peruvians, particularly the lawyers and judges and prison officials, come in for a good deal of verbal abuse, they are seen, spiritually at least, as mere agents of divine retribution — and also victims, snared in their own corruption.

His sermon concluded, Gary bade all stand as he again read
from Isaiah:

> You will open the eyes of
> the blind and set free those
> that sit in dark prisons.

And from the Psalms:

> From heaven did the Lord
> behold the earth; to hear
> the groaning of the prisoner.
> ... Thou art my hiding place;
> thou shalt preserve me from
> trouble; thou shalt compass
> me about with songs of
> deliverance.

18

NAZCA

*She lived in a flophouse, hitchhiked into the
pampa, and wandered alone for days at a time.*

Thousands of human skulls stare hauntingly from the desert
floor.

With trigonometric precision their brains once executed the
enigmatic "Lines of Nazca" — riddles that have divided the houses of
anthropology and astronomy and sold frenetic press runs of "UFO"
potboilers.

Brittle but intact, with matted raven and oddly reddish locks
still clinging to patches of dried flesh, they lie ripped from their tombs
and commingled with a million cousin bones.[61]

So wanton is the disinterment at Chauchilla that one might
have intruded upon an ancient genocide or the feeding ground of
some insatiable paleo–carnivore. How odd that this vast necropolis —
once an incomparable trove of pre–Columbian archeology — could
have survived Incan reduction and Spanish plunder to yield to the
fury of modern greed.

Among the carrion strolled tourists, some nearby, others in the
distance wobbling like specters in the midmorning heat. Scampering
urchins ingratiated themselves by retrieving fragments of faded
fardos. These are exquisitely woven shrouds, some over a hundred
feet long. Most have been unraveled in looting that has continued
unabated since the cemetery's discovery in 1936. One child presented
a skull to a Danish teacher who accepted it, thoughtfully.

In the middle distance, against a backdrop of dunes, five taxis
shaded their napping drivers. Hoods agape for engine cooling, they
appeared as parched animals or disgusted passersby assuaging thus a
presumed stench of death.

Earlier we had driven by an enclosure planted with white
crosses and small stucco grottoes. There were candles and porcelain
Madonnas and plastic wreaths. Why did the *huaqueros*, grave
robbers, not rob these?

"*Está consagrada,*" consecrated ground, Tacho, our driver, said
sternly. "It is very wrong to disturb the Christian dead."

But no offense to end the rest of pagans.

"*Son infieles,* infidels," he said.

But Mario, the senior driver, scolded the *huaqueros*:

"*Son profanadores de tombas.*"

He had quit his nap to arrange for us several *fardos* into photographic order, crowning them with random crania.

Efforts by archaeologists to enlist government officials and the church hierarchy in protecting the graves had come to naught. The latter did not consider the heathen dead among its priorities. As for the constabulary of Nazca town, what goes on in the desert is beyond its writ or care.

Looting is still a profitable business and the corpses are, after the mysterious lines, Nazca's principal attraction. For the *taxistas*, it was $5 each for as many passengers as could be impacted into their chromosaurs for the 30–kilometer round trip. We seven had rebelled at an eighth. There were unkind words and gestures. At length Tacho relented though he yet sulked from our importunity beneath his Packard — his chagrin doubtless exacerbated when the rejected tourist made a tenth fare among the less mutinous Danes in Mario's '61 Impala.

Although I missed the jeep it was good to be traveling light once again. The hitchhiking was hard, three rides in three days down from Lima, but buses were frequent and cheap. Besides, the jeep, safe for the moment in Alan Davis' garage, was best husbanded for long cross–country stretches. Just now, I had set out to explore easily accessible ruins, my only baggage a backpack and light duffel. Nazca, in the department of Ica, was my first destination. I was rested, mostly recovered from the miseries and eager for whatever these fresh, new days might bring.

Ica is but parcel to the continuum of rolling dunes and fog mists of south–coastal Peru, an emptiness seemingly as barren as the dead ergs of the Sahara. Yet there are intermittent fissures of life supported by an erratic aquifer and quinquennial inundations as *El Niño* momentarily reverses the Humboldt Current's sucking away of surface moisture to send ashore diluvial cloudbursts. Two such "rivers" are the Ingenio and the Nazca. Between them lie 30 miles of perhaps the most arid plateau on earth: the Nazca Pampa.[62] The face of Mars is more inviting.

The plain is strewn with fist–sized rocks and pebbles oxidized with a sooty varnish by eons of dew–sun exposure. Beneath is a rusty calcite floor, an inviting contrast to the tarry stones. It was by the systematic setting–aside of this gravel, not by scraping or trenching, that the Lines of Nazca were made.

Although "strange markings" were known from colonial times, it was not until mail flights began in the 1920s that the vast number and complexity of Nazca's "Inca roads," as some called them, were revealed.

At first only the lines themselves and the larger quadrangles, some more than a mile long and up to a hundred feet wide, were

Soft drink vendor, Nazca.

observed. These included a rectangle and various elongated trapezoids the shape of "runways." More than a hundred coiled spirals, zigzags and spindles eventually resolved themselves.

Barely visible from the ground as individual streaks or collective "star bursts," from a plane they look like the analytical doodlings of cyclopean physicists. When they were discovered in the 1950s so straight were the lines, so evenly curved were the spirals, and so proportionate were the animals that two assumptions enveloped them: they must have required Pharaonic labor and whoever drew them had to have seen them from the air.

Speculation assigned them, as well as a 600 by 200–foot "trident," "cross" or "anchor"[63] dug into an oceanside dune on the Paracas peninsula to the north, to Incan engineers, early missionaries and prehistoric aviation — four decades before the UFO musings of Erich von Däniken and Shirley MacLaine.

In 1941 the American antiquarian Paul Kosok accidentally discovered the first figure of an animal, a bird some 150 feet across. At the time Kosok was looking for canals to buttress the theory that big irrigation projects conclusively implied the rise of authoritarianism in primitive societies. No way, it was held, to build such without slaves — and masters to keep them working.[64]

Kosok saw some of the lines from a hill on June 21st, the summer solstice, and noted that they ran directly toward the setting sun. He concluded they had to be astronomical in function. With that, a third assumption was born.

Fascinated by the lines, but compelled to return to his teaching duties in the States, he asked Maria Reiche, an intrepid young German mathematician and linguist who had been working for him in Lima as a document translator, if she would be willing to catalog and study them for a year. She readily agreed, not knowing that the year would turn into one of the longest field research commitments of modern science.

Though a protégée of Kosok, she was initially shunned by most major institutions and academic prima donnas, some of whom still condescendingly regard her as a dilettante and her work as unprofessional. She did obtain a modest grant from the National University of San Marcos in Lima and she was able through her constant presence and forceful personality, to gradually overcome the suspicion of the local inhabitants. Because of her queer lifestyle — she lived in a flop house, hitchhiked into the pampa, and wandered alone for days at a time — they thought her daft or a witch.

At length, she became an accepted member of the community, was lodged at a local ranch and helped in her searches. In 1984, the government granted her a suite at the Hotel de Turistas. Adjacent rooms were set aside for her archives and laboratory. A street and the local high school were named after her. There is an annual fiesta in her honor.

To its credit the Peruvian government, through its Interior Ministry and air force, early on afforded her logistical help. The air force made photographic overflights of the lines at her direction.

During these flights and countless treks, she discovered scores of figures. Among them were a whale, monkey, lizard, dog, spider and a great many frigate and hummingbirds. Most were located near the Ingenio River.

300

At her urging the area was eventually made a "protected zone." Unauthorized entry draws a big fine and possibly jail time, according to signs. Four guards patrol it. They are paid with proceeds from sales of her booklet, "Mystery on the Desert."[65] Before they were hired, thieves stole most of the centuries of pots that had been deposited there, crippling any effort at a carbon 14 chronology.

Many of the lines became reoxidized so that they were almost indistinguishable. Reiche "cleaned" some of these with rakes and by overturning fresh stones; others she whitewashed to enhance their visibility from the air.

An airstrip north of town is the home of several small craft that fly visitors over the lines for $20 a head. This is the most practical way to view them. Some wealthy *Limeños* fly their own planes down as Nazca's dry climate makes it a favorite retreat. On rare occasions, a hot air balloon or hang glider made of indigenous materials will brave the pampa's fierce winds to show that Nazcan aeronautics, at least in theory, were possible. Midway across the plateau on the Pan American Highway there is a prefabricated metal tower from which visitors can see portions of the "spider" and the "thunderbird." A souvenir stand beneath offers smooth, imported river stones stenciled with facsimiles.

The clarity of the lines varies with time, altitude and cloud cover. Some can be seen only under certain conditions, others almost always. Between 11 a.m. and 4 p.m., the glare from the sun and the resultant flat light obscure most of the drawings. Early in the morning, between 7 and 9, or after 5 p.m. are ideal times, due to the shadow—angle of the sun. Seeing them in this way, in their full symmetry and grace, forbids summary dismissal of the possibility that their authors did the same. Yet one can also imagine "practical" shaman enlarging, to scale, drawings of their gods, or their anthropomorphic familiars so that they might see them and take a message: we revere you — send us rain on time. One also sees that the straight lines number in the hundreds and run, in no apparent order, to every direction of the compass. Plotted together, they would look like wheel spokes. Indeed, in 1949, Reiche did just that. The resulting chart showed clearly that at least one line could be found to point toward virtually *any* celestial body or event as it transits the horizon.[66]

Approaching 90, Reiche continues her research, although it is now considerably curtailed by Parkinson's disease and a demanding lecture schedule. The latter is part of the implicit quid pro quo for her apartment, yet a task she obviously relishes. Each evening at 7:00, in the Salón Maria Reiche at the Hotel de Turistas, Maria Reiche holds court.

An elegant, colonial–style facility with high ceilings, Valencia tiles and a swimming pool, the hotel is separated from the town by a concertina of barbwire and armed guards. It was built in the late 1970's to accommodate visitors attracted by sudden media interest in the lines.

Although most are tourists, there are some graduate students, "Peruvianists" as academics who study the country call themselves, and, not infrequently, a western correspondent or free–lance writer. It is rare for the scientist most familiar with such a site to be so available to the public. And the audience, which at times numbers 100, is raptly attentive to this solitary woman who has toiled for nearly a half century to unlock the secrets of what, had they occurred in Hellas, Egypt or Mesopotamia, surely would have been counted among the wonders of the world.

The night I attended, the room was full by 6:30 and people were standing in the lobby. The Danes who were at the cemetery were there with a Thomas Cook group of about 30 from London. An agency from Frankfurt and another from West Berlin each had about that many. There were four French students and a talkative couple from Montreal who were hitchhiking together and a travel club of some dozen Americans in their 60s. Two of the Danes and a German girl gave up their seats to three of the American women and sat on the floor.

An anticipatory silence fell as a hotel attendant set up a microphone in front of a lawn chair. A tall, older woman, whom some at first mistook for our speaker, entered leading a second. She also was tall, but frail, and proceeded tediously with a cane. She wore a knitted shawl, snazzy blue deck shoes and clutched a dark green tartan comforter. Seating her charge tenderly, the first woman retired to the hallway, closing the door. The helper was Renate Reiche, her sister's constant companion.

"Good evening, *Buenas Tardes* ..." The mike shrieked. Maria Reiche rolled her eyes saucily and shrugged:

"Demons of the pampa!"

With that the audience was hers.

"Now let's see," she said when the laughter had died. "How shall we proceed — in what language? French? German? English?"

A few suggestions were murmured.

"What nationality is this group?" she asked, gesturing to the Germans. After an exchange of native pleasantries with them she shifted into French, bantered briefly with the *Québecois*, then announced in Spanish that if there were no objection, we would proceed with German and English.

Reiche suffers from advanced glaucoma but the lighting was so poor that even one whose sight was not impaired would have had difficulty reading. The sharp glow of a goosenecked lamp, activated by the attendant at the last moment, was only annoying. Unfazed, she spoke as if from memory, her fingers moving over notes in Braille. These surely contained excerpts from her book since she occasionally followed it verbatim. This would explain why her style alternated between the informal and professorial. Her voice, at first hollow, soon gathered the volubility of one accustomed to speaking with authority:

>... The people who made the lines lived in these valleys for more than 3,000 years without interruption. They left millions of tombs — no exaggeration — millions of tombs of their dead.
>
>Museums and private collections all over the world are full of the unsurpassed pottery, weaving, gold and silver — even musical instruments taken from these tombs. Some were acquired for almost nothing. Others for prices that were enormous — which, of course, explains why some [local] people, most of whom are destitute by even Peruvian standards, do not hesitate to remove the artifacts. I wish I could say that this is now controlled, that the law [against looting] is enforced; unfortunately that is not the case.
>
>The drawings consist of shallow furrows, the narrowest being barely scratches on the surface. Even the largest quadrangle is no more than one foot below the surrounding pampa.
>
>Without exception, each is described by a single uninterrupted line. The line never stops or, as a child might say, "leaves the paper."
>
>The basic tool for transferring the figures to the ground was a unit of measurement. They must have first made models because an approximate estimate ... would spoil the proportions, which, as we see them on aerial photographs, are almost perfect. Those acquainted with surveying will understand what a great accomplishment this was. Prehistoric Peruvians must have had advanced surveying instruments on a level approaching our own.

Though portions of rope have been found which might have been used as measuring devices, we have not yet found one which could be said with certainty was *the exact* standard length or a multiple of it.

Perhaps the unit was so well–known that there was no need to make duplicates. In my view this unit was the distance between the thumb–forefinger [web] and the elbow. This identical distance was used by other early builders around the world, including the Egyptians.

Each figure was constructed separately from its own unique *model* — probably woven into a tapestry.

I would not at all be surprised to find a single master tapestry among the tombs. Certainly, there must have existed one for each figure. It was undoubtedly from first using the figures in weaving and pottery that gave them the idea to do them on the ground.

I still hope we will find, though, a single weaving, maybe a *fardo*, that will have the figures on it exactly as they were drawn. It should have on it the precise unit of measurement. Of course, the *huaqueros* are not likely to come running to us with such a thing. Perhaps a tapestry like this has already been found and removed to a collection in the United States or Europe. Its owner would have no idea of its significance.

The existence of woven "blueprints" would resolve the apparent conflict between the Indians' inability to fly, yet still assure the figures' perfect symmetry.

She took questions when she had concluded.

One of the young French women immediately asked whether they were done by beings from "out–of–space."

Maria Reiche lecturing in the conference room named after her,
Hotel Turistas, Nazca.

There was a guarded guffaw all around. Restrained, perhaps, because the question — not to mention Reiche's reaction — was on everyone's mind. "Not in the least," she replied, crisply.

"The people who lived here were quite evolved enough to conceive and construct them. It is not necessary to look for little green men, for extraterrestrial intelligence, notwithstanding the speculations of certain space fanciers. But then I fear they may be motivated by factors other than a search for truth."

One of the Germans, a bit argumentatively, asked, "But what about the robot, the standing figure? It doesn't look like any human to me. How do you explain that?"

He was referring to what has become known jokingly as "ET," a drawing of a manlike being standing, one hand apparently extended upward as if in greeting, the other held at his side. He is goggle–eyed or wearing what some have said is a helmet or visor.

"That is not an uncommon symbol," Reiche replied. "It is the body of a man with the head of an owl. The owl is a symbol of wisdom. It can see in all directions by turning its head 360 degrees. The same symbol was used throughout the Andes; it appears in Ramses' Egypt. There is nothing extraterrestrial about it. It is very much of this Earth."

Someone asked what she thought about the theory that the lines were simply roads or paths.

She responded by pointing out the steep angles of the lines as they approach their ends, mostly at clusters or "ray centers" on hillocks.

"These would have been impossible to stay on with dignity, particularly for novices or pilgrims, who would have stumbled and left tracks or disturbances. There are none. Of course, those on flat surfaces could have been used as paths, but why some and not others?"

She said that tracks of people and cars had proven ineradicable.

"It's like the surface of the moon out there. If you make tracks, they'll stay for centuries. That's why the lines are still there."

"Were the lines used by everyone or just the chiefs?" someone asked.

"The line builders were an elite who dominated the others, no doubt about that," she replied. "This was done either directly or through the tribal leaders, the chiefs. Maybe they were one and the same. But the line builders were the ones who could study the heavens and tell when would be the best time for planting and whether it would be a good harvest or not and whether austerity and sacrifice would be needed."

"Do you ever get lonely out here all by yourself?" an American woman asked.

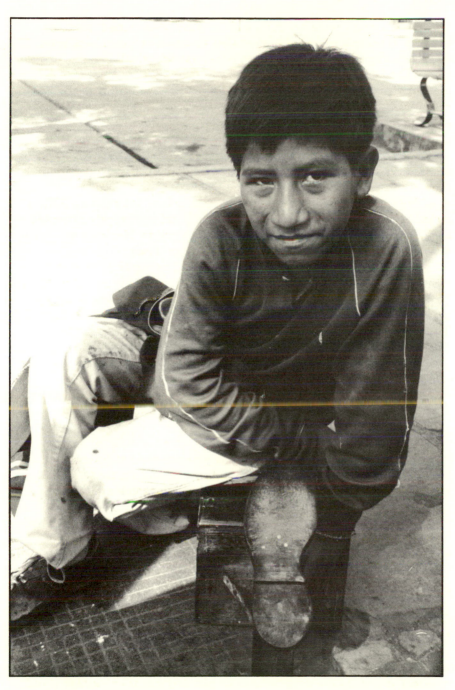

Shine boy, Nazca.

She was silent for a long moment before replying.

"Oh, I used to sometimes. But this is my life, my work. Peru is my home. Its people are my friends. I find the pampa a source of great strength, great inspiration."

Reiche is self–taught in archeology, somewhat after the fashion of Mary Leakey and her son, Richard, in Kenya, neither of whom have formal degrees. But like many dedicated field scientists, she has only published sporadically, changed her mind often and omitted from her writing what academics normally consider vital detail.

Although she cataloged the lines for years before looters removed the pottery deposited there, she has never indicated whether a study of the crockery was made and, if so, the results. She is also reluctant to reveal the data upon which she has based her shifting conclusions over the years as to the most likely unit–length of measurement used by the builders. The thumb–forefinger web/elbow, 38–40 centimeters, is only the most recent. Her estimate has ranged from 32.5 centimeters to 84 meters!

Some critics have accused her of laboring in a vacuum.

"Working in such isolation, Maria has had little opportunity to keep up with advances in the study of ancient astronomy and [anthropology]," says Evan Hadingham, a young British anthropologist and popular science writer whose superb 1987 book, "Lines to the Mountain Gods," is without question the best current treatment of the subject.

Hadingham suggests that Reiche mistakenly "sees [the lines'] designers as levelheaded intellectuals, methodically solving one mathematical problem after another ... obviously project[ing] qualities of her own onto the people of the distant past." She too readily accepted, he says, Kosok's "astronomy book" view of the lines as fact. This colored her judgment, leading her to garner evidence to support that theory while unintentionally turning a blind eye to other more plausible explanations, such as the lines' use as ceremonial pathways.

Hadingham presents substantial evidence of this use of *ceques*, ceremonial lines, by the Incas and their predecessors, a practice continued today in some parts of the Andes. He includes a photograph by American anthropologist Johan Reinhard showing Bolivian villagers marching single file along a two–mile straight line to a summit "altar" in the Bolivian mountains near Tiahuanaco, origin of the people who in the seventh century conquered or co–opted the Nazcas.

He details how dark areas in the Milky Way, not individual stars or the "constellations" into which we arbitrarily group them, form the core of Andean astrology. Straight–line ceremonies are deemed crucial for supplicating the benign progress of the "animals" — frog,

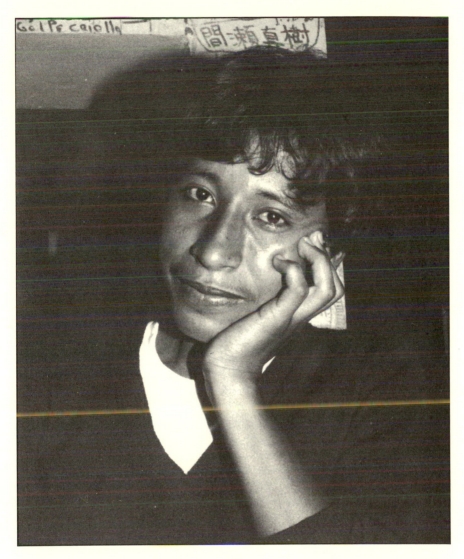

Troubadour at rest, Nazca.

snake, llama — formed by these gaps. Each gap, as it "moves" through the night sky, mirrors the seasonal comings and goings of its earthly counterpart.

Also depicted by the voids are sacred mountains and rivers. Plotting the azimuths of certain of the straight lines, Hadingham contends that a great many point, not at anything celestial, but to the 7,000–foot high dune–mountain, El Cerro Blanco, which towers over the valley. Said to be the largest in the Americas, the dune has slowly been blown inland over time from the Pacific 30 miles away. It is revered by local inhabitants, who leave offerings on its summit, as "The Volcano of Water," the mythological source of the aquifer that fills Nazca's underground "canals." The channels appear to have been dug at roughly the same time, ca. A.D. 900, that the straight lines were drawn.

According to Hadingham, the few pots found on or near the figures have been carbon–dated at the first century. Most contain drawings identical to the animals of the figures, including a great many frigates and hummingbirds. Separate datings of shards found on the *lines* are at around 900.

Finally he relates how, in a single afternoon's experiment, an American archeological team was able to nearly replicate on the pampa half of one of the more complicated figures: the monkey. They used no measuring devices, merely estimating dimensions as they went along.

Reiche, though, remains convinced of the simultaneity of both lines and figures and their celestial alignments. She contends that certain of the lines indicated solstices and equinoxes, others eclipses and yet others the risings of various constellations depicted by the drawings — the spider, Orion; the monkey, the Big Dipper, etc.

"Their existence can only be explained by their makers having in view the movements of celestial bodies."

Why is she so adamant about this?

"All over the world, monuments can be found which were built for the observation of the solstices."

Within a few thousand years of each other, a mere second in evolutionary time, widely separated groups of Homo sapiens suddenly undertook monumental works. Many of these, such as Stonehenge in Britain and the Mayan observatory at Chichén Itzá, were used to track the paths of the sun, moon and planets. Divination, not research, however, was the ultimate objective — predicting propitious times for planting, harvest, marriage, war, etc. The structures were both "practical" and priestly in function.

Whether the Nazca lines, regardless of their exactitude, were another of these aboriginal almanacs or merely metaphysical traces has become the central question surrounding them. Possibly both views are correct. The lines could well have been astronomical in focus — but toward the Milky Way, not our constellations. And perhaps the "mountain gods," such as Cerro Blanco, were cosmic viceroys.

The weight of the evidence has shifted against the aboriginal almanac view. Dr. Gerald Hawkins, the Boston University astronomer who in the early 1960s demonstrated, using a computer,

Schoolboys marching, Nazca.

that Stonehenge had been aligned by its builders so they could precisely follow the ecliptic, ran a similar program on the Nazca lines. He concluded that, while certain alignments occurred, they did so in no discernable order and their number was only slightly higher than that which would have been expected from mere chance.

Depending upon one's point of view, the debate has been clouded or enlivened by a third "hypothesis." That one, anticipated by the French student's first question after the lecture, holds that the drawings are the work of extraterrestrials or were done by the Indians, too backward or stupid to think of them themselves, at extraterrestrial direction — most likely as signals to spacecraft to "land here."[67] This fantasy, popularized by Swiss writer Erich von Däniken's "Chariots of the Gods?" and subsequent similar books by others, has done more to draw attention to the lines than the work of Reiche and others who have labored over them.

The three theories might be referred to as the mathematical, the metaphysical and the tabloid. The metaphysical seems to be in the ascendancy: while the drawings are remarkable, their construction was relatively simple compared to the works of the Mayas, the Stonehenge builders and the Egyptians. They were made for use as ceremonial pathways, still a common practice in the region. Any cosmic alignment is purely coincidental. But new finds have a way of quickly upsetting conventional wisdom in Peruvian archeology — and more researchers are digging there today than ever before. Who knows what they will next uncover.[68]

The parched bed of the Nazca River which severs the town is described in guidebooks and by popular writers as "empty" or as the place where youngsters "gather each evening to fly homemade kites." The few scrubby trees along its banks blossom during the day with drying laundry, billowing in the wind like errant spinnakers. At night, standing on the single narrow bridge, you can see the flickering from the campfires of the dispossessed. It is too hot for them to remain there during the day.

The riverbed is also the town dump and latrine, making it Nazca's olfactory governor. Citizens relieve themselves at all hours, unabashedly. Butchers from the abutting market toss their offal there. Great rubbery vultures swoop and ramble about, more agile than the children who are their competitors.

Just then the air was cool and clear and stars were emerging, although the weird dune Cerro Blanco shone purple and orange in the — for it — still setting sun. An odor of freshly scythed hay from meadows north of town blended curiously with smoke from the fires and the pungency of the riverbed.

Through side streets I came to the Taverna, the principal place where Westerners congregated. The walls were splotched with graffiti which was encouraged: Names, hometowns, witticisms, that kind of thing — but there was no profanity. The young son and a nephew of the owner played guitars and the travelers sang along. The food was good and there was beer and wine from Ica, which is renowned for its wine.[69]

I went to the plaza the morning of the independence day parade. Pubescent boys in neatly pressed school uniforms, with wooden rifles fixed with rubber bayonets, goose–stepped to drums and bugles. High school girls of the "Simón Rodríguez" brigade strutted past, some in

Interest compounded daily at 41% at savings bank in Nazca.

blue jeans, others in jungle utilities — all toting toy submachine guns with black straps.

A sign painted in black and red above a bank promised 41 percent interest, compounded daily, on deposits. For a moment that seemed impossible until I realized that the rate was flat, fixed — against an inflation of more than 200 percent. The people who gave 100 intis to the banker would get back 151 in a year, but their principal would have shrunk to 25 intis in value. The banker, smart, would himself buy notes indexed to the rate of inflation in dollars or other convertable currency. At the end of the year, the banker would have the dollar equivalent of 400 intis, or more, riding ahead of the inflation wave. Plus his interest, also indexed, at around 10 percent. Subtract the 151 which he pays to you, and he has made a tidy profit. After I had gone, inflation would exceed 1000 percent. I wondered, when I read of that, what rate the bank was now offering and if the people had any idea what was happening to their savings.

A blind mother with two infants came to the bank's portico to beg from parade goers. The poorest among them were responsive. The owner of a hardware store had the baby monkey I had seen him earlier display in a cage. The animal was now on a leash tied to the aerial of the man's car. Frightened of the small children and drunks who crowded around, the baby had crawled out as far as it could on the sun–hot hood.

Young men, fiesta dressed, browsed the wares of itinerant peddlers. One displayed guitars, flutes and mandolins. Another proffered booklets of "songs of the countryside." They carried titles such as "False Love," "I Don't Want You to Cry," and "Orphan" — "I travel the road of life remembering the flowers on the coffin of my dead mother ... blossoming memories of my sad childhood. I drink at night to forget my bad luck."[70]

One folio was called *"Jilguero del Huascaran,"* Goldfinch of Huascaran, at 22,200 feet, the undisputed sovereign of the Cordillera Blanca. It was hard to tell if that was the title of the collection of songs or the pseudonym of the troubadour, one Ernesto Sanchez Fajardo, who appeared in full costume on the cover.

A copy was purchased by a young man I had seen one evening singing in the riverbed behind the market. The last verse reads:

> I sorrow to see my country
> In the hands of the bourgeoisie
> Ay! How the poor manage only
> Barely to endure
> While the rich defend
> Themselves with rifles
> The poor die by the thousands
> Of hunger, of thirst, and homeless
> Awake, my people, awake!
> In my ignorance I will tell you how
> Not to flatter the rich
> But to fight for your liberty!
> Arise, Arise Dear Motherland!
> Brave Peruvians will not permit this evil
> Life of our nation to continue![71]

Captive monkey on roof of car, Nazca.

I caught up with the marching children and followed them until they halted in front of a school. A sergeant barked orders to the girls' brigade which disbanded. Above the entryway in large letters was the school's name: Maria Reiche. My thoughts returned to the elegant hotel, the esteemed scientist and her privileged auditors, the debate about the lines, the cozy erudition of it all — all that existed in an evanescent bubble, a fragile refuge from the gathering havoc on the other side of the barbwire.

19

MACHU PICCHU

'One year's world potato crop is worth more than all the gold and silver taken from Peru by the Spanish.'

The Inca Empire conquered by the Spanish in 1532[72] had been in existence for less than 100 years. In that brief time, what was but one of a number of quarrelsome tribes around Lake Titicaca had suddenly burst forth to subdue all of western South America between the Pacific and the upper Amazon. Inca suzerainty ran from Colombia to central Chile, a distance of more than 3000 miles — greater than that from New York to Los Angeles.

While military prowess facilitated this eruption, the realm was cemented by an administrative acumen that rivaled Rome's and emulated Machiavelli. Children of conquered chiefs were housed in Cuzco as surety for their fathers' allegiance. There they were taught the superiority of Inca language and culture. Gods of the vanquished became subordinate deities in the Inca pantheon ruled by *Inti*, god of the sun. Loyal populations were transplanted to the lands of rebellious tribes who were forcibly dispersed. A network of stone roads was constructed, each day's march along which were silos of foodstuffs — for the commissariat and for the community in time of famine. Warehouses were also built in larger towns. Cuzco's *entrepôts* held enough grain, dried potatoes and other staples, as well as spears, shields, cotton and leather, to sustain the populace for years.

Each subject not exempt — soldiers, artisans, fishermen — had to set aside a portion of his crop for the commonweal. Some 20 days' labor per year, called the *mita,* was reserved for government service. This usually consisted of road or aqueduct maintenance, masonry and the suspension of bridges. The bridges were made of thickly woven rope fiber and many spanned abysses challenging even to modern engineers.

Among their most monumental endeavors was the construction of a series of terraced agricultural bulwarks, "cities," principally along the "sacred valley" of the Urubamba River. In these were grown not only reserves of the pulpy, white-kerneled Andean maize, but tropical fruits and vegetables vulnerable to frost at higher elevations. One such redoubt, built during the mid– to late 15th century, was Machu Picchu, arguably the grandest architectural achievement of the descendants of Siberian migrants.

Flowing playfully beneath Pisac, itself a stupendous citadel 18 miles from Cuzco, the Urubamba gives no hint that in 60 miles it will surge through verdantly explosive jungle impenetrable to all but the most adept and resolute. Twenty miles beyond Ollantaytambo, the last Inca city known to the Spanish, the channel horseshoes in a gorge so sheer that the sun, when not blocked altogether by hovering mist, has but a fleeting glimpse into its depths.

Three thousand feet above, the chasm is commanded by a sugar–loafed crag, Huayna Picchu, the great horn of a saddle–ridge. There Inca sentinels could see travelers, or invaders, two days before their arrival. The peaks and glaciers of the distant cordillera, crowned by the summit of Salcantay, rim the vault of an azure sky to bestow upon the place an Olympian grandeur. Original stone roads leading to the saddle are still intact, though beyond the immediate perimeter, most remain swallowed by the forest. An exception is a 20–mile stretch to the south known as "The Inca Trail" to those who hike it from the tunnel at kilometer 88 of the Cuzco–Quillabamba railway. From the sugarloaf, trains snaking along the single tracks cut from the riverbank seem like electric toys. While there, I watched an afternoon "express" and a slow freight shrink the distance between them, their whistles suggesting catastrophe — until at "impact," I saw that the freight had cleverly yielded into a siding camouflaged by tentacles of the rampant canopy.

Around the upstream bend of the river's horseshoe lies the boisterous, seedy hamlet of Aguas Calientes. Once the site of a royal spa it now serves as bed and bar room for visitors to the ruins.

Four soldiers crouched beside the stall of a fruit vendor. They were engorging bananas and mangos handed up by the vendor's daughter, a lanky girl with rumpled, trailing hair. They chatted with her as they ate, she giggling as one tugged at her skirt. Their rifles rested against the stall but within seizing distance. Their sergeant, standing apart, carried an AK–47, the butt of which he nervously held into his right hip. He had a thick mustache but his hair was crew cut like the others. Occasionally he would look cautiously up and down the tracks which were congested with merchants, shoppers, children and animals.

One old man was pulling at a rope tied to two stalled burros laden with produce and wood. His efforts became frenetic when the whistle of the train from Quillabamba sounded in the tunnel a quarter–mile down. Wares and toddlers were whisked away leaving only the old man and his burros. The soldiers charged over and began shouting at him. One thrust his rifle at the animals and threatened to shoot them. The train emerged less than a hundred yards from the platform, its speed such that it clearly could not stop in time to avoid hitting the animals, even if the engineer wanted to try — which, from

318

his grin and the obscene pumping gesture he made with his fist and forearm, he did not. His other hand was sounding the whistle in rapid, deafening blasts.

Just then a very tall, serious–looking young fellow, a student from Lima I had met briefly earlier in the morning, ran up and whacked the second burro on the rump with a board. Startled, the animal lurched forward, pushing the other. The two of them stampeded to the village steps, dragging the old man with them. There, he regained his dignity and acted as if he had been in control all along.

The soldiers fanned out the length of the train, nervously watching the crowd. The vendors seemed oblivious to their apprehension. Many were women with baskets of hot bread and chicken and fruit and pails of tepid juice. These they peddled to passengers through the train's windows. Several were permitted to enter the cars but others were barred by conductors, wary, as were the soldiers, since the Cuzco bombings the month before.

A boy accused of trying to steal a passenger's camera was collared and frog–marched to the rear of the train where he was released. He thumbed his nose, waddling exaggeratedly away, doubtless to try again at the first opportunity.

The student, Julio, was in anthropology at San Marcos University and was working on a "schematization" of Andean languages. Quechua, he pointed out, is today almost the same language as in the time of the Incas. He was with his fiancée, a pretty young woman from Arequipa. They were here on holiday. I told him how quick thinking and bold he had been but he demurred.

"No es nada."

But he might have been killed.

"Yes. The old man and his animals were nothing to them. That is the way it is in Peru today. But this will soon change."

I started to pursue that but he said they had to hurry to board the train. He asked if I had found a place to stay. I said no.

"You should try 'Gringo Bill's.' He will always make room for another gringo," he said half jokingly. He had been told there was no vacancy, "but I don't think Peruvians are welcome there." He showed me the way, on the left through the small paved plaza.

I had come in the night before and crashed in the lobby of the overbooked Hotel Caminantes down near the station. The friendly manager had agreed to keep my gear until five; then I had to move on.

I thanked Julio for the tip.

"No problem. There's always room at my place for a travelin' Razorback." The somewhat portly, thinly bearded American spoke through the doorway of a rustic kitchen. A potbellied stove rumbled warmly behind a communal table. The strong odor of raw meat escaped from a vintage icebox.

"Power's off a day now," he said, nodding toward the fridge. He turned to stir a pail of milk boiling on the stove.

"Fresh this morning. Local cow."

The place's official name was *Q'oñi Unu* — "hot water," in Quechua. But everyone called it "Gringo Bill's."

William Kaiser, about 35, was from Michigan, "by way of Homestead, Florida." He had first come to Peru some fifteen years back, "when it was still undiscovered." After hiking the Inca Trail he got the idea of establishing a hotel at kilometer 88. He actually "made the beginnings" of a hostel there but his application for a permit was denied.

"So I came on down here."

He'd met Margarita in Cuzco and they married.

"She's definitely not your typical *Peruana*. She won't take no for an answer when she knows she's right. Like, she can't stand to see kids dying from dysentery because politicians steal chlorination funds."

In fact, Margarita had gone into politics. Municipal elections were coming up and she was an independent candidate for the council.

"She'll get a lot of votes from the women. She helped start the kindergarten and has been a leader on what passes for the school board. Women's club. She was even the secretary to the local Aprista party leader, an ex–army major. That kind of thing. Of course the men are all terribly macho. She's opposed by all the present council members. They resent having a woman argue with them, and they know she would keep them from stealing."

The town gets $2,500 from the national government each year to spend as it likes.

"That's a hell of a lot for the council to filter off — and they do it. They steal three–fourths of that allotment. That's why there are no services or improvements around here."

Margarita spoke up from the stove where she was flipping hot cakes.

"I'd like this to be a town that everybody can enjoy and feel comfortable in — not just a tourist trap but a place you look forward to staying at. Even prefer to Cuzco. You know, clean water, bathrooms, that kind of thing."

"Gringo Bill," hotelier at Aguas Calientes, below Machu Picchu.

"Clean up the hot springs, for example," Bill said. "The temperature of the water up there has dropped so low that it's a bacterial breeding ground. Lost five degrees in just the past year. It doesn't have the medicinal qualities it once had. Hell, it's a health hazard. What they did is they took a cat up there and ruined the original Inca pool. Dug it twice as deep, twice as big. Thought that would accommodate more people. What it did was muddy the water and lower the temperature. Its no longer a spa. It's a goddamned urinal. The Peruvians, not just the locals but people from Lima, pee in the water. One of my workers got a chronic ear infection from it. Another one has a cyst — the doctor says from swimming in the springs. None of the clinic people ever go up there, doctors, nurses. You sure as hell wouldn't catch me dead in that water.

"But their priorities are completely opposed: A new church! Can you believe that, a new church! The one they've got is too big for them. And brighter street lights! It's for the fiestas — they love their fiestas. Every week there's another one. Noise and drinking all night long. Nobody goes to sleep — not even if you want to. They would rather have parties than save their kids from dysentery. They finally did vote to do the chlorination but then they went ahead with the church and lights anyway and forgot all about it.

"... And transportation. They've needed a road out of here for years, ever since they built the railroad over the old river trail. For three years we've tried to get them to petition Public Works or Interior or whoever in Cuzco to build a new road but you'd think they'd been asked to insult the commanding general. People get electrocuted, cut their arms and legs off with machetes. The railroad won't take them without special permission. Last year a guy died who'd lost an arm. Stationmaster wouldn't let him ride. The doctor begged but it was no use. Next day permission came from Cuzco. By then it was too late."

His goal, Bill said, was "to build a hotel with 25 rooms, each one with a small private bath." They had a ways to go. The main structure was still a stone and cement–block shell. Tardy delivery of supplies and heavy rains had delayed completion. The two unfinished floors were serving as platforms for the storage of toilet bowls, sinks and other fixtures and an assortment of scrounged and bulk–bought hardware. Three unpedigreed dogs made the place their home. Few gringos were turned away, even if they had to throw down their backpacks among the nail buckets and scaffolding. The dogs remained suspicious, even when admonished that intruders had become guests. The animals became frenzied if a Peruvian, other than Margarita, approached.

"This is strictly a gringo hotel," Bill said. "We would like to welcome Peruvians but they steal the sheets, the soap, the towels —

anything they can get their hands on. They even steal our tools. These are middle–class, even rich, *Limeños* — none of them poor. As cheap as we are, no poor person could stay here. So I finally said the hell with it, no more. They can't stay here."

He wanted to finish up, sell out and move on. "Pretty soon we'll have the office and lobby done. Then this place'll have some class. Then we'll sell it and head back up to Florida. My dream is to build a sloop and sail around the world. Just me and Margarita."

A room at the time was 30 *Intis* about a buck–eighty. A night with the dogs was only 10.

I asked if there had been any sign of the *Sendero Luminoso*.

"Not here. Not yet. At least to know it. There's a pretty tough garrison here. 'Beret types. No way the government could let the most famous ruin in South America be taken by those guys. But there've been 60 vigilante killings between here and Cuzco just during the past year. Nighttime things, remote villages. Take the mayor out, castrate him, cut him up with a machete. That kind of thing. That doesn't include the seven tourists blown up in the train. They've taken control of the wilderness on the other side of Vitcos. Vilcabamba, you know. All that's now terrorist–run. Or liberated, depending on how you look at it."

Bill sometimes guided backcountry trekkers and private groups seeking ruins missed by earlier explorers. "The Indians hid more gold back here than the Spanish stole," he said. "Sometimes I go out by myself — several days, even a week at a time. I've found some mighty unusual things — pots, ax heads, pestles — but no gold. The Incas lived back in here more than people think. And there's no doubt in my mind they brought gold with them. But I just like to be out in the woods. Whatever I find is secondary. Besides, there's laws against removing antiquities."

The path to the hot springs led half a mile up through truck plots and hovels with hogs, burros, rib–protruding cattle and scrawny chickens. It was past dusk and clusters of flashlights and candles, winking like fireflies, described the way. There were no racks or tables so you used the first available clump of moist earth you could find. Thieves were out, so most bathers brought only the ten *Intis* fee, which was taken by an unofficial looking young man who volunteered to watch your things. Relentless tykes and adolescents in cutoffs and multicolored polyester trunks dived and splashed and pursued one another. There was a hint of sulfur but it was drowned by a surliness of urine and excrement. There was no lighting, except for the Milky Way and an unrisen moon and the peripatetic flashlights and candles. I watched for awhile, but decided against going in.

Machu Picchu remained hidden from the Spanish and their successors for almost four centuries. The honor of its discovery fell to American explorer Hiram Bingham. He was led there by a Mestizo settler and some Indians who had cleared and were farming a small portion of its terraces without realizing their significance. The date was July 24, 1911. Bingham had just broken camp on the fourth day of a mule–train expedition out of Cuzco in search of Vilcabamba the Old, the "lost kingdom" of the puppet–turned–renegade, Manco Inca and his sons.

At first complicitous with the conquistadors following their kidnap–murder of his hapless predecessor, Atahualpa,[73] Manco was chained and tortured when he failed to produce further gold. He was whipped, urinated upon and his wives were raped in his presence. Released through the intercession of Juan and Hernando Pizarro, who sought to befriend him, Manco bided his time. The next year he rebelled, very nearly capturing Cuzco and destroying the invaders. But after a long battle, the Inca army of 100,000 was repelled by the 160–man Spanish garrison. The engagement conclusively established the invincibility of armor and horse over aboriginal infantry, no matter how numerous or brave.

After a few equally futile rear guard skirmishes, Manco retreated into the jungle. At Vilcabamba he established what, for 35 years, was a government in exile. Spanish deserters and clerics were admitted, though not prospectors, who were killed for fear of a gold rush.

Manco's son, Titu Cusi, even achieved a fragile détente with the war–weary Spaniards. He became a Christian and welcomed more missionaries. Yet he cunningly postponed abandonment of Vilcabamba for the hereditary estate promised him by the viceroy, well knowing the treachery and abatement that attended Spanish munificence.[74]

Bingham died in 1956 still claiming that Machu Picchu was Vilcabamba. This was understandable, given its size and splendor. Recent archeology, however, indicates that while Incan royalty did come here to "take the cure" and enjoy the jungle climate, their presence was incidental to the site's agricultural function. The excavations of American explorer Gene Savoy, 1964–66, and others have now conclusively established Espíritu Pampa — not Machu Picchu — as the site of Vilcabamba.[75]

One morning, I hiked down the tracks to Puentes Ruinas, the substation for the ruins. With me were a Canadian botanist and two German school teachers, also early risers and coffee drinkers at Gringo Bill's.

Interior view of Machu Picchu.

The first train from Cuzco was late, leaving the flotilla of shuttle vans idle, their drivers at horseplay. We waved off a lift by a dump truck full of park custodians and grittily strode onto the goatlike climbing trail. It took three hours of vertical toil through tangles of vines, roots and briars to reach the saddle. The dank forest sounded with myriad birdcalls and anonymous rustlings. These, and the physical exertion of the climb, itself, were exhilarating.

Needless to say, we were disappointed when we found, upon reaching the "stirrup," the Hotel Turistas — a recent concrete intrusion with cafe, soda bar and rock music. The train had long since arrived below and the vans, revving and dusting back and forth on the switchbacks, had released hundreds of passengers. Some were already breaking for coffee and breakfast. A dozen or so British and American backpackers hiked in off the Inca trail as we entered. They were "stupefied," one said, by the quantity of garbage on the trail.

"You wouldn't *believe* the litter, the filth," she said. "And it's the Peruvians who do it. Smashed beer bottles, tin cans, tampons. Feces right in the campsites, even in the spring water."

Armed robbers, gangs from Cuzco but also from nearby villages, had begun to make the hike hazardous. Forewarned, these people had traveled together in two large groups, one departing from each end of the trail. Others had not been so cautious. Later in Cuzco I met two couples who had been robbed at knife point and the women raped.

Even seasoned archaeologists are awed by Machu Picchu. More than a hundred great terraces pyramid up from the forest below. Their precise number is uncertain since some that were cleared have again grown over.

Walls and doorways, the doorways trapezoidal for greater earthquake strength, are of the finest ashlar masonry: blocks hewn and snugly fitted with neither space nor plaster between them. As at Sacsahuamán and other sites, it remains a mystery how so many varied polygonal shapes resulted — leading some to conclude that each stone must have been cracked and removed from singleton slabs of granite, then fitted back together against its neighbor just as they had lain naturally. Yet this cannot explain the dearth of chinks, gaps or fillings.

An elaborate network of aqueduct sluices, cut laserlike through the stone, still canalizes fresh water to most of the city.

In addition to a score of major dwellings, temples and warehouses — some of whose open roofs are "authentically" re–thatched from time to time by the park staff — there is a magnificent sundial known as *Intihuatana*, "The Hitching Post of the Sun." From this and a similar device at Pisac, it is clear that calculation of the solstices and related phenomena had reached an advanced level in the Urubamba valley, perhaps even exceeding the technology of Nazca.

On a darker side, what can only be a torture and execution chamber is situated in a lower, forward level. Two stocks and two butchering pens are enclosed by a large rendering pit. A victim could be secured in a stock by a rope tied around his neck and pulled taut through a small hole to the rear, choking him if he resisted. Prisoners held there would be able to see what went on in the pens below and to their left. A victim would be forced to crawl into one of these grottolike spaces. His arms would then be pulled backward through small, pillorylike holes, one on either side. His wrists, barely protruding, would then be tied. His head would just fit into a cleft at the rear. It was obvious from the uneven wear in the clefts that they had been slowly ground out by the agonized squirmings and wrenchings of a great many victims. Thus trussed, one was totally at the mercy of the priest–butchers in the pit. The blood and viscera of the unfortunate victims would flow through sluices into a "dish" beneath the chamber which was carved in the shape of a vulture's beak. Presumably, buzzards and condors would be offered this grisly fare in supplication. Some have argued that human sacrifice was a rarity among the Incas and that animals, such as llamas, were used instead. While such ritual renderings may also have occurred, the design of this facility left little doubt as to its insidious purpose. Oyantaytambo, a hillside stockade whose ruins still stand, is said to have kept up to a hundred doomed prisoners at a time. No such "holding pen" has been identified at Machu Picchu, but its existence may be inferred.

One notices the abrupt change in animal as well as plant life. In addition to many bird species not seen at higher elevations, there are suddenly scores of insects and spiders. I spent the better part of an afternoon photographing several of the spiders, doing so in the company of Cedric, an elderly English naturalist who had come here for a month to study arachnids. One met a number of people doing research of one form or another.

Julia, a Yale senior from Los Angeles, was finishing a paper on "Orientalism in the Hispanic Tradition." Karen, a "medical geography" major from Minnesota, had been "working for six months" on a project near Arequipa seeking to determine "why diarrhea affects some Indian babies and not others and why some mothers refuse the World Health Organization rehydration packets" dispensed by their local clinics. José, a graduate student in archeology at New York City College, had just "spent three months talking to the people in one small valley. They gave me presents of pots and hand axes they had found in their fields and even in their houses," many of which had been built over Inca ruins. "Of course, I left them behind," he said. "They can't legally be taken out of the country." He had "already sketched out a grant" to explore the valley as a project for his doctorate.

I caught one of the buses back to the depot and a train to the village. Ragged waifs bade farewell to the buses then hurtled down the mountain to reappear and shout goodbye again on every switchback straightaway. At the bottom they panhandled tips for this exhausting stunt but, weary of incessant cadging, few gave.

After several days I returned on the afternoon train to Cuzco. The abrupt change in climate and topography was more vivid than on the outward journey, which had been taken by crowded van and pickup to Pisac and Oyantaytambo, the last place you could catch the train for Aguas and the ruins. There was a steady rolling back of the distance, like a film reversed. I had the sensation of rising out of a cavern into the sunlight, as the possessive green clung, then touched without clinging, then thinly fell away, as rain forest yielded to desert scrub and patches of evergreen on basins and foothills beneath white ice.

It was dark when we came to the rim of the trough which holds Cuzco. At first the lights of the city were hidden except for a vague haze so you couldn't tell for sure that we had arrived.

The main tracks ended at the edge of the precipice where, instead of a single line to the bottom, there was a stair–step series of separate sets of tracks, each no greater than three or four degrees grade. These leveled out, then rose a degree or two before ending. The train crept down the first of these inclines, stopped for a few moments as the switch was turned, then reversed itself down the next, and so on, back and forth, until at length it reached the valley floor. The lights from the coaches fleetingly bathed the Stygian world of the Indian barrio through which the right–of–way descended: destitute women clutching infants; hollow–eyed, emaciated children staring emptily; old men staggering, hunkered in defecation, sleeping; young men watching, waiting.

Hernán Luza Calvo had taught at Cuzco's principal high school for 40 years. Three generations of the heirs of the conquerors and the conquered had tasted with him their country's history. He filled the cup from which they drank not only in the tawdry, crowded classrooms of the *secundaria* but in the streets, temples and battlements of Cuzco, itself, capital of the last and greatest aboriginal empire to be ravaged by Europeans, living relic of the glory and shame of both lineages. Now retired at the early age of 61, he spent his days and supplemented his small pension pouring that same past for visitors.

Wall of the Incan Fortress, Sacsahuamán, above Cuzco.

You could tell he was uncomfortable hustling tourists. He would place himself conspicuously, with a book, ruler and note pad, at key points — at the base of Sacsahuamán, for example, where I met him. The combination of his merry countenance and studious air invited questions. And no sooner was one asked than you were inside the good professor's time machine.

"How do you talk to the ones who don't speak Spanish?" I asked him during a pause in his one–man reenactment of the final siege.

His face broke into a grin.

"Excuse–me. I–can–teach–you–about–the–history–of–my–city," he said slowly and in reasonably intelligible English. "See, I–can–speak–English–not–bad! Anyway, there is usually someone in each group who speaks a little Spanish and they are able, more or less, to translate."

His credibility was enhanced by an occasional "*no lo sé*" — I don't know — when asked for arcane details such as the deployment of particular units or the name of a lesser commander.

"I must go to the library and look for those facts," he said once.

Sacsahuamán, Hernán said, could house 10,000 soldiers "for at least a year — longer if they were resupplied from the city." Its three walls are roughly 2,000 feet long by 60 high. They zigzag to expose the flanks of any attackers to two ranks of defenders. The stones for its construction, some weighing more than a hundred tons, were rolled on logs from quarries up to 25 miles away. More than 20,000 men labored under the Inca Pachacuti to make the fortress the most impregnable of its day. Yet, in its moment of trial, it failed against the superior armor and maneuver of an enemy every bit as daring as its defenders.

"The two bravest men died in the battle," Hernán said, meaning Juan Pizarro, who was prevented by swelling of a previous injury from wearing a helmet and suffered a blow to the head, and an unknown Inca noble who single–handedly rallied the demoralized defenders to fight off repeated charges until, seeing all was lost, he jumped to his death rather than surrender.

My guide rushed first one way, then another, filling the air with simulated thrusts, parries, screams and confusion.

"This was the last chance the Indians had to save their way of life," he said, becoming professorial again, but still out of breath. "After the fall of Sacsahuamán, especially after they had been so close to victory and then let it escape them, many lost their confidence. Also the majority of Manco's soldiers were farmers who had to go back to their crops or lose them. They faced starvation. You must see that this was not a disciplined army like before the civil war, before the fighting with the Spanish in 1532–33. Even though there were a hundred thousand of them and in spite of their loyalty to the Inca. In the end, they just melted away. Except for the regular army, but they were few compared to the others. Of course, there was still Vilcabamba, but that was really a retreat, a hideout. Never again would the Inca really challenge the power of the Spanish."

Hernán insisted on treating me to a hot local delicacy *mate de coca,* coca tea, at a cafe on the Avenida Sol.

So many former students and acquaintances greeted him that his own cup grew cold.

Perfectly fitted 13–sided stone in Incan Wall, Cuzco.

Later, we walked up the narrow street beside the andesite–walled mausoleum of Koricancha, the "Golden Enclosure of the Temple of the Sun." Built at the juncture of the Huatanay and Tullumayo rivers, which the Incas canalized and culverted, this holiest of shrines was on the "tail" of the snarling jaguar–shape with which Cuzco was laid out. Sacsahuamán was the head with its massive staggered rows of limestone walls the cat's teeth. The temple is now consecrated as a Dominican church and monastery.

Here were kept the mummies of the Incas, adorned with gold and jewels and each attended by its own retinue of priests and *mamaconas,* holy women. They were daily fed and ministered to as if alive, the food being offered, then ceremoniously burned.

On high occasions they were brought out and paraded with great pomp. Most were removed and secreted in caves after the fall of the city to Pizarro. So revered were these corpses by the people that their new Catholic governors placed top priority on finding and destroying them. But of more immediate interest to the Spaniards as they arrived on November 15, 1533, a year less one day from their capture of Atahualpa, were the temple's cornices and skirts and the sacred disc of the sun, called *Punchau,* which was more than six feet in diameter. All were of pure gold and little time was wasted melting them down along with other priceless treasures.[76]

At the time of my visit the church was closed by the bishop in protest of the refusal of the city council to increase its maintenance allotment. There is irony here: much of this budget is for structural restoration of later masonry. Mortar cracks, collapsing in earthquakes, such as that of 1953 when half the town was toppled. In the midst of the rubble, Incan walls still stood. It is common to see telephone poles and heavy timbers propped against recent buildings to keep them from buckling.

Invariably, nearby ashlars, perfectly joined over 500 years ago, remain proudly in place. Among these is Hatun Rumiyoc, "the great stone," a mammoth, 12–sided block of diorite porphyry in the remaining wall of the *cancha,* enclosure, of the Inca Roca near the corner of Choquechaca and Triunfo–Hatunrumiyoc streets. This is halfway between the church of San Blas and the cathedral on the Plaza de Armas — a distance spanning half a millennium of architectural style.

We visited the main market near the Machu Picchu train station where Hernán persuaded merchants to lecture us on the various qualities of wool from sheep, llamas and alpacas and coaxed from a spice vendor her secret source for a particular red chili of which he was fond. Finally, on the Calle Tupac Amaru, we came to the potato sellers — at least a hundred of them vending from blankets, baskets and the backs of trucks.

Plaster walls of recent construction must frequently
be propped with poles. Cuzco.

Hernán went from spud to spud, holding forth on different ones
— "There are over 250 species," he said — and the best methods of
preparing them. Only a few were bakers; some were more suited for
making flour, others for drying and storing and still others "for
alcohol." Hernán allowed that he didn't go in for potato mash but he
knew others who did.

As we were leaving he said something offhandedly which was
truly profound:

*"Sabes que la papa es el regalo más precioso del Perú al mundo.
La cosecha mundial de un año vale más que todo el oro y la plata que
sacaban de aquí los españoles."*

"The potato is our most precious gift to the world. One year's
world crop is worth more than all the gold and silver taken from Peru
by the Spanish."

We said goodbye at the Plaza de Armas. He waved away my tip
so I had to stick it in his coat pocket.

"It is your business," I told him. "You can't just work for
nothing."

"But we are friends," he said.

He was right and I hoped I wasn't being another "ugly gringo" in
making him take the money. But he needed it. And he had earned it.

An odd sight in Cuzco was western backpackers walking about
with their packs forward, over their chests and stomachs. This was
the result of a pestilence of thievery unequaled anywhere in my
experience. The more aggressive knaves had learned how to slit open
a pocket or pouch with a razor, remove its contents and be gone
before the victim was aware of anything amiss.

So pervasive was this larceny that it seemed to have become the
pastime of every young male over the age of twelve. It got to the point
that one reflexively avoided walking close to young men, no matter
where you were. It was assumed that they would try to rob you. Once
mentioned reverentially as "the Katmandu of South America," Cuzco
was now referred to by some as "the City of Thieves."

More deplorable than the stealing, itself, was its tolerance by the
citizenry.

I at first thought that this was due to fear of the perpetrators,
but I became convinced that it was the result of an ingrained
passivity, an acquiescence to conduct considered normal in a culture
where theft is simply a way of life, not a threat to the social fabric —
particularly when practiced against foreigners.

The western ideal of civic rectitude, vigilance, betterment and order, of "all for one and one for all" is alien to Latin America. Such philosophical observations, however, were of little consolation to those who had lost their travel money, cameras and passports. One German youth had $5000 taken from his *front* trouser pocket. Almost every traveler I met had been the victim of at least an attempted theft and several, like the German, had suffered major losses.

Cuzco buzzed with cafes and coffee houses. Among the "in" places at the time was the "Café Literario Varayoc," on a side street across the little Plaza Regocijo from my hotel. The habitués were mostly students and intellectuals, many from Lima and Arequipa. A brash young mime, Adolfo Rodríguez, expressed a superb character in saturnalia, "Pepe Limón." He parodied in turn, the president, Alan García, the army, the police and the bureaucracy. The left did not escape: his last effrontery satirized the *Senderistas* as boorish, indiscriminate assassins.

Thinking that I might avoid the 40–hour bus ride to Lima, I went to the airport to try and catch one of two daily shuttles. The harried woman at the Faucett Agency warned me when I purchased the ticket for $50, twice the fare for residents, that it was worthless without a boarding pass which could only be obtained with great difficulty at the terminal. How great, I had no idea. Having had some experience with Peruvians at banks and railway stations, I did anticipate some disorder. But I was utterly unprepared for the upheaval that awaited me.

People were rioting in front of the counters of the two carriers. There was a contagion of fists, feet, elbows, teeth, sweat and hair. While senior staff sat nonchalantly — some eating sandwiches and drinking coffee — bewildered subalterns attempted to board 200 passengers from an overbooked mob twice that size. Even those who claimed reservations were shunted to the rear. The only thing that counted was a numbered pass and only those who had previously obtained one or who were able to make "special arrangements" with the official issuer in the back room had any hope at all.

After fighting my way through this suffocation of humanity, there was no ventilation and the stench from the toilets was overpowering, my inquiry was answered with one of those arrogant little wags of the finger with which Peruvians parry annoying questions: *"No hay."* Nothing. Complete. Sold out. No chance. Stupid of you to ask.

I returned to town and checked back into the Hotel Royal Inca. I called to invite Hernán down for dinner but there was no answer at the number he had given. After a walk and a couple of beers I padded down for what turned out to be the longest siesta of my journey: 14 hours!

335

The interior courtyard of the hotel, once part of the adjacent residence of the 16th century writer Garcilaso de la Vega, was a gardened aviary. Parrots, parakeets, toucans and other birds of the forest fluttered about, trilled and squabbled.

The window of my room opened onto it like a prison sill or a forecastle porthole — recessed, so that you had to crane to see out. The room, gained by a circular mahogany staircase, was overly furnished — stuffed, really — with a ponderous elegant bed of darker wood, a matching armoire and straight-backed chairs of red leather. It might have housed the children's governess, a favorite old servant or aides of visiting grandees.

It was an "inside" room, one of only a few not rattled by street screeches and combustions. Because the room had no "view" it was half price, about $30, but I would have paid double, so fatigued was I after climbing strenuously through ruins for two weeks, still without acclimatization to the altitude and, for the past day, riddled with a resurgent punch of Manco's revenge.

The birds were not, as I had feared, obtrusive. Rather they were a distant, soothing chorus, which would settle for a time, then rise again, echoing softly in the chamber of tile and stucco.

Hernán Luza Calvo, the retired Cuzco history teacher
who became the author's guide and friend.

20

MARAJÓ

*Our cargo thus spread through the town and up the
rivers and into the forest, as if in obedience to some
ineluctable law of quantum distribution.*

The old freighter toiled in the river sea, its 120 rusted tons
saddled with salt, Pepsi, kerosene, flour, rice, beer, fruit jars, and
behammocked peasants, all of which shifted with each shudder of the
bow against the wind–swept swells.

The spray from these collisions was blown aft with such force
that the tarpaulins lowered by Tatu, the cook, and Sergio, the
captain's callow son, were useless. Hammocks were drenched and
belongings swirled adrift amongst pop cases and nets of produce. How
odd, I thought, that cabbages and carrots could be carried for profit
into the planet's botanical Newcastle.

The storm had almost not come.

It had tarried coyly in the western distance beyond Bagre for an
interminable time, a teasing display of power with a promise of
magnanimity, its thunder barely grumbling overhead long moments
after yellow blades of lightning stabbed into unseen forests from
oultry puffs of cumulus. It appeared to toy with the struggling hulk
and her crusty captain, Antonio Monteria Teixera, to whom the
swollen labyrinthine tongues of the Amazon's mouth seemed as
appendant as his own varicose hands.

Teixera was a dry goods drummer, a barterer who took payment
for his merchandise as much in hearts of palm, coconuts and other
extracted fruits of the forest as in cruzados. His territory was Marajó,
an island domain larger than Switzerland, and the hundreds of
splintered islets and peninsulas of the ambiguous estuary it bestrides.
Through here, one–fifth of all the freshwater on earth pours into the
Atlantic — a volume greater than that of the Nile, the Mississippi, the
Congo, the Zambezi, the Ganges, the Don, the Columbia and the
Yukon combined. So massive is this emptying that for a hundred
miles out to sea sailors and fishermen still dip fresh water.

His métier was as old as European penetration. How else to
supply those who live beyond any thought of roads, where currency is
to some still a curiosity — and to all an inflationary certainty — and a
man's worth is measured by his prowess with knife, saw, gun and at
making children? Our captain was a successor to the *aviador*, the
grocery and hardware outfitter of the rubber boom, 1860–1920, who
swapped shoddy goods for ever greater quantities of the precious

latex laboriously gathered by solitary tappers. Those ignorant souls were thereby kept in perpetual debt to their suppliers, not unlike Dixie sharecroppers and Appalachian coal miners of the same era. But Teixera gave good weight and brooked no sharp dealing by his crew or associates. Nor did he suffer interference in his command by the owner of the vessel, one Aires da Costa, a garrulous but quickly quarrelsome sawmiller who served as titular first–mate.

The craft was customarily employed in the portaging of lumber between da Costa's mills and Belém. In slow times, such as the present, when demand for the great trees was slack and his for cash was dire, the boat would be leased to a trader whose own *navío* was dry–docked as was Teixera's, sunk or disappeared.

Navigational hazards facing the *Presidente Vargas* were as formidable as the political ones of her populist namesake:[77] hull–bashing driftwood, shifting sandbars, channels suddenly filled with flood–washed silt and *murure*, a kudzulike plant that spreads over acres of water to form floating islands that foul propellers and capture small craft. And there were the human perils of inebriated helmsmen, pirates and slipshod maintenance.

I came aboard through the auspices of Anthony Anderson, an American botanist who had lived in the Amazon for a good many years. He and his charming Brazilian wife, Suely, and young sons, Tamil and Benjamin, had been Teixera's neighbors on the Praca Amazonas, a quiet middle–class neighborhood in Belém. Pronounced Ba–*lang*, this is the capital of the eastern Amazonian state of Pará and the river basin's principal port. The city was tranquil compared to the bedlam of Lima, from which I had escaped on Varig, the Brazilian airline, leaving the trusty jeep safely stored in Alan Davis' garage. Actual flight time was ten hours with layovers of four and 12 hours, respectively, in Iquitos and Manaus. I would take sixty–five days to make it back upriver.

Anderson was a consultant with Belém's Museo Goeldi, one of the first–rate ecological research institutions in Latin America. He and his family graciously lodged me for several days, even throwing a surprise birthday party. He broke the mold of the normally reserved tropical scientist. An example was his informed speculation that an extinct "monster" once preyed on one of the region's toughest plants, the babassu palm.

He and Suely had collaborated on a two–year study of the palm, *Orbignya phalerata*, in the neighboring state of Maranhão. They found it to be a veritable arboreal soybean, a "tree of life," that thrives in forests ravaged by fire. This is because "its apical meristem, the part of the plant that is actually growing, is pushed underneath the surface during germination [enabling it] to survive ... even if [its] aboveground portions are completely destroyed."[78] When the young

The *Presidente Vargas* taking on lumber at a Marajó sawmill.

sprouts push up after a fire, they flourish in the detritus of their own stalks and that of incinerated competitors — to such an extent that the latter are wholly excluded from what eventually becomes a natural "plantation" of babassu. Such stands, the Andersons found, contain an incredible 31 tons of biomass per acre, most of it usable as food, fuel or building material.

The kernels from the inner fruit are processed to make cooking oil, soap, cattle feed and a milk substitute similar to mother's milk. From a woody middle layer flour is ground and a variety of fossil–fuel substitutes, from methanol to charcoal, come from the husk. Trunks

341

and leaves are superb beams and thatch for houses. Major enterprises have gradually developed from what was long a cottage industry, creating a market economy for the landless poor who are the palm's principal harvesters.

"To get at the fruit you have to break the husk and the only thing alive today that can do that is man — a big man with a sharp ax," Tony told me.

The only other thing that can get inside is the larva of a beetle, the bruchid, that burrows in through the husk's germination pores. The beetle is not a pest in the usual sense because it does not harm the palm itself and rarely eats every seed.

"The fascinating thing about this palm is that it's always there, always in the forest even the primary forest. But until the forest burns or is cut over, you hardly notice it. We counted over 2,500 per acre in one place. But they're small and grow very slowly — until they get free run. The plant is so well dispersed and such an excellent food source it had to have had a significant predator prior to man."

But its two–inch thick husk takes an enormous *five–and–a–half tons* of force to crack.

"My feeling is that it was the main course for megatherium, the giant South American ground sloth that became extinct in the late Pleistocene, just about the time man got down here. It was probably the only animal alive even then that would have had jaws powerful enough to break the husk — and it was a ground feeder, a perfect eating machine for babassu," Anderson said.

Although the palm can start producing at around 12 years of age in a pure stand, that doesn't happen until 70 or later in a diverse forest. But they can live more than 150 years.

Babassu's productivity per acre of only 1,800 pounds of fruit compares unfavorably with the African oil palm's 22,000. And the African trees take only four years to produce. While this makes babassu unsuitable for plantations, "it's ideal for subsistence agriculture in destroyed forests throughout much of the Amazon."

Tony suggested that I accompany Teixera on his Marajó route.

"You couldn't get a better close–up look at downriver life than on one of his boats," he said.

Suely agreed, and next day she and the boys took me over to Teixera's for lunch, a multicourse Paránese repast prepared by his wife and daughters. I was lucky he told me. The next boat had been delayed until Monday. I could have a place for $40. I had best purchase a hammock.

Children on the wharf of a remote Marajó Island trapiche
awaiting the arrival of the *Presidente Vargas*.

At the turn of the century, Marajó was the home of some of
Brazil's wealthiest cattle barons. Their meat fed Belém and the delta
during the rubber boom. It was also exported on the hoof and in cans.
Although a half century of small farming intervened, subsidies and
tax credits have again led to the concentration of holdings. Displaced
caboclos, mixed–race peasants of black, Indian and European descent,
have moved upriver into the interior, adding to the press of humanity
against the forest. Marajó's primary forests were cut by 1900 but the
harvesting of secondary growth is a major enterprise. Most lumbering

343

is done by small sawmills which are moved as locations become depleted. Rafts of logs floating toward one of these mills is a common sight.

Monday's hour of departure passed with only Sergio and myself at dockside. Beer and pop distributors made deliveries as did a produce market. Teixera would send his considerable list of needs around for competitive bidding. The wily trader thus maintained commanding leverage at both ends of his business: In Belém he bought cheap, selling dear in the bush. A case of beer that cost $10 at retail might be had by Teixera for four or even three. In the forest, this could fetch 20 dollars' worth of palm hearts or other produce.

The international market for palm oil had recently been hurt by concern over its high cholesterol content. "Jungle grease," its vegetable oil rivals called it. But according to Teixera, this had no effect on his trade.

Shortly after noon Tuesday, the *Vargas* got under way. Sergio and I strung our hammocks just forward of the quarterdeck, the best place to catch a breeze. Some peasants were made to vacate in our favor.

"You are our guest," Sergio insisted when I objected. The lad's secondary school English had caused him to be impressed to serve as my interpreter. "My father ordered it. Besides, it is nothing to them."

The crew lay forward as we headed into Marajó Bay. Teixera sat among them, arms folded, one eye closed, one shaded, in a kind of riverman's half sleep.

As Belém receded, I was struck by its sleek and reflective highrises, so explicit were their statements of privilege and gain. There were housed the Bank of America, Volkswagen, Citibank, Bank of Brazil, Chase Manhattan and scores of freight expediters, forwarders and shippers of timber, cattle, aluminum, palm and a hundred other products of the forest. Were they, I wondered, the citadels of a benign commerce that would light the Amazon and its vulnerable parceners to an era of harmonious prosperity — or Ozymandian temples doomed to be licked by the funereal dunes of the emerald vastness before us.

The storm abated toward midnight and we entered a channel barely 200 feet wide. The engine surged but our progress relative to the bank, slowed. Partially submerged whole trees hurtled past, some clawing at the hull. There was a heavy, dank odor untouched by the freshness of rain and you could tell that the weather had avoided this place. The engine cut to idle and we drifted broadside, the swirling galaxy resolving a wharf at the mouth of a slough. There were hurried flickerings of lanterns and impatient voices. Our searchlight revealed a massive, decaying dock with rotted posts. Behind was a mill or warehouse. Two figures advanced mechanically to catch our

344

Antonio Monteria Teixera, captain of the *Presidente Vargas*,
and his son, Sergio, in front of the wheelhouse.

mooring lines. A third emerged wearing a white tropical shirt and a
red–banded panama cocked go–to–hell, a miner's headlamp affixed to
the crown. He carried a cane and his manner was one of sarcastic
condescension, like that of a drill sergeant.

"That is the *patrao*, the brother of the guy who go crazy and kill
the people." Sergio's voice startled me. I'd thought him asleep.

It was one of the stories told the night before as an example of
the delirium or "fits" — a kind of Amazon cabin fever. Even the
toughest *caboclos* and their overlords were not immune.

345

As the story went, there had been a theft of supplies and when
the suspects were confronted, an altercation ensued. The brother, a
heavy drinker, went berserk and attacked the accused, slashing one
with a machete and shooting his accomplices. Someone said a woman
was involved and she too had been killed. Indeed, some cold tale of
violence shrouded almost every *trapiche,* settlement, serviced by the
Vargas, each embellished over time. There were rapes, mutilations,
drownings, beheadings and hauntings by spirits of victims seeking
revenge. The upshot here was that three were dead at the hands of
their *patrao* and though there was an inquiry, nothing had come of it.
But the crazed brother had left and two families of the victims had
remained, some of whom were presumably among the men now
heaving freight onto the rollers which fed the warehouse.

Teixera had decided that the ramshackle wharf was too
unreliable to tie to, so he had secured the mooring lines to posts
ashore and kept the engine ahead at sufficient speed to neutralize the
current. A bridge of planking was improvised to facilitate the
offloading. This was soon accomplished and the *Vargas* resumed its
passage through the night, its searchlight probing the way like a
Cyclops eye.

We came one day at dusk to a village called Mojo and were to be
docked for a time. Drawn by the sound of singing to a back street, I
found a black evangelical service in progress. It had rained and the
earth was spongy and clung to the bare feet of children who ran
through puddles. Worshipers, the men in white shirts and narrow
black ties and the women in floral print dresses, were seated on
planks between crates in front of a grocery. An electric guitar
overbore rather than accompanied and a burly woman banged a pair
of cymbals. The preacher, a peaked mulatto, waved a Bible. His
deputy, sway–backed and with huge moon eyes, directed the singing.
The hymn concluded, the preacher held the Bible aloft as if to signal
someone far to the rear. He then brought it down with a slap into the
palm of his left hand, his feet leaving the ground as he did so, his
voice moaning in "tongues." The audience responded to the thumping,
drawing breaths as the book was raised, then sighing collectively as it
was struck. The guitar was silent as if its player knew that its discord
would break the spell. People were now off their seats, jumping and
shimmying, some of them splashing in the red–orange mud.

There were among them persons of a wide variety of color and
complexion, including several white children, one with red hair and
freckles. These were clearly not intruders but very much a part of the
group. Whether they were the natural children of black women and
white fathers, or whether they were adopted, or how they came to be
here, it was not possible to tell. But no special note was taken of their
presence. They gathered with the other children to gawk–stare at us,

346

A giant moth attaches itself for a time to the *Vargas*.

affecting the same speech cadences, gestures and mannerisms as the black children.

I would see this same "universality" of behavior throughout the Amazon among children and adults of all races. But it was at this settlement that I first noticed the apparent lack of racial awareness among the region's poorer people. With the upper classes, particularly those from the European southern part of the country, racial and ethnic prejudice is very much alive — although officially Brazil claims to be the world's most tolerant nation. But the *caboclos* seemed oblivious to such artificial differentiations and would have been as much puzzled as offended by them in others.

Once we had to anchor to await high tide before entering a shallow channel. The air sagged with the heat of 30 bodies suspended, cocoonlike, one against the other. Nine night boarders from a nearby *trapiche* added their mass. I tried restringing my hammock beyond the overhead to catch a bit of breeze but to no avail. How miserable must have been those slung over the engine room. Finally, I abandoned the hammock, grabbed my sleeping bag and poncho liner and sprawled topside under the stars. There were mosquitoes but a dousing of repellent kept them at bay and sleep came.

I was awakened by Sergio who said that Tatu had the hot water, *Agua quente* — pronounced here *"cain–she"* — ready for my morning Nescafe.

This separate boiling of water had come about only after a good deal of coaxing. Normally I loathed the metallic tasting instant blend but it was far preferable to the crew's coffee, which was so laced with sugar that its texture approached that of taffy. José, the cook's real name, at first had balked at this additional chore but I gradually won him over by praising his cooking — and that not inaccurately. At least for river chefs.

The fare on the *Vargas* consisted of rice, *acail* — a bitter, nutty red berry ground up with flour in a hand–cranked mill and eaten cold, onions, tomatoes, beef tips, chicken livers and armadillo — called *tatu* and the origin of the cook's nickname. This was not a bad tasting meat, not at all gamy or rough, although it is quite greasy and for that reason I was unable ever to get used to it. It was looked forward to as a kind of "down home" special by several of the crew who were "Northeasterners" — from Pernambuco and neighboring states on Brazil's Atlantic hump. They said that there, armadillo was a cheap substitute for more expensive meat and poultry. This remained the case throughout the Amazon, a fact I attributed as much to the availability of the *dasypus* as to the preponderance of Northeasterners among the migrant population.

José prepared the animal as a roast stuffed with various vegetables and well garnished with onions and garlic. Before placing it in his propane oven, he beat the carcass with a mallet to crack the scales and soften the flesh. My unease at the delicacy was noticed, and I was subjected to a good deal of ribbing. Later, I turned the tables a bit, taking advantage of the Belém members' weariness at yet a third serving of armadillo, and referred to José as "Senhor Tatu." The crew picked this up and began chanting "Tatu...Tatu...," and this got his goat, an outcome I had in no way intended. Yet he eventually bore all in good humor and, toward the end of our voyage, had actually begun to take pride in his newfound sobriquet.

Mess was served during two sittings at a table just inboard from the stern. At the second, with Teixera, Sergio, the two mates and myself, the quality was decidedly superior.

"Tatu" the cook with his favorite dish. Armadillo is a dietary staple in the Amazon.

We had chicken breasts instead of wings and necks, and hocks instead of drippings in the rice. Armadillo was not Teixera's favorite. When that was the primary dish, a more appetizing entree would be served on the side.

The head was opposite the galley and was kept more or less clean. The odor of the solvent used in cleaning was almost as unpleasant as the alternative would have been. The shower being over the toilet helped in the cleansing but left the enclosure damp and humid.

Taking a shower, which was expected at least twice daily of both crew and guests, involved a ritual more cosmetically rigorous than hygienic.

Although the door could be latched, one never bathed naked but in swim trunks or cutoffs. Soap was particular to each bather as were talcum, aftershave and cologne. The aromas of each were sharply distinctive. From these constant applications we could as well have been a Seine *péniche* of courtesans as an Amazon riverboat.

To my surprise there was a comfortable privy seat — the first except in private homes since the States. But the Latin American custom of tossing the paper into a box or basket was adhered to, even though both effluent and other refuse was dumped directly into the water. This daily discharge from thousands of boats and settlements facilitates the rapid spread of disease and dysentery, making the river one of the deadliest places on earth.

The plodding *Vargas* was a suitable platform for bird watching. Scores of separate species were clearly visible in slack waters and in the branches of trees along the banks. The species included several very large parrots, a regally gray–blue fish hawk with bright orange wing tips and shanks, and any number of small ducks and herons.

It was from the foredeck of the *Vargas* that I first saw the famous electric–blue morpho butterfly which boasts a wing span of up to seven inches. It was plain to see why it has been called "the bluest thing in the world." Its iridescence of azure and silver gave it an aspect surreal — as if it were a mirage or a cleverly peripatetic hologram. It came upon us suddenly from the mouth of a slough and kept a steady distance abeam for many minutes.

When it occasionally vanished behind intervening foliage, I would hold the binoculars steady until it invariably reemerged in the same position relative to the vessel. We parted only when the helmsman suddenly headed into midstream to evade a rush of shoals.

The *Franz Rossy*, a typical diesel–powered riverboat.

Among small craft sighted were tiny dugouts with inverted cloth sails. The head or top of the triangle was secured in the boat, with the foot or base aloft. These were sailed with great agility by solitary fishermen who threw nets from them and by groups of up to three boys at play. The craft did not go into the wind but only ran with it, albeit at times against the current. The foot of one of these sails, a rather large one, had two vertical battens dividing it into three equal sections. Another suggested reefing, from the "foot" down, but I could not tell for certain that this was the case. There was a strong, but not heavy, wind.

We called at Serraira Sao Benedito de Irmaos Dios, The St. Benedict Sawmill, where rafts of the giant *assacu* tree, stretching for more than a quarter of a mile, were being fed up the ramp. At the other end, an acre of lumber in various sizes was being readied for barging to the shipping yards of the Lawton Company, an American firm said to be the largest wood exporter on the island. Its ultimate destination was no secret: Yokohama.

One of the most astounding facts about Amazon lumber is that most of it is shipped to Japan which imports more wood than all other countries *combined*. Imported not only for processing but for hoarding against what the Japanese fear will be a total wood product cutoff during the next worldwide depression. This in spite of the fact that Japan has more than half of its national territory planted in forest, a greater percentage than that of any other major industrial nation.

The average Marajó mill worker's wage was around 1,600 cruzados per month, about $80. An injured worker could expect a maximum monthly benefit payment of some $60, much less for partial disability. I saw several single amputees still on the job at these mills; double ones loitered at *trapiches* and in village streets.

There were at least a thousand active sawmills on and around the island although activity had recently slowed due to a falloff in export demand. Many of these were small operations such as those run by da Costa, the *Vargas'* owner. He said that his average time in one place was six or seven years before the mill was moved to a new site. Neither he nor anyone else he knew practiced reforestation.

"It is not worth the effort," he said. "If the forest will not grow back naturally then it won't grow back no matter what you do."

Bom Jardim, Good Garden, was a prosperous palm heart operation which supported a dozen large families. On the pier, workers slashed and chopped at bundles of palm stalks with machetes, vying with each other to see how fast they could cut out the hearts. Inside, young women deftly jarred the fruit and boxed it. There was a vivacity about these folk unlike that of any other *trapiche* we visited.

352

Hardware store, Afuá.

It even boasted a one–room school full of 8– and 9–year–olds reciting multiplication tables for a determined teacher who wrote the answers on the blackboard as they gave them. Her contract was for two years at a salary of 1,600 cruzados a month plus lodging and food.

In spite of the apparent prosperity of this outpost, it also received a sizable shipment of produce, including several crates of tomatoes and oranges and some nets–full of cabbages and potatoes. I asked Sergio why so many *trapiches* had to ship in vegetables and fruits when they lived on such rich land.

"They have some small plots," he said, "but they can't grow enough to feed themselves. And the owners don't like for them to take time away from their work to farm." It was also true, I was to learn, that the soil gives out after only a few years' cropping — a fact that has contributed to the destruction of interior forests as new lands are strip–cleared for planting and ranching.

Little note was normally taken of our comings and goings but at Bom Jardim people actually waved farewell. In the Amazon such spontaneity is seldom seen, even among children.

We reached Afuá, our farthest port, the fifth day out of Belém.

This town of 2,600 is situated near the open sea on the northeastern hub of Marajó, at the juncture of the Pirhiauara and Marajozinho tributaries. Although primarily a timber community, fishing had become a mainstay due to layoffs at the government–supported TIMBRAS mill across the way. Employment then was 300, less than half the normal payroll, according to workers.

Founded in 1854, Afuá was built on posts up to 10 feet high to withstand tidal wash and river flooding. Graves are occasionally disturbed by these inundations, leading to the local bromide that Afuá's dead always return. Another saying is that you can tell how long it has been since the last tide by the height of fecal piles under outhouses. These are situated on the town's raised boardwalks, some dangerously decrepit — except for the recently concreted pier front, the Avenida Micaela Ferreira. So important was its paving that the president of Brazil attended its dedication on December 7, 1984 — an event recounted on an official plaque. Most street names are historical. There is one for Vargas; Rua Joao Pablo II honors the pope. None carry the names of trees or animals.

It was here that the youth of Brazil's population was made indelibly clear to me. True, there were romps of tykes at the *trapiches*, their numbers at times making the few adults oddly conspicuous.

At Afuá so many thronged the avenida and wharves that I thought there must be a holiday or festival. Before we even made fast, a troop of them had scampered aboard, some pulling themselves up by the bowline. They plunged one after another into the river then clambered back up to dive again.

Neither Teixera nor the crew made any effort to stop them and for our time here, the *Vargas* endured these indignities like a tolerant mother bear. A question that came to mind earlier in the barrios of Mexico City and Guatemala and later in Lima returned: In the minds of the adults and of the children, themselves, is the concept of childhood with its essential tenderness and forgiveness devalued by so many children at large?

Merchants, including a very tall and muscular East Indian, who could have been Sikh, and a Chinese came to review manifests and give off–loading instructions. A third of the *Vargas'* orders were for Afuá whose trading area extends for more than a hundred square miles and includes a great many dependent villages and *trapiches*.

Although keeping her berth at the principal wharf, major deliveries were also made to those more convenient to her customers. One of these, a robust Portuguese who was apparently the "Sikh's" chief competitor, became outraged at what he said was tardy delivery of goods: some cloth and tools were different from those he had ordered. He shouted and gesticulated at Teixera, who remained cool throughout, nodding and faintly smiling as the fellow continued his diatribe. Finally, Teixera took out his notebook and, making penciled entries, told the merchant that he would gladly cancel his order and sell it to other shopkeepers.

The Indian had come out of his shop and at the mention of the cancellation said he would take the lot at the contract price.

The Portuguese had second thoughts. After a face–saving proviso, which was meaningless, he withdrew his threat and accepted delivery. This was the only time that I saw Teixera insist on payment in cash instead of bartered goods. That further riled the consignee but he paid and stalked away.

It was on our return from this delivery that the engine quit and our remaining sorties were made under tow of two jury–rigged local craft, the *Deus Me Vale, God Values Me,* and the *Concepcion Imaculada, Immaculate Conception.* Their young skippers were not as cautious as Teixera and he had a time of it keeping their speed under control.

On one of these outings, to Sitio Agualefo, a plantation landing across the Pirhiauara where we delivered five cases of Tatuzhino Armadillo Brand white lightning, the captain of *Deus Me Vale* sampled the merchandise. On the return he almost rammed us into the garbage scow *So Deus, Under God,* whose noxious odor, as if emitted in consternation, lingered behind it for a quarter of an hour. When they were not assisting us, these craft raced each other up and down the waterfront.

It was discovered that our problem was a faulty fuel pump which ̣s replaced with one cannibalized from a vessel beached for repairs.

Meanwhile, Teixera also had small orders for individual ̣ants who came alongside in canoes and flatboats and, in two ̣, makeshift schooners whose sails doubled as tarpaulins over ̣abins. One of these, *Ebenezer*, housed a family of 10.

̣hese boat people took mostly sacks of rice and flour, but an occasional toy or dress was also dispensed. A little red plastic tricycle that had been shunted about on deck for days was so delivered. There were also spontaneous sales from our beverage and fuel stores, the purchaser's cooler or barrel being presented for filling by one of the men.

No private dealing by the crew was permitted and each transaction was carefully recorded. Teixera and the second mate were constantly alert for pilfering. On a recent trip the captain had caught a crewman red–handed stealing a crate of tomatoes. The thief pulled a knife but Teixera stared him down and he fled.

Within an hour of tying up, some of our freight was in the street: cans of Pepsi, the town's first in a week; bottles of Brahma Chopp beer, relieving a similar drought; apple cider, Sidra Gereser — mildly alcoholic; and Belagua mineral water.

These were first purveyed from a restaurant, just up from our pier, which was patronized by Teixera and the crew. We were favored there with lunch on–the–house the day of our arrival. At the rear was a pedestal onto which the owner reverentially placed each morning a 30–inch color television set. The box performed until the town's generator shut down at midnight.

The programming, satellite dished, was familiar: soap operas, *fútbol*, rat–a–tat news by earnest, coiffured heads with unctuous modulation and twinkling, sales–close smiles. Commercials for cigarettes, beer, pop, banks and tennis shoes dominated, in that order. In one hour I tracked more than 35 minutes of advertising.

Among the first items unloaded were several bales of T–shirts. These now blossomed on older children and teenagers, who strutted about like *boulevardiers*. They were as oblivious to the English inscriptions on the garments as had been their Belém designers: OH BOY!, CITY ROCKER, GIVE PEACE DANCE, ACTIVE — front / AVAILABLE — back, PRAY FOR SURF, CALIFORNIA FRUIT, SPORT SPEAK GOLF.

Cold storage freight worker, Santarém.

A wing of kites lofted over the promenade. Seeing them, children without scurried to the store of the Sikh who sold them as fast as they could be wrapped in perfunctory brown paper and handed over the counter. Green, purple, yellow, blue — no swimming now, no tag–and–run, but kites! — if you don't have one, you're a goat or poor — or both!

Our cargo thus spread through the town and up the rivers and into the forest, as if in obedience to some ineluctable law of quantum distribution. In the late afternoon long nimble dugouts sleuthed past, paddled by gaunt men and women, with eight or 12 eyes of children peeping out from between sacks and crates and nets of things that so recently had lodged in the belly of the *Vargas*. In one, the red tricycle added its soft weight to gunwales precariously flush with the brown water.

Teenage boys pose at Santarém. Note meaningless
English words on T-shirts.

21

ITAITUBA

'If he is shifty and green, then I will have to kill him. The one thing I fear is a coward. A coward will kill you.'

"The only way to 'save the Amazon,' as you put it, is as a resource for the people who live here. They won't 'preserve' it because someone from New York or São Paulo tells them it is 'the lungs of the world,' which anyway is absurd. But they will *conserve* it, if they think it's in their best interest.

"'Wilderness preservation' — to peasants, talk like that is crazy. One way to look at it is to accept that both the trees *and* the people are the forest. Politics is part of ecology — *real* politics with *real* people, not some philosophical notion of 'humanity'. These people won't go away, disappear. This is their home. So to have the trees you must have the people — not as enemies but allies."

Virgilio Viana was 26 and a Harvard doctoral candidate in "secondary forests." He had moved from his native Minas Gerais state to settle with his wife, Lili, and infant daughter, Cecilia, at Belterra, Henry Ford's defunct rubber plantation founded in 1934 on the banks of the Tapajós near that clear water river's confluence with the muddy Amazon. His study was aimed at determining whether man's commercial use of the forest could be "synchronized with its natural rhythm."

Ford envisioned Belterra — and Fordlandia, a sister plantation 70 miles upstream — as providing cheap rubber for decades of tires. Some Brazilians thought the projects would restore their country as king of the rubber trade, a status which it had been deposed from by colonial Malaysia during World War I. There British plantations of trees transplanted from the Amazon proved more competitive. But the development of synthetic rubber in World War II extinguished forever the automotive market for tapped.

Abandoned in 1945, the plantation has limped along as a government experimental station.

Perhaps the primary reason for Ford's failure was *Microcyclus ulei*, the fungus which causes South American leaf blight, SALB. Plantations rarely work in the tropics since clustering facilitates the rapid spread of parasites and pests that prey on the same trees.

The Malaysian transplants had none of these, at least initially. Perhaps "because" of this, trees of a kind tend naturally to disperse goodly distances, even up to a mile or more — unlike those in northern climes where tightly bunched stands of pine, fir, oak, cottonwood and aspen thrive. Within months after it first appeared, SALB rampaged through Fordlandia, infecting whole stands in days. Although Ford used fungicide at Belterra, the blight stymied profitable production there as well. Today Brazil imports half its natural rubber from Malaysia.

Wide dispersal is not noticed by the casual observer, since an acre of rain forest can contain more than 80 species. By contrast, an acre of forest in the United States normally contains no more than four. The entire North American continent has fewer than 400.

No one knows for sure how this phenomenon occurs. How do some seeds "know," for example, not to germinate because they are too close, say only a half mile, to a parent or sibling when they "ought" to be further?

On a less profound level, Virgilio was studying the mechanics of seed distribution in several marketable species to see if they could be part of a scheme of "self–interest" conservation. He was methodically collecting fallen fruit, trying to note the location of each in relation to the crown of the parent tree.

"Many just fall on the ground," Virgilio lectured. "These are much less likely to germinate than others taken farther away by birds."

One tree, the *morototo*, is widely used for making match sticks. It abounds in secondary forests, flourishing in open spaces left by large fallen trees or fire swaths. One of the misconceptions about the Amazon basin, Virgilio explains, is that it is completely flat.

"Frequently, there are rolling hills, some of them with pronounced ridges and valleys — although they are tiny in comparison to Andean foothills. When you get a clearing, from fires or a big tree that's fallen, there will be an open space or even a meadow. That's where *morototo* does best." The other two subjects of his study — the *parapara*, widely used for pulp, and the *guaruba*, in construction — also sprout in such spaces.

Three birds eat a lot of *morototo* seeds: the wild pigeon, the parrot and the *japu*, a kind of yellow–beaked blackbird. Locating other trees visited by these birds, "either because they like their fruit, too, or prefer the air currents up there," helps predict where seeds previously eaten are likely to be deposited.

"Sometimes the rule is broken, and you'll find several trees of the same species in the same small area. But usually you have to walk quite a ways."

Young girl tending cook fire near Belterra.

Fewer than 25 of the Amazon's thousands of tree species are used commercially. Fewer than 10 of those are exported. If plantations exacerbate the spread of pests among cropped species, logging widely dispersed ones kills many times the number of trees actually harvested. Chains and cables indiscriminately smash and uproot and many trees are pulled down by mutually clinging vines as neighbors fall. Thousands are destroyed in the construction of log roads, which then allow squatters access to strip–clear the rest.

Virgilio thinks "contained dispersal" is one solution. This would mean closer planting of harvestable species but with constant pest control. "Clean" removal by dirigible or helicopter could avoid incidental damage.

We headed along a trail almost overgrown, taking turns on Lili's old one–speed delivery bike. Virgilio's own bike's chain was broken. Coming to a freshly cut side path, we followed it Poohlike, until we arrived at a tall tree with stubby boards nailed every foot or so until they disappeared into the foliage. On the bottom rung hung a cotton jacket and an opened, felt–lined binocular case — circumstantial evidence of an earlier ascent. We climbed, my host leading the way, I taking care to distribute my weight as much as possible on two planks simultaneously. The tree is a hotel of insects, some lazing, others scurrying. I recall that, on average, each two–and–a–half acres of rain forest has more than 40,000 species of insects. Most are unnamed, much less catalogued and studied. The average tree hosts 400 species.

Virgilio eases onto a crude platform already occupied by a person excitingly pointing at something far below. I follow clumsily. My guide adjusts some binoculars and without looking up, introduces me to Bebe, a phenologist and co–worker in the seed study. Bebe has been coming for a month to this *louro* perch to watch the goings–on in its immediate neighbor, a fruiting *morototo*. The *morototo* is full of *japu* including a particularly large cock not seen in some time. Virgilio passed me the glasses. Most birds, he says, prefer certain patches of the forest over others. They eat, visit and scatter droppings in a regular pattern. Each not only has its own territory but a fairly predictable daily path through that territory.

He planned to catch and feed a few of each species who eat the fruit of the *morototo* and the other trees in the study, keeping the birds long enough to get stool samples. The length of time a bird takes to pass a seed, together with its flight pattern, gives a good indication of how far seeds will spread.

Beneath the *morototo*, plastic sacks catch fruit and droppings. These will be compared with samples from other trees.

We spent an hour birding, Bebe studiously adding to long columns of numbers on his clipboard. The *japu* are easily distinguishable but other birds, to my unpracticed eye, are hopelessly intermingled.

Afterward we made our way to Belterra's nursery at the far side of the village. There, seeds from many sacks have been planted in boxes. Virgilio painstakingly notes the condition of each. He transplants some sprouts and jars others. His enthusiasm for this tedium is contagious, and I find myself an eager supernumerary, fetching first one specimen, then another, and taking closeup photographs of ants and other insectile intruders.

Toward sundown, refreshed by a cold shower that briefly fends off a fresh hatch of mosquitoes, I stepped from the back door of the town's only lodging, the Pensión Sonabrisa. I walked through its unfenced yard of pigs and chickens and down a lane of tidy cottages floating on roses and bougainvillea — the upend of Belterra with a view of the distant Tapajós. At Virgilio's, a stack of logs and a bench of tools bespoke an industriousness not elsewhere evident. Doors and windows were being redone, the porch enlarged, a deck added on. There were odors of supper. My host, Cecilia giggling from his shoulders, welcomed me with a refrigerated Brahma Chopp.

"They simply don't know how to cope with a volunteer," he lamented. "It's something beyond their experience. Everyone there has a salary. They never think of doing something for nothing. It's the same at the hospital. It took Dr. Moraes to say, 'Hey, I want her to help so she will.' Otherwise, the administrator would never have allowed it."

Liliana, an occupational therapist, had also volunteered her services at the local school, an offer summarily rejected.

"I think I'll eventually tutor, even if under supervision," she said. "But it was really weird, you know. I could *feel* the fear and resentment when I walked in. I suppose you can't blame them. They've fought hard to get hired, usually by a family member or through his influence. They have little or no qualification. They must carefully guard their territory and that means sticking to their own ways of doing things. Letting an outsider in to show them up is not doing that."

Together she and her husband had prepared an "environmental curricula" for the school, "a mix of everyday phenomena they seldom see or misunderstand when they do."

"For example, we included the taking of microbiological samples from the village sewer, samples of plants — their roots, stems, flowers, and so forth, and scat from all kinds of animals. It would show them close–up how nature works; how man affects it. You can imagine how exciting this would be to these kids who are surrounded by the most complex varieties of life on Earth, yet who know less about them than kids in Europe and the States. But there's a critical element you can't plan for, the teachers. Without their cooperation you can't even begin to start such a program.

"As long as they follow the government curricula, they keep their jobs, their security. If they take a chance on something new, the best thing that can happen is that it succeeds and the old way is shown to have been bad and them with it. If it fails, they are blamed for wasting time and money on a foolish adventure. They are very clever bureaucrats, these teachers. So nothing has been done. But we are hoping. Maybe the next term."

Ever conscious of employee morale and ever the missionary of commonweal and hygiene, Ford modeled Belterra after a typical Midwestern town, bestowing upon its several square blocks the only paved streets in the Amazon outside Belém and Manaus. There was electricity from gasoline generators, running water, sewers, a firehouse with a red hose truck and matching Detroit fire plugs on every corner, a city hall, a school and even a church. The architecture was Michigan–summer–lodge: screened porches, red–tiled roofs, dark green siding.

A life–sized statue of Tom Sawyer was raised in the park, perhaps as an inspiration to peasant schoolboys of that rambunctious irreverence that, in presuburban America, augured enterprise. This nemesis of decorum still gazes mischievously toward the Tapajós.

Ford's other structures slouch in disrepair. The inn for staff and visitors is now the seedy Sonabrisa. Operated as a private concession, its tenants are largely bush women in advanced stages of pregnancy or comforting sick children. All have come on a pilgrimage of hope, some from more than a thousand miles away. They wash, scrub, sweep and peel to defray rent on cubicles of treble and quadruple occupancy.

Their mecca and the settlement's showcase is the hospital Ford ordered built to the highest US field–surgery standards of the time. It remains the redoubt of a medicine and pharmacology locked in state–of–the–art Deco: delivery beds, hemoglobin counter, microscope, sterilizer, oxygen bottles, drug vials — desks, chairs, lamps, operating table, even the library: all 1929 originals.

Closed with the plantation in 1945, the hospital for many years ran on an on–and–off basis under the reluctant governance of the interior ministry, sometimes with a resident physician, more often not. A feud with the ministry of health, which refuses certification, continues. The result is niggardly funding, with salary delays of sometimes several months and little allotted for new equipment and supplies — most of which must be purchased on the open market rather than through the rival agency's procurement office. There is the equivalent of one full–time LPN and two nurse's aides. Several

366

Belterra Hospital, built by Henry Ford in 1929.

"trainees" come in during emergencies or when the number of patients swells toward the infirmary's 50–odd bed capacity.

That the place was open at all was due to the singular tenacity of its 37–year–old physician, Dr. Ivaldo Moraes. An honors graduate just out of a São Paulo residency, he was hired by the national police — a good first appointment for a young Brazilian doctor. Assigned to Belém, he developed a successful reputation, acquiring on the side a small but prestigious private practice. He married, had children, then learned he was to be transferred to Rio. Hearing of the vacancy at Belterra, he applied and was accepted, thinking it would only be a short tour to finish his government contract. But 12 years had passed and he was hooked: "I do not think I could leave now," he told me. "There is so much left to do."

He delivered on average 45 babies a month and performed a hundred other procedures — from tying off traumatic amputations to tonsillectomies and cyst removal. A ruptured appendix delayed him that evening so we started dinner without him.

He came at 10, as we were finishing up. Lili had kept his meal warm and we talked while he ate. Later we sat in the front room, drinking coffee and *caipirinha*, a drink of crushed lime skins and sugar over ice with a jigger of *Cacaca*, the potent Brazilian brandy. Lili, whose English was very good, interpreted.

"I didn't see this as my life's work. It was just a temporary expedient."

His wife tried living here but found it socially stifling. And the school was laggard compared to the private one that the children, now three of them, attended in the city, although "there are things they learn here that no school can teach."

He tried to phone them every night on the station's shortwave. Once a year they came for a month and he returned to Belém periodically during which time he saw private patients. Their fees kept the hospital stocked with aspirin, soap, Q–tips, towels and hypodermic needles. He unabashedly solicited from colleagues and pharmaceutical detail men who slipped him sample cases of everything from Tylenol to penicillin.

He had not sought U.N. or other such help.

"I'd like to do that, but first we need to solidify our government support."

Interior had tried to close the hospital, saying it is obsolete. "But it serves more people than any other rural hospital in the Amazon. They want to build a big modern one in Santarém. But they should rebuild this one. It is known and trusted by the people."

The next day, with Liliana again interpreting, he showed me around. We walked down a hallway past rooms of mothers and infants, one having just been delivered that morning. Beyond was what once had been the recovery room, a large sunny ward the width of the building. One row of beds with dusty sheets was long vacant. Frames of cots were stowed at one end, their springs and mattresses stacked separately.

I asked why the space wasn't used.

"Bats!"

When repeated spraying and smoking failed, he boarded up their attic roost. Still they came, burrowing through the rotting ceiling.

"You never know when they will attack," he laughed.

368

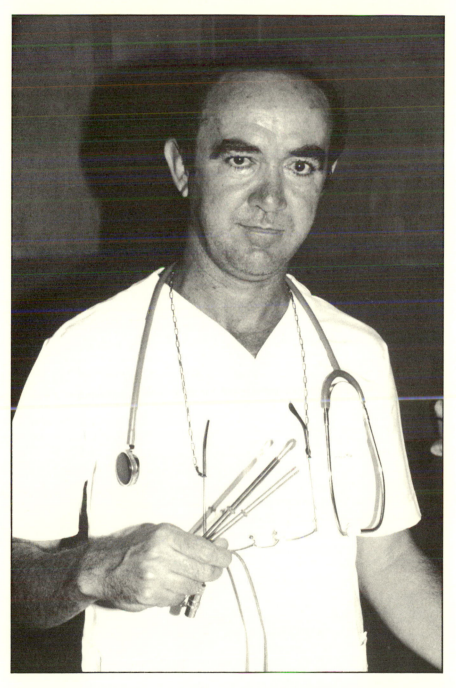

Dr. Ivaldo Moraes of Belterra

An emergency request for fumigation funds had been denied. But what about the townspeople mounting a community effort to drive off the vermin and repair the building?

"There's no way you could get them to do that. They don't understand such things. 'Who would buy the chemicals, the lumber and paint? Who would pay us for our time?' That is what they would ask." Lili had anticipated the doctor's response. When she repeated it for him, he smiled resignedly, throwing up his arms. "No way," he shrugged. He walked over and opened a window, pausing to brush off the dust on one of the beds.

Now Lili spoke less as interpreter than advocate:

"What makes his practice so beneficial is his concern with *preventing* health problems instead of just treating them.

"He tells them to get their kids vaccinated, sterilize knives before opening boils or cutting umbilical cords, how to bandage small wounds, how to boil water. Personal sanitation, malaria tablets, boiling water — these are things the people can do, themselves, immediately, at no cost. Many obey, because he doesn't boss or preach, but talks to them like a friend."

We were in the "lab," a room spotlessly clean, though stacked with cans of chemicals, the labels faded or nearly so. The doctor toyed with Ford's microscope for my photographic benefit.

"Some women have lost babies before. They want to make sure this one is born. Other ones, with many children, know he will 'fix them' so they can stop having kids, bang bang, one after the other. For this, he is condemned by the priests."

The last stop was the operating room. I asked what was his most challenging surgery there. He said one in which, using the exact procedure outlined in a 1920 Johns Hopkins medical text, he had repaired a man's testicles.

What about anesthesia. Who administered it?

"I do it myself. It is the trickiest part — more dangerous than the surgery." The first thing he would do, he said, if Belterra had all the funds it needed, would be to "hire a resident anesthesiologist. That is, after killing the bats."

Virgilio agreed to take me along on a day's foray into the Tapajós National Forest. Officially, such areas are rather wilderness preserves than livestock and logging concessions, as in the United States. In practice, depletion is far more relentless and renewal nil.

At the last moment, the nursery's pickup was commandeered by a warden so I rented one from the village prefect for $20. Lili packed a picnic and a thermos of coffee.

370

Stretch of the Trans–Amazon Highway near the Tapajós National Forest.

Beyond Belterra, on either side of the heavily eroded earth road — a branch of the Trans–Amazon Highway — the forest was turning into smoldering stumps and charred heaps of brush. Occasionally, on the far periphery of the burns, leaps of flame would explode into fresh stands of timber.

"I'm afraid it will spread into the preserve, if indeed it hasn't already," Virgilio said as we reached the cutoff. The sanctioned verdure was a respite from the desolation behind us. Yet the air was already sooted and there was a morbid stillness among the leaves.

"It's impossible to patrol such a large area with only 20 rangers, much less fight fires," Virgilio said. Once we stopped to photograph an anteater, from whose sluggishness at our approach I thought diseased. On closer inspection we found it to be dazed by the smoke.

At length we found deep greenness, and the young Brazilians delighted in exhibitions of their sylvan prowess. I was shown *mandioqueira* the size of Douglas fir, *piquia*, a straight and sturdy tree prized for construction; and the *cecropia*, home of the sloth, whose roots hold stores of clean fresh water. Virgilio chopped one up with his machete; Lili tilted it to her mouth and drank like a parched legionnaire.

We continued thus for hours. Once we stopped in a thicket of the sinewy *titica* vine and Lili pantomimed chair weaving. This was the region's most pliant "wicker." Furniture made from *titica* is a major export. The *ambe* vine, the vital fastener for babassu palm huts, was proliferous. These two plants alone were literally interwoven with the human life of the Amazon.

When one considered merely the economic value of the standing forest, leaving aside ecology, scholarship and aesthetics, it was absurd to permit, much less encourage, its destruction for any reason. Were a foreign invader to threaten annexation of its coveted Amazon, there would be a patriotic call to arms. Yet Brazil was turning that very patrimony into desert. Was there no hope? The Tapajós was but one of several score enclaves officially set aside against man's onslaught. Surely its rangers would afford it some practical measure of protection, however shorthanded they may be. They could, after all, deal summarily with poachers. And all able–bodied persons could be conscripted as fire fighters.

I recalled the "debt–for–equity–swap" urged as a solution to the Third World's trillion–dollar loan arrearages. Some environmental groups had proposed using the idea to "save the rain forests." Brazil, for example, would agree to place huge tracts in preserves, such as the Tapajós. Billions in debt would then be forgiven. The director of one group said he was working on such a plan that would "lock up half the remaining Amazon for posterity." But how could such an agreement be physically enforced on the ground? It likely could not.

We found 10 of the rangers at a temporary camp more than an hour from forest headquarters. They had been there for a week felling trees and trimming the logs for hauling out. Each had a chain saw with which he was proudly efficient. Two of them gave a demonstration by cutting down a very large tree in under five minutes. Jairo, the guide assigned to us by the superintendent, said that this was "controlled thinning," but the trees were choice brazilwood and mahogany, whose rapid depletion for the Japanese export market has become a national scandal. The logs were collected twice daily by trucks of a company said to be operating under government license.

Wash day on a creek near the Tapajós River.

The men were just having lunch when we arrived, and they invited us to join them, which we did, Lili breaking out her chicken sandwiches to add to the rice and beef stew that had stood for days. It was to take a week for me to survive its effects.

One of the men, Lira, had become a hero among them for shooting a jaguar several days previously. It had attacked him, he said, as he was walking through a clearing not far from camp. He had with him part of the tail and an ear. He proudly reenacted the event, using the single shot small–bore rifle that had by his account saved his life.

"They get fired for killing the animals," Virgilio said later. "I don't really think the cat was attacking. Only females with cubs do that. He probably just saw it and shot. A lucky hit. Then he got scared and made up that story."

Itaituba. The church stood at the juncture of a nondescript side street with the riverfront road. Although it was half past 10 Sunday morning, its ponderous doors were shut — firmly, in the Latin way: iron latches removed; a solid beam braced across inside. But the vestry entry in back was ajar, an implied invitation.

No one was in the sanctuary, whose sparse and colorless interior might have belied its function were it not for a contorted crucifix hewn from a grainy crimson trunk. Its swirls and knots would, even without the hand of its sculptor, have declaimed anguish. On the altar, draped with simple lace, was a Portuguese Bible opened to the 13th and 14th chapters of Proverbs. Next to it was a stack of the month's programs.

I sat in a rear pew, relishing this calm against the storm of avarice outside. At length, a lame, chubby lad about 15, evidently a choirboy, peeped from the doorway, then vanished to return with a formidable matron and several small girls whose bewildered stares became unsettling. The woman approached hesitantly to advise that morning services were concluded; I would be welcome that night at seven, but in the meantime no one was allowed within. "*Abrogado,*" I thanked her and followed them out. She removed the handle, hurriedly shackled and padlocked the door, then gathered the children about her like a fretful hen and bustled them away, the choirboy struggling to keep up.

They gaped back at me as they fled.

"Old prospectors? Ha! There are no 'old prospectors.' The old ones are all dead. They die quickly here. The Amazon is a great eater of people. The moment the *caboclo* reaches the interior jungle, he's a dead man.

"Lira," the Tapajós National Forest laborer who had just killed a jaguar with his rifle.

"There's, of course, death by mosquito — yellow fever, two kinds of malaria, and wildfire. You know what that is, wildfire? It's a disease of the nervous system spread by a mosquito that lives in the top canopy of the forest. It was unknown until they started cutting down the trees to build the Trans–Amazon Highway. Once you get it, it drives you crazy, like rabies. There's no cure.

"If he's black — really black, dark — then he has an advantage. His sickle cells, the ones that cause anemia, will protect him from most of the mosquito–borne diseases. But then there's hepatitis and the intestinal parasites, hundreds of them, for the slow death of dysentery, dehydration. Diarrhea kills half their children — birth control on the other end, I call it — then it kills them. For the really unlucky ones there's leprosy. The largest concentration of lepers in the world is right here in the Amazon. But you know what the deadliest disease is? *Gold fever!* It kills more than all the others combined."

We were at a fish house called Porfirio's on the riverbank south of town. My lecturer was Alex Coelho, resident buyer for Cobalt Metais, a São Paulo gold trading outfit. We had met in the lobby of the Hotel Central that morning. He had overheard me asking for a room and being turned away. "Try the Tapajós Plaza," he said. "It's a working hotel, if you know what I mean. But the girls won't bother you if you don't ask. And it's clean, and cheap." It was indeed the latter: $4 a night. And for an extra dollar I got a second sheet. The women were friendly but not solicitous. My room was across the street from a seamy disco–bar that cranked up at 10 and went till dawn. Next to it was another bordello whose roof was curtained off into extra "rooms." By day, the curtains were drawn and the ladies sewed, sunbathed and frolicked about like so many sorority sisters, joined by others from neighboring establishments. They also did their washing, dumping tubs of dirty water into the street. Splashed pedestrians, at first irate, mellowed when they saw the authors of their discomfiture, some even making engagements.

We had ordered broiled *tucunaré*, the house specialty. The waiter, a barefoot son of the owner, brought beer. The buyer lit an *Amerino*, a bitter Brazilian stogie.

"You're under my wing here now, whether you like it or not. They already say you're my new man. They believe you are an agent or partner. It doesn't matter. You are safe now."

I hardly thought I was in any peril, I told him.

"This is no place for gringos, and I include in that all white people, foreigners, myself included. My race makes me a stranger in my own country, at least out here. Many of these people would quicker cut your throat than shake your hand."

Tapajós turtle shell with eggs, Itaituba.

The restauranteur made a show of guiding to our table some children with a large turtle shell full of the reptile's eggs.

The buyer waived them off.

"Not for me. You care for some?" I said not.

"They catch them during the full moon when everything is hiding on the bottom. But a turtle has to come up for air. They run a boat around in circles until they surface then they throw a net over them." But this one was killed on the beach after laying her eggs.

I'd asked if he could steer me to some "old prospectors." That had triggered the lecture on the trade's short life expectancy.

"... And don't think they spare the women and children either," he picked up the theme again, relating that only the week before two *garimpeiros,* gold diggers, had killed another in a barroom dispute over mining shares. The dead man's family had hunted down and killed the attackers then kidnapped the wife and two children of one of them. They found them the following day on the riverbank, hacked to death with machetes. Another couple were shot, by mistake. The family of the second assailant hid with terrified neighbors until the killers gave up the search.

"People won't talk about it, at least in public. They are afraid to show interest. It might get around that they're somehow involved. Before this feud is over there'll likely be another dozen killings and mutilations."

Later, we drove to the office of Cobalt Metais, a few blocks from Coelho's hotel. It was in one of scores of tawdry little *ouro,* gold merchant, storefronts in the town and appeared to be just another one of them. But Cobalt was the town's largest buyer. Its clients, however, were mostly other buyers — only rarely would *garimpeiros* wander in. *Ouro* stalls occupied virtually every space that wasn't an eatery, bar, hardware store or undertaker. Their contents were simply a scales, propane tanks and a burner — a skillet inside a glass–doored oven.

A sample of ore is placed in the oven to burn off mercury, an element almost always associated with gold. Next, the sample is passed under a magnet to remove any iron. Finally, it is soaked in hydrochloric acid to determine its silver content.

"The greater the silver," said Coelho, "the darker the sample becomes — and the less valuable it is. The less silver, the yellower the ore. The silver is worth a little something, of course, but it has to be removed before the gold is melted down into bars in São Paulo. That cost further reduces its value. Ten years ago, silver was worth 10 times as much. But today it's worth only a little more than the cost of extraction.

"For nearly pure gold they pay 80 to 85 percent of the New York price; we pay 88. For the really adulterated stuff, we pay as low as 60. We usually pay in cruzados, but sometimes in dollars if they really press for it — but at a damned good discount, say 19 or 20. The rate is now 24 to the dollar. Our broker in São Paulo checks the New York price at least three times a day, and I get it from him by radio."

It was not uncommon for a miner to shop several stalls before finally selling. The dealer then would come to Cobalt to resell the gold for the best price over cost. Coelho — or one of his two assistants — would assay the ore yet again before doing a deal.

Garimpeiro, Itaituba.

"The diggers are *caboclos*, not white like me. I can almost never do business with them, even though I don't cheat them and actually give them a better price. They go to their own kind — who, of course, cheat them. When they weigh the gold they take a little in the palm of the hand, spill a little on the floor.

"You will see what a great display they make to sweep all the dust up very carefully back into the pouch. That is bull and the *garimps*, most of them, know it. But they prefer to be cheated by their own to doing business with a foreigner. What they don't know is that three–fourths of these buyers work for me. I pay them a small profit but it comes out the same for me. The miner gets less than if he came here directly. The difference is the buyer's profit — and what they can steal on the side from each assay, which I suppose could be figured as profit, but I call it theft, which it is. It's a shame, but that's the way it works. They may think it's a free market when they deal with each other, but I run it from this room."

We were back at the Central and he was going over his books. It was a sizable room over an alley at the end of the hall, softly air conditioned, a luxury, and equipped with a small refrigerator and hot plate. He had lived out of it, he said, almost three years.

When he said the part about running the market from his room, he reached under the bed and pulled out a portable safe, which he opened. It was stuffed with 100–cruzado notes and a few bands of 100–dollar bills. "Aren't you afraid to keep all that here?" I asked.

"Theft from me would be frowned upon. My men would be hard to restrain." At his request, the hotel had assigned one maid to clean the room. "She would never steal — probably because she's an honest soul. But she has children she loves very much."

"How much would you say the average *garimpeiro* makes in a month?" I asked him.

"Three kilos, $10,000 net, for a good month's work. Can you believe it? That's more than most Brazilians earn in a year. And $20,000 isn't uncommon. For a Northeasterner, for anybody who's had nothing, who was born starving, that's worth fighting and dying for. And most of them do."

"What about their families, their children?" I asked. "What happens to them while the men are in the gold fields?"

"Some take their families with them, out to the *garimpo*. But it's a hard life. The ones who are left behind, here or in the northeast? Well, it depends on if he can hold onto his money long enough to get home with it. Whores here cost a lot. And there's all kinds of gambling — cards, craps. For every one that makes it, 50 don't. And while he's gone, his family has to eat. Feeding 10 or 12 children is hard for a woman alone. So kids go off on their own damned early. A lot of them head out here to try their own luck at the gold."

Residents of an Itaituba hotel.

At Itaituba the legions of children without childhood continued their march, many alone, others in small groups scavenging for handouts and odd jobs. Because of the remoteness of the place and its inhospitality to life of any age, it was surprising how many there were.

Yet some had left homes thousands of miles away — either out of adventure or desperation or because there was simply nowhere else for them to go but up the great river and its tributaries. Some, particularly girls, had escaped or been evicted from households in jungle settlements.

They were as varied in race and color as in other parts of Brazil, although those with darker features predominated. While life for a boy urchin was hard enough, that for a girl was grim. Many became victims of unscrupulous employers who cheated them of their wages and subjected them to beatings and worse.

There was frequently no alternative but to become a prostitute. Itaituba had at least a hundred. Managers assigned them to preferred clients, usually *garimpeiros* just in from the bush with their satchels of gold. A curious comradery prevailed in these places, with the older women supportive, even protective, of the younger. But in the end such solace could not stave off the inevitable destitution that follows such a life. Some prostitutes, barely 30, looked twice that.

"It's the rule, not the exception, for a girl to have a child before she's 15," Coelho said. "Three–quarters of all births are illegitimate, most of them to teenagers. Of course, the filth catches up with them — dysentery is birth control at the other end, remember, that and the yellow fever."

I was having a steak and salad one night at the Cleison Lanchonete–Pizzaria, the town's only decent diner. A beak–faced young man at the next table leaned over and in Arab–accented English wondered if I were American.

We passed pleasantries. I asked what he did.

"Games of chance, my friend. Games of chance," he replied, looking in the direction of the noisy establishment next door where people had been coming and going rather urgently. "You should give us a chance to play with you. Not many rich Americans come our way!"

Baghdad's was a "spin the wheel" joint, with a tractor–wheel–sized disc painted with numbers and pictures of animals. An assistant would, on Baghdad's signal, give it a turn. As it spun, an arrow at 12 o'clock would flop in and out of slots beneath the numbers. Each animal occupied the space below four numbers and bets on them won at 25–1. A hit on a number brought 99–1.

Residents of an Itaituba bar roof emptying wash water.

As best as I could tell, the game was straight, relying on obviously favorable house odds to pick players' pockets. I placed small single wagers on the "goat" and hit twice, enough to keep even.

The lighting was poor, and the smoke from the beery patrons reduced it further. Their shouts and groans as the arrow flicked to a stop rolled up the street. A scratchy amplifier over the doorway pealed old rock and a bouquet of balloons promised happiness. The place summoned like a beckoning finger.

This casino was a haunt of Coelho's and the gold buyer came in while I was there, running up winnings of nearly a thousand cruzados in short order. The other players began following his lead and in a while the house was losing. Baghdad, however, showed no concern and maintained a pleasant banter with his clients, whose luck could not last. The Arab — he was Palestinian, actually — was unctuous toward Coelho, whom he addressed as "my dear friend, my brother."

"Baghdad's a quicksilver man," Coelho said later, as he counted his spoils, about $90 worth, over a beer and pizza. "He would make money wherever he was. Trouble is, he's going to make too much here one night and pay for it with his life."

As we parted, the buyer said he thought he had worked out a "problem" he had been having with some "claim jumpers."

"If you want to see how things really work around here, come over to my place in the morning, early. I'll take you with me."

There are no private mineral rights in Brazil. All subsoil interest belongs to the government, who issues exploitation permits provided that an applicant can show sufficient capital and expertise. Legally, a *garimpo* claim must produce within three years or it is lost. An exception is made for those who can show "continuing exploration." As a practical matter, this means that anyone with clout — and a little money under the table — can lock up rich tracts indefinitely.

Some hire miners for wages, but normally a permit holder subdivides his claim into strips around 30 square meters each. These he sublets to *garimpeiros* for a kilo — at the time about $18,000 — of gold, paid in ore assayed by the lessor during the period of the sublease. Whatever the *garimpeiro* digs out over and above that is his.

The lessor makes his best profit in the time–honored fashion of the *aviador* by selling food and supplies to his miners at tremendously inflated prices, again, payable in gold. Only his aircraft are permitted to land at the *garimpo*, assuring a monopoly on goods and transport. The fare to *Batahla Garimpo*, for example, was 2,000 cruzados, about $90 each way, with an extra $10 per kilo for freight.

Although Cobalt was primarily a buyer, it did have its own claims. One of these had been discovered and worked by a cooperative of local *garimpeiros* who did not file — out of ignorance or laches or, more likely, for fear their strike would be stolen by the likes of Cobalt in league with corrupt officials. When these men left, temporarily they now said, Cobalt occupied the site and obtained a permit. For some reason, Coelho was vague about this, the partners decided not to work it and removed all but a token crew, whereupon it was reoccupied by the cooperative who sent Cobalt's custodians packing.

"I've tried to reason with them," Coelho said as the trusted maid brought coffee and Danish. "They're just bullheaded. Now I have to use force, and someone will probably get killed."

He had offered to let the miners have "free and clear" all the gold they had taken during the 18–month occupation, "plus I'd buy all their equipment for exactly what they paid for it. They got it all here and I know the suppliers, and the prices are easy to determine." This included a bulldozer, several generators, air compressors, pumps and hoses.

"Everybody would get a free flight out and on to Santarém or Belém or wherever they wanted to go — except we'll offer all the *mansos*, veteran workers for wages, jobs with us." *Bravos,* young or "green" workers, would have to leave with the "claim jumpers."

Opening the bedside drawer, he removed a pink chamois pouch which contained a Heckler and Koch .45 recoilless pistol with red and white bands on the breach.

"But all that's over now. Now they'll get nothing but pain," although he did intend "out of sympathy" to pay them half price for the equipment.

He looked at his watch and said it was time "to meet Tania." By this he meant Cobalt's local bookkeeper and "ear to the ground." Tania was a thin, frail–looking woman about 40 whom I had met briefly at the office. She superintended the assaying and purchasing there, although technically the shop was run by the brother–in–law of the senior partner.

"She's my connection with local authorities," he said. "She's been in touch with the legal power and will be able to tell us if the little project I need sanctioned has been given the green light."

The bookkeeper's white frame house could have been in any modest American suburb. There was a small garden against the street watered by worn plastic hoses. Toys and tools littered the yard. Tania's daughter, an attractive young woman in tight jeans and half a shirt, twentyish, stood with her mother to greet us, then disappeared.

Seated in the living room was a stocky, smooth–fingered gent in a designer jump suit who rose obediently and strode to embrace Coelho in a manner suggesting success at long last. The order had been signed.

"The judge has done for us in five days what normally takes five years! And all clean, without a hearing — no publicity, no bull!" Coelho introduced me to Sousa: "The only lawyer I know who wins his cases in bed!" He repeated this for the others to a peal of laughter. The reference was to the lawyer's alleged affair with the young woman judge who had signed the order.

"But do we get the police?" Coelho asked, implying that a crucial element might have been overlooked.

"Sí," the lawyer responded. "All we need."

"I just need one, to make it legal all the way. Our men can do the rest."

What he meant was that a police officer would serve the order of eviction on the *garimpeiros*. His own men, he said, would "handle any rough stuff." They would be deputized so that whatever happened would be under official sanction. The lawyer had already notified the constable, and he would be waiting for them at the office of the flying service whose pilots would take them out to the mine.

"Let's don't waste anymore time," Coelho said. "Le Comme Vivo is a busy man."

"Who," I asked, "is Le Comme Vivo?"

"He's the physical power in these parts," Coelho replied. "He's my back up when the rough stuff starts. Le Comme Vivo means, 'He eats them alive.' You'll see what I mean."

The daughter returned and stood with her mother as we left. Her jeans and tank top had been shed for a fluffy white dress with pink bow, her sandals for high heels. It was not yet noon.

"She got dressed for you," Coelho said.

I was embarrassed. "I don't think so," I replied.

"I won't argue with you, but it is true. An American would be a great catch for a woman here. Particularly a good, pretty one like her, with no money or property. But she is very beautiful and she would make you a devoted wife. You ought to think about it. Don't dismiss it so lightly."

Changing the subject, I asked how long he thought he could count on Sousa's special relationship with the woman judge.

"Don't believe that crap for a minute about Lover Lawyer," he retorted. "That order cost me $5,000 US — half for him and half for his sweetie. She's not a judge for being dumb."

We drove to a dingy warehouse, the headquarters of the *Canta Galo*, Singing Rooster, Mining Company, one of several gold outfitters and flying services along the town's dusty back street. A knot of toughs with rifles and submachine guns had already collected in the shade out front. A taxi cloudlet swept past, disgorging others. There was a chorus of flies. The lawyer had rushed ahead and, as we pulled up, he appeared with three policemen in fatigues and khaki, including their constable who had the court order. They greeted Coelho obsequiously, then stood off by themselves eyeing the irregulars.

Inside, seven taciturn men in the worn flannel and leather habit of *garimpeiros* stared at us coldly. The plane to their mine had been diverted to haul Coelho's posse. They awaited an uncertain lift to a neighboring dig.

The Singing Rooster's owner was in his office and would see us shortly, a woman announced. From a glassed–in cubicle came the hiss and squelch of a shortwave transceiver monitored by a pock–faced young man with earphones. Seeing the armed men, the woman admonished them to unload their weapons and stand inside. They squatted and perched among sacks of flour, barbwire and hardware. There was little conversation. You could tell that they were not held in high esteem by the *garimpeiros*, two of whom were taking long pulls from a jug of Logan's, a Brazilian "Scotch" that tended more toward stump water than whiskey. One had a digital wristwatch that chimed "Dixie" and "The Yellow Rose of Texas."

"That's Le Comme Vivo's son, there on the radio," Coelho said. "They call him LCV II — he brags that he's already killed three men. He's only 20."

LCV's muscle and transport, Coelho said, was normally not for hire, the operator taking great pains to keep out of other people's quarrels. Cobalt, however, had done the Singing Rooster some big favors recently — flying out SR's ore to São Paulo in Cobalt charters when LCV's planes were on the fritz and package–dealing it for higher prices. Additionally, some of the miners pestering Cobalt had bucked LCV in an earlier squabble over prices. So Coelho had asked for a plane and some rowdies, and LCV had obliged. All that remained was the working out of "some minor details," such as compensation for the retainers, which had to be negotiated with them separately for this job.

"Senhor will see you now," the woman said tersely.

A bullish, beady–eyed gent rose from a desk and shook hands all around with an efficient, businessman's courtesy. It was Coelho's turn to be supplicatory. He was almost fawning as he introduced me to "Senhor Rondo, Le Comme Vivo!" The man wore a cross necklace hammered from two substantial nuggets. On the wall behind him was a life–sized open–heart print of Christ. Opposite, hung a geological map of the region with multicolored pins indicating prospects and landing strips.

Aides brought extra chairs. The lawyer, the lead goon and the constable had joined us. There was a side exchange, obviously about my presence.

"I told him you were an American writer who's doing an article on the Amazon," Coelho said. "He said you can come in for an interview after we discuss some confidential matters, like who is to be paid how much to kill whom — I think I said that correctly. Then you're welcome, provided you don't make us look civilized. He doesn't want anyone to think we're soft and easy."

Le Comme Vivo smiled tolerantly as Coelho finished, then signaled the woman to show me out. An hour later I was asked to return and, with Coelho interpreting, he gave this brief account of himself:

"I was born in a rubber camp near Breves in Marajó. My father was a *seringueiro*. We were very poor. I was rubber tapping with him before I was 10 and by 16 I had my own trails of trees. The life we knew was the forest. Sometimes there would be no other people for months. I got to know the animals and the different trees and plants, what you could eat or use. There were still Indians in the forest then. They taught me how to track and keep silent and not get lost. I went to a one–room school where I learned to read and write.

"I worked at small jobs in Breves. Loading and unloading cargo, in a sawmill, etc. There was no future there, and you could get injured for life and have nothing. Many men, young boys too, lost hands and arms or were crushed. In 1957, I sailed on a Brazil–nut boat as a turner. You have to turn the nuts constantly or they ferment. The ship went to Liverpool, in England, three times, but we had to stay on the ship. They fed us goat meat. I ate so much goat I almost died. Mother of God, how I hated goat! That was all they gave us — no beef, no chicken, no pork. The ship also went to Miami, but it was the same thing for the nut turners — nobody allowed to leave the ship. Two years sailing all that distance and never shore leave.

"The work was hard, but it paid well. A hundred and fifty cruzados a month. But you had to join the syndicate [seaman's union] and they made you wait your turn before you went out again. I was lucky at first, but later I had to wait. I would get to the top of the list and someone with more seniority or who had bribed the steward would pass ahead of me. And the dues kept going up. So I quit and went to the manganese mines near Marapa as a machine oiler. But in a month everybody got laid off.

"I was making 48 cruzados, about $20, a month. Quite a loss from the ship. An old worker told me if you weren't making 500 cruzados a month you're not a man. So I headed into the jungle and found a job on a *garimpo* on a tributary of the Anapali river. The pay was better, around 200 a month. But I got malaria and almost died. I fought it for two years. It was the Indians who taught me how to use quinine, not just the tablets given by the government doctor but from the forest there. That saved my life."

His strength finally restored, he proceeded up the Tapajós to Itaituba. That was in the summer of 1959. He was 23.

"Bocas das Tropas, the first *garimpo* here had just been discovered. I got hired and made enough to get a stake, then started looking for fields on my own with a friend. On foot. We cut our way through the jungle with only mules to carry our gear. We hired some Indians to guide us. They were clever scouts. While we panned one prospect, they would blaze a trail to the next. There were no topographical maps like today; it was just guesswork, but by talking to the Indians, carefully asking them questions, you could get a good idea of the terrain ahead and the best way there. Without them it would have been impossible. It was on this first expedition that we found the deposit that became *Canta Gallo*.

"When we started operations in the early 1960s there were no bulldozers, no backhoes, no air compressors. We picked and dug by hand. We didn't have money. We bought supplies with gold dust and nuggets. Three grams of gold bought a machete, five grams a can of corned beef — a delicacy. Mostly, we killed our own meat — small animals, fowl. But sometimes you wanted beef, even in the can. A kilo of jerky was less expensive — four grams.

"In those days the only other people in the forest were rubber tappers and nut pickers. You could go for days and never see anybody, weeks even. Today, there are colonists everywhere. They have boats, trucks, airplanes, radios, motors. And the mining is mechanized — Caterpillar, John Deere, Cummins, Westinghouse. Who would have thought it 30 years ago that all would be done by machine? The *garimpeiro* is still indispensable — and they all know it. You can't keep good men working for you like then. When they hear there's a strike in another place, they head there. Nothing like the cry of gold to set them running. I have one fellow who has been with me 15 years and another 12. After that, the longest is two–and–a–half."

He married and brought his wife out to the Singing Rooster, where they had eight boys and two daughters. Son number three was the pock–faced boy in the radio shack. Another was a gold pilot.

"But the time of the independent operator, even the *garimpeiro*, is passing. The big mining companies will eventually control everything. It is the way of the future, those who have technology, unlimited capital, foreign connections.

"At first, the Trans–Amazon Highway was a good thing for everyone. The road brought settlers who raised crops and provided fresh meat and produce for the miners. A stable population at last. But the problem is they don't stay. They burn the forest, raise crops for a couple of years then move on, leaving only dead land behind. And the road itself is now a joke, impassable. I think that it was a mistake. The government doesn't maintain it, so just when you depend on it for supplies they can't get through. Days, weeks wasted. And when it is passable, the people who come on it! Not workers, not tough people, but the weakest of all, people who burn down the forest to make a farm but after only a year or two they leave — or die, which is all the same for the land."

Was it true, I asked, that he had killed 33 men?

Coelho relayed the query with trepidation. The others shifted nervously. LCV's eyes remained fixed on mine. Then he smiled:

"Shouldn't you give me first your police warning so I will not incriminate myself?"

Laughter blew the room. The lawyer slapped his thighs and the constable, who was sitting across from LCV, flayed his hands in the air like pistols, shouting "boom! boom! boom! boom!" Coelho, swiveling in his chair, was again amiable and feigned to scold me for my importunity at posing such a question.

"Life in the Amazon is dangerous."

Silence returned to the room.

"Some men act without thinking, without respect for life. Either because they are drunk or stubborn or crazy. One must protect oneself and one's property, or one will cease to exist. No challenge must ever go unanswered."

With that he stood, propelling the others to their feet. He spoke rapidly to Coelho and to the lawyer, then strode from the room.

"I'm afraid you can't come with us," Coelho said. "It's going to be worse than I thought. He says the *garimps* told a pilot yesterday they will fight."

The constable and headman hastened to the supply room where each spoke to their men. Dissatisfaction was obvious. The men wanted a bonus for hazardous duty — and they wanted to be paid in advance of departure. Coelho huffed at the rising cost and further delay, but there was naught to do but pay. He rushed to the hotel and returned with the cash in a briefcase. They would get their money, he said, as they boarded the plane and not a moment before. So it was agreed. The men reloaded their guns and piled into taxis. Coelho lined up the constable, the lawyer and several of the gunmen for a photo.

"Here's one for your book," he jested. "Law west of the Tapajós!"

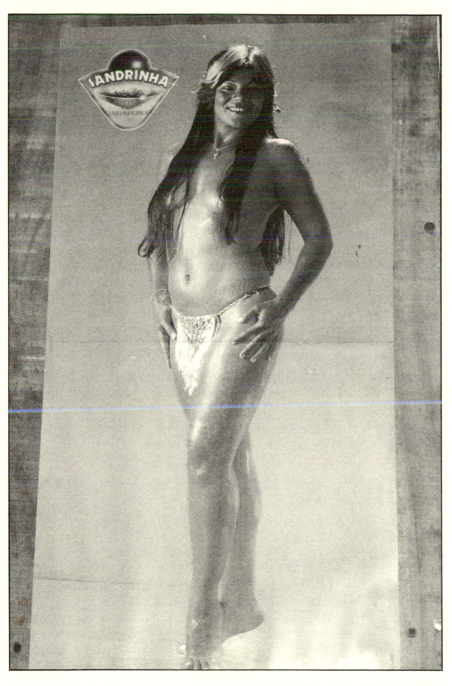

Poster girl, Uropa, Pará, Brazilian Amazon.

He, LCV and the lawyer then boarded the lead cab and the convoy became a cyclone of dust. I went back and sat with the miners. "The Yellow Rose of Texas" announced the hour.

The plane took off, without Coelho, it turned out, and its progress was followed on the radio — augmented by the bemused animations and choppy English of my fellow standbys. Coelho later filled in the gaps.

The pilot negotiated a raise with the lawyer, who was riding in the copilot's seat wearing headphones, and LCV II. He was hired to haul supplies, not get shot at, he broadcast. Besides, the posse got more: why not me? The landings, it turned out, were unopposed. And the miners were quiescent, agreeing to vacate by the weekend. That would have been that, except that a crashed plane from a nearby *garimpo* diverted both aircraft to look for survivors, stranding evictors and trespassers together.

"They won't eat or sleep for three days," Coelho joked impishly. But LCV's face became drawn. The pilot of the downed plane had been a protégé.

With a dignity that eluded the others, he delivered a kind of elegy.

"He would have gone a very long way with me," Coelho translated. "It is a very sad day."

That night Coelho joined me in my search for a boat to Santarém. We passed the undertakers. Some carpenters were hammering coffins.

"You can tell when a plane's crashed by the coffins," he said.
"How's that?"
"The tin. They have to line the boxes with tin. Look!"

The carpenters were flattening strips of corrugated roofing against the casket bottoms.

It was rumored that six people had died in the crash and that it was caused by a deranged miner who was being flown out in irons.

"They say he grabbed the stick and fought with the pilot," Coelho said. "A wing clipped a brazilwood tree at the end of the runway. What a stupid disaster! It's a big fine for cutting down brazilwoods, so they gash them and leave them to die and fall on their own. Every airstrip has the bastards."

A newspaper in Santarém said two days later that this was pretty much what had happened — at least what "the authorities" had deduced from sounds of shouting and a struggle heard over the radio. But, of course, no one knew for sure, since there were no survivors.

Coelho sat on the wharf dangling his feet like a schoolboy and shouting *"Bon Voyage."*

The *Viageiro IV* arrived in Santarém at 8 a.m. the next morning. It was a smooth, uneventful ride. Afterward, when I read that a vessel named *Viageiro* had sunk on the Tapajós with 200 drowned, I remembered the faces of the braceleted girls who sang and patted hands and celebrated their escape from Itaituba. The capacity plaque had said 90 but there were many times that.

I thought of Coelho's histrionic plans for the leader of the expelled:

"Didn't you hear the woman at the warehouse keep asking me, asking me something? She was asking: 'When are you going to put him away?'

"I'll wait until he comes to talk to me about the equipment. If he looks me in the eye when I tell him I'll only pay the half price, then I will do nothing. If he is shifty and green, then I will have to kill him. The one thing I fear is a coward. A coward will kill you."

Hundreds of paddle wheelers churn the Amazon. Some began as steamers in the 1800s and were only recently converted to diesel. Scars on their weathered plating suggest histories that, if known, would inspire shelves of dark novels. One hag launched in 1872, the *Yurimaguas*, yet plies between Iquitos and Tabatinga, Brazil's mud—wallowed appendage of Colombia's cocaine port of Leticia.

Regulated passenger fares lag months behind inflation. Freight, on the other hand, commands what the traffic will bear. Still, no skipper neglects to top off his cargo with suffocating hammocksfull of humanity.

I crept westward on these machines, stopping sometimes for a week or longer, as the notion struck, to explore a town or yield to the promise of a road, such as that to Belterra and Itaituba. Among my conveyances were: the *Fe Em Deus IV, Faith in God No. 4*; the *Salvador*; the *María*; the *Cisne Branco, White Swan;* and the hapless *Teixera Junior*, whose rudder was smashed by a submerged log at midnight two hours out of Santarém.

Her hull shivered from three impacts, but it was the last which crippled her. The helmsman was diverted by two women with whom he was sharing a bottle of rum. His eyes, earlier shaded and suave, bulged as he shouted from the wheelhouse. The captain, a wan, disconsolate sort, suddenly rushed about berating the crew. But there was nothing any of them could do but stand helplessly with the rest of us as the craft spiraled into the blackness.

After a while, an outline of land fell ahead and there was a thud as we carried aground on a low island, a sandbar really, with tall grass and scrub. The engine surged then failed, taking with it the lights. Off somewhere was a clanging, like a fog bell or someone striking metal. It drew nearer and with it came the lowing of cattle. They collected on the bank and watched us.

A comforting wind died and we were swarmed by mosquitoes. There were slaps and curses. Mothers vainly fanned their children. I shared some repellent with those closest by, then strung the mosquito net over my hammock. A few people huddled on the wheelhouse deck where there remained a gasp of breeze, but most simply endured the torment as best they could.

It was clear that our predicament required aid from another ship. Several did pass, shoving their prows eerily up to our quarterdeck. They offered no help, but only stole what they could of our passengers before disappearing into the night.

Shortly before dawn we were hailed by the *Cisne Branco*, who cast a line and towed us to Santarém. I returned with her to Manaus.

Amazon gold pilot drinking *mate*, a strong herbal tea,
with a silver straw at Itaituba's landing field.

22

DUCKE

*Something moved to my front. There was a rustle
of leaves and a soft snap. A heavy, musklike odor
filled the air.*

I was awakened by the silence. Lingering "rivets" and chirps from the long disbanded symphony of frogs and insects had quit. No breeze stirred. There was only the toss of Igarapé Acara, the little creek near camp. I sat up in the soft humid coolness. The clearing was brushed by an ephemeral shaft of starlight denied to the forestal depths beyond.

"Go wherever you like," Marc Hero had told me. "Just mind where you step and don't go out of your way to sneak up on anyone. You're a long way from help, even if you could make it back to the *cantina*,[79] which might prove difficult."

The mindful stepping was in respect for *Bothrops atrox*, the fer–de–lance, a potentially though not usually deadly cousin of the larger and more lethal Central American viper by the same name. Here stretching perhaps to four feet, its presence across one's path was rare but ominous. The previous year a student had suffered weeks of excruciating pain and swelling despite receiving antivenin within five hours of a bite.[80] Friends carried her to the *cantina*, themselves nearly stepping on another of the grayish–brown snakes camouflaged in leaves on the trail. Two others were spotted later near camp. These were the first seen on the prowl in a long while and none had been spied since, except patiently coiled in hollows waiting for something that would justify the energy of a strike.

There were other reptilian dangers, to be sure, notably the illusive Bushmaster or "sucurucu," *Lachesis muta*, but most were colubrids — nonvenomous species. Against the hypodermic fangs of the vipers, canvas or "jungle" boots were useless and anything heavier would have been ludicrously impractical. Thus everyone, except myself at the beginning, traipsed about barefoot even after dark, protection entrusted to a head lamp, coal–miner style, and a good eye.

"Clothing out here is an uncomfortable bloody nuisance, as you'll see," Marc warned. "Besides, you have a much better feel for the forest with your feet." While a shirt might be used against the night air, the only other attire was cutoffs and, for the young women, a T–shirt or thin bra, a deference less to modesty than to brush.

I had been alone now for a week, the others having returned to the Institute for Amazon Research, INPA after its Portuguese initials, in Manaus. I had so exalted in the zoological bountifulness of the place and in its quietude, a desperately needed respite from the press and decibel of Brazilian humanity, that I'd volunteered to remain behind to tend camp and check traps. The duration of my watch was indeterminate, although I had half expected Marc the day before, a Friday, so eager had the feisty Aussie been to "see who we catch this time."

"Catch" was banter. These were "print traps," patches of earth cleared along game trails so that whatever passed would almost certainly step into them. Opposite sides of fallen logs, forks and thickets were preferred. Passersby over time included anteaters, otters, opossums — including six of the nine Amazonian species, three of which are pouchless — and the solitary tapir or *anta*, a shorter version of the Belizean "mountain cow," a Shetland–sized nocturnal herbivore with a long snout that looks like a cross between a hog and a burro. Seldom seen are the tracks of the lesser cats, such as the ocelots, rare here because of the paucity of rodents and other small game. The margay, an ocelot look–alike, is frequently seen but it is arboreal.

But the major felines were regular visitors, the jaguar being the most common, followed closely by the puma — *felis concolor* — the same as the North American cougar or mountain lion, but smaller. Almost all rain forest species, though not the jaguar, are smaller than their temperate counterparts. With an amenable temperature and constant food supply, more energy is invested in reproduction than in the creation and maintenance of body mass.

"And don't forget to look for droppings," Marc admonished. "It's the scat that counts. The tracks just let us know who's been here." I'd known that scat could indicate what an animal had eaten. But a skilled eye could distinguish between types of plants and animals ingested and in what order, digestive irregularities, parasites, disease and so on. From it all, inferences could be drawn not only about an animal's diet, but its health, age, range and probable interaction with its own and other species. Significant tracks were measured, sketched and sometimes photographed. Dung was saved in plastic bags.

Jaguars are wide–ranging; covering a territory can take several weeks. But because there were so many in the area, tracks were spotted every four days or so. The cats are "cryptic" — subtle, devious, the nonscientist might say — with a knack for hiding, watching, reversing course. Backtracking researchers commonly found their own prints, some only minutes old, topped by a jaguar's.

Marc Hero at Igarapé Acara Camp, Reserva Florestal Ducke,
north central Brazilian Amazon.

An exception to the compactness–of–species rule, the Amazon
jaguar tops 400 pounds full–grown, somewhat larger than its
almost–extinct Mexican cousin. The big cat was of especial interest to
my hosts, it having been adjudged the villain in an intriguing local
mystery: the violent demise of *Paleosuchus trigonatus*, the dwarf
caiman.

With an adult length of from four to five feet, the animal is not
large by crocodilian standards. Indeed, it's not really a crocodile at all
but a cousin of the North American alligator. It is the dominant
reptile in the vast network of small streams in undisturbed primary

forest. Although long known to share the mouths of most tributaries with three larger caimans, the extent of its upstream occupation only recently became apparent from the remote stalkings of the likes of herpetologist Bill Magnusson, the de facto duke of *Reserva Florestal Ducke*, the 25,000–acre wilderness sanctuary 20 miles from Manaus in which I now found myself. Officially, a *pesquisador associado* — associate researcher — with INPA's Department of Ecology, this brilliant and spirited Australian is one of the world's leading tropical biologists.

"The major predator of these crocs is the jaguar," he said as we stood, the week before, knee–deep in Acara Creek far above camp. Though jaguars eating caimans was no news, dwarfs were not thought to be among their prey. But the killing of a Ducke dwarf a few years back couldn't be laid to territorial fighting or poaching — usual causes. When jaguar scat was identified with the croc's remnants, the cat became the primary suspect. Cinching the case was the finding, based on jaw–force projections, that only *Leo onca,* not even the puma, has the strength to crack open a dwarf croc's body armor.

According to Magnusson, "Recent work has shown that the dwarf caiman is not only the dominant reptile, it has the highest biomass [of any] large predator [animal weighing over one kilogram] in the entire Amazon rain forest. In fact, they have a higher biomass than all the large mammalian predators put together — despite the fact that no one could find them." But unlike many species, the dwarf caiman's population dynamics renders it vulnerable to the mortality of its *adults* rather than its young. "The [Ducke] population could not afford the loss of several adults, [even] over a period of a few years," he said. Hence, the grave concern about the jaguars.

"A jaguar follows the creek, looking for one careless enough to be out on the bank or in shallow water. Once he sees a croc, it's dead. A crocodile depends for his survival on being unseen. As fast as the old boy is, unless he's near deep water he can't escape a jaguar."

I had met Bill and Marc, a Queensland zoology graduate on a world travel "sabbatical," at the herpetology lab on the second floor of the INPA research center. I had gone there looking for "a guide to the deep bush." They and two Brazilian student–assistants, Albertina Lima and Tania Sanaiotti, were headed to Ducke the next afternoon. "You're welcome to tag along," Bill said. "Just bring your own tucker and a sleeping bag."

Acara camp was an hour's hike from the *cantina,* a cluster of aging cabins and a barracks. A suspect bridge over a marsh led to the trail head. A few paces farther and you knew you'd entered a place like no other. So lush was its greenness, so aggressive its odors, that

Bill Magnusson at Igarapé Acara Camp, Ducke.

one's linear progress was accompanied by a proportionate mental distancing from the peopled world without.

A half hour on, an old NASA meteorology tower penetrated 130 feet of bird–rich canopies. From its platforms, ornithologists followed the mating, nesting and flight patterns of hundreds of species. The trail then shrank to a spongy ribbon rutted with mudholes until, regaining solid ground, it descended to the creek.

A canvas shelter, open at the bottom, was supported by nine poles. From a horizontal center pole hung kits of measuring tapes, rulers, tweezers, scissors, protractors, twine balls, rubber bands, paper clips, Formalin solution, index cards, pencils, heavy–duty flashlight batteries, film canisters and other notions and widgets of the naturalist's armamentarium.

A plank sagged under a disarranged pantry of soggy saltines, imitation Oreos, *Sao Luis* cream crackers — "Extra" "Extra", *Vega* strawberry and orange jam, *leite em po integral* — powdered milk, tea, coffee and vegemite, the bitter high–protein yeast extract as vital to the Australian palate as peanut butter to the American. The paste is shipped via Miami in the "gringo pouch," an irregular but dependable circumvention of the theft–plagued Brazilian post: Whoever goes stateside carries outbound mail. Incoming mail — and the vegemite — is collected from the office of a Florida colleague,

The creek's sweet water, tea–colored from soft leafy acids, was drunk without qualm. A wide pool above the first of two modest waterfalls was reserved for spontaneous skinny dips and bathing. There was nothing more invigorating than a cool splash in the midafternoon. Yet the slightest exertion afterward brought back the torpor. Upstream from the swimming hole was a space for cooling meat and fruit, and above that for drawing water for cooking and drinking.

"These streams are naturally clean and safe," Bill said. "You have to have people to contaminate water. All the harmful bacteria, viruses and parasites and whatnot come from people. Until it flows past a settlement, it's as pure as a mountain spring."

Some 20 color–coded plastic bowls were arranged to one side of the shelter. Each had been filled with a dozen tadpoles of different species and a minnow–sized fish — principals in an experiment to ascertain the toxicity of the larvae and any repellent effect that might have on the predator. In most instances, all or none of the tadpoles remained; in a few, there were eleven toxic ones: "He got one down before he found out what it was," Marc laughed.

The ultimate aim, he said, was "to determine the effect of predation on the distribution of these larval amphibians."

"It's likely that evolution of reproductive strategies takes place very rapidly in rain forest frogs in response to constantly changing pressure from predators. Tropical frogs breed all year, unlike those in North America and Europe that have only one breeding season. So the evolutionary pressures here are much more intense."

Whether to have two or three reproductive stages — egg–frog or egg–tadpole–frog — and where to place the eggs — ground, water or in trees over water — is governed in large part by two considerations: the energy required, less in three stages than two, and attrition from predation, usually greater for tadpoles in open streams than in marsh or "perched" ponds.

"We work almost exclusively in pure primary, not secondary, forest," he said. "Normally, different species colonize each." Of the 33 species of frog identified in Ducke, several by Marc himself, fewer than a half dozen would make it outside.

"It's a lot harder to survive with three life stages anyway, no matter where you live. Maybe there's no place to put your eggs because the creek dried up, maybe a big fish is waiting to gobble up your tadpoles. There are lots of possibilities. To throw a species who's adapted to all that into a secondary forest where all the rules are changed is disastrous. That's why deforestation kills off so many species even when you get a rapid secondary regrowth."

Some frogs deposit several thousand eggs in the water. Though fish may eat most of them, or their tadpoles, there's still a survival rate of around one percent, which is enough.

Others have only two reproductive stages, bypassing the larval altogether. Their handful of eggs — as few as a dozen — are deposited in the ground and hatch directly into frogs. "We believe that's an evolutionary response to avoid predators in ponds, but we've not yet done enough research to say that conclusively. One possibility is that terrestrial ovipositioning evolved simply because ponds dry out."

But for now he proposed to determine the distribution of tadpole species and their predators in each habitat and which predators were likely to influence the distribution of each. "I'll then try to find the adaptive traits which allow the tadpoles to survive those predators." Toxicity was definitely one, he was convinced. Whence all those bowls full of tadpoles and hungry minnows.

Much of each night's work consisted of foraging for adult frogs and the entire party would bend to this effort. Croakers would be lifted from logs, leaves, branches, puddles. Most were located by their calls, although others were simply run upon by accident. A remarkable aspect of frogs is the ability of each species to home in on prospective mates' voices in the nightly babble, sometimes converging from hundreds of feet away. This is an especially astonishing feat for tiny ones whose signals are infrequent and barely audible. Males squabbling on branches above the creek feed the dwarf caiman, which waits patiently for the loser to fall.

Many a small splash in Igarapé Acara is followed by a larger one.

"In order to know which frog is living where, you have to catch the buggers and mark them and indicate precisely where they are each time they're caught," Marc lectured.

Once captured, by hand or with a mechanical grasper on the end of a long pole, the animal was marked by cutting off one of its toe pads. Careful note would be made of the precise marking "coordinates" — limb and digit, the date, location in the research area and condition — injuries, defects. A separate index card was later prepared for each subject.

Miles from camp Marc would suddenly shout that he'd found "Ol Jumper" or "Mr. Bigmouth" and "the bastard's doing fine, doing fine, thank you, mate!"

Marc's gathering was not limited to frogs. He was confident in his ability to distinguish colubrids from vipers, so nonpoisonous snakes would be snatched from limbs or off the ground, examined, measured, marked — by removing precise belly scale segments — and released. During the day lizards would also be taken and catalogued.

Tania was the group's "arachnologist." Once she called us over to see a woolly *Ancylomedes,* hunter spider, she had captured, holding it expertly to keep it from biting but not to harm it. She later led us to the beer–mug–sized opening of the lair of a giant female tarantula, *Theraphosa.* "Keep your light on the hole," Bill said as Tania hit the ground with a stick. Nothing happened. "Too hard," Bill said. She tapped more lightly, whereupon the spider struck with suddenness and force, its furry body, the size of a saucer, glistening with dew. Taking the stick, I could feel a determined grinding and gnawing, like that of a small dog. Objects of known weight had been dropped in front of the hole to gauge the occupant's reaction. "She won't strike at anything less than nine grams or more than 22," Bill said. "Big enough for dinner but not big enough to turn the tables." Mice and frogs were favored. Like its smaller cousin in the United States, *Eurypelma californicum, Theraphosa* is not poisonous although its bite can be quite painful.

The wasp is the tarantula's nemesis, having evolved the specialty of locating the spider in its den and paralyzing it with its sting. The wasp then deposits its eggs in the spider, which is eaten alive by the larvae when they hatch.

Tania was preparing to defend her thesis on the ecology of an ant bird that makes a living by following swarms of army ants to catch flushed insects. When not helping Bill and Marc she was off birding. One ancillary project was a study of a hummingbird hen, *Topaz apella,* and two chicks she had found downstream from camp and which she observed from a leafy blind. While groping about for gear adrift during a cloudburst, I saw Tanya's neatly stowed but the student was nowhere to be found. As the squall grew, Bill, who was normally blasé about comings and goings, became concerned at her absence. But at dusk she returned with pages of notes on hummingbird storm behavior. Eating cold stew, she patiently lent a hand to Marc with some frog cards then repaired to the blind, notwithstanding a resumption of the downpour that brought the creek to within inches of the hut.

Tina worked with frogs and lizards. She had coauthored with Magnusson and others several articles on the latter, one of which reported communal nesting of teiids based on a deposit of 827 eggs

Giant female tarantula, Ducke.

over many years in the dry hollow of a creek stump. Unlike crocodile eggs, those of these lizards could withstand temperature fluctuations of as much as 13 degrees Centigrade. "All of the eggs ... had probably hatched successfully. The only holes in the [shells] were neat slits in one end. [None] showed ragged holes that might suggest that a predator had chewed its way in."[81]

Another article dealt with wide–foraging and sit–and–wait teiids which necessitated hours of tedious following and watching. Speed, frequency of movement and hunting area indicated that wide–foragers' diets, termites and smaller insects, were appreciably more varied than those of sit–and–waits, who "may specialize on large prey to diminish the number of prey chases and thus avoid predation [themselves]."[82] In a typical brief to the journal *"Biotropica"* in 1983, she and Magnusson reported a symbiosis between Black Vultures and trees with boxlike root buttresses at the confluence of the Rio Negro and the Amazon. The structures provide roosts and nest sites for the heavy birds whose nutrient–rich droppings favor the trees.

To Tina usually fell the job of holding down crocodiles during examination and marking, though she was perfectly capable of capturing them herself. According to Bill, she was a "compulsive note taker, a scientist's scientist." She was also something of an acrobat, with a lumberjack's prowess at shinnying trees. No edible fruit was beyond her reach, particularly the plumlike "jambo," a favorite. She climbed one of these trees outside the *cantina's* office, shaking down fruit to the amusement of the sedentary employees who seldom ventured beyond the bridge.

Student and professor combined again in the "Journal of Herpetology" in 1985 to report a remarkable dependency of the dwarf caiman on the lowly termite:

> It is strange that crocodilians have not evolved to incubate their eggs at lower [than ambient] temperatures like the majority of reptiles.
> … *P. trigonatus* has little alternative to the use of termite mounds if it is to maintain warm temperatures within its nests."

Crocodile nests are universally built with mud, leaves and other vegetable matter, energy from the decay of which normally provides sufficient heat. But this habitat, at 22 to 24 degrees Centigrade, fell well below the 27 degrees Centigrade minimum required for incubation. Dwarf caiman females, therefore, steal from the best thermal source available. A bustling termite colony can boost a nest's temperature to 32 degrees Centigrade.

Male dwarfs have territories averaging around 300 yards of streambed. Woe unto smaller males that intrude. Young crocs have to avoid such bailiwicks to survive, a difficult task since most sections of a stream are already taken by a dominant adult. "They can detect the slightest violation of their domain," Bill said. "And they don't show much compassion." Sometimes one big male will venture into the territory of another, "and then you have a hell of a fight."

The dwarf caiman, *Paleosuchus trigonatus*,
held by Albertina Lima near Igarapé Acara Camp, Ducke.

Lately he had been gathering supplementary data on the
termite–mound phenomenon. The morning after our arrival he
summoned me along on a nest hunt. We hiked up the creek,
crisscrossing its smooth, sandy bottom on game trails, which often
ran in the stream until brush or a log diverted them into the forest.
There were pesky gnats and no–see–ums, which abated once you got
moving. Bill would probe clumps of mud and leaves until he located a
nest — usually on or very near a termite mound. He would take
temperatures within and at specific distances from the nest, then dig
into it to find the eggs, which can vary in number from ten to 15. He

would collect one to determine the age and condition of the embryo. Incubation takes about 100 days. To protect her eggs from predators, a female will remain in the vicinity, although we saw none that day. From time to time, she will brush the nest with her tail. When the embryos are ready to hatch, they start "squealing" inside the eggs. She hears them and knocks away the overburden and carries them to water. She may watch them for a few weeks, but then they're on their own.

After painstakingly examining one nest, Magnusson pointed to a grass–covered stump not 10 feet away and asked, "How would you like to photograph a Bothrops close up?" At first I didn't understand, but when he added, "He's been coiled up in there for at least three weeks," I realized he meant the fer–de–lance. "Bring your camera and follow me." He casually walked over to the stump, motioning me to the far side. "Focus on the hole at a slow shutter speed and let me know when you're ready." At first I could only see a tangle of leaves over a dark background. Then my vision adjusted and I saw part of the coiled flesh, though not the head.

"Ready," I said after a long moment.

"Now don't get nervous. No sudden movements. He won't strike if he doesn't feel threatened." With that, Bill reached over and pulled away the foliage. Barely an inch from his hand the snake's head faced us with cold sinister eyes. I shot methodically, changing settings back and forth. "That's good," I whispered dryly at last, and Bill let back the brush.

One night we swam for crocodiles.

Bill had decided to check on "Ol' No. 5," so with underwater headlamps, and snorkel and masks, he and Tina waded out into the creek. An hour's fruitless search caused fear that the fellow had departed his territory, perhaps as jaguar fare. Then at the end of a long pool Tina called that she'd found him resting under a ledge.

It was necessary, she said, to swim under a submerged log and then loop into a small cavern. The croc would be up and to the right. After Bill, Marc and Tania had each taken a look, my attempt to beg off was greeted with hoots of derision. Chastened, I waded into the soft muck until I was chest–high then inhaled and kicked for the bottom. How clear the water was! Small fish, tadpoles and insects darted ahead. The current gently nudged some grasses and a frog sped away. I found the log, swung underneath, and up and found myself staring at a five–foot crocodile sitting lengthwise, his head to the right. Unable to resist, I reached out and touched his tail, whereupon he spun about and faced the opposite direction. I was about to pester him again when he whipped violently and was gone, leaving only a cloud of grit. There was concern when the log appeared

Bothrops atrox, *fer–de–lance*, Ducke.

to have sunk, blocking my escape. But I worked my way to the clearance, pulled under and pumped to the top.

Searches for crocodiles were routine and sometimes led to their capture for examination and marking. Bill usually did this, slipping a noose around the back of the head and bringing the animal to the surface where its snout would be tied shut with twine. It would then be held by one of the women while Bill performed various measurements and checked for injuries, deformities and parasites. A first–time captive would be marked by the cutting away of a tail ridge section. It would then be weighed on a hand–held scales, unbound and released.

Magnusson would pronounce these findings in the manner of a surgeon lecturing interns — except that his slippery patients were not anesthetized. In this, as in all else that I observed him do, the man exuded a serene self–confidence and dry humor, doubtlessly molded by years of endeavor under conditions of chronic discomfort and semisolitude.

One would think that the Institute would have offered unparalleled opportunity for the country's scientists. Fat grants from the World Bank, World Wildlife Fund, and other international groups provided huge contract–work payments which often exceeded government financing. Getting locked into one of these projects, such as compiling statistics on this or that ecological effect of highway or dam construction, cattle ranching, etc., could result in a meteoric career path or at least a sinecure. In addition, there was the prestige and hands–on experience unobtainable in academia. Yet there were disproportionately few natives compared to foreigners — an odd ratio which held true in other research facilities throughout Amazonia.

"I'm afraid they demand too much of the good life, the 'creature comforts,'" one researcher told me. "They can have those in the south of Brazil, but not here."

Even with the international grants, he said, "the Institute is grossly underfunded. Often there's not enough to pay for maintenance, toilet paper, air conditioner repair, and the like.

"World Bank and hydroelectric money keeps the Institute alive, but there are so many strings attached that often decent long–term studies can't be done. Funding agencies use the incomplete results, often unethically, for their own promotion. Too, allocation of grants often gets bogged down in the bureaucracy and the money devalues from inflation before it can be used.

"Fortunately, there are some really good people here, some of the best tropical research people in Brazil — the world for that matter. Unfortunately, we also get some difficult types. Did you know that it's possible to get a [biology] degree in Brazil without ever having touched an animal? People like that are literally lost in the woods, worse than useless."

INPA, it seemed, was no exception to the universal rule that in large institutions, particularly governmental ones, the sedentary accumulator who excels at caution, ingratiation, infighting and self–promotion will advance to the detriment of field workers. Many a combat leader has been sacked by club–soft staff generals for the very audacity that wins battles and saves lives. In academia, the accumulator tries to divert students from the field, where he may be incompetent and his authority threatened, to the classroom, where nomenclature, description and theory, in which he is exquisitely conversant, predominate.

A Ducke worm and Marc Hero's foot.

Graduate students, Magnusson said, are chosen, "based on their interest in areas we're working in. They decide their own topic but it must be one within our power to supervise." Just then, there were 17 — 12 pursuing masters degrees and five doctoral candidates. Of course there were several, like Tina, who were still undergraduates. Marc was a doctoral candidate, at Griffiths University in Brisbane. In the field his bearing was professorial, which Bill encouraged.

Both men were critical of "descriptive biologists," a term used for those who write flatulent general descriptions of animals and plants they've only briefly observed.

"We are quantitative scientists," Marc said during a break for tea, his hands dripping with frog slime, an ugly scratch down a forearm. "We don't just write, 'the plant had a marvelous little flower some 'x' centimeters long and 'y' centimeters wide which, when seen, radiated a yellowish color. A large bee was seen to settle into it'. We write that the plant was seen under 'abc' conditions and really report a wealth of data, which we have gathered not only from observation but from controlled experiments. Most people in the States and Britain now do this, but in Europe you still have the old Darwin descriptive school which, don't get me wrong, was good in its time but which today has lost its usefulness. Those people were pioneers, innovators. They were seeing these things for the first time. Somebody had to describe them and catalog them. But now that work has basically been done. We pretty much know what and where everything is. What we need to know are all the many complicated little details about its cycle — its growth and reproduction and its precise relationship to its environment — not just that it looks nice and bees suck honey out of it and a frog sits on it and something else eats it and we saw all this during our two-week stroll through the woods last summer."

Others earning opprobrium are Americans who duck down for three to four months with big grants but little time.

"It takes you a month just to get acclimated, get over the dysentery and sweats, and then another two to find out just where everything is and get set up," Marc went on. "Then you have to head back home to teach — can't lose that tenure, can we? So all that funding and clout — it means nothing really as far as true research, true science, goes. It's a trap. You get caught in the [academic] system. It demands most of your time and energy. It may give you the illusion of doing research but you're really just another bureaucrat with a fast clock."

In spite of the demands of research and writing made all the greater by his burgeoning reputation, it became apparent that Magnusson considered his role as teacher paramount. Taped above his workbench back at INPA was the following handwritten admonition:

> Such are the best teachers: a dogma
> learned is only a new error — the old one was
> perhaps as good; but a spirit communicated is a
> perpetual possession. These best teachers climb
> beyond teaching to the plane of art: it is
> themselves, and what is best in themselves, that
> they communicate.
> — R.L. Stevenson, May 1887.

I took care to perform the small, and clearly make–work, tasks assigned me — keeping equipment and provisions dry, gathering a bit of firewood and checking the trails. Otherwise I felt free to improvise my own "projects," which needless to say did not include handling crocodiles and snakes. I made regular climbs up the NASA tower where I was treated to splendid avian displays. Among the most colorful were the parrots, blue–and–yellow and hyacinthine macaws, and toucans. There were hawks, wrens, finches and troupial blackbirds and even an owl. Following them with the binoculars at dusk, as they swooped about and added their own voices to the sonic cauldron, drew me inescapably toward the essence of the rain forest. Derelict though it may have been, the old tower still served as a relayer of messages.

Taking pictures of the birds, and of the more interesting flowers and fungi, was nicely combined with long game–trail walks. Most of the prints in the traps were those of small animals — anteaters, opossums, armadillos and the like, though occasionally something larger would leave tracks. A tapir, four toes in front, three behind, seemed to have used a length of trail one morning, but the tracks were disturbed by birds scratching for grubs. Afternoon rains also did their work, so it was best to make the rounds early — at dawn, and again from three to four. It got dark around six.

My more or less constant companions at camp were a Morpho butterfly who would unexpectedly flutter in and out; a knotty black spider who captured these and moths in its web — the Morpho was lucky, but an "owl" variety was not; two "forest captains," seldom seen brown little birds whose siren–whistles whiplashed incessantly in the middle distance; and a woodpecker that drummed rapidly like someone driving a nail inside a barrel. A column of eggheaded army ants took a day to march through, two of its kamikaze sentinels leaving their wretched pincers in my leg.

And so I had gotten used to Ducke, reducing my compulsive pace to its sedative rhythm. Even in such a short time, I became so sensitive to its syncopations that appreciable variations were noticed. Which is perhaps why I was awakened by the silence the morning of the jaguar.

I lit the Casio digital: 3:15, far earlier than usual. I thought I might as well get moving. I built a fire, dipped the coffee pot in the creek, and after four cups and a pack of instant oatmeal, *Avena em Flocos Quaker*, headed out with a jump on the day.

Hardly beyond earshot of the falls, something moved to my front. There was a rustle of leaves and a soft snap. A heavy, musklike odor filled the air.

413

As I reached to flick on the headlamp, there was a sudden thrashing. The light's tardy beam caught a blur of yellowish gray bounding out of sight around the bend ahead.

Walking as noisily as possible, I approached the fork in the trail. There was no indication of which way the animal had gone. Electing the branch, I continued a hundred yards to a print trap on the other side of a fallen samauma tree.

There I found the evidence: four pan–sized jaguar tracks headed north. But there were none returning and none on the main trail either. At daybreak I photographed the prints, using an oatmeal box for contrasts.

They measured nine inches long by six wide. In case Marc and the others came while I was away, I put up a cairn at the fork with a stick pointing south then made my regular rounds, watching in vain for droppings.

"Nice jag tracks, eh? But you bloody missed the scat! Can't tell about you Americans!" Marc grinned as I strode in expecting a compliment but getting a ration instead. "Don't worry. Almost missed it myself," he hastened to add. He had found the cat's stool not far from the tower — beneath some trees well off the trail but still visible if you knew what you were looking for, which he did. "No doubt about it," he said, "Ol' jag was here. He was headed into camp, and you spooked him first."

I could tell he was amused at the reverse prospect.

"Doesn't appear to have been eating any crocs," he went on, referring to the scat. "We'll have a closer look back at the lab. 'Appears rather sickly, if you ask me, runny and all."

We returned to Manaus the next afternoon, hiking the eight miles to the highway and hitching a ride to the city limits with a family out for a Sunday drive in their new red Toyota pickup. They dropped us at a bus stop. Among the passengers were young men in T–shirts: RUM AND COKE, WHISKEY, GIN AND TONIC, MILK SHAKE. WHISKEY nursed an oversized radio from which there was no reprieve.

Thomas Malthus, in his 1798 *An Essay on the Principle of Population*, held that human populations expanded exponentially against static or gradually increasing food supplies. The result, inevitably, was famine. A half century later, Charles Darwin applied Malthus' theory to all life, seeing in it the triggering mechanism of natural selection whereby the fittest win the struggle for what's left and all others perish.

Rob Bierregaard, ornithologist and Amazon resident agent of
the World Wildlife Fund, Manaus.

Neither foresaw the advent of modern technology whose bounty would fuel such an explosion in man's numbers and power that he would threaten the very existence of earth as a life–bearing planet. What an evolutionary anomaly: a species, through its very success, drawn toward extinction — and all else with it.

Nowhere is man's onslaught against nature more telling than in the rain forest, repository of three quarters of all known life — in variety as well as volume.

Brazil's Amazon contains more rain forest area than *all other regions of the world combined*, an area equal to one–third of the continental United States, some 1.2 million square miles.

Since 1970, more than 10 percent of this area has been deforested by colonists, squatters, cattle ranches, gold mines, sprawling settlements and hydroelectric projects. Such rapacity in northern climes would bring televised havoc to the doors of politicians. In Brazil there are only shrugs of indifference or smug self–congratulations among the power elites, many of whom profit personally from forest destruction.

Few journalists venture into the "green hell" and those who do leave quickly, filing yet others of those seemingly endless Chicken–Little reports to whose anecdotes and exasperations we have become impervious.

There are, to be sure, some devoted naturalists but much of their work is specialized research within narrow parameters, and most are here for only a very short time before returning to their colleges and bureaucracies in America and Europe. Few are as seasoned and savvy as the taciturn Magnusson.

Surely, one would think, somewhere there must be an advocate in the field, a champion against the torch, the chain saw and the bulldozer — in other words, a Defender of the Forest. To many, there is such a person in Manaus.

A few days after our return from Ducke, Marc arranged with his friend, ornithologist Rob Bierregaard, World Wildlife Fund's resident director, for me to go with a field crew to one of their "minimum size reserve" projects, *Fazenda Esteio*, about 80 miles north of Manaus. He would take me over on his motorbike in time to catch the van which left at two. An American public television crew filming a "Nature" program on monkeys would be along.

In the lab that morning I drank coffee, leafed through reptilian tomes and watched Tina dissect frogs. Suddenly, the door opened and the secretary from across the hall announced, in a manner not unlike that adopted by federal judges' clerks toward mere lawyers: "Dr. Fearnside will see you now."

I was at a loss, but then recalled dropping by for a chat with the elusive American, to whom almost everyone deferred on the Very Big Questions: How long can the Amazon survive? Can anything be done to save it? What effect would its destruction have? Her boss was terribly busy, she'd said. It would be at least a week before I could schedule an appointment. I replied that I would be in the lab off and on the next few days so just holler if he could spare a moment.

Phil Fearnside was tall, intense, imperious and articulate. Only 39 at the time of our meeting, his bearing was that of a general buckled in for a long siege — but with time for an occasional round of chess or handball.

Condemned by conservatives as an "alarmist" guilty of "strawmanship," he was suspect to the left because of his eight–year consultancy at INPA, an arm of the Brazilian government, *bête noire* of environmentalists. There he performed computer studies of Trans–Amazon settlement patterns, horticulture, soil and burn samples and satellite photographs. Much of his work was concentrated in the far western state of Rondónia, which served as a great ecological field laboratory. As devil's advocate, and a foreigner at that, his tenure implied a tenuousness that would have cowed the prudent and made sycophant the timid. Yet with perseverance, and with a wiliness approaching the Machiavellian, he had survived detraction to see his ideas gain ascendancy — in discourse as well as policy, though enforcement, stymied by cultural inertia and corruption, lagged far behind. He was an incubator of projects and ideas for projects, incessantly percolating articles, notes, conference papers and letters–to–the–editors of an array of journals. He was the author of two books on rain forest "carrying capacity" and like chapters in the books of others. Pulped battalions of the trees he championed now soldiered this formidable bibliography. Controversy, which he seemed to relish, followed in his wake. Yet his work was so respected by major international foundations that a grant proposal with his blessing was virtually assured of acceptance. "Fearnside's a grant wizard," someone said. Chief among these was the World Wildlife Fund, field–wise standout among those sometimes noisy, pious and administratively sated junk–mail solicitors of critter balm.

"... Education is the answer — isn't it always? Primary school is where you start — early, from the first grade, teaching them, showing them the fragility, the complexity of the forest." He was wary at first, eyeing me pensively, tugging at a ferocious mustache. But soon he was relaxed, leaning back in the chair professorially, warming to yet another occasion to edify the ignorant.

"But it's being destroyed so fast that sometimes I doubt there'll be time for education to take effect, for respect for the forest to become a part of the culture. It's hard for Amazon settlers to believe that its survival and their own are tied together. That's a radical idea for them. For them the forest is infinite, and infinitely exploitable. A change in that perception isn't quickly brought about, particularly when the way they're doing things is so advantageous. They simply move on as soon as the resource depreciates. Some just clear and sell out and leave without planting at all. There's a very rapid discounting of future benefits and costs here, as well as the feeling that 'if I don't cut it down someone else will.'

"But you've got to have government support for education — and for enforcement. Not just from the forestry service and the military, but from the whole bureaucracy. Right now it reflects the cultural attitude which says, 'if it's profitable, then cut it down.'"

There had, he said, been some political progress. For one thing, regulations providing subsidies and tax breaks for large scale cattle ranching had been rescinded. These included a disastrous provision permitting half of all income tax owed from any source to be "invested" in clearing rain forest — a bonanza for large speculators and ranching concerns, including ventures tied to the likes of Citibank, King Ranch, Armour, and Volkswagen. By the mid–1970s such interests had utterly co–opted the Trans–Amazon colonization program either through direct investment — the rules were changed to permit corporate acquisition — or subsequent purchase from the small colonists that the program had been devised to resettle. All reforms, however, are prospective and vast previously approved projects remain intact.

Since 1970 over 40 national forests and preserves have been established, though poaching and squatting have severely encroached upon many of them. Silviculture, tree plantations and selective harvesting, is officially encouraged over clearing in some areas and in others extension services now emphasize longer fallows between crops, though not the 20– to 30–year periods of the shifting swidden cultivation practiced for millennia by forest Indians.

Good rules were one thing. Enforcement was quite another. For example, the requirement that half of each homestead along the Trans–Amazon Highway had to be left in forest was either ignored altogether or circumvented by allowing the sale of the forested half to another colonist — or rancher — who could then clear half of that, and so on.

"You see," Fearnside continued, "there's a tradition in Brazil called *jeito*, that treats the law as good in principle but that condones, even extols, evasion: 'The law is for other people, not me,' is what it says. There's always a way for anyone with money or connections or ingenuity to get around it. You have literally thousands of laws on the books but enforcement is random, selective, capricious.

"The tradition goes back to colonial times. It's particularly evident when it comes to deforestation because this is a frontier country with the idea that you can have what you use. 'Use' meant 'clearing.' That was the determinative act that proved ownership, title. It became the law. Anything else — fishing, hunting, collecting medicinal plants, herbs, even wild rubber, didn't count. So you modify that law by, say, restricting how much of a man's land can be cleared and you've got a real problem with enforcement."

Terra firma, unflooded high ground or uplands, accounts for more than 90 percent of the region. Most of the rest is *várzea*: rich, annually flooded semiwetlands along the river and its tributaries. Constantly stirred, replenished and fertilized by this process — "the river is the plow," is a local saw — the *várzea* is among the world's richest riparian soils. Indians and *caboclos* have cultivated it for centuries without posing a threat to the forest. Its isolation and difficulty of occupation — floors of houses must be literally raised and lowered with seasonal fluctuations in the water level — and the preemption of better *várzea* properties by earlier settlers have all served to shift the recent waves of colonists onto adjacent terra firma. The Trans–Amazon Highway, completed in the mid–1970s, and its rapidly expanding network of branches and secondary roads has exposed thousands of additional square miles of virgin forest.

"A road brings colonists; the population grows and demands more roads. With more roads come still more people, and so on. The process feeds on itself," Fearnside said.

We discussed settlement patterns and incentives — free land and start–up loans for clearing and planting, etc. "But most migrants today come on their own. They become *posseiros,* legitimate settlers, or *invasores,* squatters, usually on private land. If they enter government land which is not an Indian reserve, the government usually just goes along. Private land is another matter. It depends how many *invasores* there are — and how many *pistoleiros,* gunmen, the rancher can send out to evict them. Sometimes the *pistoleiros* evict settlers from their own land — government land they've cleared and lived on for years or bought from someone who did. But they neglect to get the title changed over or maybe they tried but couldn't get the paperwork done. The bureaucracy is slow if you are ignorant and illiterate and poor. It takes a lot of travel back and forth — days, weeks even, by riverboat — to different offices, and a farmer can't be away from his land that long. Maybe the rancher says the *caboclo* owes him money. There's usually a reason. But more often the *caboclo* just sells out to the rancher and leaves and the land is turned into pasture. That's eventually the most profitable use for it under the present system, anyway."

419

Fearnside refers in his book, *Human Carrying Capacity of the Brazilian Rainforest*, to the classic "tragedy of the commons" in which farmers grazing a common pasture eventually destroy it by adding more and more stock. By analogy there was an inherent conflict between profitability and ecology in the Amazon because of the "basic disparity between [rain forest] sustainability and the investment patterns producing the highest economic returns ... Unfortunately, the rate of return that can be sustained ... is limited by such biological factors as the growth rates of trees, which have no logical link with bankers' discount rates."[83]

What about the oft heard homily, I asked him, that the Amazon was the "Lungs of the World?"

"That's an unfortunate exaggeration that's used by deforestation interests to discredit valid environmental concerns. The inference is that the world's oxygen supply is dependent on rain forests. That's not true. Oxygen levels from climax forests are in a state of equilibrium in terms of biomass, meaning as much oxygen is produced as is used. Like the water: most of it evaporates and falls right back to earth in the forest. The real atmospheric concern is the huge quantities of carbon dioxide produced by rain forest burning. Carbon dioxide, as you may know, causes the so–called greenhouse effect, which is a shorthand way of saying that solar energy, most of which normally reradiates as ultraviolet rays, is trapped by an atmosphere too heavy with carbon dioxide."

In an article in the journal *Interciencia* the year before, he had given a startling picture of the consequences of continued carbon dioxide release from Amazon deforestation:

> The West Antarctic ice sheet is vulnerable to rapid melting.
>
> ... Floating ice shelves on its perimeter presently impede the sheet from undergoing a "surge" or accelerated sliding into the sea. The[se] shelves are pinned against the Antarctic mainland by grounding on several rock high points or islands.
>
> ... Should air temperatures increase [the shelves] would melt ... releasing the back pressure that now limits the rate of ice flow. [The resultant rise in sea levels] would flood many of the most populous parts of the globe. [O]nce critical temperatures [are] attained to begin melting polar ice, the long delays [necessary for remedial action] would render ineffective any human countermeasures at that late date, such as reduced carbon dioxide emissions.[84]

Philip M. Fearnside, Manaus.

Combined with fossil fuel combustion, by far the largest source of atmospheric carbon, rain forest clearing would, if continued at the present rate, create enough carbon dioxide in the atmosphere by the mid–21st century to increase the earth's temperature as much as 4.5 degrees Centigrade. Polar temperatures would rise more quickly than those elsewhere "due to a positive feedback relationship between albedo, reflectivity, and ice cover, since melting ice exposes darker surfaces, which absorb more heat." The Arctic, he said, would heat up even more quickly because of the larger area of open water there and the "smaller seasonal change in snow cover." This would cause a "shift of climatic zones northward," turning some of the world's richest farmland into desert and substantially increasing rainfall in what are now relatively dry regions. The effect on the Amazon, which surprisingly has a hard dry season with some areas experiencing occasional droughts of from 40 to 60 days, would be devastating.

Carbon dioxide has already reached 330 parts per million of atmospheric volume, he said, and is still rising due to delayed effects of previous pollution and burning. This compares with an average of 270 parts per million measured in air bubbles trapped in ice before the industrial revolution.

This ominous prophesy was by no means accepted by everyone. Two US Department of Energy researchers at the University of Illinois responded:

> Fearnside ... clouds rather than clarifies
> important questions about the role of tropical forests
> ... in the global carbon cycle. [He] is clearly alarmist
> ... offers no new information [and] confuses the issue
> through misinformation ... bias and strawmanship."[85]

They accused Fearnside of using "old," pre–1980, citations, "unsubstantiated opinion" and "a contrived scenario" — the complete destruction of the Amazon rain forest, an event that they doubted was occurring at all and that would have little effect on the Earth's ecosystems even if it were.

Among their targets were Fearnside's statistics on the Amazon's total biomass and the rate of carbon release from changes in land use, particularly conversion to pasture. Their own studies, more recent by several years than those used by Fearnside, showed that pastures actually *accumulated* carbon. They also condemned the Fearnside time frame, 62 years, for the forest's destruction, together with his purported failure to allow for carbon retention in soil, mature as well as secondary forest growth, and in "sinks" — charcoal, ocean water, etc. All this, they averred, showed that the author, instead of following all available evidence to a rational conclusion, had marshaled only those facts which fit his "preconceived idea" of total rain forest destruction.

In a vigorous rebuttal,[86] carried in the same issue by supportive but oddly defensive editors, Fearnside refined his argument, although the paucity of exact data remained a problem, particularly with regard to the total volume of forest involved and the portion converted into carbon dioxide as opposed to being retained as carbon in soil and sinks.

He dismissed his critics' own biomass studies by stating that their samples included only larger trees, many from other regions, and that their results showed less aggregate vegetation than all save one of 16 separate estimates by others throughout the basin. Their assertion that secondary forest would contain enough carbon to offset felled primary growth he disputed by stating that the latter was mainly replaced with cattle pastures which, contrary to their opinion, would hold little or no carbon. With regard to the 62–year period, this was used, "to make it equal to the number of gigatons of carbon which the total burned biomass would yield." Most commentators, he said, would think that far too generous a time.

The net effect of the exchange was to leave the detached reader convinced that continued deforestation could not but add substantially to atmospheric carbon dioxide. However, whether the end result would be a rise in temperatures sufficient to alter the earth's ecology would appear, in the present state of knowledge, to remain an open question. Even so, it is not a risk that any but the most devoted defenders of the industrial status quo would wish to run. The unspoken reality, however, is that the decision is entirely in the hands of the Brazilian government, which, even were it able to do so, would unlikely use its police power to disrupt present resettlement patterns — the key to halting deforestation.

What should be done, I asked.

"The key is a diversity of uses, each compatible with the environment — plantations, farming, even ranching in some areas," Fearnside replied.

He put it this way in the book:

> The creation of self–sustaining communities capable of maintaining their populations at an acceptable standard of living without regard to benefits accruing to other parts of the country.[87]

He might have added: "or the world." Extraction of its resources for the benefit of foreign interests has been the lot of the Amazon

423

since European man came here. Timber, rubber, gold — now the land itself.

Rip off what you can, then move on. To hell with conservation. Massive resettlement programs to alleviate population pressure in the sprawling but economically stagnant cities of northeastern Brazil have been a big factor. The Amazon was going to be the safety valve for the inequitable system of land distribution: less than 10 percent of the people own three–fourths of the land. But more people are born every year in Brazil than have been resettled in twenty!

"Do you actually believe all of that could be deforested by the year 2050," I asked as we wound things up. I suppose my tone implied that I suspected he might have been posturing after all — giving a histrionic worst–case "scenario."

He turned to look at the map on the wall behind him. After a long silence he faced me again, an unexpected sadness in his voice: "Yes, I'm afraid so. Much sooner than that, really."

Fazenda Esteio was one of three still substantially forested cattle ranches that had been voluntarily placed by their owners in a World Wildlife Fund project designed to determine the "minimum critical size" a reserve's ecosystem had to be in order for animals to maintain themselves in "continuously breeding populations."

Too small, and there was not enough territory to support diverse groups, especially of wide–ranging species like monkeys and big cats. Too large, and the area would not be politically sustainable with the resource–hungry human population.

Plants were integral to the experiment, since each animal depends on the forest as a place to hide, stalk, nest and eat. Each has its own root, bark, fruit and flower menu — or entrees of lesser beasts who do.

The whole is woven together in a complex mosaic of interdependency which ecologists refer to as "coevolved relationships." Every species theoretically might be moved to a zoological garden in California, but coevolved relationships, like good wine, don't travel well. Once disrupted, they are lost forever.

Rob Bierregaard had persuaded the ranchers that participation in the project could only inure to their benefit: extensive crop, grass and hydrological tests — done on pastureland as well as forest soils — would be shared with them.

The owners were impressed and agreed to go along.

Crucial to the projects were the efforts of a dedicated staff of young Brazilian workers and students trained to observe and record animal movements and conduct the soil studies. Some of this work involved trailing species for long distances, as was the case with the local variety of *Cebus apella*, or capuchin monkey.

424

Virtually living with these primates was a 32–year–old zoology graduate from Minas Gerais, Wilson Spironello. He was assigned by Bierregaard to guide the PBS camera crew, two men from Jackson, Wyoming. I would accompany them.

Wilson's task was to observe the monkeys throughout their 900–hectare range, which necessitated his clearing more than 100 miles of meandering trails. The distance was usually covered in two to three weeks, although it could take longer since the monkeys tarried for days where food was especially plentiful.

Working out of various base camps to which he returned at night, he would plot their movements in a notebook, later transferring the data onto a master grid–map of the *fazenda*. He had traced the particular group to be filmed for more than 700 hours during the previous six months.

They were seen in this time to eat more than 180 species of plants, some of which Wilson had sampled himself. They also ate a variety of insects and spiders, which our guide had not sampled, he assured us, but no rodents or other mammals: cebidae, unlike some monkeys, and chimpanzees, are not even occasional carnivores.

The monkeys had become so used to his presence, he said, that he was able to approach them almost at will, sometimes to within a few feet. Occasionally, they would come to him. He told how recently he had broken fruit husks by striking them together against a stump, an effort several of his subjects had readily imitated.

Assisting Wilson was a young woman biologist, Tania Linhares, who was sent along as interpreter but who was every bit as familiar with the project as any of the others, including Wilson.

We were briefed before heading into camp by WWF director Tom Lovejoy, technical advisor on the TV series. An affable, articulate fellow, Lovejoy had a shrewd grasp of the exigencies of the struggle for the world's rain forests. Like Fearnside, with whom he had coauthored several articles, he held the view that the fight would be won or lost locally, in the rain forest nations, themselves.

Fazenda Camp No. 41 was established in a clearing about a mile into the forest from an access road. It was a semipermanent base, with a long tent shared by crew and guests and a pavilion for cooking.

There was space for your hammock and a few provisions beneath or suspended from the overhead. The food was tolerable. A kind of chicken–and–rice broth with tough singed beef and overboiled potatoes was the first night's fare, and it proved to be the best.

The crew stayed up past midnight listening to full–blast radio rock and playing dominoes, aggressively slam–cracking the pieces onto the table. These reports carried to the road, where I walked to escape the bedlam and listen to the forest. The roars of howler monkeys rippled in the distance, rising then falling like gusts of wind.

Next morning after fritters and eggs we made a column of eight, Wilson and a tracker leading the way followed by the TV men. The first toted his camera over his shoulder at-the—ready; the second carried a case with a microphone sensitive enough to catch the faintest sound. They prided themselves on using only actual sounds recorded simultaneously with the footage. Nevertheless some dubbing, but only of on—site noises they insisted, was inevitable since some animals are silent when filmed.

Three porters carried backup lenses, film, batteries, tools and cleaning equipment. In the rear were Tania, myself and a senior tracker whose job was to see that no one fell behind. There were a number of false sightings and straggle stops resulting in an accordion effect in our progress. Nor was its cohesion aided by the failure of the cameramen to relay Wilson's marching signals. This was doubtless due to their disdain for the presence of Tania and myself, though it was she who at long last spotted the monkeys and saved what would otherwise have been a filmless day.

This committee pursuit of the spider monkeys was a minor adventure, but the most instructive aspect of *Fazenda Esteio* was the scope of the project, the commitment of its young Brazilian scientists, and its example of cooperation between ranchers and ecologists for the advantage of both.

Bill and Marc graciously invited me to crash at their place near INPA during my remaining time in Manaus. Bill flew off to a convention in São Paulo, and Marc returned to Ducke, so I had the little house to myself. I read, caught up on the journal and slept. The doors were bolted and the windows meshed against burglary, a constant nuisance. Even wash hung out to dry was not safe. Conveniently, the *Coroado 2* bus belched a route to town from the bottom of the street, stopping only a short walk from the lab.

I went to the *Teatro Amazonas*, the famous opera house built in 1896 during the rule of Governor Eduardo Ribeiro. In the rubber collapse after the first world war, it fell into disuse, suffering neglect, pilferage and fire. In 1974, it was restored at a cost of several millions of dollars. Curtains and bunting trimmed in gold, emerald and blue framed busts of Wagner, Racine, Mozart, Goethe and 20 other maestros. Against a background of cherubs and Greek columns, an angel crowned Mark Twain and Governor Ribeiro. A series of lobby frescoes portrayed horrible imaginings: a stalking jaguar stared menacingly; a "savage" carried off a Rubenesque damsel. There is no resident company, road performances are few and no local groups use the hall. Its majestic lounge at the time housed a curio shop selling portraits of bug—eyed American teenagers.

426

Wilson Spironello, World Wildlife Fund primatologist,
Fazenda Esteio, north of Manaus.

Passing an imposing building with the Citibank logo, I went inside to find Flavin J. Ferreria, resident vice president.

"We do everything a Brazil bank can, and much more besides. Our expertise is in foreign exchange, export–import agreements, letters of credit — whatever you need to do international business. And we can loan more money on better terms than anyone."

The Manaus branch was heavily involved in the *Zona Franca*, a free–trade zone designed to boost the Amazon's economy with jobs and overseas markets. This would get the region on its feet while generating some badly needed export earnings for the national treasury. To get set up, firms were given tax immunity, subsidized power from hydroelectric projects whose reservoirs flooded millions of acres, free rent for up to five years, and other inducements. More than 60 of the enterprises were plants assembling Japanese products under franchise: watches, stereos, TV sets, and computers. There were a few American and German surrogates too — razors and diesel engines, for example. Most of the *Zona's* customers were, however, not foreigners but Brazilians, many of them bureaucrats who flew up from Brasília, Rio and São Paulo for the weekend at government expense. For those without free rides, the savings on subsidized goods bought tax free still more than paid for the fare. Little of benefit accrued to the poor Indian and *caboclo* inhabitants since even these bargains were beyond their means, and most *Zona* jobs were held by workers brought in from the south.

I left Manaus late one afternoon in October on the N.M. *Avelino Leal*, bound for Tabatinga. She eased into the channel just below the mouth of the Rio Negro, whose viscous ribbon of black silt against the blond Solimões some consider the beginning of the Amazon. But most cartographers hold that the Solimões *is* the Amazon, from its nativity at the confluence of the Ucayali and the Marañón above Iquitos.

It was necessary to pick through a jam of boats to which we had been rafted. Many, like our own craft, were festooned with hammocks. Disentangled, we drifted between two ocean liners, European cities afloat, their pink inhabitants smiling down at us.

My journey to the extremity of Brazil, where it shoves back Peru and the thumb of Colombia that just grasps the river, took seven days. Enclaves of humanity tolled past with names like Fonte Boa, Jutai, Tonantins, São Antônio do Icá, Amataurá, São Paulo de Olivenca and Benjamin Constant.

Each received its portion of passengers, so that toward the end our number was reduced almost to the legal capacity of 80: 40 for each dingy, four for each life jacket. But for the first few days our hammocks, suspended at improbable angles in whatever space could be forced, swung against each other like potato sacks.

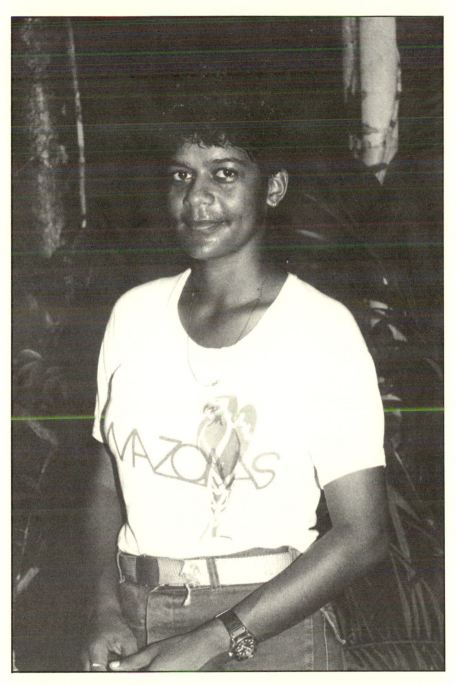

Tania Linahares, World Wildlife Fund biologist, *Fazenda Esteio*.

Mess was served in relays at a long table near the head, from which wafted an incessant pungency. Meals were announced by a crewman who walked about crying "eat now" and poking three fingers at his mouth. Some would anticipate the call by loitering at the table; others, caught by surprise, fended as best they could. Those unable to get a place for the first sitting positioned themselves to contend for the second, and so on. There was something almost ceremonial about it. People with hammocks over the table had to remove them.

One served oneself with care. There were rarely enough first servings to go around but others were quickly ladled up from the galley below. Rice and manioc with fish and chicken were regular fare.

Fish were purchased from overtaken skiffs, the captain heaving to to deal with them. Catches varied in species and size but were invariably tasty; the other items less so. There could be some delay with the fish, depending on when we might hail a lucky boat. Once, lunch fell past three and there were suggestions of mutiny. Food and the customary heavily presugared coffee were prepared with water drawn directly from the river with a bucket attached to a rope. Hoping to extend the respite from fecal contamination begun at Ducke, I tried sticking to mineral water, bread, fruit and tinned beef bought in Manaus. But eventually my appetite bested me, and I suffered the consequences.

The captain busied himself transferring records from ledgers and cargo manifests onto an Apple II computer, at which he proudly pecked in his office amidships. A compact disc sound system broadcast a concussive blend of Brazilian rock and martial airs. Equally annoying was a daily reveille of fireworks at the wheelhouse attended by the captain, himself. These cherry—bomblike devices were ignited and tossed by a junior crewman, many exploding just off the passenger deck.

Our arrival at Benjamin Constant coincided with a kind of regional fair. People from nearby villages had set up stalls to sell vegetables and fish. An evangelical group sold handicrafts for their church and a guitarist busked. A few Peruvian Indians had come across the border to sell their distinctive pottery and colorfully painted mussel shells.

I mailed letters and sat under a tree next to the T—shirt boutique "Donkey Donkey Donkey." In its tidy yard, a very large child, perhaps 12, played with a toy dump truck, pulling it by a string.

Two young men left a bar up the street in fighting stance. A crowd gathered around them. When I glimpsed the disputants again, they were sitting astride motorcycles, glowering. It was a standoff. The mob, cheated, taunted them.

Tom Lovejoy, then Director of the World Wildlife Fund at *Fazenda Esteio*.

Then a vendor pedaled up with a cart of *guarana* soda, a bland but refreshing pop made from the seeds of a bush by that name. "BARE — Antarctica, S.A.," it said on the bottle. His arrival distracted the crowd, who bought him out.

As they dispersed, a dog hobbled down the street in plain view, a rear leg severed but with the shank and paw still dangling by a thread of flesh. The wound was only half clotted. The animal wagged its tail at the oncoming faces. I lost sight of it, and when it reemerged, it was in front of the bar where the nonfight had taken place. Someone, perhaps the bartender, came out and stoned it away.

We spent an entire day and night at this place. Tabatinga, the official port of entry, was just over the river, and none of the freight and passengers waiting here could be boarded for the return trip until the vessel had cleared police and customs there. Permission to dock came by radio the second morning and in a surging downpour we crossed over and tied up at a modern pier out from streets swirling in red mud.

It took half an hour to slog into the town. Merely another run–down bidonville, it seemed. The first few houses were shanties no different from those of a hundred Podunks downriver. But then dwellings with a newness about them caught the eye: fresh blue and yellow paint, for example, and the use of concrete and brick and ornamental tiles. On the main street the houses had satellite dishes, trailered swift boats with double 135–horse motors and snazzy late model pickups, Japanese mostly, but also Fords and Dodges. From one garage, a new Mercedes peered out arrogantly.

I had been told that a transit visa could be obtained from Colombian *migración* in Leticia next door. I had my passport out, ready to present. But there was no checkpoint. Tabatinga–Leticia were one. Not even a flag demarked the actual border. Every Latin American border crossing I had ever approached, no matter how remote and insignificant, had been manned by grim *machos* prepared, at least in liturgy, to die for *La Patria*. But not here.

Now, to be sure, there were Brazilian customs and border officials, but they were a mile away. And Colombia, too, had its apparatus, also in *el centro*. Most impressive were five gray patrol craft, which doubtless had seen US Coast Guard service. Whistles, pipes, bugles and klaxons summoned the sailors to shipboard drills. Twice the entire fleet *ahooga–ahooga–ed* to battle stations and churned the river in nautical dressage to intercept imaginary foes. And the soldiers, too, paraded smartly in the town. No slovenly, unkempt sad sacks these, but trim, starched, trained and ready troopers.

But what was it, I wondered, that could explain the absence of formal fencing at proud Leticia, Colombia's only port on the Amazon?

Surely there must be a sound commercial reason for such extraordinary comity. For if Tabatinga was well–off, Leticia was wealthy. Jaguars, Porches and even a Rolls–Royce, cruised the streets. Mercedes were almost plebeian. Bars and sidewalk cafes were adorned with dapper dandies and slinky, diamond–bedecked vixens.

Ordinary merchants exuded a sheened gluttony of gain. Wads of $100 bills were commonplace. Yet there was not a single smokestack to be seen. The docks, while superior to most of those downriver, carried no bustling commerce. There were no major trading houses or brokerage firms. What was the source of so much wealth?

The answer was in the air: Leticia has one of the busiest small airports in the western hemisphere. And the freight is, in a manner of speaking, agricultural. It is exclusively a derivative of a single crop, the coca plant: precious kilograms of cocaine paste ferried from Peru and Bolivia where it has been distilled from tons of coca leaves in jungle laboratories. At Leticia, this concentrate is warehoused and transshipped to northern Colombian and, increasingly, to nearby Brazilian, processing plants to be turned into the fine white powder destined for smuggling into the United States and Europe.

Drones and whines of arriving and departing aircraft, mostly twin–engine Beeches and Cessnas and the like, are such a part of the background noise as to be unremarkable. Most avoid overflying the town itself, although the morning of my arrival, three unmarked DC–3's in apparent formation buzzed the riverfront on both sides of the border at under 500 feet before landing. There have been many fronts in the so–called War on Drugs, but none has ever been opened on this vital — and exquisitely vulnerable — rain forest bottleneck. Considering the billions of dollars involved and the remoteness of the site, it is not difficult to imagine why.

The ancient steamer–now–diesel, *Yurimaguas*, lay near the mouth of a creek that emptied offal, crankcase oil, excrement and spoiled produce from the market into the river. Children splashed and swam. Dugouts brought shoppers from the bush, some slaking their thirst in the brown water. Night fell and the time for departure approached. Relatives and friends congregated and there was food and beer and singing, although a sadness too. Finally, almost as an afterthought, the vessel slipped her mooring line. One of the PT boats circled abeam, its red light flashing. The skipper exchanged shouts with our captain, then shrugged his shoulders and motioned for him to proceed.

We crossed into Peru barely half an hour upstream, stopping at their border post. Our captain and the commander had a long talk together in a back room. There followed a meeting with the mates, then the captain and the commander went into the room again and shut the door. Soon afterward we sailed.

At the post–village of Chimbote next day, the garrison were at soccer. After the match the troops formed a boarding party to inspect for contraband. They confiscated portable radios, sacks of grain, comic books, a novel from a man who was reading it at the time, cartons of cigarettes and boxes of candy — those from the ship's store. No one protested. The captain smiled obsequiously, replying, *"Sí, mi capitán,"* and *"No, mi capitán,"* when questioned by the sergeant in charge.

We halted again below Pluvial, a fort with a commanding view of the river. There was another of those thunderstorms that were increasing in intensity. A private, drenched and miserable, stumbled down to command all *extranjeros* to report at once to the post *Comandante.* I and a French Canadian obeyed, grasping roots and limbs as we climbed. The *Comandante* only smiled and looked at our passports and told us we needn't have bothered to come up. A corporal showed us around. In a small cage was a juvenile *tigrina*, eyes hollow and bulging, ribs protruding, fur mangy. It had been taken as a mascot when its mother was shot by soldiers on patrol.

The *Comandante* would conduct an inspection when the storm passed, we were told, but it only got worse, and it was decided that the inspection would be done by the two guards on duty. We struggled down with them to the boat. The inspection was halfhearted, and we were cleared to proceed. The storm became a deluge, reducing visibility almost to nothing. I fell asleep to the beat of the rain and the drive of the engine. The night passed.

The engine sputtered and died and the current forced us toward the bank. Three moans of the horn broke the unexpected stillness. Crew and passengers exchanged shouts with some Indians who emptied their village to watch the spectacle. Naked boys darted about in canoes, one under an inverted sail. A mate heaved ashore a rope which was caught and coiled around a stump. It looked good to hold but the stump uprooted and was dragged along behind. A snag was tried but the rope snapped, whistling in midair and narrowly missing some children. We were fast swept away when two men grabbed the remnant and ran to tie it to a tree but the captain shouted for them to let go, which they did, disgustedly flinging it down and throwing up their hands.

The boat careened into mud and appeared to be stuck, to the apparent satisfaction of the rebuffed Samaritans. But the engine coughed to life again and thrust mightily between reverse and forward until the *Yurimaguas* wrenched herself back out into the channel. Spinning awkwardly at first, she soon steadied and resumed her way upriver. The people on the bank stared after us and I looked back at them until they were indistinguishable from the forest.

Dugout with inverted sail near Benjamin Constant
on the upper Brazilian Amazon.

23

ORURO

*'Son terroristas. Somos perdidos,' he
whimpered. His voice was choked with
fear. 'We are lost,' he was saying.*

I arrived in Villazón, Bolivia on November 13th, the 14th month
of the journey, after a rough jaunt. Stalled by breakdowns, I was
sidetracked in a snowstorm, detained by irregulars, pursued by
ghosts and robbed of the camera gear. In this time, I saw terror in the
eyes of brawny peasants, knew fear again myself, felt the profound
peace of Lake Titicaca and witnessed the scourge of Bolivian cocaine
and the futility of efforts at its control.

"Adventures?" replied the irascible British geologist to a pesky
reporter. "I had none. Only incompetent people have adventures."
Easily enough said. Yet even the best preparations can go awry. And
luck, competency's silent partner, can be pressed beyond her
willingness to smile.

I flew back to Lima from Iquitos, finding the jeep and equipment
secure in Alan Davis' garage. María and the Velázquezes were as
happy to see me as I them. I restocked with coffee, dates, raisins, rice,
oatmeal and dried beef. All was now ready for the road to Argentina.

Two days after my own arrival, Alan returned from a month's
vacation in the States resolved to marry Monique. She accepted his
proposal, and I threw a dinner for them in a steak house on the
Pardo, buoyed by a special bottle of *Ocucaje*.

There was a stack of mail at American Express and another
twice as large at the Embassy — the latter held hostage by an
officious clerk who scolded me for "abusing APO privileges." She
huffed that she was "returning all to sender. We have no choice." I
profusely apologized for the imposition, fairly well begging her
indulgence. At last, she relented "just this once." I would be forever
grateful, I assured her. Alan was blameless in all this, having notified
my office in my absence to use American Express thenceforward. I'd
done the same in my Amazon correspondence, but it was too late for
those who'd already written care of his AID address.

Anyhow, there was a happy ending. Nothing is more lifting of
morale than mail after a long stint in the bush.

I went out to Lurigancho for last interviews with the prisoners.
The Americans were hungry to see a fellow countryman, consular
visits being fewer and further between. I took along several recent
issues of the Miami Herald, which they read ravenously. There was

not much change in the status of most of their cases, and despondency was pervasive. However, the Frenchman, Patrick, had just been released on parole to the Good Shepherd church. Ron Babb and Gary Harris rejoiced at this turn of events.

Later I would hear that all three escaped Peru; Ron down the Amazon and Gary and Patrick down the Madre de Dios into Bolivia. A new law revoking parole for certain classes of criminals, defined ambiguously, raised rumors of reinternment of foreign felons. After five years in that hell pit, they would have been daft not to make a run for it — although Babb and Harris expressed regret for giving up their ministry. In fact, neither did. They have, as of this writing, founded chapters of Foreign Prisoners Fellowship in six other countries, including Brazil. There are no more compelling witnesses against the evils of drug trafficking. The Fellowship has been recognized by a growing number of relief organizations and clergy. Patrick disappeared and has not been heard from.

> ... the spirit that I have seen may be the
> Devil, and the Devil hath power to assume a
> pleasing shape.

"Sorry to interrupt."

"No, no, no. Do come in and sit down! I was just listening to Act III. I do them by acts, one each day if I can, at about this time. You're the American that was here asking all those questions back in July, aren't you? Did you ever get down the Amazon? Sit a spell and we'll talk when it's finished."

Maria Reiche flicked the cassette player back on and "Hamlet" resumed its engagement in the Nazca pampa. Next would be "Romeo and Juliet" and "King Lear," she said, followed by her favorite, "Julius Caesar."

> ... the undiscovered country, from whose
> bourne no traveler returns ...

The porter brought an ewer of coffee, quietly passing it to me through the door. My host, lost in concentration, declined with a brisk shake of the head.

When the act was done we talked about it for awhile. She was intrigued with the device of the play–within–the–play and by Hamlet's failure to act even after seeing the king's guilt–betraying response. At length, she asked about my turn on the Amazon and I covered a few of the highlights.

"Where are you off to now?"

When I told her, she mentioned some recent reports of the Shining Path guerrillas and various *narcotraficantes*. I assured her that I would most assiduously attempt to avoid them.

Her lecture that evening was much the same as the previous summer, although the question–and–answer session was less than amicable, with a group supporting the UFO theory of the Nazca Lines squaring off against some graduate students in anthropology. Maria eased things by observing: "We can all speculate, can't we? And I suppose none of us really knows for sure." She was assisted by Dr. Phyllis Pitluga of the Chicago Planetarium, her newly arrived understudy.

I made Arequipa at two in the morning after a long day and half a night on relatively good roads.

The part along the coast in the late afternoon was rich with desert and seascape colors — an orgy of orange and pink pastels and shadows played against wind–sculpted pinnacles, outcrops and dunes. Later, the Milky Way was resplendent overhead, bringing to mind again the ancient drawings on the pampa and the awe with which their authors must have held the cosmos.

There being no answer to my knock at the Pensión Guzman, where I had lodged the previous July, I splurged on the Hotel Turistas in the verdant Selva Alegre, the city's great eucalyptus park. Hovering behind were the twin ice–fringed volcanoes, Chachani and El Misti — "Guardians of the White City" — each reaching above 19,000 feet. The town's principal buildings are of *sillar*, white rock cut from the base of these mountains.

Misti is one of the premiere nontechnical climbs of the Andes. It can be done in three days, two up and one back. I had gone halfway in July, defeated not by the topography but stomach cramps from the local revenge.

Arequipa remains one of the most colonial of all South American cities. Founded by Pizarro in 1540, only a mule trail connected it with the rest of the country until 1870. Perhaps because of its remoteness its powerful families constituted a virtual state unto themselves. It is still a bastion of the old ways, undergirded by a strict Catholicism — architecturally exemplified by the Monastery Santa Catalina, one of the most splendid structures anywhere in New Spain. Built in the 17th century in the Arabic or *Mudejar* style of interconnected catacombs, closes and cloisters, it housed 500 nuns. Admission was the highest honor for a young woman and aristocratic families vied for vacancies. Eventually a school for girls was established and, in 1970, the convent was opened to the public.

In spite of its outward piety, however, Arequipa honored the eighth commandment more in the breach than in the observance: thievery there was a high art form.

Teams of muggers roamed the Plaza de Armas and adjacent streets, snatching purses and cameras and filching wallets. One was most vulnerable at the bus and rail stations and the visitor's bureau. The lamentations of young American and European victims of these punks were common. It was impossible to believe that such blatant larceny could have gone on without the complicity of the local police.

In vain I sought what I had heard was the "new road" to Puno. I was given first one direction, then another, and finally a third. Among my uncertain respondents were college and secondary students from wealthy Lima families here for the Todos Santos holiday. Arequipa, considered a refuge from assassination and abduction, had become a retreat for the elite. Their teenagers prinked and postured in the main square and at *Manolo*, a cafe and ice cream parlor with many mirrors. The boys wore chic leather jackets with sweaters draped over their shoulders; the girls, jerseys stenciled in English: "Hey Child," "Boy Look!," "Harvard Polo."

I climbed out of town on the road indicated by the prefecture of police, to the southeast. Reaching a quiet crossroads, I found an Indian, maybe 25 years old, squatted on a coarse, sooty blanket.

"*¿Puno? ¿Puno? ¿Va usted a Puno?,*" he called as I leaned over to ask the way, for there was no sign.

"*Sí, cómo no,*" I replied and was about to inquire if he wanted a lift but he was already stuffing his gear in the window.

He quickly corrected my route, indicating instead a steep, badly pocked grade to the left. He dozed again, bundling up like a mummy in his kilts and blanket and emitting a dank, sour odor of charred wood and garlic. Yet when the trail petered out or splintered into improbable fragments, he would awaken and again point the way — proving himself a worthy pathfinder. I thus, over the next 18 hours, avoided every wrong turn — except one.

There were pronounced slopes, such as that at the beginning, but for the most part the ascent was gradual, at times unnoticeable. I was, of course, rising to over 12,500 feet, to the great Altiplano, that vast arid basin ringed with Andean peaks. At its northwestern edge, like a turquoise pendant stripped from some cyclopean neck, is Lake Titicaca, the highest navigable lake in the world.

I had covered almost the same route four months previously, by train, also at night, unfortunately. The railway, built by American and British companies in the late 1800s, lay somewhere just to the north of my route. There were day trains twice a week and one nightly in each direction.

The further we traveled the more comfortable my guest, who gave his name as Alfredo, was with the country. From time to time he would come to and motion for me to slow or stop, and he would listen

440

and look about as if gauging the weather or pondering a landmark. Once, after we had crossed a low water bridge, he bade me backtrack and take another fork. Another time we halted on a high crest while he scanned the horizon. Grunting confidently at last, he motioned "straight on." There were stretches of sand or soft dirt, but mostly the road was potholed and corrugated. Some of the washboard was so spaced as to make it necessary to creep at 10 to 15 miles per hour or accelerate to 40. It was during one of the latter options that we hit a dip that tore loose the top rack and cracked the left rear spring hasp. It still held, but precariously. It took an hour to bolster it with a length of chain and to secure the rack, whose plates and bolts had luckily remained attached. Three jerry cans were emptied into the fuel tanks, removing that weight. The trunk of camp and mess gear was repositioned and tied with sisal cord.

When it became apparent that we would have to travel well after dark to make Puno, my guest became agitated:

"¿Qué hora es?" he would ask.

"Son las cinco ..."

"Vámonos, vámonos ... más rápido. Es peligroso la noche por aquí ..."

Why wasn't it safe? I asked.

"Hay terroristas," he replied. There are terrorists.

Although we passed a number of vehicles during the first few hours, the traffic thinned as the day wore on. Toward late afternoon it was rarer still and after dark there were only occasional groups of two or three, the last ones stopped for the night.

I recalled Maria Reiche's remark about the Shining Path but dismissed it since the conventional wisdom was that the guerrillas stayed for the most part in the provinces of Ayacucho and Cuzco. Then I remembered that they had hit near Puno a few weeks back, killing some officials and peasant leaders. Maybe those truck drivers we passed knew something we didn't. As much as they'd like to deliver their loads and get paid, they were in no hurry to press on. But then Alfredo was afraid to stop. Hard to tell. Funny, the thoughts that run through your brain when the seat of your britches is hanging out like mine was now.

The snow was no longer runny but wobbling down like sourdough patties plopping toward the griddle. Yet it was not terribly cold, barely 30 degrees it seemed, hardly lower. The wipers mashed the flakes to the bottom of the windshield where they banked up. Vision became problematic, forcing stops to scrape away the slush. Alfredo would start at each of these and renew his admonitions: "No, no ... don't stop, we must keep moving. Very dangerous, it is very dangerous ..." Trying not to seem too finicky I let it collect. Just as I was flying blind we hit another hole that rent the rack again. Alfredo huddled inside until I frankly commanded him to hand up the rope and tie–chains.

Past midnight, the storm easing, we crested a ridge and headed down a saddle. At a rutty crossroads, I sensed uncertainty. My scout said first right, then left, then right again. I obeyed, reluctantly. We had gone maybe three miles when the road abruptly dead–ended in a narrow turnaround occupied by two covered trucks. Men with rifles blocked our way.

Alfredo moaned, *"Terroristas, terroristas."* I figured this was the Big Soup.

I pulled over as directed and one of the men approached the passenger door.

"Get out!" he ordered in Spanish and evidently the same in Quechua.

I started to obey but he shouted, "No! Only you!" and pointed at Alfredo.

"Es un turista, Norteamericano," my guide said, as he fumbled to find the door handle. I reached over to help but a flashlight played in my face.

"Don't Move!"

I obeyed.

Alfredo at last managed the door and was made to stretch over the hood and frisked. A resumed explanation in Quechua was cut short. I was next for the pat–down. Then they had a look inside.

"Peruano o extranjero?" asked the one with the light, his breath foul, cadaverous.

"Extranjero," I replied. *"Norteamericano. Yo soy turista."*

He asked for papers. In the glove compartment. I asked if I could fetch them. He motioned with the light.

The two of them studied the photo.

"What is your business in Peru, señor?"

I described the trip. Mexico to Argentina, the lot. He asked the names of the towns in northern Peru I had passed. I said Tumbes and Trujillo, which were the only ones I could think of.

He ordered Alfredo to accompany him and spread me back on the hood. They walked to the forward truck. The other one covered me. When I shifted my weight he stiffened, nervously, raising his rifle. I began to chill, having only a light sweater and windbreaker, but decided it was best not to ask to get something heavier. At length the interrogator returned with Alfredo, head down and trembling, in front of him. A backup crew, maybe a dozen, drew closer.

Just then there were other footsteps and a detail appeared pushing three peasants, their hands tied behind them, faces bloody. They were shoved to the first truck and lifted aboard, still bound.

I was told to take everything out of the jeep and unlock the tool boxes. This I did alone as none of them would help and Alfredo, as usual, did not offer. The one with the light toyed with the spare water pump and distributor cap assembly. Then, apparently satisfied, he told me to replace the gear, get back in and wait.

"What about him?," I asked of Alfredo.

"You, too," they said, directing my guide to resume his seat.

Neither of us spoke, although the men moved out of earshot. The lead truck started and they signaled us to follow it. The other one fell in behind.

"Who are they?" I asked Alfredo.

"*Son terroristas. Somos perdidos,*" he whimpered. His voice was choked with fear. "We are lost," he was saying.

"How do you know they're terrorists?"

"*Son terroristas*" was all he would say.

Whatever they were, they certainly did not appear to be regular army or militia. They wore no uniforms but an assortment of native garb, slacks and sweaters under surpluslike parkas, pea coats and flight jackets. The interrogator and one other fellow had on jeans and hairy pullovers. They offered no explanation or identification and I certainly demanded none. I asked if he knew where they were taking us but he only responded the same as before. "*Terroristas … perdidos.*"

Up ahead, the first rig reached the crossroads and turned left. Someone was in the road telling us to make a right. I couldn't believe it. As I obeyed, he made a "get moving, dammit" motion, arms high over his head, pushing rapidly. I didn't have to be told twice. The other *camión* was so close I thought it would ram us. But it peeled off to follow the first.

I kept a steady speed, not fast at all, but steady — and a constant watch in the mirror, but there was nothing. Alfredo didn't go back to sleep. He didn't talk nor did I.

Moisture had barely returned to my lips when there was a burst of light from the left accompanied by a metallic roar: the night train from Arequipa, window lights streaming, converged on us like some mythological predator. No cross bucks or other sign had warned of tracks; nor was there a whistle as the machine sliced across the road not a hundred feet ahead. Brakes locked, the jeep skidded to within an arm's length of the last hurtling coaches.

Then, just as suddenly, we were alone again with only our dust to prove that the encounter was not ephemeral.

We had taken an inadvertent detour, for shortly we came to the town of St. Ramon, well north of the main road. Alfredo broke his silence to say that he'd get off here. I said I thought he was going to Puno, but he was adamant:

"Aquí, no más."

As he walked away, I hollered, *"Adiós, ¡buena suerte!."* He flipped a hand limply to one side without looking back.

A half hour on, I made Juliaca, the village just out from Puno where the tracks from Arequipa meet those from Cuzco. Its people make a living peddling sweaters and blankets from the railroad platform. Each purchase is a new deal, a lengthy haggle, with the market favoring the buyer the closer it draws to departure time.

Catapulted by a surge of adrenaline from the night's activities, I suddenly realized that it had been over 20 hours since I'd slept. It was at this moment that I saw Lake Titicaca, pearl of the Andes, gem of the Altiplano. Its surface mirrored the cosmos. Dark now, it would be as blue as a robin's egg at daybreak.

Puno was rather a squalid little place, even for a Peruvian town. I had seen what there was of it back in July while laying over for the train to Cuzco.

There was little to do but sleep and move on. I thought of kipping in my rig next to the station which berthed the now–sleeping steel–wheeled monster that had almost killed me but I thought better of it. The friendly night manager at the insular, land–filled, Hotel Turistas north of town, unused to the likes of me, offered a room for 20 bucks, a 60 percent discount. The jeep was safe out front.

From my window I saw the lake in all its splendor come alive: lavender, peach, chartreuse, every golden hue, and, finally, the legendary turquoise. A sunrise unsurpassed. In this kaleidoscope, fishermen in reed boats glided about their ancient labors, netting my thoughts with them.

El Mar Pertenece a Bolivia. Recogerla es un Deber.

The sign is a reference to Bolivia's loss of its nitrate–rich coast to Chile in 1880 during the War of the Pacific. Since then, school children and soldiers and, yes, its landlocked sailors, have been told that, "The sea belongs to Bolivia. To recover it is a duty."

I was delayed by an auto race.

Traffic was halted for the racers, some of them Europeans driving "Formula" this and "Formula" that. There were Argentines with oversized sunglasses and sleek leather habits that matched the upholstery of their Maseratis and blue jeaned Peruvians with Camaros and Trans Ams. All of Puno was there — small boys amok, each an incipient Andretti.

444

Trackside vendor of sweaters, Juliaca, Peru.

Kasani is the little border post on the peninsula that squeezes the lake almost in two. Its very tip is Bolivian territory. I was the only petitioner which always means either quick clearance or *problemas*. During my prolonged stint in the Amazon, the AAA *carnet de passage* for the jeep had been extended for 30 days at the request of the efficient Peruvian auto club. Today was the very last, or one over, depending on how you counted. The customs man counted me delinquent and talked of a $100 *multa*. My protest only strengthened his resolve — and suspicions: All the gear was once again spread out. But when he found a paperback copy of my Africa book, he relaxed. "Is that you, señor?" he asked, looking at the pictures. "And the same camión! Ah, I see it now. You were much younger then."

It was the only time I had official help repacking.

Copacabana. The name brings images of svelte, suntanned women, sambas and rum. But this is not the celebrated place of Brazilian decadence but Bolivia's hag–town port on Lake Titicaca. Except for an elegant colonial cathedral within a Moorish plaza, recently restored, the town is not memorable: Dirt streets strewn with refuse; odors of burned fish and tethered pigs swilling in ditches of raw sewage; meager shops shuttered against some vague uncertainty; averted, watery eyes. Yet from its promontory, one has an Impressionist's view of Titicaca and its weather. Thunderclouds stumble out of the Cordillera Occidental and cross the lake trailing curtains of water, rainbows and prismatic sunsets. Both citadel and temple from pre–Incan times, the hill now bears the fourteen "Stations of the Cross."

Pilgrims come from La Paz to walk the stations and stand gazing over the lake. They install at one of the town's several *pensiones*, the most adequate being the Hotel Prefectorial, 1914. That was the year of its construction. There had been a remodeling in 1940 according to a plaque. Another was overdue. Still, there was a coziness to its shabbiness — its sagging gate, its mismatched crockery, the stained jackets of its unkempt waiters, and the gabby couple who did the cooking.

I slipped into the back of the town's cathedral toward the end of the All Souls Eve Mass, attended mostly by women and small children with candles and flashlights. Afterward, many gathered in the plaza to form a procession. Some carried vessels of food for the dead.

This occasion was neither festive nor solemn. There was none of the riotous saturnalia of Mardi Gras or the trickstering of Halloween. Nor was there the morbid fatalism of the Mexican holiday. Rather, there was about it a methodical purposefulness, as if it were a necessary chore to be performed.

Train leaving Puno for Cuzco on track elevated
over Lake Titicaca near shore.

I remembered reading of the festivals of the Incas at Cuzco, the frequent removal of the mummies and their parading about the city. Implicit in Andean metaphysics was the idea that the living and the dead remained part of the same continuum, the same community. Only the forms changed.

"They go to the cemetery to visit the dead ... *para hablar con los muertos*. Would you like to go watch them?" It was the custodian at the hotel.

"Yes, if it's possible," I replied.

I gathered that this was not something that he would attend himself, but that he had thought it interesting to show to me, a stranger. We had talked briefly that morning about the *muy folklórico* customs of the place. They had them in La Paz, his home, but not as *primitivo* as here.

We fell in with the procession as it left the plaza. I tried to remain as inconspicuous as possible with my turtleneck, windbreaker and clodhoppers. At the next street, another group merged with us, and I lost the fellow. I tried to wait but was caught by the surge. When at last I was able to slip to one side, he was nowhere to be seen. I was about to continue, when I felt a sharp tug on the arm and was confronted by two men with cloaks drawn up under the long muffs of their alpaca caps so that they appeared hooded. One wagged his finger in my face and the other pointed back toward the center of the town. They then dissolved into the flow. I lagged, then followed behind some stragglers. But at what I later judged to be the entrance of the cemetery, the way was blocked by these same men and others like them.

One raised his arm and there was movement in my direction. I turned and headed back down the street. Looking over my shoulder, I saw that two of them were following. I dodged down one side street then another. Just as I feared I had become lost, I recognized a street that led to the hotel. The custodian was locking the gate. He smiled quizzically and shrugged. Did I go to the cemetery? Part way, I replied, and told what had happened.

"No problem," he said. "They will not bother you here."

At dinner that night I ate at a table with Gustavo, a sales manager from Cochabamba, and María, a librarian from Sucre. María suggested that I had overreacted by fleeing. "What authority did they have, anyway?" she asked. After a pause in the conversation, Gustavo said that he did not trust the villagers, that they were sullen and strange. People had disappeared without a trace. "They could do anything to us and get away with it. These men, the hotel employees, would say nothing." What an odd thought.

Later we adjourned to a large table in the sitting room where we were joined by several young professionals from La Paz, a petite but

448

precocious widow, a watchful aunt and her ingenue niece and a stuttering Argentine lawyer. We discussed the history of the place, the Incas and their predecessors of Tiuanaco. Someone brought up ritual sacrifice and burial practices, and all that led to a discussion of the festival at hand and, perhaps inevitably, to stories of ghosts.

Cinematically, in the midst of this the lights dimmed then went out. A waiter brought a candle and the night clerk lit another at the reception. When I went to get a blanket from the jeep, the clerk had gone and his candle had burned down to a crater of molten tallow. Outside in the courtyard, I heard titters of nervous laughter from the sitting room and the wary bark of a distant dog.

La Paz. The cries of *cholitas*, market women peddling produce and sundries, rose above the combustion of morning traffic on the Avenida 16 de Julio. Calling from blankets in favored doorways they hawked their wares to passersby, including housewives, clerks, functionaries, soldiers and cops. Among their weights of fruit, potatoes, tea and richly earth–colored spices was an elixir whose use antedated the Incas by a thousand years. Jaws masticating contentedly, the *cholitas* drew the millennial Andean high of coca.

In the throngs pushing toward offices were pale, lean young Americans in sunglasses and narrow ties and middle–aged Bolivians in brown suits. Together, they climbed the Calle Colón to the US Embassy and the morning briefing by Thomas Orum, coordinator of Operation Blast Furnace, the Reagan administration project for the destruction of Bolivia's cocaine laboratories.

A hundred and seventy US agents had arrived in July to support troops of UMOPAR, Bolivia's drug–busting unit. In four months, only 22 labs, all undefended, had been sacked, with fewer than 10 arrests — all small fry.

"The bosses are always 'on vacation' — can you believe? Vacation! We hear that every time. Or 'He just flew out on business!' Did you know that over 70 percent of the inmates in Bolivian prisons are narcotics violators? But none is a major trafficker."

Orum's morning staff briefing had run over by two hours and the last thing he needed now was another meddlesome writer. He quickly thumbed through a stack of stateside newspapers, one of which referred to "the comic opera escape" of drug kingpins.

Since 1980, Orum said, cocaine had become Bolivia's primary enterprise, with earnings surpassing tin, silver, coffee and tourism combined. More than 300,000 people, in a nation with more than 40 percent unemployment, now owed their livelihoods to the growing, processing and transport of coca and its base–paste derivatives. One hundred thousand people alone were involved in the smuggling and delivery of so–called "precursor chemicals" — dimethyl ketone, kerosene, industrial ether, and sulfuric acid — across the Argentine and Brazilian frontiers. Forty thousand workers had been laid off by government–run tin mines in the past year. Many, half by some estimates, had become involved in the cocaine trade, some by migrating to the lowland Chaparé region to farm coca. The leaf was already averaging a 10 percent annual increase in production, to over 100,000 metric tons.

"In the poorest country in South America, where the average individual income is less than $500 a year, some peasant growers are making over $10,000; lower–level processors, $30,000; 'mules,' persons smuggling paste or powder to Brazil or the States, $50,000 to $100,000. That's beyond the wildest dreams of most Bolivians."

Newly established government pay rates, he pointed out, paid a rookie cop $60 in pesos a month and a UMOPAR lieutenant colonel, $440. Yet *narcotraficantes* were offering $25,000 to the latter just to look the other way long enough for them to move a major shipment — usually by air to Leticia in the Colombian Amazon.

"Did you know that over in Chaparé there are more than 37,000 individual coca farmers? These guys are not just lone rangers, mavericks, like US pot growers. They're organized into unions — over 500 local *sindicatos*! Can you believe it? That translates into political power. It gives you some idea of what we're up against." Each of these peasants, he said, farmed an average plot of about 1.3 hectares, about three acres.

He mentioned the part of the eradication effort which called for growers in "nontraditional" areas — where coca had never been grown for chewing — to be declared illegal, given a year to shift to other crops or face confiscation. A new law empowered the Bolivian president to decide which areas were "traditional." Trouble was, he refused to make the decision. And the country's congress was unwilling to make it for him.

In truth, everyone knew which areas they were, Orum said. The mountainous Yungas region between La Paz and Lake Titicaca produced a small–leafed plant preferred for chewing by natives over the larger, more acidic, Chaparé shrub. The latter, however, produced 2.5 tons per hectare per year compared to one ton for the Yungas variety. By far the greater part of illicit growth was concentrated in Chaparé, which is mostly in the province of Cochabamba. But with so many farmers making so much money from the nation's only profitable enterprise, putting teeth into the law was hard to do.

"The health–danger aspect may be our best hope. It didn't sell as long as it was thought of as a gringo problem. But now it's hitting close to home. There's hardly a middle–class family that's not been touched by it. *Patillos*, crack cigarettes, have become the in–thing with Bolivian students and young workers. The number of cocaine addicts in this country is now estimated at well over 100,000."

Lab workers, he said, were getting hooked and many were paid in "rations" of paste.

"They take their habit home with them and spread it to other people. Coca use here has gone way beyond cud chewing. They're into paste and crack as bad as we are in the States."

Another thing, sadly, that had shifted opinion was the murder of Dr. Noel Kempf, a botanist who just happened to stumble into one of their labs. The professor and a Spanish colleague, it seemed, had been mistaken for drug agents. The Spaniard escaped unharmed.

"That blew the lid off. The public demanded that the killers be punished. Many people who had never spoken out did so. One group, in Santa Cruz, formed a citizens committee and demanded that the names of *narcotraficantes* and their families be published and that all of them be ostracized. We flew our whole drug assistance section up there to the pubic forum, to listen to the outrage. One feisty little lady got up and said, 'we must call these people what they are: criminals. And their families too, because they all are part of it.'"

A congressional committee, Orum said, had just published a list of more than a dozen families, "who were nothing, dirt poor, just three years ago. Now they're multimillionaires, driving Mercedes, Rolls–Royces, Porches, children with fancy bicycles."

But there was a danger, Orum sighed, that the indignation "might just blow over" and business as usual return. There was a growing cottage industry, not only in Cochabamba and Santa Cruz but in La Paz and even in places like Oruro — the old tin mining town far removed from historic coca cultivation. People were beginning to distill paste at home.

In La Paz, he said, this had become "almost as fashionable as homegrown pot in the States, a way to have your own stuff and make a little extra money on the side." Small amounts of the necessary chemicals were easily available from legitimate sources. Not only crack, but cocaine powder, could be had in La Paz bistros and bars — including, I found later, the Café Brulot, a Bohemian *rincón* filled with university students, where I was offered a toot from three different people within half an hour. None believed I'd never touched the stuff. One young couple, college students, laughed in my face when I said it would kill them.

Would "Blast Furnace" continue, I asked, referring to its approaching end the following week unless the Bolivians requested a third renewal.

"We'll wind it up formally, but we're leaving them, UMOPAR, six new Huey choppers to carry on after our departure. The pilots are being trained now. You have to realize that even though the results

451

look a bit scanty, we've given the Bolivians a great boost in confidence. We've shown them they can hit hard and win. It's up to them to push on and finish the job."

I asked what had been done to stop kingpin tip–offs. He said that from now on only the pilots would know lab targets and even they wouldn't be told until they were airborne.

"To tell the truth it's not the troopers who do it; it's the brass. And just having 20 choppers taking off suddenly from the airport tells everybody what's up. There's only a few places the strike force could be headed."

Walking back to the hotel, I saw that the *cholitas* were still smilingly about their business.

I moved on south two days later, making a troubled ascent out of the 2,000–foot chasm that cradles La Paz. The engine sputtered, which I attributed to bad gas or a low carburetor setting. A brief surge followed an adjustment, enabling me to make the Altiplano grade, but in another 20 miles the motor died. A friendly tow brought me to the isolated garage of one Ignacio. The place was overrun with chickens, goats, llamas and humpbacked dogs that ate poorly. Acres of crumpled chromosaurs stretched into the plain, the rising sun blindingly refracted by their fossil alloys.

Ignacio blew out the fuel lines with an air hose, spat into the carburetor and started the engine. Thinking I was at last free of downtime, I picked up the pace, but outside Oruro a pot hole did its worst, splitting the right spring hasp and shifting the opposite one to the edge of its retaining chain. I crept into the town and was guided to a curbside welder by an apprentice at another ramshackle garage. I stepped next door for a coke, leaving him to watch the jeep. In the minute of my absence, thieves — who either intimidated or were alerted by the sad sack — stole the camera bag. The lad at first said nothing but when he saw my alarm, he begged forgiveness, pleading that the culprits had threatened him.

I was as angry at the indignity of the rip–off as at the loss itself. Particularly annoying was that my picture taking was over just at one of the most picturesque moments of the voyage.

Sad feelings were cut short by the knowledge that the theft was due entirely to my own carelessness in failing to lock the jeep and in relying on someone in whom I had absolutely no reason to place any trust. Yet, in moments of fatigue and fret, it's easy to let down one's guard. I had slept poorly for a week and was fighting a new strain of revenge.

Much time was wasted in reporting the robbery to the police and in their severe interrogation of the welders in my presence. Although it was plain, according to the detectives, that they knew who had taken the property, there was no evidence linking them and they were released. Known yeggs from the neighborhood were questioned, also severely, but to no avail.

Next morning I continued on to Potosí, little rested and still blue over the incident. Yet it seems that even in the most distressing times something invariably occurs which removes the burden and restores one's sense of humor and perspective. So it was with me at the pueblo of Cuchuingenio, with a single store–*cum*–pensión, the Villa Imperial.

A room was had for a buck–fifty, and I sat alone with a beer in the wide back common room which was cluttered with old card tables, rickety chairs and unswept trash. Outside, dusk had just settled when there came a lowing and bleating and the tread of many hooves.

I opened the door and walked into the yard just as a man and woman came into view driving a herd of sheep and llamas. They and their animals soon disappeared behind a hillock. The scene was so natural, so uncontrived, so ancient, so serene that in the soft moment of their passing I was renewed.

The following day was one of the most exhilarating of the entire journey, with a long easy descent from the Altiplano, some stretches lasting for an hour and more without interruption.

The route was through little traveled grazing country. I paused to chat with shepherds and, at the hamlet of Cotagaita, with an old man in the market who told of the great armies that had passed here during the War of Liberation from Spain in the 1820s. He led me to ruins he claimed dated from that period. No foreigner had stopped in a long while, he told me, and it was an honor to be my guide. He asked for nothing and gripped my hands firmly when we parted, wishing me Godspeed.

24

PERITO MORENO

Who can take away the dance after you have danced it?
'All profits are private; all debts are public.'
'There is much silence. Then it speaks.'

Hummingbird–sized bumblebees, copper and black, slaked on the meadow's wildflowers, their drones an apian cello concerto. Leafy velvet butterflies and tiny orange ones wobbled in and out of the forest. Somewhere a woodpecker hammered. A flock of ducks settled onto the lake below.

I munched a cake of Patagonian cheese and a spicy chorizo bought several days before in Calafate, the last settlement fifty miles back. A long–neglected windbreaker pocket yielded a loaf of dried apricots. All this was washed down with mossy sweet water from a crashing brook. A crumpled map redlined the route from La Quiaca on the Bolivian frontier to my present position at the mouth of the great Glaciar Perito Moreno on Lake Argentino, 12 ice–miles from Chile.

The evenness was shattered by a concussion like the crack of incoming artillery, its echo overwhelmed by a second and yet a third explosion as successive towers of the 150–foot–high glacial wall calved into the lake. Waves from these collisions creased shimmeringly across the surface. The emergent bergs yawed and rolled, then, captured by the wind, ghosted out like phantom brigs. Their imagined shapes — a fist, a skull, the cocked head of a bull — the surreal whimsies of an unseen sculptor.

Once one of the world's ten wealthiest nations, "Rich as an Argentine" was a '20s cliché, this most European of Latin American states had become an economic cripple riven by political malpractice, terrorism, and a disastrous war with Britain. Its foreign debt was one of the largest and most defunct on the international books. There was 20 percent unemployment, inflation had destroyed savings and three–fourths of the country's youth schemed to emigrate. And yet —

"Italians who speak Spanish and think they're English," was an oft heard saw repeated even by some Argentines in ironic self–deprecation. Indeed, every other name in the morning papers, Viola, Galtieri, Dozo — some disgraced generals, for example — was unmistakably Roman. And Buenos Aires' warrens of tailors, Longstaff and James Smart among them, had stitched the city's nabobs and subalterns into regiments of Saville Row ringers. With their pinstripes, derbies and umbrellas, they made the Avenida San Martín an ersatz precinct of the City of London.

"And we hate like the Germans." A reporter in La Quiaca had expanded the metaphor. As I recalled his words, a chunk of ice with the mass of a locomotive let go, the ducks scrambling at its report.

"Take the disappearances. They were certainly more than counterattacks against the communists, whoever they were." We were sitting in the bar of La Quiaca's Hotel Turistas discussing the "Dirty War" — the Argentine police and military's brutal response to leftist kidnap–murders in the 1970s.

"The *manos,* death squads, killed thousands of *inocentes. Communismo* was an excuse to liquidate democrats."

The respondent was a math teacher and acting principal: tall, thickly bespectacled, swaybacked. He was lodged in the hotel at national expense. It was a hardship outpost. A veterinarian joined us. Also a government man, he substitute–taught animal husbandry. Teachers throughout Latin America are federal retainers. National guilds control bureaucracies. Placement is a powerful prerogative. An American school board would not tolerate such intrusion. The teachers chain–smoked, the vet L&Ms, the principal Camel Filters. The reporter drew a small cigar, but didn't light it.

"I had a friend who was taken. She was a secondary teacher in Córdoba. *Una maestra de Geografía.* Nothing was ever heard from her. It has been ten years." The reporter was a big fellow, fortyish and a bit flabby, though you could see he had once had the build of an athlete. He was returning to Tucumán from La Paz, he said, with a feature on Bolivian archeology. At the mention of the geography teacher, whose husband and children had come home to a whirlwind of glass and test papers, his voice waxed husky. She was more than a friend. An uncomfortable silence fell over the table. The others stared, then, apparently satisfied, nodded. They, too, had known ones who had vanished.

The hotel was a two–story walk–up fronted with golf–green grass. It was the town's only agreeable hostelry, the other being an hourly rental above a pawn shop and disco. Some twenty *cholitas,* several with swaddled infants, huddled on a street near the market. Technically illegal after six, the women were tolerated as long as they kept to themselves. Sales to such Bolivians, hundreds of whom crossed back and forth daily, were the bulwark of the local economy. Some were in the unlikely employ of two young *contrabandistas* whose racket was smuggling Argentine hams, considered the most succulent in Latin America.

Operating out of the Pensión Pan Americana in Villazón, where I had met them, they retained these women for the equivalent of 50 cents a ham — six hams, one per crossing, being a usual day's work.

456

After clearing pliant customs inspectors, the *cholitas* toted the pork to the train station. On a good day in Sucre one of the hams would fetch $30, in La Paz, $40, maybe $50 — ten times cost. It was somehow refreshing, this bit of mundane skulduggery, in a country where corrupt officials were pulling down millions from cocaine.

Crossing the border from Bolivia into Argentina was like entering the United States from Mexico, or South Africa from next door. Such abrupt demarcations between want and plenty are uncommon. There is usually an ocean, or part of one, separating them. But here, suddenly, there were clean streets, tidy houses, quiet neighborhoods, brimming stores, potable tap water. Gone was the stench of soot and excrement. There was a four–pump gas station with garage bays and uniformed attendants who sponged the windshield and checked the oil. A plaque said the station had been built in 1964 by the Jujuy provincial government and the Automobile Club of Argentina. The club is a formidable lobby, twisting political arms for roads and bridges and building way houses in remote areas. After locating the hotel, I walked through the town. In a church a choir practiced. A volleyball bounced into the street from a game in progress. There was California television noise: an engine revving, teenagers wowing, tires screeching. "You're under arrest! — Aw c'mon, sheriff."

La Quiaca was primitive compared to what came as I dusted the steppes of the sub–Andean plateau, dirt yielding intermittently to gravel — *tramo* — but the road graded and rolled and rarely corrugated. I met but three vehicles in a hundred miles, including a highway patrolman who issued a warning for my not having emergency flares. He saluted, courteously, and clicked his heels.

With its bonsaied shrubs and smart steel and glass lowrises, San Salvador de Jujuy, the main town in Argentina's far north, could have been any middle–sized city in the American Southwest. The surrounding topography consisted of undulant emptinesses with promises of mountains on far horizons. Sugar plantations had endowed a gentry only recently supplanted by a middle class. Parks and plazas were promenades, not dormitories for the poor which, for the first time in my journey, were nowhere to be seen. Shops, from bakeries to haberdasheries, were bountifully merchandised and boasted well–lit display windows, unmeshed and unshuttered. Restaurants and cafes boiled with buoyant burghers and students from the local college and a private school. Extended conversations raised pessimism about the future: "I don't know what's to become of us"; "Things will get much worse"; "I should have emigrated long ago." But in talk of the present there was only that lighthearted, almost brash, exuberance for which Argentines are famous. National stereotypes are dangerous, but I think it can be said that Argentines by nature have an invincible day–to–day optimism but expect the worst tomorrow — unlike Peruvians, for whom almost no day holds brightness. Maybe that is why Argentines are thought of as living for the moment, an outlook captured in their proverb: *¿Quién te quita lo bailado?* Which is to say: Who can take away the dance after you have danced it?

"That might have been the aim at first — you know, going after the communists: 'These *hijos de puta* are blowing up trains and bridges and killing our comrades. The law can't deal with them so we'll do it ourselves.' But then it was not long before anyone who criticized them was the enemy." The reporter was back on *los problemas*, responding now to the suggestion of a truck driver at a neighboring table that what the army did really hadn't been all that bad.

It had begun around 1970 when a dozen or so ragtag insurgent groups appeared. They were merely annoying at first, but their attacks became more bold and, by 1973, they had coalesced into two forces, the *Montoneros* and the People's Revolutionary Army, the ERP. Their efficiency markedly improved.

The *Montoneros* were mostly young radicals disillusioned with politics–as–usual. They sought a greater expansion of state planning and wealth redistribution, but with some private enterprise. They attempted a takeover of the Peronist Party, to which many belonged. Defeated, they turned to violence, killing a number of party officials. They were alternately embraced and chastised by exiled founder, Juan Perón, who had dominated Argentine politics for 30 years, including nine, 1946–1955, as president. During his brief restoration, 1973–74, he repudiated them.[88]

The ERP on the other hand were a self–styled "Guevarist" outfit that demanded a total leveling and rebuilding along Maoist lines. In this they closely resembled Peru's *Sendero Luminoso*. They disdained *Montoneros* and moderate Peronists alike as "bourgeois reformers."

The groups were too small to mount sustained engagements. At their maximum strengths, in 1975, they probably had fewer than 2,000 combatants apiece — though each had a much larger fifth column. They therefore opted for hit–and–run attacks on outposts, ambush murders and Robin–Hood–style kidnappings of foreign industrialists. Ransoms were handouts to the poor. Vying with each other, they staged ever more dramatic escapades. Policemen, conservative politicians and military officers — one a former president — were abducted, tortured and killed.

The right was slow to respond, but wanton when it did. In early 1974, avengers in the Army and national police formed the *Alianza Argentina Anticomunista*, the "Triple A."

They struck at not only the complicitous but at the innocent as well: artists, teachers, journalists, relatives of the *desaparecidos*, "the disappeared ones," as the victims became known. Even high school students who made offhand remarks critical of the regime were taken. They were held, sometimes for years, in dungeonlike conditions, unspeakably tortured and many were killed. Mass shootings in remote pampas, live burials and throwing from aircraft at sea were some methods of execution.

¡Nunca Más! — Never Again! — , the 1984 report of a special Argentine government commission, concluded that as many as ten thousand may have died. The result was the eradication of both guerrilla groups but at a cost of the nation's inner peace and dignity. The commission condemned the military, who formally seized power from Perón's widow and successor, Isabel,[89] in 1976, for using counterinsurgency as a pretext to exterminate moderate opponents. Many of the disappeared were teachers, shop stewards and union officials with no ties to the guerrillas. They included Peronists and other socialists who opposed scrapping the welfare state for a market economy.[90]

The military regime finally relinquished power in 1983 to an elected government. This followed a failed attempt to annex the Falkland Islands by force, a contrivance designed to divert attention from the junta's economic failures.

Known here as "Las Malvinas," Argentina's legal claim to the islands, dating from Spanish times, was as good as Britain's. The latter had simply occupied them in 1832 as a coaling and naval station on the strategic South Atlantic approach to Cape Horn. They are a bleak archipelago inhabited by fewer than three thousand sheep farmers — "kelpers."

Argentina was humiliated as Britain easily retook the colony with fewer than 500 casualties. Seven hundred and twelve Argentines were killed — over 400 went down with the unescorted troopship, *General Belgrano* — and 14,000 captured.

The new civilian government in Buenos Aires prosecuted the junta and a great many lesser officials for the terrorism of the Dirty War and the bungling of the conventional. Most were convicted and sentenced to prison. All were later pardoned under a general amnesty, which was also extended to former guerrillas.

With the trials concluded, guilt assessed, punishment imposed, memorials erected, and a system of survivors' pensions — still unfunded — established, most of the disappeared remained unaccounted for. They will probably never be found. The Dirty War and its Falklands coda were the nadir of the tumultuous modern history of Argentina.[91]

Porteños, as Buenos Aires natives call themselves, think of the world's ninth largest city — 1990 population: 11 million, one–third of the country's inhabitants — as "The Paris of the Americas" and not without cause. Its great avenues imitate those of the French capital as it was restored by Haussmann under Napoleon III. It is an expansive, open city that diffuses sunlight and captures fragrances. The architecture is late 19th century imperial rather than colonial, more baroque than capitol. Its gardens burst with roses, gardenias and bougainvillea. Its parks — *espacios verdes* — are adorned with exotic plants and trees. Jacarandas line the streets, their brilliant purples blending into memory with the rustic strains of *milongas* in smoky cafes, the sweet strength of Turkish coffee and the shrieks of ruddy children at soccer.

I took a room in the declining but still quaintly elegant Hotel Lancaster. The jeep, parked out front, attracted a small crowd. The doorman explained what I had told him of my journey, then summoned me for an impromptu lecture. I obliged, until a cop whistled an end. The manager arranged free parking in a nearby garage.

After a good night's sleep, the first in weeks, and a steak and egg breakfast, I headed over to collect the mail at American Express. It was closed, so I wandered through town.

Given media alarms of "economic chaos" and "goods vanishing from shelves," inventories were impressive: Television sets, VCRs, home computers, all manner of kitchen appliances, vanity items, hardware. I'd half expected vacant fronts, seedy pawn shops and those weird emporia of wristwatch carousels and chained–down radios superintended by pale, diamond–fingered men with tattoos. Yet here was smooth department retailing, particularly on the Avenida Florida. Natty office workers, mothers with children and fashion–crazed teens had clerks ringing cash registers like slot machines. There were painted battle matrons in the tonier shops, as one might expect, but they did not predominate. Credit cards, Visa, American Express, were flashed, but cash was most used, frequently dollars. Indeed, the greenback had become a sort of second currency — though change was invariably tendered, Greshamlike, in australs. Expensive items like cameras were listed at monthly or quarterly payments, not full prices. For example, a Minolta's tag read "552"; Inside, you learned this was the amount of the layaway payments. The price was 2760 australs — over two thousand dollars!

This sprightly commerce held more or less throughout, even in working class areas. I didn't visit the destitute *villas miserias*, shantytowns, but their inhabitants came into the city. While the severe dress and faces of many told of need, there was not that collective, wretched hopelessness that overwhelms one in Mexico City

460

and Lima. In sum, news stories and official statistics told only part of the story. While Argentina was in dire straits, there was a strong cash economy keeping life, at least temporarily, comfortable for some and tolerable for most.

One morning I entered the narrow Avenida Bartolomey Mitre in the financial district. Four armored cars squeezed about their duties. Edgy soldiers with rifles covered colleagues grimacing under sacks of currency. An imperious plaque at the corner conferred upon the Bank of Boston of Argentina, now First Boston, the "Distinction of Honor" for its "extraordinary character and contribution to the economic and social development of the Argentine Republic." A senior US bank here, it sprang up in 1914 just as European interests were consumed by World War I. Unable to gain an audience with their Brahmin excellencies, I walked around to First Chicago. The trucks followed and were soon swapping australs for dollars there, too. I was led to a small room. The walls were bare. A young man arrived with a satchel of arguments.

"Look at the people in the street. You can't tell who is a corporate executive and who is an employee because they all look the same. They're well dressed, well fed, white. There are no colored people here, hardly any Indians. Everyone does relatively well — quite well, in fact, compared to other South American countries. So we get by, no matter how difficult the crisis of the moment."

The Argentine banker's title was "credit policy manager." He was a former Fulbright scholar and a 1966 graduate of Dartmouth He had been home—mortgage vice president at an Argentine bank. I asked whether he set credit standards for First Chicago and reviewed loan applications.

"No, I only check documentation — nature of business, licensing, that kind of thing. The Country Risk Management Committee in New York makes all credit decisions. They don't ask for my opinion."

"Do you keep track of the foreign loan crisis, day to day developments, that kind of thing?"

"No more than what I read in the papers. You must realize that the debt problem has very little impact on everyday life for most people. After so many crises — we overuse that word, don't we? — they've learned how to protect themselves. They have dollars, here and abroad, so they have a cushion against inflation, against austerity. Not only executives and bankers but other people. My butcher, for example, asked me how to convert his australs into dollars and send them to a safe place. This is a small individual, and he didn't mention it, but I felt twenty thousand [dollars] was what he had, his life savings. A list of Argentine depositors in Miami banks would show people like that in addition to the big ones. Of course, it's

461

only a cushion as long as it lasts, and if it does not improve, we will, most of us, be in difficulty. But that is still in the future."

First Chicago was one of 320 foreign banks with outstanding loans to Argentina. Negotiating with that many creditors was impossible — somebody could always block an agreement. So they set up a steering committee in New York headed by Citibank and Chase. Those two had over five billion dollars' exposure. The Argentine government sent a "special mission" whose job was not so much to negotiate repayment terms, as to nitpick, wheedle and delay. The banks were over a barrel, and everyone knew it.

How did so many different big banks all get into the same mess, I asked.

"There were highly advantageous interest rates. Better than almost anywhere in this time frame, 1976–1982. Our economy was growing and there was the sovereign guarantee of the Argentine government. A big consideration for the United States banks was your system of deposit insurance. Also, the knowledge that your government would always stand behind them. That was — excuse me, that *is* — the assumption behind all Third World lending by American banks."[92]

I confronted an American banker with this at a Thanksgiving reception later that week. "Surely," I told him, "some of those loans are secured by land, product, equipment. Can't you just foreclose?"

"Ah, yes," he sighed, looking down at his gin. Swishing it so that the ice seemed about to escape, he looked at me indulgently, like a teacher might survey a dullard student. "It's not so easy to do. And besides, it's better for everyone if a loan is nationalized — as we say, 'co-opted into the sovereign portfolio.' Ninety percent of them are. That precludes asset seizure and at the same time adds leverage to the Argentines' bargaining position. It helps the bank, because Uncle Sam's more likely to help out if the debtor is a country. There's a saying in this business: 'All profits are private, all losses are public.' Do you think if everything was hunky-dory we'd pay dividends to the taxpayers in Peoria? Hah, Hah, Hah! But don't quote me on that one. Hah, Hah, Hah!"

The young Argentine manager made a further point, hitting the palm of one hand with the fist of the other:

"You must realize that it's not like all of the money vanished, though some was lost to mismanagement, some to corruption. Much of it went right back in profits. Your banks have taken billions out in interest and the companies they finance — Nestle, Goodyear, Fiat, Massey Fergusson, Ford — all have taken out many times more in profits than they ever invested." Ford, he pointed out, had just merged with Volkswagen to form Autolatina, the largest car manufacturer in Latin America. The multibillion dollar project would be financed in large part by "foreign loans" from American banks. Its primary beneficiaries would be US and German shareholders of the two multinationals.

"There are many other examples. So when you hear about Argentina's debt to the American banks, remember that much of that money is in American pockets. If you count Argentine deposits in Miami banks, probably most of it is."

I thought he glossed over corruption too easily. By some estimates, half the Argentine debt — half the entire Third World debt, for that matter — is money stolen, mostly by skimming bureaucrats and politicians but also by kickback clutching managers and contractors who padded, double–charged and invoiced for phony work. This is in addition to the bankers' bonuses and the enormous fees charged by US lawyers, lobbyists and "consultants" — many of them former members of Congress or the executive branch.

First Chicago was a newcomer to Argentina, buying into a local bank in 1981. The deal made the local a "representative office," agent. Scores of foreign banks have them. But First Chicago wanted to do the same business here that it does in the Loop. So it bought controlling interest in the agent, whose outlets immediately became "full–scale" First Chicago branches.

"What does that mean, exactly?" I asked.

"You know, a full–service bank. Checking, savings, safe deposits, commercial paper. All services, just like in the States." In this they had joined Bank of America, Chase, Morgan, Manufacturers Hanover, Irving, Continental Illinois, Republic National and others.[93]

A few days later I cornered another young surrogate, resident vice president, for an American bank. He still had that boyish blush of do–right earnestness. He was ambitious, "Sure, I'd like to be finance minister; why not president?," but genuinely, I felt, concerned for his country. He had given a great deal of thought to its dilemma:

"Argentina can no longer pay its debts by incurring more debt. Baker Plan or no, those times are done. Local taxes can't even fund half our budget. The only place the money can come from is from foreign trade. But, you see, we're trapped: our only exports are corn, wheat and beef, which are at historically low prices and subject to severe import restrictions, especially in the US. So we're left with sending precious capital to New York for interest payments! How absurd! What little seed money we have must go for debt service!

"If we could just bring back half the capital that fled the country we could build a manufacturing base. That would let us pay the debt and still compete with Europe and the States. But first, the government has to get serious about reform: Sell off all the state enterprises, make labor and management — everybody — compete in the market place for their jobs."

But wasn't there still a terribly unfair distribution of wealth? Wouldn't going back to laissez faire make the rich richer on the backs of the poor, just like before?

"Only a free market can allocate resources fairly," he replied adamantly, raising his voice. "Government cannot, will not do it. The era of redistribution is over. There's nothing left to distribute, except misery."

After work, he was to meet two friends at Matias' Irish Pub on San Martin. He asked me along. Over our third round of Guinness, I posed the hypothetical question: Suppose you made the Casa Rosada, the Argentine White House, would you use your office for private gain?

There was a long pause. The others smiled wisely; one patted him gently on the back.

"I don't understand the question, would you repeat it?" He said, quite seriously. The others nodded, still smiling.

"If you were finance minister or president, say, would you accept money in return for official favors?

"I really can't say such a thing," he replied at last. "It would depend on the circumstance, the situation."

Glasses clinked.

I faced a vital trip decision. The jeep had performed well after Bolivia, but the clutch began slipping on the descent of the Altiplano and was almost gone by Buenos Aires. I carried no spare. The long exposure to the Pacific, particularly on the deck of the *Lykes*, had taken its rusty toll. The occasional drip in the auxiliary fuel tank was now a steady leak. It was no longer reliable. The loss of its 23 gallons cut my range to 450 miles, less than that needed for side–trip flexibility in Patagonia, where gas off the main roads was speculative at best. I could "maybe" get a clutch in three to four weeks, according to the garage that serviced Toyotas. Finally, the only sea transport further south was out of Punta Arenas, Chile, and that would cost half again as much as from here. So I decided to ship the jeep to the States and finish the trek by thumb and public transport.

Tim Bell and Associates, a British–Argentine freight agent, arranged space on the *Ana B.*, sailing in ten days for New Orleans. I took three sets of clothing, two medium sweaters, a windbreaker, sleeping bag and light mess kit and stowed everything else in the jeep, chaining it and the tool boxes securely to deter pilferage.

A rancher in Metán had offered me eight thousand dollars cash, "paid in Miami," for it, more than three times its container freight and twice its trade–in value. The night before I drove it to the holding garage the gent called the hotel to up the offer to ten thousand. He had traced me through American Express. I thanked him but said I

464

was under bond from the AAA to return it stateside. Besides, there was a strong sentimental attachment.

The American Society of the River Plate, pronounced, one quickly learns, like dish, not map, contributes substantially to local charities, including an orphanage, a school for the deaf and several British–sponsored relief agencies. Its good works are a steady beacon of friendship in sometimes turbulent US–Argentine relations. It is also the very pinnacle of gringo society. Membership is by invitation only and is striven for. The society's big event is its Thanksgiving dinner. Thinking any American would be welcome, particularly a lonely one so long on the road, I put on my one pair of light wool trousers and a clean cowboy shirt and went over to the spacious hall that the society shares with the American Club of Buenos Aires at 1133 Viamonte Street.

On arriving, I found a cocktail party at midroar. Everyone was finely attired, some of the diplomatic corps in ribbons and sashes. I felt like Huckleberry Finn in church. Bank hot shots and Ford and John Deere reps mingled with exchange students from West Virginia and New Jersey. Tickets were required, but no one seemed to mind my not having one. Spirits bubbled and flowed. I plucked some champagne from a passing tray and ricocheted from the fringe of one buzzing group to another:

Ten years? I can't believe it. Who could do without a phone that long? My wife would go crazy. What do you do if you have a business? ...

Oh, for a little something extra in the right place you can jump to the top of the waiting list. The going price just now is six to eight thousand US. No wonder those boys want to keep their jobs ...

I couldn't sleep for a week after the first *Psycho*. People went back two and three times. This thing is so boring it puts you to sleep. I think it's demeaning for Hitchcock's estate to let them do such a dumb film. Anthony Perkins should be ashamed ...

Could you believe it? A half million in counterfeit hundred dollar bills. They were making them in somebody's basement. There must be zillions in phony dollars down here ...

Yeah, but you know the only ones smart
enough to bail out lock, stock and barrel? The
ol' stagecoach bunch, Wells Fargo! Left last
year. Said the hell with it. Even they waited
too long. They got burned, sure. But at least
they had the guts to admit it and cut their
losses ...

I'm putting my money on Miami, pal.
The 'Cane's time has come ...

We still feel that strong attachment to
the English Race. You can hardly call us
Anglo–Argentines. We're British ...

We're taught from the earliest time in
school that the Malvinas belong to Argentina.
It's a very emotional thing with us ...

You don't say? Did you hear that, Marge?
Muffy's going to Harvard ...

The corruption is a Spanish thing. We
inherited it from them and we're probably
stuck with it as long as we're a country. But
the way of life! Ah! That is Italian, through
and through ...

I'm tellin' you, Kib, just stay away from
the old bitch! Don't spoil Thanksgiving dinner.

Chimes were sounded and all 280 guests began moving toward
the stairwell that led up to the dining room. The now attentive
attendants, for whom I could present no ticket, shook their heads. I
was saved from ejection by the kindly Belém and Robert Torres, who
insisted that I take an empty seat at their table. He was a supervisor
here with Boeing Aircraft.

Behind the ambassador's table was a 48–star US battle flag
which had been presented to the club by the crew of the landing craft
Lou Gehrig. It had been flown at Normandy on D Day in 1944,
according to an inscription. We faced it and recited the Pledge of
Allegiance.

466

There was grace by the Reverend William Timothy Hamilton of the United Presbyterian Community Church. "Montanans like to be brief, especially before eating," he said as he concluded.

"Bring on the turkey," someone shouted. White jacketed waiters complied. A woman who was helping buy audio equipment for hearing–impaired children discussed the project. "The Argies aren't big ones for that sort of thing," she observed. "I'm afraid if it weren't for us and the Brits, there wouldn't be much private charity."

We talked about cultural differences blurring. The spigot of American television was wide open here, from voiced–over soaps like *Dallas* to a tot–wise Spanish adaptation of *Sesame Street*. Someone mentioned the opening of McDonalds' outlets to half hour lines of the world's greatest beef eaters. Selling hamburgers here, I thought, was like selling Bartles and James wine coolers in Paris or Chile Con Carne in Jalisco. There was no limit to Yankee ingenuity. Americans really could do anything.

"Have you been to the basketball games?" one of the exchange students asked. "Man, that's a real trip! Lots of US players. The league here is a kind of pro farm for the States."

I hadn't, but I described my encounter with Chris Hardin and A.M. Battle, two black cagers, in the little suburb of Zárate where I had stopped for a few days on the way in. They were the first Americans I had seen since La Paz and were as surprised to see me as I was them. Their team was the *Defensores Unidos* — United Defenders. This was an odd name for a ball club, I thought, who ought to be attacking, not defending. They were signed to nine–month contracts and were in their second year. Each was 25 years old and a college graduate — Hardin from McNeese and Battle from Memphis State. Salaries averaged $30,000 per season. That was in addition to housing and food, which was "outstanding, no complaints." There were some 200 American players in the country, they said, most of whom played on teams in the Province of Buenos Aires. After another try at the majors the following year, they planned to pursue their professions, Hardin in coaching and Battle, real estate.

Someone pounded a glass and Ambassador Theodore Gildred rose and read the president's Thanksgiving Proclamation. The mike fed back annoyingly so he turned it off and finished in a bizarre croak–shout. The "whereases" and "wherefores," which he had difficulty pronouncing, sounded silly, but that wasn't his fault. There was dutiful applause, and we stood for the hymn, "We Gather Together to Ask the Lord's Blessing," which was sung with great feeling. All residual stuffiness now effervesced with the champagne. Few occasions are more convivial than a holiday gathering of Americans overseas.

I spent a few days enjoying the city and doing some shopping for family and friends. I tried to talk to as many *porteños* as I could — in cafes, markets, on the street. The United States Information Service library was a good place to meet students and business people. Several of the latter were having a go at selling nonfarm products to the States, including a microscope eyepiece. That was encouraging.

On the whole, Argentines are an agreeable and courteous people. There is, however, one habit that I found most unpleasant, particularly in Buenos Aires. I refer to the "tsk–tsk–finger–wag." This is, to one not accustomed to it, a quite rude way of responding in the negative, such as "all sold out," "I don't want to do it," or "you can't do that." Other Latin Americans use the gesture, but it is exquisitely a part of the Argentine culture. Shopkeepers, hotel and bank clerks, cab drivers, ticket sellers and cops — all use it. An index finger is aimed generally at the person being addressed and wriggled back and forth. Simultaneously, the tongue is smacked rapidly against the roof of the mouth, resulting in a sound rather like that one might make in mildly scolding a child. A respondent in a particularly lethargic mood might simply stare into the distance and wag his finger limply without tsk–ing.

Buenos Aires is catacombed with chess and domino parlors. One, near the Lancaster, had two dozen tables which, in the evening, were rarely vacant. The chess players tended to be intense young fellows with well–worn wooden sets in leather cases. A few would sit and wait for a challenge, which almost always came in short order. Others would enter hurriedly in pairs, set up their pieces and go to it. Serious players timed their moves with a clock. A minute was average; some set 20–second limits. The domino tables attracted large, boisterous crowds of older men and clouds of smoke. They played rapidly, cracking their pieces on the table tops amid schooners of beer. *Quilmes Imperial* was a favorite brand. Some places also served espresso and wine. Many of these were wagered games. Money was not displayed, but exchanged discreetely. The same was true of billiards, which was the classic variety of long table and small holes. Although sometimes an establishment would host all three games, billiards for the most part were separate. These places were well kept, with an air of civility — if not gentility — about them. There was none of the tawdriness and menace associated with some American pool halls.

Eagerly now, I turned toward the end of my journey, catching a bus for the 300 miles to Bahía Blanca. From there I planned to hitch to Península Valdés, a sea–mammal sanctuary 300 miles on down. It was not until the day was almost gone that we cleared Buenos Aires. I knew it to be large but its hugeness belied nighttime impressions gained entering Zárate and during the freeway drive downtown. Claustrophobic tenements, decked with laundry and resignation, mushroomed precariously for miles. Lumpen towers of socialist paradise; Babel–legacies of Perón.

A lift through Bahía was managed quickly, but the next ride was six hours coming: a lowboy hauling a bulldozer to Viedma. The driver took me to his home across town. Dinner was succulent hunks of roasted mutton and potatoes, washed down with bottles of *Pierre Johanette*, a hearty *tinto*, broken out in my honor. Afterward, there was *mate*, the strong rusty "tea" distilled from the Ilex plant that macho Amazon gold pilots had used but which here was commonplace. There were seven children, ages two to 20 — all boys save the last. I was offered the eldest one's bed but it being a mild night, and looking, mistakenly it turned out, for an early start, I asked to sleep instead on the rig. My headboard was the Caterpillar's blade, my pillow a pair of jeans in a T–shirt. Next morning the wife brought tea, bread and jam, and I kicked at soccer with the kids until the first ride, a 10–mile lift on a neighbor's load of garbage. Long after his pickup had gone, I watched the wind lick the bleach jugs, diapers and lottery tickets into the pampas. Next, I joined five horses in a six–horse trailer. The people in the cab stared at me, uncertainly. They were convinced of my dementia when I clamored to be let out as they turned off to their *estancia*. A tile salesman next dropped me at the Puerto Lobos bus station, where I slept until the five a.m. bus for Trelew.

Valdés is a strange spit of land, shaped like a hammer head or pickax. The "handle" is a slender isthmus that connects with the Patagonian mainland. Most of its flat semidesert interior lies well below sea level. Like the rest of Patagonia, the principal summer events there are wind and heat. Sheep, nevertheless, thrive on the thorny scrub and meager grass. At the peninsula's top end is one of the world's largest colonies of elephant seals. Penguins thrive along the coast, some even migrating as far north as Brazil during the winter. Golfo Nuevo, the larger of two miniature gulfs, is the Scammon's Lagoon of the Atlantic: migrations of humpback whales converge there during the August–to–November mating season. Sea lions, permanent residents, make their rookeries on the shore.

The mainland was settled by Welsh farmers beginning in the 1860s. Their *estancias* still produce the highest grade of wool. These settlers, led by a Viscount Madryn, built the small port in Golfo Nuevo, which bears his name. Later arrivals pushed inland and founded Trelew. British influence is evident throughout Chubut province, from place names like Dolavón and Rawson to architecture. Some enduring Victorian homes have become inns and tearooms.

Nicky Ripley, an Australian from the bus, joined me for Pirámides, Valdés' sole village. For ten bucks we persuaded the owner of the seedy *posada* to reopen. Next morning, he demanded an extortionate 50 dollars for the only "taxi." He was adamant, but so were we.

The sea lions were an interesting study, larger and furrier than those off Baja California. I did a rough sketch of a mother and pup. Two humpbacks rolled in the distance.

We started hitching toward the elephant seals late, well past ten. It was 100 degrees and rising. In ten miles there were three vehicles, tinted–glass tour vans and an old Ford. The vans bulleted past. The Ford hesitated, but kept on. We were resigned to an ignominious retreat. Then it braked and returned.

"Where are you going?"

"Trelew," Nicky said.

"Well, it'll be a tight fit, but get in."

It was Lt. Col. William J., *Bill*, Greenwalt, US Army (Ret.), his Argentine wife, Carolina, and some Italian friends on a Sunday outing.

We drove with them back to Trelew and past it to Gaimán, a staunch Welsh community. I sprang for scones and coffee at the town tea room. The hostess brought an album of five generations — from faded Gothic daguerreotypes to feisty school day glossies. There were snapshots of cousins who had moved to Australia.

The Italians were Francesca Sepe and her mother, Coco, Neapolitans presently of Buenos Aires. Francesca was a photographer. When I mentioned my camera theft, she volunteered her own work for any illustrations I needed of Argentina. Just send her a list. She was true to her word.

Eric Sletten, a longtime equipment salesman on the continent, was now State Department liaison for US businessmen in Buenos Aires. "What do you tell Americans who want to invest here?" I had asked.

"Don't come to Argentina," he replied. "It's not worth it. You have better odds in Las Vegas."

Greenwalt, who had come down in 1972, disagreed:

"There was opportunity here then, and there is now. You have to have a feel for how Argentines do business. Most Americans think that because their lawyers came down for the closing, the money's in the bank. Not so. Legal bullying doesn't work here. You've got to be tough when you know you're right, but fairness and consistency go a lot further than they seem to lately, back home."

He had set up a branch of his investment company, Bestline Inc., a firm he'd begun on leaving the service. Things had been slow at first, but within a few years Bestline Argentina was turning a steady profit, somehow managing to avoid the vicissitudes of Perón's restoration and the junta's paranoia. It had done so well, in fact, that he had relocated his headquarters here, leaving his Connecticut office with associates. He also found a new wife and family: Carolina, with her three children from a previous marriage. They had one child together, 3–year–old Butch — home with a nanny.

But the previous January he had "turned over the active leadership" to his Argentine vice president and was preparing to move back to the States.

"It's best for the family, and for me at this stage, to go home. The older kids are getting ready to go to college and our business now involves many more countries than before. It's hard to keep on top down here." They had "substantial personal holdings" in Argentina which had to be sold first, but he was confident that could be done in reasonably short order.

But not long afterward, President Raúl Alfonsín's government ceased functioning in all but name as the economy spun out of control. Liquidation into dollars became impossible. What had been tolerable became, the colonel wrote, "a disgracefully rotten economy which is the constantly recurring … history of Argentina." But he was lucky. His business was at least paying its way, which was more than could be said for the New York banks.

Hitching on south from Trelew proved fruitless. One short hop into the desert, then nothing. I counted fewer than forty vehicles in eight hours. Hiking five miles back to a garage, I talked the owner into a ride across town to the airport.

Waiting room plaques in Patagonia commemorate the first air mail run in 1929 by pioneer French aviator and author Antoine de Saint Exupéry. The novelist immortalized the Argentine service in his books, *Night Flight,* 1930, and *Wind, Sand and Stars,* 1937. The former is a blow–by–blow account of a mail courier's duel with a Patagonian thunderstorm; the latter, the story of two fliers, downed in the Sahara, who survive against odds by following the advice of an old Andean pilot: no matter what, walk east.

A second, more austere, plaque in Comodoro Rivadavia bore the names of Chubut sons who perished in the Falklands War — referred to, not as *La Guerra,* the war, but as *"La Gesta,"* the gesture. There were two vice commodores, one major, seven captains, 11 first lieutenants, 13 second lieutenants and 25 enlisted men. Some of the surnames: Meisner, Falconier, García, Krause, Castagnari, Castillo, Bono, Sevilla, López, Luna.

The plane, which showed up as Flight 662, was not the same 707 that had left Buenos Aires that morning. The first had hit the runway too hard at Viedma and broken its landing gear. The replacement was

471

five hours late arriving and it was almost out of fuel, necessitating a further delay.

"*¡Siempre hay problemas! ¡Siempre hay problemas!*" Always there are problems, an auto parts salesman kept saying as he paced back and forth. Perhaps in tacit recognition of this, Aerolíneas Argentinas does not post exact times of arrivals and departures. There is only "flight south" and "flight north," sometimes but not always twice a day in each direction. The gent had hoped, he said, to be in Comodoro Rivadavia by noon. It was now past five. None of the ten of us waiting was assured a seat, but as it turned out exactly that many disembarked.

During the 200–mile flight the aquamarine pampas spread inexorably to the south and west. Comodoro Rivadavia was the first interruption in contour. This oil–drilling port in the Gulf of St. George is fought over by gales from the Andes and the south Atlantic. One had to bend double walking into the wind; going away was like being shoved by an invisible bouncer.

It was from here that the unlucky *General Belgrano*, formerly the World War II cruiser, U.S.S. *Phoenix*, sailed to its fateful rendezvous with the British submarine, H.M.S. *Conqueror*. I imagined the soldiers, laden with duffels and rifles and singing their battle hymns, weighing out of the gray, whitecapped harbor. Their pathetic end belied the fustian name of the town's main bank: "Bank of Tierra del Fuego, Antarctica and the Islands of the South Atlantic." Maps kill soldiers, someone once said. The bank's map replicated the admiralty's, which showed *La Patria* extending not only to the Falklands and South Georgia but down an absurd pie–shaped slice of Antarctica to the South Pole, notwithstanding the latter's international status. Except for a handful of scientific research stations, such as McMurdo Sound, there are no settlements there. Nor are there any bankers. Though perhaps there should be.

The 400–mile flight on to Río Gallegos was long enough for lunch. The all–male cabin crew first stuffed themselves in full view and smell of the passengers.

I sat next to two Finnish botanists who had come to study the flora and geology of Tierra del Fuego. The University of Helsinki had underwritten the project as part of research into extreme climates. They had only left Amsterdam that morning but showed no fatigue. We passed a good time discussing their work and the natural history of the place. They continued on to Ushuaia from Gallegos.

The *estancia* Cerro Buenos Aires was the westernmost of several ranches sprawled along the south shore of Lake Argentino below the glaciers. As the pampa stepped into the Andes foothills, desert scrub yielded grudgingly to scrawny grassland, patched here and there with drifting clouds of sheep.

"Go there during the day, in full view," the ranger said. "Be prepared for discourtesy." The owner didn't cotton to neighbors or people from town; strangers could expect summary eviction.

The shuttle bus dropped me at the crossroads, the driver half smirking as I alighted.

"Es un loco allí, también," he said, pointing toward the ranch. That fellow is crazy, too.

His engine still intruded when I flushed a mother ñandú, the ostrichlike rhea of the pampas. Eight chicks as plump as full–grown Rhode Island Reds scurried after her. A Mora eagle, silent partner to our encounter, swooped away. A herd of sheep approached in the distance, patrolled by two dogs and a high dirge of condors. Two horsemen followed. Cows with calves and some fat heifers grazed in a fenced pasture. They were mostly Herefords, with a scattering of Angus.

The road played out at some sheds and a barn. Behind was a rundown ranch house, the paint peeling, the roof sagging. So was the barn's. There was a pungency of dip and dung. Shouts and whistles popped above the unsteady *punk–ca–punk–punk* of a generator and the stop–go whine of a motor.

A gate opened to accept the sheep. Two men brandished poles. Some ewes bolted, but the dogs headed them up. The procession poured inside, leaving its dust

I leaned on the fence. The herdsmen funneled the sheep into a chute, which led to the dip trough. There, other men inspected the animals individually, then dunked them and shoved them into a holding pen. Jerky and frisky, the sheep collapsed when seized. A few were separated for shearing in a shed to the rear.

"¿Qué necesita, Señor?" What do you require?

I started. The lead drover had circled around and ridden up behind me. He was as one with his lathered horse, like a centaur. A wide–brimmed black hat with red band was cocked back; his face was deep–lined and grim, the eyes cold green. A lasso coiled in his shoulder, the loop–end dangling to the ground.

"¡Buenos días!" My voice was cracked from the dust. I cleared my throat. "I'd like to talk to the boss. I'm a *yanqui* writer."

"A El Patrón no le gusta." The boss was not interested. I nodded, but tried again:

"Tell him the *guardaparques*, Jeronimo, sent me. He said I was okay, would not make trouble. We are friends."

At the mention of the ranger he managed a stiff smile, wheeled, and rode around the compound. In a moment, a tall, muscular,

473

balding man, about 70, walked into the lot from the shearing shed and beckoned me over.

"... Scab is a problem, always, and lice. That's why have to dip so often, several times a season. But here we lose more to predators — gray fox, condor, eagle, sometimes puma. The puma don't come much, but when they do, they kill many. The dogs are protection, but a puma can kill a dog.

"Raptors carry off lambs, but the foxes kill the bigger sheep as well as the little ones. Pull them right down by the neck. The foxes even seem to prefer the bigger ones. We try to save the hides, but that's not always possible."

How many animals did the ranch run at one time? I asked.

"No, that is not a good question," he replied. "But it enough for us to have meat and make a living."

Where was his principal market? Río Gallegos?

"No. Those prices are too political. We sell meat only direct to the processors — *fabricantes* — and they come for the sheep in their own trucks." The political reference was to the recent inclusion of wool, long exempt, on the price–control list.

Shearing is done by wool buyers, who bring their own men, or by roving contractors. Some use a specially adapted trailer. They pass the sheep through the trailer, a few at a time, where two to four shearers fleece them.

"These men can sometimes be in a hurry or inexperienced and hurt the animal," he said, so he has to watch them carefully. The year before, he had to get up his own crew locally, "like in the old days."

Mid–May is the normal time for bringing the animals in for the winter. It is so cold here, –50 Fahrenheit, that unless penned and fed they would not survive. Indeed, most are herded or trucked to lower pastures. The men there that morning were regular hands. In a clutch, he said, they could do whatever shearing and slaughtering had to be done but it was "much work." The foreman, the one who had come to question me, was "the best gaucho in the country. *Tengo mucha suerte. Todos son muy buenos hombres.*" He was lucky to have all good men.

Did the lake ever flood? I asked.

"No. It is always the same. Except when the ice breaks at Brazo Rico. Then it rises very quickly, maybe a meter or two. Not really a flood, although it could be dangerous. Since I can remember, that is the only time."

"How long have you been here?" I asked.

"Since I was born. Now, excuse me, I must get back to work."

"The rancher's name is Ivo Stypicich," the ranger said when I returned. "He came here right after World War II, in 1946, from

474

Yugoslavia. You were lucky to talk to him at all. I think that there are people from the time before that he does not want to see."

With leathery face, steely–eyed gaze, jutted jaw and penciled mustache, Jeronimo Miguel Soule could have been a cavalry sergeant in the Montana Territory.

He sauntered, bowlegged, into the Moreno lodge kitchen one morning a little after sunup toting an 18–month–old baby girl in one arm and a stuffed monkey in the other. He smelled of resin, tobacco, horseflesh and talcum.

"Emilcita!" the cook took the tot and swung her about as he trilled from *Carmen*:

"La,la,la,la–la–la–la–la–la ..."

Jeronimo pulled a mug off the wall and filled it with steaming coffee. It was still 40 degrees outside. The child, released by the cook, seized the doll.

"His daughter!" The cook shouted from the stove. *"¡Número una!"* He had grown kids from a previous marriage, but this was his first with his new wife, Emilca — at 26, half his age. I had thought the child was his granddaughter.

When the second pot was empty, he invited me to his cabin. It was tightly built with sweet–smelling evergreen beech, *nothofagus betuloides*. Here called *guindo*, it is the region's tallest tree, climbing over 100 feet. The cabin had a living room–kitchen, and a bedroom to the rear with a window facing the glacier. There was a storeroom: canned goods, snowshoes, boots, tack, rifle, the lot. In a commodious stall, two contended chestnuts chewed their hay.

Emilca, lanky with large eyes, interrupted her needlepoint to take the baby and bring bottled beer: *Breckert Especiál*. One led to two. It was early, but the company was good. Then Jeronimo pulled ahead with a third. He put some wood in the cast–iron stove and settled back.

He had been a park wrangler for 21 years before this job, he said. Some of their mounts came from a wild herd of two to three hundred over near the Onelli Glacier, 25 miles to the north. They were good horses but hell to catch and demons to break. Then, in 1980, desperately needing a resident replacement, they promoted him from gaucho to *guardaparques*, ranger, and assigned him here. Perito Moreno was one of only three stations in the 1.6 million–acre *Parque Nacional los Glaciares*, a roughly 2,000–square–mile wilderness of ice pack and untrammeled forest. Its crown jewels were the Moreno Glacier and Monte Fitz Roy, an 11,040–foot spire on the park's northern border that is considered one of the most difficult technical climbs in this hemisphere.

The station had two deputies in the summer. Winters were a one–man operation — although now he had Emilca and little Emilca, born, luckily, just before the winter set in. Snow drifted up to 15 feet, all but covering the cabin. Mobility was by snowshoe; there was no dogsled or snowmobile. The horses went to pastures far below.

Winter communication with the outside could be difficult. Park headquarters in Calafate wasn't always "up." His own radio ran off a generator. Back in '84, the supply officer said he had stocked enough diesel, but the drum ran dry in July, just after the first big snow socked them in.

"A plane with skis landed after a month, and I told the pilot the problem, but we didn't get fuel until September." A good lesson. Since then he has personally double–checked all provisions.

"They should get you a backup battery model," I told him. "Your family might get hurt or sick."

"Yes, this I have told them, just that. They say soon, always soon — but now I keep plenty of diesel."

In summer and fall, he walked the lakeshore with his dog and fly rod, hooking a few trout for breakfast and listening to the glacier, not just the calving, but the cracking and crunching that go on deep within the ice as crevasses shift and collapse.

"Sometimes there is silence for many hours. I think maybe it has stopped. But then it moves again. *Es algo de otro mundo.* Something from another world. It is alive." It was most restless, he said, at dusk, after a long day's exposure to the sun.

Once in a while there might be a winter rescue — a crashed plane, a rancher taken ill. Those were rare and were mostly done from Calafate. He felt he could go a week on his snowshoes, if necessary. He kept a survival pack with enough rations for a month, but limited himself to routine day patrols of the nearby area.

November to May was easy weather–wise but more prone to visitor emergencies: stranded mountaineers, poachers, lost and injured tourists. Though forest fires were a threat, there was no plan to fight them. "So far, they have always burned themselves out," he said. "There is too much water and ice for them to go far."

"If it's a very serious matter," he said, "a bad injury or a poacher for example, I call for the seaplane. Normally that is not necessary." The Calafate shuttle bus usually came by ten and left at two, taking with it any walking wounded.

At least once a month, he said, someone was struck by falling ice. Most injuries were minor. Lost climbers had a harder time of it. Some never returned. Forest searches were difficult; glacier rescue could be impossible, particularly from deep crevasses. "We might be standing right over him, but see or hear nothing." Two climbers had fallen into one of the fissures the year before. By the time the one who climbed out returned with a rescue party, his partner had disappeared.

476

Gauchos breaking a mount, southern Patagonia. Photo by Francesca Sepe.

I had already had a brush with the ice. Robert Eigenman, a Swiss engineer who had gone in with me on a cabin, found a trail to the glacier base. We even tried slipping into a fissure. As we emerged, a couch–sized chunk hit not ten feet away, splattering us with its vertical blue shrapnel.

"Muy macho pero muy peligroso," Jeronimo said when I told him about it. Translation: What a dumb thing to do.

He had been told by a geologist that the glacier moved a hundred meters a year, more or less. At that rate it would take 500 years to flush the farthest ice from its 50–kilometer length — considerably faster than the "thousands of years" suggested for some arctic moraines. No, he had not found any frozen mammoths or saber tooth tigers, he said, smiling. He was fascinated that such animals, preserved intact for millennia, have been found in Siberian ice.

Jeronimo cherished *"la tranquilidad"* of Peninsula Magallanes, the knob of land opposite the glacier that holds his cabin and the lodge. It abuts *Canal de los Témpanos,* Kettledrum Channel, so named from the echoing rolls of falling ice.

Since 1947, the glacier has actually shoved into the peninsula just where Kettledrum joins Brazo Rico, the south arm of the lake. This was where Robert and I had walked, although we hadn't realized at the time the significance of the place.

The ice acts as a natural dam, causing the arm to rise 50 to 100 feet higher than the lake proper. The water, warmer than the ice and under increasing pressure, gradually tunnels underneath, taking from three to five years, until it bursts out the other side. The result is a deluge of ice floes, logs and trees.

The trees are swept by the flood, itself, and by a wind as powerful as that generated by an avalanche. The tunnel's "arch" lingers momentarily but is quickly caved in by the surge. From breakout to stabilization takes 24 hours.

These spectacular events have been filmed since the 1950s. A bar in Calafate rolls 40 minutes of them at happy hour.

The glacier was discovered in 1905 by Perito Moreno, one of Argentina's most intrepid explorers, while surveying the country's border with Chile. The same day he was attacked by a cougar, Jeronimo said. He shot it and left its hide on a tree where it remained for many years.

"How long would you like to stay here?" I asked one afternoon as we watched banded ibis scarfing fish. The red grass was overlorded by insolently yellow daisies and dandelions as big as softballs. The glacier was quiet.

Glaciar Perito Moreno on the border with Chile at the top of Lake Argentino, southern Patagonia. Photo by Francesca Sepe.

"For the rest of my life," he replied. "I know this place, I feel its spirit. *Es algo de otro mundo.* For me, I would not like *El Hogar de los Ancianos.*" He referred to the Calafate nursing home.

"I am Argentine. There is no other place so much like Argentina as this glacier: Stupendous, beautiful, unpredictable. There is much silence. Then it speaks."

Jeronimo Miguel Soule, forest ranger at Glaciar Moreno.
Photo by Francesca Sepe.

25

USHUAIA

*Only two Fuegians survived in what had become a
simultaneous planetwide extinction of aboriginal cultures
— all occurring in the name of Progress.*

From the plane's window, there were glimpses of the Strait of
Magellan, the link most favored by mariners between the southern
oceans. I imagined the Portuguese retainer picking his way through
in 1520, followed by Drake in the *Golden Hind,* in 1578. The sea dog
was looting Spanish galleons while seeking the Northwest Passage.
He would sail to within a fog's breath of the Golden Gate before
turning across the Pacific. Separated here in a storm, and fearing
Drake lost, a sister ship returned to England. Drake arrived two
years afterward, becoming the earliest captain to survive a voyage
'round the world. Magellan was killed in the Philippines.

Joshua Slocum's valiant *Spray* entered the strait in February of
1896 on the first solo circumnavigation. Howling gales shoved the
38–foot, yawl–rigged sloop back into the western reach through
perilous crags. Pirating Indians boarded from canoes but were
repelled by carpet tacks the wily skipper had sown on deck.

The coast of Fireland's main island, Isla Grande, loomed
forebodingly just as the thunderhead snatched us back inside,
buffeting the fuselage so violently that its joints creaked. There was a
momentary respite, whereupon the plane plunged into a vertiginous
spin that sent snacks and flight attendants into weightlessness. Then,
as quickly as it had dropped, the craft leveled. A cooing voice
apologized for the turbulence and urged seat–belt usage at all times.
The chief steward forked sauce from his blouse; his mates, one with a
bloodied nose, swabbed the coffee–scalded with towels. They then
collected trays as if nothing had happened.

We broke through over Ushuaia at under 300 feet. The town
clung to a thin plain between snow–banked peaks and the Beagle
Channel. Its tiny inlet churned with whitecaps. The capital of Tierra
del Fuego with 9,500 souls, "The World's Southernmost City"
resembled those bleak enclaves of the far north: squatty cabins,
weathered pastel houses with single gables, boxy government offices,
a semimodern hotel, a fish cannery. There was also a naval barracks
and ivory clumps of what proved to be repositories of cracked toilet
bowls, retired refrigerators, chromosaur fossils, power–line bushings.
We buzzed the short strip, floated back out over the town, then glided
in above dogs fighting, a couple strolling, a runway fire truck.

The big hotel was called the Albatross: 50 dollars a night. Superstitious — and a tad penurious — I settled instead for the 12–dollar Las Malvinas. My room faced the street above a stoplight and offered a partial view of the harbor. Twenty flatbeds braked, revved and turned during the night. They carried electrical components from the *Chaco* and *Cana Beagle*, two small container ships, returning to them with radios and television sets. Appliance assembly plants, mostly Japanese, employ more than 8,000 workers in the territory, half of them Chileans. Wages, untaxed, are triple those in Buenos Aires. Most of the plants are up near the Atlantic port of Río Grande, 60 miles to the north. Ushuaia's port is smaller but less congested. The Beagle Channel is too shallow for most shipping, which uses the faster and deeper Magellan Strait. Cruising sailors like the channel's milder weather, though progress is hostage to violent westerlies. The hotel manager, one Jean Marie, said he was "correspondent" for *Nautique*, a French sailing magazine. His assignment was interviewing transiting yachtsmen.

It is in the nature of the sedentary burgher to become content, smug even, in his ignorance of things beyond his *ville*. He relishes reports of hazard and magnifies every mishap, however slight, into calamity. The seasoned traveler finds that most inhabitants of remote towns know little about the surrounding country. They seldom, if ever, venture there and are full of dire warnings to one who might do so: "There are guerrillas," "The road is closed," "You will be turned back at the border," "There is an outbreak of cholera," "It's a bad year for grizzly attacks." Nazcans were woefully ill informed about the desert "lines" and most of Cuzco's "guides" so misspoke of the Inca that it was painful to hear them. Local knowledge in the Amazon was next to nil. Thus it was not surprising to find the citizens of Ushuaia unfamiliar with the mountains and marshes of the channel, its fauna and the weathers at its Atlantic and Pacific mouths — in spite of the fact that the waterway is the town's *raison d'être* and chief source of livelihood. They were also unaware of its variegated history.

Captain Robert Fitz Roy of the H.M.S. *Beagle* discovered the channel on the ship's first voyage in 1830. The expedition was part of a British Admiralty project to study and chart the world's oceans. Fitz Roy captured four Indians here and took them back to England. One died of smallpox but the other three, called by the crew, "York Minster," "Jemmy Button" and "Fuegia Basket" — a 10–year–old girl — were taught English, woodcraft, the Bible and etiquette. They were privately presented to King William IV and Queen Adelaide, who gave Fuegia a ring and a lace cap. The Indians returned to Fireland in January 1833 on the Beagle's second voyage, the geologist for which was a 24–year–old ex–divinity student named Charles Darwin:

484

This channel is a most remarkable feature in the geography of this, or indeed of any other country: it may be compared to the valley of Lochness in Scotland, with its chain of lakes and firths. It is about one hundred and twenty miles long, with an average breadth, not subject to any very great variation, of about two miles; and it is throughout the greater part so perfectly straight, that the view, bounded on each side by a line of mountains, gradually becomes indistinct in the long distance. It crosses the southern part of Tierra del Fuego in an east and west line, and in the middle is joined at right angles on the south side by an irregular channel [Murray Narrows, which is] the residence of Jemmy Button's tribe and family ...

Three whaleboats and the yawl, with a party of twenty—eight ... entered the eastern mouth of the channel, and shortly afterward found a snug little cove concealed by some surrounding islets. Here we pitched our tents and lighted our fires. Nothing could look more comfortable than this scene. The glassy water of the little harbor, with the branches of the trees hanging over the rocky beach, the boats at anchor, the tents supported by the crossed oars, and the smoke curling up the wooded valley, formed a picture of quiet retirement. The next day we smoothly glided onwards in our little fleet, and came to a more inhabited district. Few if any of these natives could ever have seen a white man; certainly nothing could exceed their astonishment at the apparition of the four boats. [Fires were lighted on every point hence the name of Tierra del Fuego or the land of fire], both to attract our attention and to spread far and wide the news. Some of the men ran for miles along the shore. I shall never forget how wild and savage one group appeared: suddenly four or five men came to the edge of an overhanging cliff; they were absolutely naked, and their long hair streamed about their faces; they held rugged staffs in their hands, and,

485

springing from the ground, they waved their
arms round their heads and sent forth the most
hideous yells ...[94]

The boats turned south through Murray Narrows and deposited
the three natives at Wulaia, a seasonal fish camp. The next day
canoes full of Indians converged there, among them the family of
Jemmy Button. According to Darwin, "There was no demonstration of
affection; they simply stared for a short time at each other [like
horses reunited after a long separation]."[95] Discharged with the
returnees was one Richard Mathews, a young clergyman who wished
to begin a mission. Fitz Roy's crew built three wigwams and planted
gardens. Newlyweds York Minster and Fuegia Basket, now 14, would
occupy the second hut, Button the third.

On his way back to the Beagle two weeks later the Captain
found Mathews on the edge of terror: his stores had been stolen, the
buildings destroyed and much of his beard plucked out. The three
"parishioners" were unable or unwilling to stay the attacks. Fitz Roy
insisted that the missionary return to the ship, which, according to
Darwin, they reached the next night in rough seas "after an absence
of twenty days, during which time we had gone three hundred miles
in the open boats."[96] Mathews continued on to New Zealand.
Concluded Darwin of the Fuegians, "[Here] man exists in a lower
state of improvement than in any other part of the world."[97]

Not until 1848 was another mission attempted — by a
56–year–old retired naval captain named Allen Gardiner, recent
founder of "The Patagonian Missionary Society." Before he could get
his tents pitched his camp was looted. Luckily, the ship hadn't sailed
so Gardiner re–embarked for England, vowing to return. Two years
later he and six acolytes off–loaded enough gear for a permanent
mission. Unfortunately, they left their gunpowder and shot on the
transport. The natives swarmed their camp, stoning them and
making off with their stores. The party fled in longboats to a
cave–pocked cove where for a year they subsisted on washed–up fish
and seaweed. They died one by one from exposure and scurvy,
Gardiner being the last to succumb.

Following instructions in its founder's recovered journal, the
society launched another attempt some eight years later. Yet it, too,
ended in disaster when the Indians killed everyone but the cook.
None other than Jemmy Button led the attack. Some said he
begrudged the hospitality shown Fuegian converts in the Falklands.
More likely, he simply took advantage of an easy opportunity for
plunder.

Nine years later, the Reverend Whait H. Stirling landed at
Ushuaia and won the Indians' trust. Ushuaia means "Inner Harbor to

the Westward." He started building a church, cut firewood and preached the Gospel. After six months, he was appointed Bishop of the Falklands. His successor was Deacon Thomas Bridges and his new wife, Mary, both aged 28. They came ashore on October 21, 1871 to begin one of the boldest and most colorful pioneering adventures of all time.

Bridges was a tough, take–charge type who quickly moved to expand Stirling's fledgling outpost into a thriving community. He finished the church and added crop sheds, a smithy and a carpentry shop. He apportioned garden plots and built a road up from the beach. Next, he constructed an orphanage. Many a father was killed in the Indians' constant feuding. Abduction of mothers was commonplace. The canoe users of the channel, the Yahgan, were fishermen and mussel gatherers. Their rivals, the nomadic Ona or "Mountain People," were ferocious hunter–warriors. The principal source of meat was the *guanaco*, a large auburn ungulate related to the llama. It was common game, but for the Ona it was the dietary staple and they claimed the better hunting grounds. The Yahgan took otters and fox from channel islands and an occasional seal, though these were rare. Both tribes fervently scavenged blubber from beached whales, events which sometimes led to battle.

In the early years, the Yahgan predominated among the mission's residents. Although a few erected wood and metal huts, most lived in traditional wigwams. This consisted of a branch–and–sod roof over a pit floor surrounded by a berm of bones and mussel shells. Some of these were more than six feet high. Shrubs and grass would sprout on them, solidifying and insulating the structures. Openings were shifted to avoid the wind.

Bridges showed the Indians how to make dugouts from logs. This resulted in sturdier and more durable craft than their traditional bark canoes which had constantly to be replaced and could not be beached on the hard shingled rock of the channel. They had to be anchored–out, preferably in the channel's ubiquitous kelp, a chore of the women, who then dog–paddled back to shore in the icy water!

The missionary practiced first aid, setting broken limbs, washing wounds and establishing basic hygiene. He mediated disputes, some of them quite violent. Once he was almost axed from behind. On another occasion he stood down a warrior who held a spear against his chest.

As tenacious settlers coping heroically in the wilderness, Thomas Bridges and his family were hardly unique. Making a living in the Amazon or even in the nearby Falklands was an undertaking just as speculative; and others built far more lucrative plantations in equally hostile milieux. But what distinguished Bridges from most of the rest was his commitment to a methodical understanding of his environment and its aboriginal occupants. He brought to the task a boundless good will and a painstaking scholarship equal to that of the best field scientists of the day.

While a boy in the Falklands, Bridges learned Yahgan from transported tribespeople. He compiled a dictionary of the language which grew to more than 30,000 words. Contrary to what many scientists, including Darwin, then thought, all languages contain the same basic structure, including most verb tenses, and are "refined" according to the environment of the speakers. Thus, an aboriginal tongue will have a wealth of names for animals, trees, plants, waterways, weather, relatives, etc., but be devoid of industrial nomenclature. Included in Yahgan, for example, were five words for snow, more than fifty of consanguinity — oldest brother–in–law, first cousin once removed — and verbs which required whole sentences in English to translate. "To hunt," for example, had many variations, depending on the game sought, how the quarry was to be pursued, where, etc.

The missionary kept a journal in which he described the geology of the archipelago, its animals, plants, weather patterns and even astronomical events. He imbued his sons with his love of natural history and with an appreciation of the importance of good note–taking. Among the highlights of his journal were descriptions of hunts, food preparation and native ceremonies — including a mock battle to avenge a killing. Relatives of an accused who had fled were "stoned" by the victim's family, but in a manner that permitted them to dodge the missiles.

In 1886, after sixteen years at the mission, Bridges resigned and sought a government grant of 15,000 acres to start a sheep ranch.

Traveling by steamer to Buenos Aires, he personally presented his petition to the colorful Argentine president, Julio Roca, "Conqueror of the Wilderness." The request was granted. It was the birth of Harberton.

After Bridges' death in 1898, the ranch was maintained and expanded by his six children, of whom the third, Lucas, was paramount. Lucas later recounted the family's history in a rich autobiography, *Uttermost Part of the Earth,* a book that rivals Karen Blixen's *Out of Africa* in prose and story telling.[98]

By 1902, Lucas had started a second Bridges ranch, called Viamonte, on the Atlantic coast some 50 miles to the north. An earth road, laboriously cut through marsh and forest, connected the two farms. Viamonte combined 125,000 homestead acres with an equal parcel under government lease. One hundred thousand sheep ran there, compared with 20,000 at Harberton.

Shearing the Sheep, Tierra del Fuego. Photo by Francesca Sepe.

The Yahgan not only provided dependable labor but became skilled husbandmen. The best workers from Ushuaia followed the Bridges to Harberton. Many kept their own small flocks. The Ona also came, hesitantly at first, but then in increasing numbers, until they were a majority of the work force.

Controlling intertribal quarrels was a problem, but the Ona feuded more often among themselves. There were massacres of whole families, made all the more bloody with firearms. Each fresh killing required revenge. There was an outbreak of typhoid in 1884, within days of the arrival of the first Argentine garrison. A catastrophic measles epidemic struck down many Indians in the 1920's. But homicide remained the leading cause of death.

Conflicts were exacerbated by the displacement of the Ona from their northern range by white ranchers and miners. Territorial feuding took a heavy toll, but so did white raids — many of which were organized as much for sport as for security. Such pogroms were given impetus by Ona killings of gauchos, prospectors and shipwreck survivors.

Gold was discovered on the southern shores of Fireland in the late 1880s. Miners tried but failed to find lodes in streams and valleys. The metal had evidently been rafted as part of sediment dislodged by icebergs from alluvial sources in Antarctica. Sailors today commonly report chunks of earth clinging to floating ice.

After these surface deposits were sluiced, little ore remained and the "gold rush" quickly ended. Nevertheless, pressure on the Ona continued as hundreds of sourdoughs stayed on to ranch.

Other visitors included castaways, adventurers, and scientists. Among the latter, were French astronomers who came to observe a Venusian transit of the sun and some Italian archaeologists whose ship, with Bridges and sons as "guides," ran aground. All narrowly escaped. One self–styled explorer was Captain Frederick Cook, whose claims to have climbed Mount McKinley and reached the north pole were subsequently discredited. Cook persuaded the elder Bridges to entrust him with the Yahgan dictionary. Years later, and after fearing the work lost, the family learned that Cook was attempting to have it published as his own. The plagiarism was blocked, but rightful publication was disrupted by World War I and the manuscript again disappeared. Fifteen years later it was found in Austria and after phonetic and editing obstacles were overcome, finally published: 1933. The original document, however, vanished into the vortex of Hitler's war. By chance, a professor who had hidden it in his Hamburg kitchen heard an appeal for its return in 1946 and came forward.

The Indians found champions in the Bridges brothers, especially Lucas, who all but "went native" in the tradition of Burton and Lawrence in Arabia and Sam Houston in Arkansas. He hunted with the Ona, took them on his explorations, challenged their strongest wrestlers and stood down renegades unarmed. The Indians adopted him and inducted him into their *hain* or secret lodge. Its seat was a sacred wigwam forbidden to noninitiates, including women. There, members masqueraded as pastoral spirits in elaborate costumes. These beings were rather elves than demons — though they were capable of black magic and could hex or dispatch anyone who displeased them. Accidents and disappearances were attributed to them. They had no religious significance, however. "[T]here was no worship, no prayer, no god, no devil" among the Ona or any of the other Fuegian tribes, wrote Lucas. Nor was there any concept of an afterlife, blissful or punitive.[99]

The morning after my arrival came dark and wintry, though summer was only a week away. A cutting wind shot the air with sleet. I trundled with it down to the Prefectura Naval, the naval station, taking care not to be upended. In front of the gate was a traffic circle that contained a concrete head emerging from what looked like a conch or pasta shell. It was smooth-crowned, as if shaven or encased in a sock or helmet. The mouth was curled into a sneer, suggesting that the sculptor had been influenced by Mussolini poster art. According to a plaque, the metaphor was of the Argentine republic emerging from the sea, guarded by her ships, sailors and marines. The latter were represented by three supporting "waves." The statuary was the town's tribute, it said, "to the civilizing actions of the Argentine Navy ... faithful custodian of national freedom."

The flaccid garrison's flotilla consisted of two old US Coast Guard PT boats and a tug. Marches and flourishes — interrupted by announcements — echoed from a loudspeaker in the courtyard behind the sentry box. Its corporal eyed me suspiciously. There were few visitors and none approached on foot. The original penal purpose of the structure, now partially stuccoed, remained manifest. There were massive stone walls, slits for windows, narrow entryways, turrets. Here, at the turn of the century, recidivist felons and hapless Indians had mingled with disfavored politicians and the insane. Official graffiti — the first seen since Nicaragua — was sprayed on the outside walls: "The government has restored human rights and rejected the actions of the English pirates!"

There was a 40-minute wait to mail a letter at the post office. Most of those in line smoked. More cigarettes are sold in Argentina than in any other Latin American country except Brazil. Common brands are Chesterfield — "Made under arrangements with the successors to Liggett and Myers Tobacco Company, Durham, N.C., USA; Massolin Particulares, An Argentine Industry" — and Conway — "Made under the supervision of British American Tobacco Company, Ltd." Cigarettes are aggressively promoted on television. There are no health warnings.

A dirt road led to Harberton, but there was no bus. Nor was there a ferry. Hitchhiking seemed out of the question. The only conveyance was the *Canal Beagle*, a discotheque-catamaran full of French and German tourists from the Albatross. A head count revealed the absence of a Lyon math teacher. I got her seat for 20 bucks. We hove to in the channel for cocktails and breakfast, accompanied by scratchy American juvenilia: *pain ... rain ... moon ... june ... muh babee jis luvs meeee ...*

491

The engine kicked in, and we puttered east past rocks and islets. Our captain–guide belittled Puerto Williams, Chile's outpost on the south shore, as "only a military base, not a town," impugning its own claim to being the southernmost city. At the time there was only one boat a week there. It left at the same time as the catamaran.

We reached our destination around noon. A sloop, about 24 feet, was anchored in Harberton Bay. She was rusty and listing to starboard. Assorted skiffs and canoes were beached near a boat house and pier. I recalled the succession of schooners, each named the *Allen Gardiner* after the mission's founder, which serviced Ushuaia and Harberton from the Falklands. The first had brought the eight martyrs of 1859; the last, in the late 1890s, had a steam engine. Seamanship was an essential skill for both preaching and ranching and the Bridges excelled at it, beating about the channel in weathers that broached others. They built their own barges and runabouts with boards sawed from tall beech.

The old homestead, with its oval Victorian portico, still stood. Nearby, was a more recent two–story dwelling connected to a warehouse by an elevated covered walk. There was a chicken house with fat fowl pecking and fluttering about and a garden with long neat rows of lettuce and cabbages bordered with flowers. The family close was surrounded by evergreens and dwarf deciduous beech, the latter twisted by the wind into curvaceous shapes, like geriatric ballerinas taking last bows. There were two outhouses just below the manor and another at the end of the pier, Carib style. Sheep were nowhere to be seen. An employee said they were far away grazing. None of the Bridgeses, the fourth generation of whom now run the ranch, were at home, he said.

Harberton is officially a port, but little freight not consigned to the ranch is unloaded here. A defunct sawmill, collapsed and rotting, once exported beechwood lumber — mostly to the Falklands and Gallegos, but some up the coast as far as Buenos Aires.

There was a guardhouse manned by two soldiers, whose light complexions, unit braids and campaign caps gave them a Tyrolean look. One, a corporal, sat inside thumping time to the same radio rock captured by the catamaran, while the other patrolled the dock. Three French girls from the boat approached the sentry and his military bearing collapsed — as did that of the corporal, who abandoned his post to join in a spate of picture taking.

A bus belonging to Rumbo Sur Touring, SA was waiting for those who wished to return by road. Six attendants prattled over a bullhorn. They instigated the singing of inane tunelets: *rinky tinky tanky tooooo ... aye yaye yaye–yaye ... my bonnie lies ... din dan don ... are we happy? yes, we are happy ...*

Outside, the mist–shrouded forest beckoned and repelled. The sleet became snow, then sleet again as we traversed a swath of earth denuded by fire. Such deforestation I had not seen since the Amazon. The lead guide purported to declaim history, his mangled French exploding from the megaphone: "The Indians were cannibals who ate their old women ... Tomas Bache, the missionary, arrived in 1830 ... The Indians killed all but him ... There is a legend of buried treasure left by the pirate, Francis Drake ..."

Finally, I could take it no longer and asked to be let out. There were gasps, then ridiculing laughter. Finally, the driver stopped and opened the door. The passengers near the front smiled and called *bonne chance* and bye–bye. My sweater and windbreaker, which had a hood, were warm enough. The fire swath gave way to growth again, but many trees bore evidence of the angular gnawings of beaver. Introduced as a source of commercial fur, but with no natural predator, they proliferated to destructiveness. Beaver now account for as much felled timber as fire. A similar misadventure occurred with transported rabbits, thought to offer a plentiful source of cheap food. The hares became a scourge, devouring untold acres of undergrowth. The massive erosion resulting from these two pests is everywhere evident. Indigenous grasses might have held but they have been largely supplanted by a species used for English lawn tennis — the seeds arriving in clothing donated to the mission by upper–class Brits. The grass is, however, excellent grazing for sheep.

The clayey gravel clung to my boots. The wind abated and the sleet again gave way to snow. An engine caught up with me at a bridge, the rusty river churning underneath. I put out my thumb. It was the two guards from Harberton. *"No se puede,"* the corporal said. When I persisted good–naturedly, they shrugged and dropped me at Francisco Restivovich's Coca–Cola bottling plant. Next to it was a dump. A sign read: Danger! Area Treated With Insecticides. Dogs Forbidden.

I took a taxi to the end of Route 3 where brackish wetlands and tundra were set aside as a waterfowl refuge. Leaving the two German professors who accompanied me to their photography, I deliberately "lost" myself among the guindo trees and muskeg. To the north, mountains barely 3,000 feet high had shawls of snow. The air burst with resin fragrances as pungent as those of a Greek or Alaskan forest. Occasionally, the brush gave way to meadows of marsh grass, which thrust above the tuft and moss before yielding to them again. Through clover the size of cabbages loped rabbits, some as big as Texas jacks, others mere cottontails, each adding its own to decades of ancestral pellets and sheep dung. There were the remains of a fence, the posts rotted but supported, like crippled old men, by recently strung barbwire. It must have been more economical for the last grazer — doubtless a short lessee or trespasser — to prop them with new wire than to cut and hole new ones. In the wilderness, wire was now cheaper than wood. Across a freshet, someone had bridged a raft of logs. A path led to a knoll from where I could see a lagoon winding into the Beagle Channel. Four ponderous geese with green and silver wings dished across the water then lifted westward.

Somewhere out there, Fuegia Basket had suckled her old age against the wind. Thomas Bridges saw her on an outer island in 1883, more than half a century after her debut at Buckingham Palace. According to Bridges, she retained only a dim memory of her London years and none of her catechism. Maybe she just let him think that. Or maybe the window into the cosmos from her atoll had revealed to her things that paled even great Albion. How quickly things pass, I thought. It had been hardly more than a century since that last encounter and my tourism, yet Fuegia's people were no more.

Though physically among the hardiest of folk, their harsh environment had long held their population to around 10,000. Winter clothing consisted of a single guanaco pelt and not even crack alpine troops could equal Ona speed over bogs and ice. Thus white disease, weaponry and greed doomed them with the coming of the *Beagle* — the most supreme of ironies.

By 1930 they numbered fewer than 300 and by 1947 half that. In 1975 only two Fuegians survived in what had become a simultaneous planetwide extinction of aboriginal cultures — all occurring in the name of Progress.[100]

The Bridges ranch at Harberton on the Beagle Channel in the Argentine Tierra del Fuego. Photo by Francesca Sepe.

EPILOGUE

What of it then? There I was at the bottom of the map, where I had set out to be. But what had I accomplished? What had been the purpose of it all? Others had been there before. And there was no deed or deposit slip to show for it.

"What did you learn?" people asked. "Was it worth it, all that time alone in strange places?" "Why do you take trips like that?" And so on.

I had no shrewd answer, no grand conclusion, no profound wisdom for any of them. I could only describe what I had found: a city, a desert, a glacier — a prison and the people in it. Perhaps that is as truthful an answer as any traveler can give. Even those who mocked my journey, most of whom were genuinely curious but enslaved by a received philistinism more shackling than cocaine, would at least see that I understood the questions they desperately wanted to ask but were afraid to.

But the "Why?" would remain unanswered. I suspect that it has something to do with making the most of the hiatus between earth's last frontier and those to come beyond.

I have done my best, then, to depict the precarious corners I have crossed so that others might gain a tincture of insight into them. I am neither poet nor scientist nor chronicler. This account is neither muse nor treatise nor history. But I have plumbed the ordinariness of the places, and exalted in their anomalies and contrasts. Opinion has undoubtedly crept in. Final judgment, though, has been left to the reader, for whom I have striven to surmount the towers of convention, and their clouds, to seek a crisper view of the forest above the tree line.

Hymas Cabin
River of No Return
Smiley Creek, Idaho
September

Notes

1. (p 46) Mexican–claimed territories, which today comprise most of the western United States, were largely ignored by both the colonial and republican governments in Mexico City. Title to the greater portion had been asserted less than a hundred years previously, boundaries were inexact, Russian, British and French claims conflicted, settlement was sporadic, and, except for some scattered trapping and mining, there was little enterprise. An exception was New Mexico, where recent Spanish immigrants had established a small but strong agricultural base. Studied exploration, such as that by Lewis and Clark, had not been attempted, government services were nil, and corruption and brigandage endemic.

2. (p 50) Adult male goat, literally. The word is normally used as a mild expletive, perhaps even favorably, as here, or in jest to denote a cuckolded husband or boyfriend. However, a few moments later, in talking about the politicians, the fisherman uses the term in its most vicious connotation, roughly translated: "disloyal, greedy, thieving bastards."

3. (p 50) State governors in Mexico are, for all practical purposes, appointed by the president in Mexico City, who selects the PRI nominee, except in rare instances the inevitable "victor." Qualifications for the job are loyalty to the autocratic system, and, in particular, to the president, himself.

4. (p 60) At 42 births per 1000 population, Mexico has the highest birthrate among the major Latin American nations. Even Ecuador, 39, Peru, 35, and Brazil, 30, have lower ones.

5. (p 61) Genaro Vásquez Rojas, head of something called the Nationalist Revolutionary Civic Association and Lucio Cabanas Barrientos, *jefe* of the Party of the Poor, operated in Guerrero in the early 1970s. Vásquez was killed in a car wreck in 1972 and Cabanas in a 1974 sweep by the army, which claims to have eradicated both movements.

6. (p 63) Most of the Indians, the country's most dispossessed peasants, supported the royalists, as did the majority of the urban poor. See MacLachlan and Rodriguez at p 315: "The danger of civil war frightened all classes, castes and ethnic groups, who perceived the insurrection as a potential threat to their interests."

7. (p 63) "Have pity upon me. I see the destruction of the soil that I have wrought, the ruins of the fortunes that have been lost, the infinity of orphans that I have made. I desire and beg that my death ... be a convincing plea for the instant cessation of the insurrection. ..." — From Simpson at pp 216–217.

8. (p 66) Voltaire reported a perhaps apocryphal story that Cortés once forced his way onto the steps of the king's coach in an effort to gain an audience. When Charles asked who it was, Cortés replied, "One who has given you more kingdoms that you had towns before." — Prescott, p 676.

9. (p 66) It is one of the indignities of contemporary revisionist history that his pagan enemy is thus extolled in Cortés' own house as his moral superior. Although after Mexican independence, Cuauhtémoc achieved the status of worthy adversary to Cortés, his recent deification was not an altogether Mexican idea. Rather, it followed the Marxist revival of the myth of the "noble savage" as propaganda designed, with supreme irony, to aid in yet another imperial imposition, totalitarian socialism, on chronically backward countries.

In debunking Cortés and his successors, who were certainly no benign governors and are no less deserving of just censure for their actual cruelties and peculations, mention is invariably made of the "horrors" of the Inquisition. The fact is that, in contrast to the tens of thousands carved alive and eaten annually by the Aztecs, fewer than a thousand were put to death during the entire 250–year tenure of the Holy Office in Mexico. Not many Indians were among the victims, they being exempted by royal decree in 1538. Several thousand persons, many of them Portuguese Jews, were publicly whipped, reprimanded, or jailed for long periods and their property seized. See MacLachlan and Rodriguez, pp 212–214 and Simpson, pp 186–195. Writes Simpson, p 194: "In the seventeenth and eighteenth centuries the [Inquisition] was gradually undermined by modern rationalism, and it went into rapid decline under the anti–clerical Bourbons until, in the words of Thomas Buckle, 'it was reduced to such pitiful straits that between 1746 and ... 1788 it was able to burn only [14] persons.'" Nor was colonial rule as wicked an imposition as the revisionists maintain. MacLachlan and Rodriguez hold, pp 1–2, that "[Colonial Mexico] was neither a dependent nor an underdeveloped region. Rather, [it] forged a complex, balanced, and integrated economy that transformed the area into the most important and dynamic part of the Spanish empire. The conquest of Mexico and the subsequent incorporation of the region into the world system constituted one of the major events in modern world history. It definitively ended the

500

relative isolation of Europe and...terminated Mesoamerica's physical and cultural isolation, integrating the area into the new global culture."

10. (p 66) While there, Rivera preached that art must serve the propaganda aims of the Communist Party and he signed the "October Manifesto" to that effect. In a letter explaining his views to his comrades there, he stated: "Proletarian art must ... penetrate by cultural means into the capitalist countries, becoming thereby a weapon of exceptional strength in the hands of the communists."

Following his own advice, Rivera returned to Mexico, where he became one of the Comintern's first and most successful Latin American agents of influence. To his credit, he publicly disagreed with the absurd strictures of Stalinist art and this led to his expulsion from the party. Yet he never ceased being a tireless, peripatetic spokesman for its totalitarian ideology, in spite of Stalin's purges and his pact with Hitler in 1939. Through his powerful paintings and incessant politicizing, Rivera did more to legitimize and give impetus to Marxism in Mexico's Academe than any other individual.

The result is that collectivist, anti–entrepreneurial and anti–American claptrap has become the tenured liturgy of Mexican scholarship, deviation from which, even in today's post–Soviet world, anathematizes a student or teacher.

While the implementation of Marxist domestic policy has been checked by the reactionary PRI establishment, meaningful land reform being abandoned after 1939 in favor of its cleverly maintained illusion, successive PRI administrations have just as cleverly co–opted Marxist foreign policy, particularly that calling for a Pavlovian anti–US response to most questions of regional concern. Outright oil grants to and diplomatic support of the Sandinistas, havens for Guatemalan and Salvadoran guerrillas, and warm — at times almost fawning — relations with Cuba are a few examples.

But it has been in the universities where the influence of Rivera has had its most insidious effect. By displacing what otherwise might have been honest, unbridled inquiry into Mexico's economic and political malaise, three generations of Mexican "thinkers" have wasted eons of thought–years in hobbled obedience to yet another imported orthodoxy — Marxism — thought–years that possibly by now might have synthesized intrepid Mexican solutions to Mexican problems.

Rivera was expelled from the party in 1929 and his repeated pleas for readmission were rebuffed until 1954, when he again became a member and toured the Soviet Union with honors. He died in 1958.

Interestingly, Rivera's Cuernavaca mural was commissioned and donated by the then United States ambassador to Mexico, Dwight Morrow, a shrewd capitalist and father–in–law of Charles A. Lindbergh. See W. Richardson, "The Dilemmas of a Communist Artist: Diego Rivera in Moscow, 1927–1928," *Mexican Studies / Estudios Mexicanos*, Vol. 3, No. 1 (Winter 1987), University of California Press, Berkeley, for an excellent treatment of Rivera.

11. (p 66) Zapata had joined forces with the naive poet and pamphleteer, Francisco Madero, when the latter began his unexpected march to the capital in May of 1911 in the wake of the renunciation of the 80–year–old Díaz. Madero had committed himself to Zapata's policy of land return — i.e. to the Indian peasants from whom it had gradually been stolen in the 19th century by the big sugar planters.

But in no time, Madero, dominated by his strong–willed brother, Gustavo, went back on his word. Zapata, disillusioned, returned to Morelos and resumed his attacks on the plantations, burning and killing with unprecedented fury.

Madero sent his top general, Victoriano Huerta, to crush Zapata but the latter retreated into the hills. The atrocities Huerta committed against the villages in his path cemented Zapata's support and resolve. On November 25, 1911, just over a year after the revolution had officially begun, Zapata proclaimed his "Plan of Ayala," the core of which was a complete restoration of all Indian lands. It is the basis of Article 27 of the Constitution of 1917, and for many remains the rallying cry of the Revolution: "Just as we took arms to raise [Madero] to power, so we take arms to depose him for betraying the Revolution. We are not partisans of men but of principles."

For the next five years, Zapata continued to fight, first against the remnants of Madero's regime, then, when Madero was murdered by Huerta, against Huerta, himself. He even directed his guns against his erstwhile ally, Carranza, who at the constitutional convention, openly repudiated the Plan of Ayala, though he later accepted its central provisions.

In October 1914, just as Europe was plunging into its great railroad war, trains full of armed Mexicans converged on their capital, but not against the old regime, (it had been ousted now for four years) but against their own third revolutionary government, headed by Carranza.

It was here that Zapata rode with Pancho Villa and the two posed for their famous joint photographs. Villa's men pillaged and raped; Zapata's begged for food then returned to Morelos. There, on April 10, 1919, their leader was lured into a trap by an agent of

Carranza and shot from ambush. Villa retired but was himself assassinated near Chihuahua in 1923.

12. (p 66) Expropriation doesn't necessarily mean redistribution, by a long shot. Through various clever means, most notably a legal writ known as the *amparo agrario*, actual execution of expropriation decrees can be postponed indefinitely. So a great public to–do may be made of signing a presidential order "returning the land to those who work it," but with a good lawyer and enough *mordida* in the right places, a *latifundista* can hang onto his plantations, seemingly forever.

Even where title to land has been vested in peasants or their *Ejidos*, communal farms, the big shots may wind up with the profits by contracting with the peasants to do the actual farming and hiring them to work at cheap wages on their own land!

Finally, after making innumerable costly trips to their state and federal capitals, for up to twenty years in some cases, a peasant may still return in failure. And even if he gets a plot, it may well be a slice of barren desert. According to Riding, p 266, "Between 1952 and 1982, 85 percent of land distributed to the peasantry was unsuitable for arable farming." See Chapter 22 for a discussion of the same problems facing peasants in Brazil.

13. (p 74) Alfred Wegener is generally acknowledged to have first deduced (1912) that all present continents were once part of a single land mass but drifted apart over tens of millions of years. Wegener was ridiculed by the vast majority of geologists until the mid–1960s, when further research, much of it influenced by NASA projects, confirmed "Wegener's Hypothesis," as the premise is now universally known.

14. (p 78) Political investigator. Such cards are frequently handed out to friends or relatives by bureaucrats and politicians. With one, a bearer can enhance his clout with traffic cops and crash sports events without a ticket. Judith took hers seriously.

15. (p 81) In the dry Yucatán peninsula, as in Baja California and other arid areas, the chief agricultural agency is S.A.R.H., *Secretaria de Agricultura por Recursos Hidráulicos*, whose irrigation projects breathe life into moribund or barely subsistence agriculture. Carlos knew the bureaucrats and engineers of S.A.R.H. personally and did not hesitate to play agency politics to secure help for his people. Twice in the past year he had succeeded in diverting projects from other ejidos to his own clients: Carlos was becoming a true *cacique*.

16. (p 81) Writers generally divide the Mayan epoch into four periods: Pre–Classic, 2000 B.C. to 250 A.D.; Classic, 250–800; Terminal Classic, 800–1000; and Post–Classic, 1000 to the Spanish Conquest in the 1520s.

17. (p 88) According to the Encyclopaedia Britannica, as late as the 1860s Christian–pagan ceremonies in Chiapas included the sacrifice of Maya men by "heart removal or crucifixion."

18. (p 89) There are 28 dialects spoken by Mesoamerica's 4 million Mayans. All were in use by 100 A.D. They are separated into three subgroups, of which Yucatecan is the largest. See Morley, *et al*, Chapter 15.

19. (p 90) *Ibid* p 351.

20. (p 91) The Mayans measured the year at 365.2420 days, just shy of its modern calculation of 365.2422; Venus' revolution they figured at 584 days, compared to a precise 583.92. See Gallenkamp, p 78. However, Mayan calendrics underpinned a metaphysics so arcane, mechanical and oppressive that, while mathematically deft it led to a cultural cul–de–sac that doomed the civilization to extinction. See Puleston (Hammond and Willey) pp 63–71. Human history, and the fossil record, is replete with overspecialized failures. Social organization, culture, has been as determinative for Homo sapiens as visual, dietary and locomotor adaptations for our ancestors. Many will label this observation "social Darwinism." But with our ability to destroy ourselves — not only with nuclear weapons but by media manipulation, language corruption and environmental degradation — we should take a closer look at how the Maya, and others, fatally misapplied their own knowledge.

21. (p 92) In Edward Herbert Thompson's initial, 1890s, recoveries at the large *cenote* at Chichén Itzá, for example, "…of the identifiable skeletons retrieved from the *cenote*, twenty one were children between eighteen months and twelve years, thirteen were adult men and eight were women." Puleston (Hammond and Willey), pp 181–182.

22. (p 92) *Ibid* p 132. They also domesticated turkeys, ducks and stingless bees.

23. (p 94) Morely, *et al*. p 487 state that, "Study of the gold and copper objects found in the [well] indicates that they were brought to

Chichén Itzá from points as far distant as Colombia and Panama to the south and from as far north as Oaxaca and the Valley of Mexico." However, it is highly unlikely that Indians from those places actually came to Chichén. The artifacts were almost certainly trade items.

24. (p 94) Landa, although devoting much of his life to the study of the Maya, committed perhaps the most wanton and stupid act of destruction ever perpetrated by one pretending to scholarship: he located the principal cache of Mayan hieroglyphic parchments at Mani and, on July 12, 1562 burned them all — destroying in one moment one of the world's greatest archeological treasures. Further codices may lie entombed elsewhere, but exposure to the region's heavy humidity makes it unlikely they would have survived in legible condition.

25. (p 95) Gallenkamp, pp 170–171.

26. (p 95) *Ibid* p 180.

27. (p 96) Morley, *et al.* p 257.

28. (p 100) All beaches in Mexico are, by right of law, free and open to everyone. Thus, the Club Med officials were without authority to evict the yachtsmen from the beach, itself.

29. (p 101) Echeverría also let Chiapas be used by the Cubans and Czechs for training Guatemalan guerrillas and opened Mexico City as the largest base for Soviet espionage in the hemisphere — all in exchange for Castro's promise not to sponsor insurgency in Mexico. The billions stolen by Echeverría, much of it through Cancun leasing, permit, construction and supply kickbacks, are exceeded only by the loot of his hand–picked successor, López Portillo. The greed of these two made even their Swiss bankers blush.

30. (p 114) Belize has hundreds of Mayan ruins, many still undiscovered. Among the largest excavated sites is Altun Ha which, with Tulum, was one of the two principal trading centers on the Caribbean coast. It is located in the north near the present town of Rockstone Pond. Altun Ha was closely allied with Tikal during its heyday, between the third and ninth centuries. The largest Mayan jade carving ever recovered, a 9.7–pound head of the god Kinich Ahau, was found there in the late 1960s by a team from the Royal Ontario Museum.

31. (p 115) There are probably more blacks living in Guatemala than in Belize, chiefly on the Caribbean coast in and near Lívingston and Puerto Barrios. They speak some Spanish but mostly the same pidgin English, "Carib," spoken in Belize. Yet, in spite of its problems, Belize has the most rambunctiously functioning democracy in the region next to Costa Rica. The PUP, People's United, and UDP, United Democratic, parties sharply contest each election.

32. (p 119) For example, gasoline, at $1.84 a gallon. It is imported not from nearby Mexico but from Venezuela. The octane is considerably higher, relieving the knocking caused by Mexican gas. Regular in Texas — Livingston, Louise and Victoria — had been only 95 to 97 cents a gallon.

33. (p 132) The skull was in fragments, including a right mandible with three erupted molars and two incisors. According to Gary Walthers, the lead archaeologist with the project, the evidence indicated that Maya children were weaned at about two–and–a–half to three years of age, "[T]hrowing them abruptly onto a harsh diet of gritty maize, nuts, roots, uncooked meat and leaves … and a heavy dosage of salmonella." The result, Walthers said, was that as many as half perished from starvation or diarrheal dehydration.

Tikal was the leading lowland Maya center due to its strategic location between two lakes, which not only provided irrigation and a natural military defense, but quick access to the sea — one draining to the Caribbean and the other to the Gulf of Mexico. Tikal was an ally of Teotihuacán in the Valley of Mexico and Kaminaljuyú at what is now Guatemala City. Tikal's principal buildings, peaked or "combed" pyramids, were constructed, most on top of previous structures, themselves imposing, between 700 and 800 under the now–verified reigns of Au Cacau and his son, Yax Kin. See Morley, *et al.* pp 101–122 and 272–293. Carbon dating has established a living site here as early as 600 B.C. By A.D. 1000, Tikal had been abandoned to the jungle. It was discovered in 1848 by Guatemalan General Modesto Méndez on a surveying and reconnaissance expedition. British explorer Alfred Maudslay was the first to photograph the site, in 1881. A succession of institutions, including Carnegie, Harvard and the University of Pennsylvania performed excavations, the latter's being by far the most extensive, 1956–1970, involving 113 archaeologists who produced as many articles. A 28–volume encyclopedia of this work is now being edited.

Tikal is distinguished from other ruins not only by its architectural grandeur, area — more than 23 square miles — and historical supremacy, but by the pristine condition in which it is maintained by the Guatemalan parks department and the *Instituto de Antropología e Historia,* which in 1970 superseded the University of Pennsylvania as the in–fact supervisory authority.

There is a small museum on the premises. Its chief exhibits are the so–called "Stela 31," a stone carved with pictorial glyphs; the image of "Stormy Sky," one of Tikal's most important early rulers; and the exhumed skeleton and burial artifacts of an earlier ruler, displayed as found in 1962.

34. (p 132) See Note 29. Little was known about these guerrilla groups or which ones operated in which territory. At the time, leftist insurgents were loosely organized under the umbrella of the URNG — *Unidad Revolucionaria Nacional Guatemalteca,* Guatemalan National Revolutionary Unity — which was patterned after the Sandinista front in Nicaragua. Included were: the EGP — *Ejercito Guerrillero de los Pobres,* Guerrilla Army of the Poor; the FAR — *Fuerzas Armadas Rebeldes,* The Rebel Armed Forces; ORPA — *Organización del Pueblo en Armas,* Organization of the People in Arms; and PGT — *Partido Guatemalteco del Trabajo,* Guatemalan Labor Party. All but the last were insurrectionists in the field, supplied and trained by Cuba. The PGT was the Moscow–line Communist Party of Guatemala.

35. (p 138) Then 2.6 to the dollar. At 108, that was an average monthly wage of $41.54; at "half surge," 160 quetzales a month, a woman would take home $61.54. "Surge" would get her twice that plus a special rate bonus.

36. (p 143) Central America Report billed itself as "The weekly review of economics and politics." It stated that it was "[P]ublished by Inforpress Centroamericana, 9a Calle "A" 3–56, Zona 1, Guatemala. Cable: INFORPRESS Guatemala." Subscriptions were $30 a year; back issues, $2.50 each. A European edition was "[P]ublished by the El Salvador Committee for Human Rights and the Guatemala Committee for Human Rights, 20 Compton Terrace, London, N.1." There were no names on either masthead. Stories began with ostensible objectivity, but suddenly lapsed into propaganda. This, from the March 21, 1986 issue: "Honduras ...This zone [Comayagua] is very much in the news now because of the detailed and gruesome allegations that some 400 of the 1,200 US soldiers [stationed there] routinely spend their free time sexually abusing local youngsters and promoting drug and alcohol abuse." This was one of the first reports of these "allegations," later disproved by Honduran and independent US and international health agencies, and was used as an unidentified source by some US journalists who reported it as fact. *Mesoamerica* billed itself as "News and Analysis of Central America,"

and was published monthly in San José, Costa Rica by an organization called "The Institute for Central American Studies." The editor was Fred B. Morris, who also directed the institute. It also promised objectivity, but it too waxed polemical. Thus, from page 1 of the March 1986 issue: "... It's about time the lies and the killings stop. It's about time the people of the US feel shame for what their government is doing to one of the poorest and most suffering countries in the hemisphere. It's about time Mr. Reagan stops posturing and lying and funding the killing of women and children in Central America." Morris at the time was ABC News resident agent for Central America. See Chapter 14.

37. (p 146) According to a private note to the author from the Swiss ambassador to Guatemala, Ursula and Marco Giterio were flown back to Switzerland the following month. Both have fully recovered.

38. (p 146) Alvarado sailed from Nicaragua to South America in 1534 with the aim of beating Pizarro to Quito. He bogged down in mangrove swamps and Andes snow storms. Half his force perished, including most of the ill clad coastal Indians impressed into service as porters. See Hemming at pp 152–153 and 209.

39. (p 162) Gast's tour with the Peace Corps expired in November 1986. His successor undertook to continue the project. Renewed efforts to obtain a medfly waiver from the USDA failed. The cooperative folded in 1988.

40. (p 173) Seventy percent of the Miskitos are Moravians, the result of decades of missionary work by the sect's churches in Pennsylvania and North Carolina.

41. (p 178) Actually, the Carter administration did not send weapons to the Sandinistas until they had already seized power. The shipments were a belated — and futile — attempt to win favor with the new revolutionary government. Among the weapons, mostly rifles, light machine guns and mortars, was a consignment of M16s later seized by Colombian police from M19 guerrillas who blew up the supreme court in Bogota, killing scores of civilians, including most of the judges.

42. (p 190) Violeta Chamorro was elected President of Nicaragua in February 1990 as the candidate of the combined democratic opposition to the Sandinistas. However, she kept so many of the latter

in her administration that some former Contras accused her of becoming a Sandinista captive.

43. (p 195) "The Necessity of a New Model of Communication in Nicaragua," delivered November 22–24, 1984 to the National Council of Higher Education, Managua.

44. (p 195) "Censorship: A Form of Resistance to the Penetration of the Enemy's Ideology," *Cuadernos de Periodismo*, a journal published by the University of Nicaragua Humanities Faculty, undated, pp 69–73. The course ran four hours a week for four months.

45. (p 195) "Don't Abandon the Nicaraguan People," *The Washington Post*, April 9, 1986; "The Sandinista Goal is the Soviet Goal," *The Miami Herald*, April 12, 1986.

46. (p 197) Christian, p 254.

47. (p 197) *Fidel and Religion: Conversations with Friar Betto*, pp 9–10, published by the Cuban *Oficina de Publicaciones del Consejo de Estado*, Havana, 1985.

48. (p 198) OXFAM, the private British relief conglomerate, the Lutheran Church of Sweden, and the World Council of Churches were among the principal contributors.

49. (p 209) Such arms might have been among those purchased with funds diverted from illegal Iranian sales. More probably, they were weapons purchased by the Contras with private donations and funds appropriated by the US Congress. Legal deliveries of such arms by both CIA and military transport occurred regularly. Finally, Hershell's information may have been false. Rumors of tricky arms deals were ceaseless. Some were the result of Soviet and Sandinista disinformation campaigns. Others were based on truthful reports of US military airlifts. See Chapter 11.

50. (p 218) The centennial of this landmark US Labor Movement protest for an 8–hour day and other reforms, the first "May Day," was the Sandinista's official theme for this particular May Day. *Barricada's* front–page headline was a giant "100." Eight policemen were killed in the Chicago disturbance. A number of strike leaders were convicted of murder, in spite of overwhelming evidence that the event had been peaceful until strikers were provoked by industry goons and the police, themselves. Four union organizers were hanged, one committed suicide and the others received lesser sentences. The

Sandinistas made no mention of the fact that all were later pardoned and their prosecution condemned by Governor John Peter Altgeld, who thereby almost certainly forfeited a presidential nomination.

51. (p 223) "Berkeley Law Professor — A Visit to Nicaragua," "The Recorder," July 10, 1985. Distributed by the "Lawyers Committee on Central America," San Francisco Bay Area Chapter, 2269 Market Street, No. 189.

52. (p 223) Even travel guide writers were swept up in the euphoria: This, from page 424 of Fodor's 1982 Central America Guidebook: "The peasants and Sandinistas had been struggling against Somoza for years, but when the wealthy businessmen gave up hope and allied themselves with the Sandinistas, and when the children of the upper and middle classes joined the Sandinistas and the gun–toting muchachos ... the Somoza empire finally toppled. The Sandinistas ... know that they need the cooperation of the businessmen, that a true socialist democracy is not created in a day. For the first time in [their] lives [Nicaraguans have] hope for a better life." And this, from Lonely Planet Publications' "South America on a Shoestring," 1990 edition: "Nicaragua is simply too convenient a pawn with which Reagan [sic] can play propaganda games with the Russians ... [V]olunteers from all over the world are going to Nicaragua to ... demonstrate solidarity with a people and a government trying their best to put into effect changes which will result in a society that enjoys the same kind of rights and freedoms which Reagan vowed to defend when he took the oath of office."

53. (p 229) Costa Rica has a 1–to–30 percent progressive income tax on net earnings, heavy sales and excise taxes — up to 100 percent on some luxury items — and a severe progressive real property tax.

54. (p 234) Cabezas, author of *"La Montaña es Algo Más que una Inmensa Estepa Verde,"* The Mountain is Something More than an Immense Green Steppe, [Published in the United States as "Fire from the Mountain" in 1985] is Tomás Borge's chief propaganda assistant in the defense ministry. His primary task is media relations, lecturing foreign delegations and "literary liaison." He received the New York Pen Club Award for the book.

55. (p 234) This is questionable on two counts. First, the United States did not enter the war until after more than 2,300 soldiers and sailors were killed at Pearl Harbor on December 7, 1941. Second, there is no evidence of any such closings. Logistical reports, troop movements, force strengths and command presence were regularly

censored — but not information similar to that routinely cut by the Sandinistas from *La Prensa.*

56. (p 244) Pastora was granted provisional asylum in June 1986, conditioned on his refraining from all military activity, including recruitment, on pain of summary expulsion. He accepted these terms and never returned to the field.

57. (p 250) "Memoirs," 1885, Vol. 1, p 195–198.

58. (p 251) *The Conquest of Peru,* 1847; Mentor Edition, 1961, p 144.

59. (p 254) A partial breakdown for fiscal 1987 includes, in long tons:

Automobiles	2,500,000
Chemicals, general	3,650,000
Coal and Coke	8,000,000
Corn	16,000,000
Fertilizer	2,700,000
Gasoline	2,700,000
Lumber	6,000,000
Manufactures	7.000,000
Oil, Crude	9,000,000
Oil, Diesel	1,400,000
Oil, Residual Fuel	6,000,000
Ores, various	2,700,000
Paper and Products	1,400,000
Petroleum/Products	370,000
Phosphates	6,500,000
Pulpwood	2,650,000
Refrigerated Food	3,050,000
Sorghum	2,625,000
Soybeans	7,800,000
Sugar	3,225,000
Sulfur	3,240,000
Wheat	4,520,000

— Panama Canal Commission, Annual Report, Fiscal Year Ended September 30, 1987, pp 117–118.

60. (p 254) PCC Annual Report, Fiscal 1984, p 8.

61. (p 297) Some were actually buried without their heads, which were shrunk and carried as talismans or trophies and buried

later with their "owners." There is evidence of both killing by decapitation and head removal after death.

62. (p 298) In Peru, the word has a more severe connotation than in Patagonia, denoting desert–wasteland instead of desert–prairie.

63. (p 300) The latter is the view of the author. The remains of a rope were found attached to the middle bar of the design, it was visible for miles out to sea, and the dune lies just before a major prehistoric harbor.

64. (p 300) Semicooperative systems with regional groups contributing an annual required share — *mita* in Pre–Columbian Peru — are now thought to have been equally common, if not the rule, although even these were not entirely voluntary.

65. (p 301) Self published; printed by Heinrich Fink Co., 7,000 Stuttgart 80 (Revised 1976); 1987 printing.

66. (p 301) If such an event were a solstice or equinox, and many are so claimed, there would, of course, be a second "valid," reverse, sighting six months later — a sort of "two–for–one" that Gerald S. Hawkins recognized as artificially raising the odds in favor of alignment during his Stonehenge computer tests — and for which he later corrected.

67. (p 312) Aside from the patently racist assumption of the intellectual inferiority of the Indian, it is absurd to posit that beings so advanced as to navigate intergalactic space would need such primitive flight instructions.

68. (p 312) Readers interested in pursuing the topic seriously are referred to Reiche's and Hadingham's books and the extensive bibliography cited in the latter, published by Random House. The former, unfortunately, has been available only at the Hotel de Turistas in Nazca, although I am told that a revised edition may soon be purchased from Reiche's understudy, Dr. Phyllis Pitluga, at the Chicago Planetarium. Those interested in UFO's are referred to von Däniken's *Chariots of the Gods?* and MacLaine's *Out on a Limb*.

69. (p 312) Most "Peruvian" wine is made from grape concentrate shipped from Argentina.

70. (p 314) *"Voy por el camino de mi vida/ recordando la flor a del ataud/ alla en la tumba donde mi madre muerta/ florecio un*

recuerdo de mi triste juventud ... en la noche voy en busca de la vida de me alegre/ y ... hacer algún deroche/ para alivio de mi suerte negra." — El Cholo Berrocal, *Navarrete*, Lima.

71. (p 314) *"Siento de ver a mi patria/ en manos de los burgueses/ caramba cuantos reveces/ los pobres hay que soportar/ mientras que los oligarcas/ protegense con fusiles/ los pobres mueren a miles/ de hambre y de sed y sin hogar ... despierta pueblo despierta/ en mi ignorancia lo explico/ más ya no adules al rico/ y lucha por tu libertad ... Arriba, arriba patria querida/ y los peruanos de corazón/ no permitamos la mala vida/ la mala vida de la Nación."* — *Al Compas de mi Guitarra*, *Navarrete*, Lima. This song was written in 1952.

72. (p 317) Some scholars, and more romantics, argue that the conquest actually was not completed until 1537 at the earliest, the defeat of Quiso at Lima and the retreat of Manco into Vilcabamba; others hold out for 1572, the date of Tupac Amaru's execution. Yet the empire ceased to exist when the Inca Atahualpa was captured in the square of Cajamarca by Pizarro's surprise cavalry attack on November 16, 1532. Although the superiority of horse, armor and firearms was demonstrated repeatedly thereafter, all of those engagements — including the great one at Cuzco — were impossible defensive gambits by the Incas. The myth, aura and writ of the "invincible" Son of the Sun were extinguished at Cajamarca.

73. (p 324) See both Prescott and Heming for excellent discussions of the capture, internment, extortion and execution of Atahualpa.

74. (p 324) Manco himself was stabbed to death by Spanish deserters to whom he had granted refuge. They evidently hoped that this ingratitude would win them the viceroy's pardon and reward. But before they could escape they were caught and gruesomely dispatched by Manco's guards. In 1572, the last of his heirs, Tupac Amaru, was captured in a daring campaign ordered by the powerful viceroy, Francisco de Toledo. Toledo, an honest but ruthless administrator, knew that in order to pacify the Indian population he had to remove all hope of an Incan restoration. This meant not only the conquest of Vilcabamba, but the termination of the royal line. Seizing as a pretext the murder of a messenger and priest by undisciplined warriors, acts which the Inca neither ordered nor condoned, Toledo had Tupac Amaru tried by a kangaroo court and condemned. The last claimant to the "Throne of the Sun" was beheaded on September 24, 1572. He died a converted Christian and, in an eloquent speech before the

scaffold, he renounced Incan deities as false gods and the sun religion, itself, as a sham concocted by the Incas to deceive the people. There was no Sun God, no sacred *Inti*, he told them. He and his predecessors had only pretended to pray and to consult such a being, then did whatever they had wanted to do in the first place, saying that was what *Inti* wanted — as remarkable a confession of shamanism ever recorded. He then urged the thousands of Indians who had been assembled to witness his execution to follow his example and adhere to Catholicism. Most of them did so. Within less than a decade following his death, his former subjects had become Church–sanctioned plantation serfs and *mita* slaves in the silver mines that for three centuries financed Spain's decadent royalty and European wars.

75. (p 324) These ruins, a hundred miles to the northwest, were discovered by Bingham a month after he found Machu Picchu. Hemming (pp 488–499) has an excellent discussion of this controversy and its apparent resolution.

76. (p 332) Including hundreds of exquisite miniature gold replicas of crayfish, spiders, bees, insects and small animals. These items had been omitted from Atahualpa's ransom delivered to Cajamarca the previous year. The Inca had unwisely sought to buy his freedom by offering to fill two rooms at Cajamarca with gold and silver. Pizarro took him up on it and Atahualpa made good his part of the bargain, ordering treasure brought from throughout the empire. Pizarro then reneged and, on the pretext that the Inca had plotted his own rescue, had him convicted of "treason" and garroted.

77. (p 340) Getúlio Vargas' 25–year dominance of Brazilian politics ended in suicide in 1954 — the only Latin American leader known to offer this ultimate gesture of exasperation at his recalcitrant people. In death he is now revered as "Brazil's FDR" — even by many who rejected his social and economic reforms. His two administrations, 1930–1945 and 1950–1954, brought massive road and dam construction, rural electrification, steel industry expansion to a level of global competitiveness, one of the region's most efficient state oil monopolies, Petrobras, and the beginnings of a system of social security.

78. (p 340) "A Tree of Life Grows in Brazil," by Anthony and Suely Anderson, "Natural History," December 1985, p 41.

79. (p 397) Literally, "canteen" or commissary, but the word was used generally to refer to Reserve Headquarters, also called "*alojamientos,*" housing area.

80. (p 397) Her ordeal was exacerbated by daily injections of penicillin to which she was allergic.

81. (p 405) "Perennial Communal Nesting by *Kentropyx calcartus,*" Journal of Herpetology, Vol. 18, No. 1, pp 73–75, 1984.

82. (p 406) "The Correlates of Foraging Mode in a Community of Brazilian Lizards," Herpetologica, Vol. 41, No. 3, 1985, pp 324–332.

83. (p 420) *Human Carrying Capacity of the Brazilian Rainforest*, Columbia University Press, New York, 1986, p 150.

84. (p 420) "Brazil's Amazon Forest and the Global Carbon Problem," *Interciencia*, July–August 1985, Vol.10, No.4.

85. (p 422) Lugo, Ariel E. and Brown, Sandra, letter to the editor critical of Fearnside, *Interciencia*, Mar.–Apr. 1986, Vol.11, No.2, p 57.

86. (p 423) *Interciencia*, Mar.–Apr. 1986, Vol. 11, No.2.

87. (p 423) *Human Carrying Capacity of the Brazilian Rainforest,* p 153

88. (p 458) Even in exile, 1955–1973, Perón's secret directives to supporters caused mischief and sometimes turned elections. In 1958, their block vote made the difference in a close presidential race — although Perón later exposed the deal when he found he could not control the winner. In 1963, Peronists cast blank ballots on the boss's instructions from Madrid, where he became a permanent guest of Spanish dictator Franco. Both had been admirers of Mussolini, whose speaking style and "heroic" posters Perón imitated. Finally, in 1973, in a masterful piece of political theater and timing, in which he persuaded even his opponents that he was the only man who could save Argentina, Perón returned from exile and won reelection to a belated third term at the age of 70. Once in power, he condemned the Montoneros, whom he had called "my young heirs" and who had championed his return. They resumed their insurgency. His second wife, Isabel, succeeded to the presidency upon Perón's sudden death the next year. She turned a blind eye to the Dirty War, which sharply escalated. She left policy to her husband's holdover cabinet, who sought to restore the discredited apparatus of the 1950's — and with

the same results: quadrupled inflation, doubled unemployment, strikes. As rioting spread, much of it guerrilla inspired, the army deposed her and placed her under house arrest.

89. (p 459) Eva Duarte Perón, "Evita," Perón's first official wife (he claimed to have had a great many "unofficial" ones) died in 1952. A popular actress and entertainer, as the dictator's first lady she became a national heroine as powerful as her husband. Publicly, she cultivated the image of ombudsman for the poor, personally supervising mass distributions of free food and clothing and leading fund–raising drives for the elderly, orphans — she had been one — and the infirm, and for schools and hospitals. In fact, each of these activities was expertly orchestrated by her for maximum political effect. She sat in the highest councils of government and her husband's party and ruthlessly manipulated the levers of power. In death she achieved popular sainthood with her enshrined remains, returned from Italy where they had been hidden for two decades, the object of idolatry. Hollywood and Broadway have marketed her myth to the world. Her story is beyond the scope of this narrative.

90. (p 459) The extreme right were not alone in their wish to dismantle Perón's welfare state. Most Argentines, even those employed by them, detested the corrupt and grossly inefficient rail, oil and gas industries. Each was a featherbedded sloth, saddled with political hacks and timeservers. Costs of oil production, for example, were the highest per barrel in the world. Old fields were rapidly depleted; the few new ones were developed by foreign companies under license. Half of all railroad rolling stock was idle for repairs, right of way was poorly maintained, accidents epidemic. Other state enterprises were equally, if not more, decrepit. Still, almost half the country worked for the government. All of this, combined with protectionism, had a stunting effect on private enterprise. According to historian David Rock (p. 326) "Among the country's 30 largest firms in the mid 1960's, state firms had 49 percent of total sales, foreign companies 41 percent and domestic manufacturers only 10 percent ... [B]y the early 1980s some 700 state firms accounted for 42 percent of the gross domestic product." For most firms, "[p]rofit was based not on mass production and falling prices, but on high prices, near monopoly, or state contracts in a limited market." In one note of irony, the generals appointed to run the various state enterprises, awash in the power and perquisites of their new offices, soon fought privatization as vehemently as had their Peronist predecessors.
Even some private concerns benefited from the status quo: Protective tariffs and quotas, dollar loan guarantees and outright subsidies — all part of what was euphemistically called "import

substitution," an effort to nurture "infant" industry against foreign competition. But manufacturing became chronically infantile, with little incentive to innovate or cut costs.

Perón, in the tradition of previous federalist governments, looked to the one consistent producer, agriculture, for revenues. Farmers were exhorted to expand acreage under harsh production quotas and threat of confiscation of their holdings. But costs of tractors and fertilizers were kept so high by protective tariffs that they were out of reach for most and used only sparingly by the few who could afford them. A government trading corporation bought all products except wool at prices far below those on the world market, which was booming in the aftermath of World War II. With the windfall profits, Perón funded his bloated public payroll and subsidized favored manufacturers. When, after a 10–year hiatus, farmers returned to private trading, they were faced with depressed markets and strict US and European quota and tariff restrictions. Only during bad crop years were these relaxed — then stiffened again as domestic production recovered.

This combination of a lopsided policy of wealth redistribution at home and uncertain markets abroad was guaranteed to stymie productivity. It did just that, shorting or fallowing untold hectares of the pampas breadbasket that once, 1890–1940, had made Argentina one of the world's greatest meat and grain exporters of all time. According to a United Nations report, by 1959 less than a quarter of land suitable for stock, crops or forestry was in use; less than one percent was under irrigation, though almost half suffered from aridity. These conditions prevailed into the 1970's.

As a result, the government was forced to look increasingly to outside sources for revenue. These included expanded foreign investment in protected domestic industry and, later, direct loans by American and European banks. Perón had used these as temporary expedients, but his successors, faced with stagnation, made them mainstays of economic policy.

The 1976 military government became so desperate that it threw caution to the winds. Minimum reserve requirements were repealed and shake–and–bake debt brokerage houses, *casas financieras*, were created. Virtually immune from regulation, they competed with established banks in hustling not only foreign capital, but local savings as well. Some exiled capital returned from Miami and Zurich, but most of the Argentine money sucked up by the *casas* was cash flow and venture capital that otherwise would have been invested in the private economy.

Like hogs to an open feed bin, the FDIC–insured US banks, led by Citibank and Chase, stampeded to the *casas*. Whenever new deposits let up, the government would "guarantee" higher and higher rates of interest — at one time exceeding 60 percent! Repatriation of interest and principal and convertibility into dollars were also "guaranteed."

Concurrent increases in the level of government spending, and a sharp rise in the costs of industrial components, triggered triple–digit inflation. Foreign banks were supposedly protected from this by a so–called "creeping peg" system of devaluation, which locked in their profits in dollars.

Thus, while destroying civil liberties in the name of husbandry, the generals abandoned fiscal prudence. The result would ultimately pick the pockets not only of Argentine but of American and European taxpayers as well. By 1983, the multinational banks, mostly American, had advanced more than $52 billion, by some accounts $76 billion, even the interest on which was unpayable — and remains so.

91. (p 459) In fairness, it must be said that Perón and the 1976 junta were dealing with a system fundamentally flawed. For 400 years, Buenos Aires has existed as a financial parasite on the Republic's hinterland. Extraction, monopoly, market and monetary manipulation, capital diversion, protection and confiscation had all been used by federalist politicians to maintain provincial dependency on the capital. Though there was resistance, much of it sustained and bloody, *porteños* inevitably won in the end. Perón merely institutionalized these practices — with a populist twist — to support his new urban constituency. Beyond this, beggar–thy–neighbor is woven into the Argentine psyche and often knotted with violence. The Dirty War, and the insurgency which precipitated it, had as much to do with this traditional struggle for economic advantage as with classic right–left politics. Simply to label the one "neofascist" and the other "communist," as much of the western media have done, or to dismiss them as terrorism and vigilantism run amok, is to ignore the shoals and undercurrents of Argentina's history. Law and reasonableness have foundered there before and may well do so yet again.

92. (p 462) This is true. In 1982, when it was clear that most Third World debtor countries couldn't pay on time, US officials lurched about, desperately cajoling debtors to try to send more and the banks to take less. As each obligation fell due, regulations were stretched to allow partial late payments to count as "performing" — to forestall write–offs, which would have required setting aside equal reserves, with stupendous balance sheet losses and possible panic. Remarkably, banks were persuaded to keep loaning money in spite of debtor default, a word religiously avoided. This is particularly remarkable in the case of banks like City, Chase and Chemical, who

were already into third world debt by amounts approaching total shareholder equity.

This brush–fire policy put off the reckoning but by 1985 it was clear that something more drastic was needed. Then recently appointed Secretary of the Treasury, James A. Baker III, a Texas banking multimillionaire whose own bank was itself top–heavy with Mexican loans, proposed what became known as "the Baker Plan." In this scheme the banks would advance just enough new money so delinquent countries could pay the same money back to the banks as partial interest due: No principal now, mind you. In return the US Treasury would continue to treat the loans as "performing." The Treasury would also lean on the World Bank and the IMF to advance still more money to the same countries so they could stay in business. Some people said that this was nothing but a fancy shell game which is what it was.

Ostensibly to qualify, countries had to give "satisfactory assurances" that they were moving away from state planning toward market economies: open doors to foreign investment, knock down tariffs, rescind quotas, trim bloated public payrolls, control inflation, balance budgets and reduce trade deficits. One marvels at the hypocrisy of Washington in insisting that destitute nations do what it refused to do, itself. In the event, of course, the requirement was so broadly interpreted that it became meaningless. Implicit was the idea that, with a few years respite, most countries would grow enough in the expanding world economy to resume payments from revenues. "A rising tide lifts all boats," someone said. But it has not turned out that way.

Several publicly unspoken factors doomed the loans from the beginning.

Bankers, from CEOs down to loan officers, received substantial bonuses for "signing up" countries into new agreements. These were based on loan sizes and were paid when the deals closed. Hundreds of millions of dollars were thus shaved in a process which, for all practical purposes, was beyond shareholder or government scrutiny.

That a loan later turned sour meant nothing. Most of the players were long gone — some to new fiduciary casinos, others to top management, where they had no interest in "finding the bastards who got us into this mess."

A number, Baker and Donald Regan among them, were appointed to high government posts — Treasury, the Federal Reserve, the White House Staff. Baker eventually became Secretary of State in the Bush Administration. They not only did not reign in rodeo banking but spurred it on — along with the runaway savings and loan industry.

From the State Department's point of view, bank loans to these countries, many run by "friendly" military regimes, were a foreign–aid end run around Congress. Such sums would never have been directly appropriated in shrinking aid budgets.

At the ongoing *real* inflation rate of eight percent, in eight years or so the banks' exposure would shrink by half, if new lending did not exceed interest received. Sandbag — set impossible conditions for future loans but pretend to "negotiate" — and the problem would take care of itself. The banks did just that, advancing less and less, until eventually they were able to begin writing off large portions of outstanding loans without the previously feared panic.

Congress, supposedly the watch dog of last resort, took little interest. Bankers, both directly and through surrogates, are the greatest single source of campaign contributions. And many retired congressmen draw five– and six–figure salaries on bank boards of directors.

Finally, everyone knew that whatever happened in the end the Federal Deposit Insurance Corporation and beyond it Congress would never let the banks go belly up. There were too many teachers' and firemen's pensions, widows' savings and state employee retirement funds in those chips on the foreign loan crap table.

Thus, prudence and good government, not to mention honesty and truth, were ill served.

Notwithstanding their sackcloth protestations to the contrary, bank and government officials alike embraced constant inflation — which they began calling "a moderate three to four percent," but which, in real terms, was eight to 10. The ordinary American's dollar shrank every year by an amount greater than he was able to earn in interest in his own bank or savings and loan account. Simultaneously, more and more of his taxes went to the international lending agencies to "fill the gap" left by the departed banks — both to maintain debtor–nation cash flow and to keep up payments to the banks, themselves, whose greed had caused the crisis to begin with. And even after all that, as of today, 1993, Third World real debt has not been reduced, but is greater than 2 *trillion* dollars. That is a great many schools, hospitals, roads, bridges, Social Security pensions and spacecraft. To be fair, much of the debt has been discounted and sold into the secondary market; some has been "converted," again after discount, into long term zero coupon bonds. More than 90%, $240 billion, of the total commercial bank debt of the major debtors, including Argentina's current $31 billion, has been thusly refinanced — usually with agreements by the banks to resume "selective" lending. With concurrent increases in federally mandated reserves, the banks have, through this creative accounting, officially lowered their bad Latin American debt exposure — at least on the books. But the money left and never came back and prospects for its return are dim. And meanwhile, more is on the way.

93. (p 463) For two centuries the United States Congress has steadfastly refused to permit banks to expand into states other than their own without the approval of the State Legislatures involved — permission rarely given. The idea is to prevent concentrations of financial and political power. It is also to insulate the national economy from the mismanagement and failures of a few — a financial fire wall, if you will. Presidents from Andrew Jackson to Franklin D. Roosevelt to Richard Nixon refused to attempt repeal, although fiercely lobbied to do so — both by the banks and by some public advocates who argued, persuasively, that such competition would result in lower interest rates and better service. Too risky. Better to keep the fire wall. And to keep local money working in each community. But since the late 1970's, with the blessings of both political parties in a deregulation minded Washington, banks have used technical loopholes to sprout a forest of overseas branches, many in places subject to calamity.

Chase, for example, can't cash checks in Cincinnati or Memphis or Boise but it can loan millions in Comodoro Rivadavia, Rosario, Mendoza and a dozen other cities that most Americans never heard of. Chase's Chairman and Chief Executive Officer, Williard Butcher, had come down a few months back with an entourage of underlings to tell the Argentines that plain banking wasn't enough, that more was on the way. Third world repayment problems, he told them, were "regrettable but temporary:"

> When I first came to Chase National Bank
> 39 years ago, 90 percent of our loans were to US
> businesses. Would you be interested to know that
> today it's [only] 11 percent? This is a dramatic
> change but the one we are undergoing today is of
> a greater magnitude ... Fundamentally, we are
> building [our own] market.

Not only was interstate banking soon to be a reality in the United States, Butcher said, but US banks now had a free hand to engage in worldwide credit card schemes, international stock and bond trading and a host of other "services." Between the lines he was telling them that multinational banking had grown too big for Congress and 50 enfeebled state banking commissioners to handle.

94. (p 486) *Voyage of the Beagle*, Natural History Library Edition, 1962, Doubleday and Company, New York, pp 218–219.

95. (p 486) *Ibid* p 215.

96. (p 486) *Ibid* p 227.

97. (p 486) *Ibid* p 231.

98. (p 488) *Uttermost Part of the Earth*, E.P. Dutton and Company, New York, 1947.

99. (p 491) *Ibid* p 429.

100. (p 494) I have relied extensively on Darwin and Lucas Bridges in my descriptions of Tierra del Fuego and its colonial history. These two authors, writing a century apart, were masters of observation who captured, as even modern photography could not, a world that literally vanished between them.

TABLE OF PHOTOGRAPHS

Giant cactus in boulder field north of Guerrero Negro, Baja California Norte. 33

Juanito and his mother, Rosa Elba Balles, Punta Norte, Cedros Island, Mexico. 37

Statue of girl with seal pelt, Cedros Island, Mexico. 39

The author's camp at Punta Norte, Cedros Island. 41

Plaza, San Ignacio Oasis, Baja California Sur. 43

Mexican Workers, Marxist, Party poster, La Paz. *"You are drugged up if you think we can pay the foreign debt. The only solution: suspension of payments!"* 55

Sidewalk poster display, Veracruz. 73

Carnival Clown, Veracruz. 79

Ruins of 18th Century church, Maxcanú, Yucatán. 83

Drinking water delivered to restaurant, Campeche, Yucatán. 85

El Castillo, the principal Chichén Itzá pyramid. 97

Washing the rig at cattle ford near Spanish Lookout, Belize. 111

Ferry crossing, Bermudian Landing, Belize. 121

Large snake ingesting a smaller one, Bermudian Landing, Belize. 123

Gamussa, diver and fisherman, Cay Caulker, Belize. 125

Tapir or "mountain cow," Belize. 129

Mother and daughters paddling down the Río Dulce to market in Lívingston, Guatemala. 133

"Madre," a bust of the ideal mother in front of the town hall in Lívingston, Guatemala. 135

Sewing machine operator in Gator of Florida textile plant, duty free zone, Puerto Barrios, Guatemala. 137

J.W. Harold, manager, Gator of Florida textile plant, duty free zone, Puerto Barrios, Guatemala. 139

Ferry passenger, Puerto Barrios, Guatemala. 141

Schoolmates, Puerto Barrios, Guatemala. 145

Statue of banana worker, Puerto Barrios, Guatemala. 147

Easter pilgrims at Lake Atitlán, Panajachel, Guatemala. 151

"Big Mama" in front of her eatery, Utila Island, Honduras. 163

Ceremonial stone head, Copán, Honduras. 167

Iguanas for sale near Tela, Honduras. 169

US troops at Palmerola Base, near Comayagua, Honduras. 183

Jaime Chamorro, managing editor of *La Prensa*, Managua. 189

"Guilty of Treason." The two were said to be CIA agents. 192

Papaya vendor, central market, Managua. 201

Window in Santa María de Los Angeles church, Barrio Riguero, Managua. 205

CUSCLIN May Day flyer, Managua. 212

Sandinista loyalist on her way to the May Day parade, Managua. 219

Mural on a government discotheque, Managua. 225

Fred B. Morris, ABC–TV resident agent and editor of *Mesoamerica*, at his office in San José, Costa Rica. 231

Some of the anti–US / pro–Sandinista publications distributed during the Nicaraguan conflict. 236

Comandante Cero, Commander Zero, Eden Pastora. 243

A drift log being washed ashore at Playa Manuel Antonio National Park, Costa Rica. 245

Policeman, La Chorrera, Panama. 249

Beer ad, La Chorrera, Panama. 253

Painted bus, Panama City. 255

Lime and tomato vendor, La Chorrera, Panama. 257

Garbage scavenger, Quito, Ecuador. 259

Beer drinker, Trujillo, northern Peru. 261

Twin boys, near Tumbes, northern Peru. 263

Author and jeep in the north Peruvian desert, near Sullana. 265

Moche ceremonial figure, National Museum of Anthropology and Archeology, Pueblo Libre, Lima. 271

Pre–Incan trophy head from northern Peru, National Museum of Anthropology and Archeology, Pueblo Libre, Lima. 273

Mummy, ca 1300 B.C., from the Paracas penninsula, south coastal Peru. Researchers claim that what appears to be an expression of terror is merely incidental to the hands having slipped from the eyes after burial. National Museum of Anthropology and Archeology, Pueblo Libre, Lima. 279

Soft drink vendor, Nazca. 299

Maria Reiche lecturing in the conference room named after her, Hotel Turistas, Nazca. 305

Shine boy, Nazca. 307

Troubadour at rest, Nazca. 309

Schoolboys marching, Nazca. 311

Interest compounded daily at 41% at savings bank in Nazca. 313

Captive monkey on roof of car, Nazca. 315

"Gringo Bill," hotelier at Aguas Calientes, below Machu Picchu. 321

Interior view of Machu Picchu. 325

Wall of the Incan Fortress, Sacsahuamán, above Cuzco. 329

Perfectly fitted 13–sided stone in Incan Wall, Cuzco. 331

Plaster walls of recent construction must frequently be propped with poles. Cuzco. 333

Hernán Luza Calvo, the retired Cuzco history teacher who became the author's guide and friend. 337

The *Presidente Vargas* taking on lumber at a Marajó sawmill. 341

Children on the wharf of a remote Marajó Island trapiche awaiting the arrival of the *Presidente Vargas*. 343

Antonio Monteria Teixera, captain of the *Presidente Vargas*, and his son, Sergio, in front of the wheelhouse. 345

A giant moth attaches itself for a time to the *Vargas*. 347

"Tatu" the cook with his favorite dish. Armadillo is a dietary staple in the Amazon. 349

The *Franz Rossy*, a typical diesel–powered riverboat. 351

Hardware store, Afuá. 353

Cold storage freight worker, Santarém. 357

Teenage boys pose at Santarém. Note meaningless English words on T–shirts. 359

Young girl tending cook fire near Belterra. 363

Belterra Hospital, built by Henry Ford in 1929. 367

Dr. Ivaldo Moraes of Belterra. 369

Stretch of the Trans–Amazon Highway near the Tapajós National Forest. 371

Wash day on a creek near the Tapajós River. 373

"Lira," the Tapajós National Forest laborer who had just killed a jaguar with his rifle. 375

Tapajós turtle shell with eggs, Itaituba. 377

Garimpeiro, Itaituba. 379

Residents of an Itaituba hotel. 381

Residents of an Itaituba bar roof emptying wash water. 383

Poster girl, Uropa, Pará, Brazilian Amazon. 391

Amazon gold pilot drinking *mate*, a strong herbal tea, with a silver straw at Itaituba's landing field. 395

Marc Hero at Igarapé Acara Camp, Reserva Florestal Ducke, north central Brazilian Amazon. 399

Bill Magnusson at Igarapé Acara Camp, Ducke. 401

Giant female tarantula, Ducke. 405

The dwarf caiman, *Paleosuchus trigonatus*, held by Albertina Lima near Igarapé Acara Camp, Ducke. 407

Bothrops atrox, *fer–de–lance*, Ducke. 409

A Ducke worm and Marc Hero's foot. 411

Rob Bierregaard, ornithologist and Amazon resident agent of the World Wildlife Fund, Manaus. 415

Philip M. Fearnside, Manaus. 421

Wilson Spironello, World Wildlife Fund primatologist, *Fazenda Esteio*, north of Manaus. 427

Tania Linahares, World Wildlife Fund biologist, *Fazenda Esteio*. 429

Tom Lovejoy, then Director of the World Wildlife Fund, at *Fazenda Esteio*. 431

Dugout with inverted sail near Benjamin Constant on the upper Brazilian Amazon. 435

Trackside vendor of sweaters, Juliaca, Peru. 445

Train leaving Puno for Cuzco on track elevated over Lake Titicaca near shore. 447

Gauchos breaking a mount, southern Patagonia. Photo by Francesca Sepe. 477

Glaciar Perito Moreno on the border with Chile at the top of Lake Argentino, southern Patagonia. Photo by Francesca Sepe. 479

Jeronimo Miguel Soule, forest ranger at Glaciar Moreno. Photo by Francesca Sepe. 481

Shearing the Sheep, Tierra del Fuego. Photo by Francesca Sepe. 489

The Bridges ranch at Harberton on the Beagle Channel in the Argentine Tierra del Fuego. Photo by Francesca Sepe. 495

The author and friends at San Francisquito, Baja California Sur, Mexico. 543

Selected Bibliography

Abbot, Patrick L. and Gastil, R. Gordon, (Editors), *Baja California Geology, Field Guides and Papers*, Reports to the Geological Society of America Annual Meeting, San Diego, 1979.

Alexander, Robert J., *The Bolivian National Revolution*, Rutgers University Press, 1958.

Alvares, Robert R., Jr., *Familia: Migration and Adaptation in Baja and Alta California*, 1800-1975, University of California Press, 1987.

Amnesty International Reports: 1985, 1986 and 1987, Amnesty International Publications, London.

Aschmann, Homer, *The Central Desert of Baja California, Demography and Ecology*, Manessier Publishing Company, Riverside California, 1967.

Bonner, Raymond, "Peru's War," *The New Yorker*, Jan. 8, 1988, p 31.

Botting, Douglas, *Humbolt and the Cosmos*, Harper and Row, New York, 1973.

Boza, Mario A. and Mendoza, Rolando, *Los Parques Nacionales de Costa Rica*, INCAFO, S.A., Madrid, 1981.

Bridges, E. Lucas, *Uttermost Part of the Earth*, E.P. Dutton, New York, 1949.

Bruccoli, Matthew J., *Reconquest of Mexico*, The Vanguard Press, Inc., New York, 1974.

Bunker, Stephen G., *Underdeveloping the Amazon: Extraction, Unequal Exchange and the Failure of the Modern State*, University of Illinois Press, 1985.

Caufield, Catherine, *In the Rain Forest: Report from a Strange, Beautiful and Imperiled World*, University of Chicago Press and Alfred A. Knopf, 1984.

Chapman, Charles E., *A History of California, The Spanish Period*, The Macmillan Company, New York, 1921 (1953 ed.).

Chatwin, Bruce, *In Patagonia*, Summit Books, New York, 1977.

Christian, Shirley, *Nicaragua: Revolution in the Family*, Random House, New York, 1986.

Clark, Leonard, *The Rivers Ran East*, Funk & Wagnalls Company, New York, 1953.

Collier, George A., "Peasant Politics and the Mexican State: Indigenous Compliance in Highland Chiapas," *Mexican Studies / Estudios Mexicanos* Vol. 3, No. 1 (Winter 1987), University of California Press, Berkeley.

Collins, Joseph, *Nicaragua: What Difference Could a Revolution Make?*, Grove Press, Inc., New York, 1986.

Crassweller, Robert D., *Peron and the Enigmas of Argentina*, W.W. Norton & Company, New York, 1987.

Crow, John A., *Mexico Today*, Harper and Row, New York, 1972.

Darwin, Charles, *The Voyage of the Beagle*, Natural History Library Edition, 1962 (from the author's 1860 revised edition), Doubleday and Company, New York, 1962.

de Biesanz, Mavis Hiltunen, de Biesanz, Richard, and de Biesanz, Karen Zubris, *Los Costarricenses*, Editorial Universidad Estatal a Distancia, San Jose, 1979.

Eisenberg, John F., *The Mammalian Radiations: An Analysis of Trends in Evolution, Adaptation, and Behavior*, University of Chicago Press, 1981.

Fairchild, Loretta G. and Sosin, Kim, "Manufacturing Firms in Mexico's Financial Crisis: Determinants of Severity and Response," *Mexican Studies / Estudios Mexicanos* Vol. 3, No. 1 (Winter 1987), University of California Press, Berkeley.

Fearnside, Philip M., *Human Carrying Capacity of the Brazilian Rainforest*, Colombia University Press, New York, 1986; "Brazil's Amazon Forest and the Global Carbon Problem," *Interciencia*, July–August 1985, Vol.10, No.4; Letter in Reply to Lugo and Brown, *Interciencia*, March–April 1986, Vol.11, No.2; "Environmental Change and Deforestation in the Brazilian Amazon," pp 70–89 of *Change in the Amazon Basin: Man's Impact on Forests and Rivers*, J. Hemming, editor, Manchester University Press, Manchester, U.K., 1985; "Agriculture in Amazonia," pp 393–418 of *Key Environments: Amazonia*, edited by G.T. Prance and T.E. Lovejoy, Pergamon Press, Oxford, U.K., 1985; "Settlement in Rondónia and the Token Role of Science and Technology in Brazil's Amazonian Development Planning," *Interciencia*, Sep–Oct 1986, Vol. 11, No.5; "The Development of the Amazon Rain Forest: Priority Problems for the Formulation of Guidelines," *Interciencia*, Nov–Dec 1979, Vol.4, No.6; "Development Alternatives in the Brazilian Amazon: An Ecological Evaluation," *Interciencia*, Mar–Apr 1983, Vol.8, No.2; "Land Clearing Behavior in Small Farmer Settlement Schemes in the Brazilian Amazon and its Relation to Human Carrying Capacity," pp 255–271 in *Tropical Rain–Forest: The Leeds Symposium*, Leeds Philosophical and Literary Society, Leeds, U.K., 1984; "Spatial Concentration of Deforestation in the Brazilian Amazon," pp 72–79 in *Ambio*, Vol.15, No.2, 1986; "Deforestation in the Brazilian Amazon: How Fast is it Occurring?," *Interciencia*, Mar–Apr 1982, Vol.7, No.2; "Explosive Deforestation in Rondónia, Brazil," *Environmental Conservation*, Vol.12, No.4, 1985; [With G. de L. Ferreira] "Roads in Rondónia: Highway Construction and the Farce of Unprotected Forest Reserves in Brazil's Amazon Forest," *Environmental Conservation*, Vol.11, No.4, 1984.

534

Gallenkamp, Charles, *Maya: The Riddle and Rediscovery of a Lost Civilization*, Third Revised Edition, Viking Penguin, Inc., New York, 1985.

Gerhard, Peter and Gulick, Howard E., *Lower California Guidebook*, Fourth Edition, Arthur H. Clark Company, Glendale, California, 1967.

Guillet, David, *Agrarian Reform and Peasant Economy in Southern Peru*, University of Missouri Press, 1979.

Hadingham, Evan, *Lines to the Mountain Gods*, Random House, New York, 1987.

Hammond, Norman and Willey, Gordon R. (Editors) *Maya Archaeology and Ethnohistory*, (14 papers presented to the Second Cambridge Symposium on Recent Research in Mesoamerican Archaeology), University of Texas Press, 1976.

Heming, John, *The Conquest of the Incas*, Harcourt Brace Jovanovich, New York, 1970.

Hyams, Edward and Ordish, George, *The Last of the Incas, The Rise and Fall of An American Empire,* Dorsett Press, New York, 1963.

Lee, Vincent R., "Sixpack Manco, Travels Among the Incas," Privately published by the author, Wilson, Wyoming, 1985.

Levine, Robert M., *Pernambuco in the Brazilian Federation, 1889–1937*, Stanford University Press, 1978.

Lewis, Oscar, *The Children of Sanchez, Autobiography of a Mexican Family*, Alfred A. Knoff, Inc. and Random House, New York, 1963.

Lipset, Seymour Martin and Solari, Aldo, (Editors), *Elites In Latin America*, Oxford University Press, 1967.

Love, Joseph L., *São Paulo in the Brazilian Federation, 1889–1937*, Stanford University Press, 1980; *Rio Grande do Sul and Brazilian Regionalism, 1882–1930*, Stanford University Press, 1971.

Lovejoy, Thomas E., "Forest Fragmentation in the Amazon: A Case Study," Chapter 18 of *The Study of Populations*, H. Messel, editor, Pergamon Press, Oxford, 1985.

Lugo, Ariel E. and Brown, Sandra, Letter–to–the–Editor critical of Fearnside, *Interciencia*, March–April 1986, Vol.11, No.2, p 57.

MacLachlan, Colin B. and Rodriguez, Jaime E., *The Forging of the Cosmic Race: A Reinterpretaion of Colonial Mexico*, University of California Press, Berkeley, 1980.

McGovern, William Montgomery, *Jungle Paths and Inca Ruins,* The Century Company, New York and London, 1927.

Moheno, Roberto Blanco, *La Corrupción en Mexico*, Bruguera Mexicana de Ediciones, S.A., Mexico City, 1979.

Moorehead, Alan, *Darwin and the Beagle*, Hamish Hamilton, London, 1969.

Morison, Samuel Eliot, *Admiral of the Ocean Sea, A Life of Christopher Columbus*, Little, Brown & Company, Boston, 1942; *The European Discovery of America, The Northern Voyages*, Oxford University Press, 1971.

Morley, Sylvanus G. and Brainerd, George W., *The Ancient Maya*, Fourth Edition, Revised by Robert J. Sharer, Stanford University Press, 1983.

Paz, Octavio, *One Earth, Four or Five Worlds: Reflections on Contemporary History*, Harcourt Brace Jovanovich, New York, 1985.

Prescott, William Hickling, *History of the Conquest of Mexico*, 1843; *History of the Conquest of Peru*, 1848 (Modern Library Edition).

Reiche, Maria, *Mystery on the Desert* (Preliminaries for a Scientific Interpretation of the Prehistoric Ground Drawings of Nazca, Peru and Introduction to their Study). Privately published by the author with Heinrich Fink & Co., Stuttgart, 1968 (Revised March 1976).

Richardson, William, "The Dilemmas of a Communist Artist: Diego Rivera in Moscow, 1927–1928," *Mexican Studies / Estudios Mexicanos*, Vol. 3, No. 1 (Winter 1987) University of California Press, Berkeley.

Riding, Alan, *Distant Neighbors: A Portrait of the Mexicans*, Random House, New York, 1984.

Rock, David, *Argentina 1516–1982: From Spanish Colonization to the Falklands War*, University of California Press, 1985.

Russell, Findlay E., *Snake Venom Poisoning*, Scholium International, Inc., Great Neck, New York, 1983.

Savoy, Gene, *Antisuyo: The Search for the Lost Cities of the Amazon*, Simon and Schuster, New York, 1970.

Schmink, Marianne and Wood, Charles H.(Editors), *Frontier Expansion in Amazonia*, University of Florida Press, Gainesville, 1984.

Schryer, Franz J., "Ethnicity and Politics in Rural Mexico: Land Invasions in Huejutla," *Mexican Studies / Estudios Mexicanos*, Vol. 3, No. 1 (Winter 1987) University of California Press, Berkeley.

Singelmann, Peter, *Structures of Domination and Peasant Movements in Latin America*, University of Missouri Press, 1981.

Simpson, Lesley Byrd, *Many Mexicos*, Fourth Edition Revised, University of California Press, Berkeley, 1966.

Smith, T. Lynn, *The Race Between Population and Food Supply in Latin America*, University of New Mexico Press, 1976.

Stephens, John L., *Incidents of Travel in Central America, Chiapas and Yucatán*, Harper and Brothers, 1841 (Dover Publications, New York, 1969); *Incidents of Travel in Yucatán*, Harper and Brothers, New York, 1843; (Dover Publications, New York, 1969).

Subercaseaux, Benjamin, *Jemmy Button*, The Macmillan Company, New York, 1954.

Thornton, Lawerence, *Imagining Argentina*, Doubleday and Company, Garden City, N.Y., 1987.

Turner, Christy G. II, "The First Americans: The Dental Evidence," *National Geographic Research*, Winter 1986, Vol. 2, No.1, pp 37–46.

Veliz, Claudio (Editor), *Obstacles to Change in Latin America*, Oxford University Press, 1965.

Welty, Paul Thomas, *Pageant of World Cultures*, J.B. Lippincott Company, Philadelphia, 1971.

Wilkie, James W., *The Mexican Revolution: Federal Expenditure and Social Change Since 1900*, (Second Edition, Revised) University of California Press, Berkeley, 1973.

Wilkie, James W., Meyer, Michael C., and Wilkie, Edna Monzon de, (Editors), *Papers of the IV International Congress of Mexican History*, University of California Press, 1976.

Wirth, John D., *The Politics of Brazilian Development, 1930–1954*, Stanford University Press, 1970; *Minas Gerais in the Brazilian Federation, 1889–1937*, Stanford University Press, 1977.

Worcester, Donald E. and Schaeffer, Wendell G., *The Growth & Culture of Latin America, The Continuing Struggle for Independence*, Oxford University Press, 1971.

I have too deeply enjoyed the voyage, not to recommend any naturalist, although he must not expect to be so fortunate in his companions as I have been, to take all chances, and to start, on travels by land if possible, if otherwise on a long voyage. He may feel assured, he will meet with no difficulties or dangers, excepting in rare cases, nearly so bad as he beforehand anticipates. In a moral point of view, the effect ought to be, to teach him good–humoured patience, freedom from selfishness, the habit of acting for himself, and of making the best of every occurrence. In short, he ought to partake of the characteristic qualities of most sailors. Travelling ought also to teach him distrust; but at the same time he will discover, how many truly kind–hearted people there are, with whom he never before had, or ever again will have any further communication, who yet are ready to offer him the most disinterested assistance.

— Charles Darwin
Voyage of the Beagle

About the Author

Born at Quantico Marine Base, Virginia in 1941, Sandy S. McMath grew up in Hot Springs, Arkansas and the Grant County community of Cane Creek where the family settled after his father, Sid, had completed two terms as one of the most innovative and progressive governors of the New South.

During high school and college McMath worked as a laborer with the Arkansas State Electric Cooperative, as an Interior Department surveyor's assistant in the national forests of Oregon and northern California, and as a merchant seaman for American President Lines between San Francisco and Hong Kong.

He attended Arkansas public schools and was graduated with honors from Castle Heights Military Academy, Lebanon, Tennessee in 1959. He received his B.A. degree in history from the University of Arkansas in 1963 and was graduated in 1966 from the University's School of Law. He was admitted to practice in Arkansas in 1966 and in California in 1970.

Following law school, McMath, who had previously earned his commission as a second lieutenant, entered the Marine Corps and was posted overseas, serving with the Ninth Marine Amphibious Brigade in 1967 out of Okinawa and the Third Marine Division out of Dong Ha and Quang Tri in Vietnam's I–Corps during 1968. He was awarded a number of service ribbons together with the Navy Commendation Medal with Combat "V."

Discharged with the rank of Captain in January of 1970, McMath spent six months traveling through Central and South America, following which he attended the University of London, receiving his Master of Laws Degree in International Law from the London School of Economics and a certification in Air and Space Law from the London Institute of World Affairs.

Returning to Little Rock, he served as Chief Deputy Prosecuting Attorney then entered private practice with his father and two brothers, Phillip and Bruce. The McMath Law Firm is one of the oldest and most successful personal injury firms in the United States.

Following his landmark victory against an automobile manufacturer for a young woman quadriplegic, the ATLA *Law Reporter*, official journal of the Association of Trial Lawyers of America, said of McMath:

> [The case] ... represents an advocacy accomplishment of the highest order. With insight which is innovative in its acuity, daring and depth, [McMath] contended that product misuse is no defense when encouraged or invited by the product producer.
>
> The lawyering that went into the preparation of plaintiffs' case in [this] tragedy exemplifies creativity along with courage, constancy and concern.

McMath and his brother Phillip hold the record invasion of privacy verdict. The case involved a 98–year–old North Arkansas woman whose photograph was used by a supermarket tabloid in connection with a wholly fabricated "news" story of sexual misconduct.

Recently, McMath has taken on the health insurance industry. He won a record verdict in 1992 for bad faith denial of benefits to a traumatic brain injury victim. His practice now emphasizes major damage recoveries for victims of head and spinal cord injuries.

An active member of the Association of Trial Lawyers of America, McMath founded (1983) the ATLA Nursing Home Malpractice Victims Litigation Group. He was named Outstanding Trial Lawyer of the Year for 1992–1993 by the Arkansas Trial Lawyers Association.

The author is a Fellow of the International Academy of Trial Lawyers, the American Board of Trial Advocates and, since 1981, a member of the visiting faculty of the Center for Trial and Appellate Advocacy, Hastings College of the Law, University of California, San Francisco.

In 1976–1977, McMath drove alone north to south across Africa. His account of that journey, *Africa Alone*, was widely praised by travelers, historians and critics, one of whom called it, "a true adventure classic of our time."

McMath is married to the former Allison Boyer Van Pelt of Sun Valley, Idaho. They have three children.

The author and friends at San Francisquito, Baja California Sur, Mexico.

Praise for *AFRICA ALONE*

Sandy McMath's lively account of his lone safari through Africa is an entertaining and stimulating read.

— Mary Leakey

McMath journeyed through Africa, often at great risk, for 18 months. He dug for fossils with Mary Leakey, was held at the point of a machine gun, and roamed widely in his Land Rover under a general air of unease. This is a satisfying travel book, written in the fine tradition of 19th century adventurers.

— *Washington Post Book World*

McMath, a lanky, good–natured, former Marine took a two–year leave of absence in 1976 from his Arkansas law firm to follow a dream: to drive from Paris to the southern tip of Africa. Along the way, he won the confidence of Mary Leakey at the famed fossil site in Tanzania ... In Rhodesia, he narrowly missed becoming the victim of a terrorist raid on a nunnery.

The author's ingratiating style and eye to detail make this a special book.

— *The Virginia Pilot*

Africa Alone captures the essence of Africa as surely as the drums beat out a tribute to the day.

— *Southwest Times Record*

From Morocco — where beggar children literally stoned him — through the Sahara with its endless sandstorms to the big game country of Kenya ... the quality of his storytelling wins over the reader.

— *United Press International*

Africa Alone is at once a spellbinding account of a grand adventure and a stirring documentary of modern times in lands that, for most of us, exist only as puzzle pieces on a map. McMath's vivid narrative brings the continent to life, without stripping it of its mystery. The reader learns and enjoys in equal measure.

— Janet Fullwood
Dallas Times Herald

A true–adventure classic of our time!

— Perrin Jones

Africa Alone succeeds primarily because of the straightforward nature of its narrative style. The language is direct and bare of literary flourishes, and McMath's intentions seemed to have been to allow the presented material to create its own emotional impact ... *Africa Alone* reads quickly, and each chapter serves as a catalyst to the imagination.

— *Arkansas Democrat*

Africa Alone is the kind of book with which generations of armchair travelers have idled away long evenings.

— *The Houston Post*

The miles of travel described by Sandy McMath create even greater wonder when one traces the route across expanses of desert, marshlands, forests and mountains ... [His] style is personal and easily read and even poetic ... The story of Africa is one of pain and struggle ... He may not have all the answers, but he has the right questions.

— *Arkansas Gazette*